AF531577

Creating Customer Delight: Customer Service and Relationship Management

Creating Customer Delight: Customer Service and Relationship Management

Dr. Anand Prakash

RANDOM PUBLICATIONS
NEW DELHI (INDIA)

Creating Customer Delight: Customer Service and Relationship Management

ISBN 978-93-5111-857-2

Published in 2016 in India by

RANDOM PUBLICATIONS

4376-A/4B, Gali Murari Lal, Ansari Road
New Delhi-110 002
Phone : +9111-43580356, 011-23289044, 011-43142548
e-mail: sales@randompublications.com,
info@randompublications.com, randomexports@gmail.com

Reprinted 2022

Type Setting by : Friends Media, Delhi-110089
Digitally Printed at: Replika Press Pvt. Ltd.

Preface

A customer is usually used to refer to a current or potential buyer or user of the products of an individual or organization, called the supplier, seller, or vendor. This is typically through purchasing or renting goods or services. However, in certain contexts, the term customer also includes by extension any entity that uses or experiences the services of another. A customer may also be a viewer of the product or service that is being sold despite deciding not to buy them. The general distinction between a customer and a client is that a customer purchases products, whereas a client purchases services.

Customer Relationship Management is increasingly recognized as crucial to the success of any organization. CRM is all about human interaction, aided by technology. It involves offering service and information about the product whenever the customer requires it and retaining a competitive edge by keeping the customer satisfied. The greatest challenge for any enterprise is to keep in mind changing customer needs and achieving customer satisfaction--and this is where CRM enables companies to remain successful.

The goal of customer experience management (CEM) is to move customers from satisfied to loyal and then from loyal to advocate. Traditionally, managing the customer relationship has been the domain of Customer Relationship Management (CRM). However, CRM strategies and solutions are designed to focus on product, price and enterprise process, with minimal or no focus on customer need and desire. The result is a sharp mismatch between the organisation's approach to customer expectations and what customers actually want, resulting in the failure of many CRM implementations.

This book should be most useful to the professional who is well versed in the technical operations of a firm and would like to get a comprehensive feel of the customer-focused perspective that is so often implied and assumed to be understood in business discussions.

– Author

Contents

1

Customer Relationship Management

A customer is usually used to refer to a current or potential buyer or user of the products of an individual or organization, called the supplier, seller, or vendor. This is typically through purchasing or renting goods or services. However, in certain contexts, the term *customer* also includes by extension any entity that uses or experiences the services of another. A customer may also be a viewer of the product or service that is being sold despite deciding not to buy them. The general distinction between a *customer* and a *client* is that a customer purchases *products*, whereas a client purchases *services*.

The word derives from "custom," meaning "habit"; a customer was someone who frequented a particular shop, who made it a habit to purchase goods of the sort the shop sold there rather than elsewhere, and with whom the shopkeeper had to maintain a relationship to keep his or her "custom," meaning expected purchases in the future. The slogans "the customer is king" or "the customer is god" or "the customer is always right" indicate the importance of customers to businesses – although the last expression is sometimes used ironically.

However, "customer" also has a more generalized meaning as in customer service and a less commercialized meaning in not-for-profit areas. To avoid unwanted implications in some areas such as government services, community services, and education, the term "customer" is sometimes substituted by words such as "constituent" or "stakeholder". This is done to address concerns that the word "customer" implies a narrowly commercial relationship involving the purchase of products and services. However, some managers in this environment, in which the emphasis is on being helpful to the people one is dealing with rather than on commercial sales, comfortably use the word "customer" to both internal and external customers.

Obsolete meaning: In the early 17th century customer was defined as a "common prostitute". This meaning is important for understanding historical literary works. ("I marry her! What, a customer?") Othello, or ("I think thee now a common customer") *All's Well that Ends Well*. Today the meaning of "customer" has been inverted in this usage.

Customer relationship management (CRM) is a widely-implemented strategy for managing a company's interactions with customers, clients and sales prospects. It involves using technology to organize, automate, and synchronize business processes—principally sales activities, but also those for marketing, customer service, and technical support. The overall goals are to find, attract, and win new clients, nurture and retain those the company already has, entice former clients back into the fold, and reduce the costs of marketing and client service. Customer relationship management describes a companywide business strategy including customer-interface departments as well as other departments. Measuring and valuing customer relationships is critical to implementing this strategy.

CUSTOMER EXPERIENCE MANAGEMENT

The goal of customer experience management (CEM) is to move customers from satisfied to loyal and then from loyal to advocate. Traditionally, managing the customer relationship has been the domain of Customer Relationship Management (CRM). However, CRM strategies and solutions are designed to focus on product, price and enterprise process, with minimal or no focus on customer need and desire. The result is a sharp mismatch between the organisation's approach to customer expectations and what customers actually want, resulting in the failure of many CRM implementations.

Where CRM is enterprise-focused and designed to manage customers for maximum efficiency, CEM is a strategy that focuses the operations and processes of a business around the needs of the individual customer. Companies are focusing on the importance of the experience and, as Jeananne Rae notes, realizing that "building great consumer experiences is a complex enterprise, involving strategy, integration of technology, orchestrating business models, brand management and CEO commitment." (2006)

According to Bernd Schmitt, "the term 'Customer Experience Management' represents the discipline, methodology and/or process used to comprehensively manage a customer's cross-channel exposure, interaction and transaction with a company, product, brand or service." Customer experience solutions provide strategies, process models, and information technology to design, manage and optimize the end-to-end customer experience process.

CEM SYSTEMS

One of the key features of successful CEM implementations is their ability to manage multi-channel interactions. Customer experience solutions address the cross-channel (contact Centre, Internet, self service, mobile devices, brick and mortar stores), cross-touchpoint (phone, chat, email, Web, in-person), and cross-lifecycle (ordering, fulfilment, billing, support, etc.) nature of the customer experience process. By contrast, CRM solutions tend to offer point solutions for specific customer-facing functions such as, but not limited to, sales force automation, customer analytics, and campaign management.

Experience-based providers also integrate both internal and external innovations to create end-to-end customer experiences. They evaluate their business models as well as business support systems and operational support systems (BSS/OSS) from the customer's point of view to achieve the level of customer-centricity necessary to improve customer loyalty, churn and revenue (Lopez, 2007).

CUSTOMER EXPERIENCE

Customer experience (CX) is the sum of all experiences a customer has with a supplier of goods or services, over the duration of their relationship with that supplier. From awareness, discovery, attraction, interaction, purchase, use, cultivation and advocacy. It can also be used to mean an individual experience over one transaction; the distinction is usually clear in context.

GROWING RECOGNITION

Analysts and commentators who write about customer experience (CX) and customer relationship management have increasingly recognized the importance of managing the customer's experience. Customers receive some kind of experience, ranging from positive to negative, during the course of buying goods and services. Thompson and Kolsky say that "an experience is defined as the sum total of conscious events. As such, a supplier cannot avoid creating an experience every time it interacts with a customer" (2004). Furthermore, it has been shown that a customer's perception of an organisation is built as a result of their interaction across multiple-channels, not through one channel, and that a positive customer experience can result in increased share of wallet and repeat business.

A company's ability to deliver an experience that sets it apart in the eyes of its customers serves to increase their spend with the company and, optimally, inspire loyalty to its brand. "Loyalty," says Jessica Debor, "is now driven primarily by a company's interaction with its customers and how well it delivers on their wants and needs." (2008)

To create a superior customer experience requires understanding the customer's point of view, say Don Peppers and Martha Rogers, Ph.D in *Rules to Break and Laws to Follow*. "What's it really like to be your customer? What is the day-in, day-out 'customer experience' your company is delivering? How does it feel to wait on hold on the phone? To open a package and not be certain how to follow the poorly translated instructions? To stand in line, be charged a fee, wait for a service call that was promised two hours ago, come back to an online shopping cart that's no longer there an hour later? Or what's it like to be remembered? To receive helpful suggestions? To get everything exactly as it was promised? To be confident that the answers you get are the best ones for you?" In short, customer experience meaning a customer journey which makes the customer feel happy, satisfy, justify, with a sense of being respected, served and cared, according to his/her expectation or standard, start from first contact and through the whole relationship.

EMERGING BUSINESS REQUIREMENT

With products becoming commoditized, price differentiation no longer sustainable and customers demanding more, companies – and communication service providers (wireline, wireless, broadband cable, satellite) in particular – are focusing on delivering superior customer experiences. A 2009 study of over 860 corporate executives revealed that companies that have increased their investment in customer experience management over the past three years report higher customer referral rates and customer satisfaction (Strativity Group, 2009).

This finding is also supported by research completed by software company Chordiant in 2008 into the customer experience management performance of large organisations across Europe. The research surveyed 450 large organisations to create a maturity model and the results showed that over ¾ of the organisations surveyed achieved level 3 (of 5) or less for CEM performance (5 being best possible result).

The results also showed that performance in four key business areas (market share, retention, profitability, and customer satisfaction) was directly related to CEM performance.

The customer experience has emerged as the single most important aspect in achieving success for companies across all industries (Peppers and Rogers 2005). For example, Starbucks spent less than $10MM on advertising from 1987 to 1998 yet added over 2,000 new stores to accommodate growing sales. Starbucks popularity is based on the experience that drove its customers to highly recommend their store to friends and family.

CUSTOMER EXPERIENCE TRANSFORMATION

Customer experience transformation (CxT) is a strategy that uses business process management to enhance customer service experience from any customer touchpoint. The objective is to provide companies and their customer service organizations with the tools needed to move customers from satisfied to loyal, and then to avid brand advocates.

CUSTOMER LIFECYCLE MANAGEMENT

Customer Lifecycle Management, or CLM is the measurement of multiple customer related metrics, which, when analysed for a period of time, indicate performance of a business. The overall scope of the CLM implementation process encompasses all domains or departments of an organization, which generally brings all sources of static and dynamic data, marketing processes, and value added services to a unified decision supporting platform through iterative phases of customer acquisition, retention, cross and up-selling, and lapsed customer win-back. Some detailed CLM models further breakdown these phases into acquisition, introduction to products, profiling of customers, growth of customer base, cultivation of loyalty among customers, and termination of customer relationship. According to a DM Review magazine article by Claudia Imhoff, et al., "The purpose of the customer life cycle is to define and communicate the stages through which a customer progresses when considering, purchasing and using products, and the associated business processes a company uses to move the customer through the customer life cycle."

B2B

Business-to-business (B2B) describes commerce transactions between businesses, such as between a manufacturer and a wholesaler, or between a wholesaler and a retailer. Contrasting terms are business-to-consumer (B2C) and business-to-government (B2G). The volume of B2B (Business-to-Business) transactions is much higher than the volume of B2C transactions. The primary reason for this is that in a typical supply chain there will be many B2B transactions involving sub components or raw materials, and only one B2C transaction, specifically sale of the finished product to the end customer. For example, an automobile manufacturer makes several B2B transactions such as buying tires, glass for windscreens, and rubber hoses for its vehicles. The final transaction, a finished vehicle sold to the consumer, is a single (B2C) transaction.

B2B is also used in the context of communication and collaboration. Many businesses are now using social media to connect with their consumers (B2C); however, they are now using similar tools within the business so employees can connect with one another. When communication is taking place amongst employees, this can be referred to as "B2B" communication.

ETYMOLOGY

The term "business-to-business" was originally coined to describe the electronic communications between businesses or enterprises in order to distinguish it from the communications between businesses and consumers (B2C). It eventually came to be used in marketing as well, initially describing only industrial or capital goods marketing. Today it is widely used to describe all products and services used by enterprises. Many professional institutions and the trade publications focus much more on B2C than B2B, although most sales and marketing personnel are in the B2B sector.

B2C

Business-to-consumer (B2C, sometimes also called Business-to-Customer) describes activities of businesses serving end consumers with products and/or services. An example of a B2C transaction would be a person buying a pair of shoes from a retailer. The transactions that led to the shoes being available for purchase, that is the purchase of the leather, laces, rubber, etc. However, the sale of the shoe from the shoemaker to the retailer would be considered a (B2B) transaction.

TYPES OF BUSINESS TO CONSUMER

While the term e-commerce refers to all online transactions, B2C stands for "business-to-consumer" and applies to any business or organization that sells its products or services to consumers over the Internet for its own use. When most people think of B2C e-commerce, they think of Amazon, the online bookseller that launched its site in 1995 and quickly took on the nation's major retailers. In addition to online retailers, B2C has grown to include services such as online banking, travel services, online auctions, health information and real estate sites. Peer-to-peer sites such as Craigslist also fall under the B2C category.

B2C e-commerce went through some tough times, particularly after the technology-heavy Nasdaq crumbled in 2000. In the ensuing dotcom carnage, hundreds of e-commerce sites shut their virtual doors and some experts predicted years of struggle for online retail ventures. Since then, however, shoppers have continued to flock to the web in increasing numbers. In fact, North American consumers adopted e-commerce so much that despite growing fears about identity theft, they spent $172 billion shopping online in 2005, up from $38.8 billion in 2000.

By 2010, consumers are expected to spend $329 billion each year online, according to Forrester Research. What's more, the percentage of U.S. households shopping online is expected to grow from 39 percent this year to 48 percent in 2010.

In October 2010, an extension of B2C, B21 was] According to marketingterms "B2C businesses played a large role in the rapid development of the commercial Internet in the late 20th century. Large sums of venture capital flowed to consumers in the form of free online services and discounted shopping, spurring adoption of the new medium." Business to Consumer e-consumer quickly developed as an alternative way for companies to sell more products to a larger market.B2C e-commerce provided not only multiple advantages to a company but also to the consumers.

The main advantages for both the business and consumer are that by opening their market up to B2C e-commerce trade they are reducing transactions costs. Businesses usually ship their products to a number of stores to make them visible to the consumer. However, by using B2C commerce they can instead showcase all of their products on the internet which reduces the cost of transaction. B2C also allows their customers to better access information about different product and sellers which broadens the selection available to their customers. Business to consumer ecommerce is valuable to the economy because it creates a more unique way for businesses and consumers to interact.

UNIQUE ATTRIBUTES

- *Negotiation:* Selling to another business involves haggling over prices, delivery and product specifications. Not so with most consumer sales. That makes it easier for retailers to put a catalog online, and it's why the first B2C applications were for buying finished goods or commodities that are simple to describe and price.
- *Integration:* Retailers don't have to integrate with their customers' systems. Companies selling to other businesses, however, need to make sure they can communicate without human intervention.

EMPLOYEE EXPERIENCE MANAGEMENT (EEM)

Along with the notion of Experience Economy, Employee experience is defined as what employee received during their interaction with careers' elements (e.g. firms, supervisors, coworkers, customer, environment, etc.) that affect their cognition and affection and leads to their particular behaviours. Employee Experience Management (EEM) is conceptualized by Abhari as an approach to deliver excellent experience to employee, which leads to the positive customer experience by emphasizing on their experiential needs-like Experiential Marketing for external customers.

Harris (2007) hinted, "It [customer experience] begins at the heart of an organization. It begins with employees who are being the strategy and living the brand". EEM, same as Internal marketing, is an internal approach by focusing on employee (internal customer) prior to external customer. The notion of EEM come from the question that how firms make sure that employee create the desirable customer experience, whenever they interact with customer or provide the information and service to them. Alternatively, utilizing employee in delivering brand value promise is remarkable concern in EEM. EEM also goes beyond standard Human Resource Management by rewarding more employee-experience in form of both professional and personal development.

ENTERPRISE FEEDBACK MANAGEMENT (EFM)

Enterprise feedback management (EFM) is a system of processes and software that enables organizations to centrally manage deployment of surveys while dispersing authoring and analysis throughout an organization. EFM systems typically provide different roles and permission levels for different types of users, such as novice survey authors, professional survey authors, survey reporters and translators. EFM can help an organization establish a dialogue with employees, partners, and customers regarding key issues and concerns and potentially make customer specific real time interventions. EFM consists of data collection, analysis and reporting.

Prior to EFM, survey software was typically deployed in departments and lacked user roles, permissions and workflow. EFM enables deployment across the enterprise, providing decision makers with important data for increasing customer satisfaction, loyalty and lifetime value. EFM enables companies to look at customers "holistically" and to better respond to customer needs.

Gartner projected that 40 percent of total feedback system deployments would be EFM solutions in 2008. Its worth noting that the motivation to pilot/deploy EFM is often to reduce the reliance on (or reduce the costs of) traditional satisfaction research.

Esteban Kolsky, when a research director at Gartner, described the market structure as follows: "The market for these tools is a highly fragmented one, with no single provider. It's going to jumpstart a bunch of acquisitions as larger vendors look to work EFM and surveying into their growth strategy."

The EFM market grew 60% to 70% in 2005 and 2006.

EFM applications support complex survey design, with features such as question and page rotation, quota management and advanced skip patterns and branching. The software typically offers advanced reporting with statistical analysis and centralized panel management. EFM applications are often integrated with external platforms, most typically with CRM systems but also with HRIS systems and generic web portals.

Unlike low-end survey tools, EFM applications provides a workflow process with user roles and permissions, so that users may be able to author a survey but require another user to approve it before it is published. Such workflow ensures consistent survey quality and enforces respondent privacy and IT security policies. Applications of EFM vary widely from HR, IT, Marketing, Sales and continues to expand on its corporate implementation and scope. Departments within an organization can collaborate on feedback initiatives, sharing results and gaining insights that enable the organization to listen, learn and react to the needs of their key stakeholders. A key part of the value of an EFM deployment is the development of the business rules (i.e. who needs to see what feedback info) and which parts of the customer/employee/partner facing process needs to be measured.

MYSTERY SHOPPING

Mystery shopping or a mystery consumer is a tool used by Mystery Shopping Providers and market research companies to measure quality of retail service or gather specific information about products and services. Mystery

Shopping should be performed by a person, so called Mystery Shopper, who is unknown to the establishment the shopper is evaluating. '*Mystery shoppers* perform specific tasks—such as purchasing a product, asking questions, registering complaints or behaving in a certain way—and then provide detailed reports or feedback about their experiences.

Mystery shopping was standard practice by the early 1940s as a way to measure employee integrity. Tools used for mystery shopping assessments range from simple questionnaires to complete audio and video recordings.

Mystery shopping can be used in any industry, with the most common venues being retail stores, hotels, movie theaters, restaurants, fast food chains, banks, gas stations, car dealerships, apartments, health clubs and health care facilities. Since 2010, mystery shopping has become abundant in the medical tourism industry, with healthcare providers and medical facilities using the tool to assess and improve the customer service experience. In the UK mystery shopping is increasingly used to provide feedback on customer services provided by local authorities, and other non-profit organizations such as housing associations and churches.

METHODOLOGY

When a client company hires a company providing mystery shopping services, a survey model will be drawn up and agreed to which defines what information and improvement factors the client company wishes to measure. These are then drawn up into survey instruments and assignments that are allocated to shoppers registered with the mystery shopping company.

The details and information points shoppers take note of typically include:

- Number of employees in the store on entering
- How long it takes before the mystery shopper is greeted
- The name of the employees
- Whether or not the greeting is friendly, ideally according to objective measures
- The questions asked by the shopper to find a suitable product
- The types of products shown
- The sales arguments used by the employee
- Whether or how the employee attempted to close the sale
- Whether the employee suggested any add-on sales
- Whether the employee invited the shopper to come back to the store
- Cleanliness of store and store associates
- Speed of service
- Compliance with company standards relating to service, store appearance, and grooming/presentation.

Shoppers are often given instructions or procedures to make the transaction atypical to make the test of the knowledge and service skills of the employees more stringent or specific to a particular service issue (known as scenarios). For instance, mystery shoppers at a restaurant may pretend they are lactose-intolerant, or a clothing store mystery shopper could inquire about gift-wrapping services. Not all mystery shopping scenarios include a purchase.

While gathering information, shoppers usually blend in to the store being evaluated as regular shoppers. They may sometimes be required to take photographs or measurements, return purchases, or count the number of products, seats, people during the visit.

A timer or a stopwatch may be required. In some states in the USA, mystery shoppers must also be licensed as private investigators in order to perform some of the tasks. After the visit the shopper submits the data collected to the mystery shopping company, which reviews and analyses the information, completing quantitative or qualitative statistical analysis reports on the data for the client company. This allows for a comparison on how the stores or restaurants are doing against previously defined criteria.

STATISTICS

The mystery shopping industry had an estimated value of nearly $600 million in the United States in 2004, according to a 2005 report commissioned by the Mystery Shopping Providers Association (MSPA). Companies that participated in the report experienced an average growth of 11.1 percent from 2003 to 2004, compared to an average growth of 12.2 percent. The report estimates more than 8.1 million mystery shops were conducted in 2004. The report represents the first industry association attempt to quantify the size of the mystery shopping industry. Similar surveys are available for European regions where mystery shopping is becoming more embedded into company procedures.

As a measure of its importance, customer/patient satisfaction is being incorporated more frequently into executive pay. A study by a U.S. firm found more than 55% of hospital chief executive officers surveyed in 2005 had "some compensation at risk," based on patient satisfaction, up from only 8% to 20% a dozen years ago." CBC Television's news magazine program *Marketplace* ran a segment on this topic during a January 2001 episode.

ETHICS

The Trade Organization for Mystery Shopping Providers, MSPA has defined a Code of Professional Standards and Ethics Agreement for Mystery Shopping Providers and for Mystery Shoppers. MSPA has also defined Standards for Mystery Shopping. The Standard is available in a full version and an Abstract version. The Abstract is available in 32 languages.Other organizations that have defined standards for Mystery Shopping are; ESOMAR, MRS and MRA.

IMPORTANT FACTOR IN ATTRACTING AND RETAINING CUSTOMERS

Recognizing that service is an important factor in attracting and retaining customers, organizations are increasingly turning to technology to help them improve their clients' experience while aiming to increase efficiency and minimize costs. Even so, a 2009 study revealed that only 39% of corporate executives believe their employees have the right tools and authority to solve client problems.

APPOINTMENT

Creating and scheduling appointments with customers is a central activity of most customer oriented businesses. Sales, customer support, and service personnel regularly spend a portion of their time getting in touch with customers and prospects through a variety of means to agree on a time and place for meeting for a sales conversation or to deliver customer service. Appointment CRM is a relatively new CRM platform category in which an automated system is used to offer a suite of suitable appointment times to a customer via e-mail or through a web site. An automated process is used to schedule and confirm the appointment, and place it on the appropriate person's calendar. Appointment CRM systems can be an origination point for a sales lead and are generally integrated with sales and marketing CRM systems to capture and store the interaction.

ANALYTICS

Relevant analytics capabilities are often interwoven into applications for sales, marketing, and service. These features can be complemented and augmented with links to separate, purpose-built applications for analytics and business intelligence. Sales analytics let companies monitor and understand client actions and preferences, through sales forecasting and data quality. Marketing applications generally come with predictive analytics to improve segmentation and targeting, and features for measuring the effectiveness of online, offline, and search marketing campaigns.

Web analytics have evolved significantly from their starting point of merely tracking mouse clicks on Web sites. By evaluating "buy signals," marketers can see which prospects are most likely to transact and also identify those who are bogged down in a sales process and need assistance. Marketing and finance personnel also use analytics to assess the value of multifaceted programs as a whole.

These types of analytics are increasing in popularity as companies demand greater visibility into the performance of call centres and other service and support channels, in order to correct problems before they affect satisfaction levels. Support-focused applications typically include dashboards similar to those for sales, plus capabilities to measure and analyse response times, service quality, agent performance, and the frequency of various issues.

INTEGRATED/COLLABORATIVE

Departments within enterprises — especially large enterprises — tend to function with little collaboration. More recently, the development and adoption of these tools and services have fostered greater fluidity and cooperation among sales, service, and marketing. This finds expression in the concept of collaborative systems that use technology to build bridges between departments. For example, feedback from a technical support centre can enlighten marketers about specific services and product features clients are asking for. Reps, in their turn, want to be able to pursue these opportunities without the burden of re-entering records and contact data into a separate SFA system.

SMALL BUSINESS

For small business, basic client service can be accomplished by a contact manager system: an integrated solution that lets organizations and individuals efficiently track and record interactions, including emails, documents, jobs, faxes, scheduling, and more. These tools usually focus on accounts rather than on individual contacts. They also generally include opportunity insight for tracking sales pipelines plus added functionality for marketing and service. As with larger enterprises, small businesses are finding value in online solutions, especially for mobile and telecommuting workers.

SOCIAL MEDIA

Social media sites like Twitter, LinkedIn and Facebook are amplifying the voice of people in the marketplace and are having profound and far-reaching effects on the ways in which people buy. Customers can now research companies online and then ask for recommendations through social media channels, making their buying decision without contacting the company. People also use social media to share opinions and experiences on companies, products and services. As social media is not as widely moderated or censored as mainstream media, individuals can say anything they want about a company or brand, positive or negative.

Increasingly, companies are looking to gain access to these conversations and take part in the dialogue. More than a few systems are now integrating to social networking sites. Social media promoters cite a number of business advantages, such as using online communities as a source of high-quality leads and a vehicle for crowd sourcing solutions to client-support problems. Companies can also leverage client stated habits and preferences to "hyper-target" their sales and marketing communications. Some analysts take the view that business-to-business marketers should proceed cautiously when weaving social media into their business processes. These observers recommend careful market research to determine if and where the phenomenon can provide measurable benefits for client interactions, sales and support. It is stated that people feel their interactions are peer-to-peer between them and their contacts, and resent company involvement, sometimes responding with negatives about that company.

BUILDING STRATEGY IN CUSTOMER RELATIONSHIP MANAGEMENT

The first step in creating an outstanding relationship with your customers is to simply listen to them. That may seem like a simple thing to do, but so often we get so caught up in sharing what we have to offer and what our product is that we forget to take the time to listen to what it is that our customers, the people that are walking through our doors, really want. For example, in my chiropractic businesses, I know what services I can render. I know what I think that I'm going to do but it's so important, in the medical field especially, to listen to the patient's complaints or concerns.

The necessity to be focused on their concerns and complaints can be carried over to any business whether it be in the technological, merchandising, or informational arena. Specifically look at what it is that the customer wants to have. Can you hear them through, over, and above what you want to put out there? All businesses know what they have to offer, but do you know what your customers want and does what you have to offer equal what they need?

CUSTOMER RELATIONSHIP BUILDING STRATEGY

Once you listen to your customers' needs, you have to let them know that you can help them. It is important to make them realize that you understand their problem by letting them know that you heard them.

Sometimes that's as simple as just repeating what you heard them say. "If I understand correctly, these are your needs" and summarizing what you heard. Then after you clarify what you heard, a great strategy to use is to ask, "Is that correct?" They will tell you whether or not you've summarized it correctly and then you can ask, "Is there anything else?" This will help you discover if they have any additional problems or concerns. This is an opportunity to re-listen; to reiterate what you heard them say.

What may be holding them back? What do they perceive as drawbacks? What are the things that could stop them? What are their obstacles? What is their budget? What is their desired outcome? All of these things are very important for businesses to know, but often businesses are more focused on their own business rather than the needs of the people that they are designed to serve.

ABOVE AND BEYOND THE CALL

The third customer relationship strategy involves letting your customers know what you have to offer. But what I encourage is that you tell them what you're going to give them and then give them more. I have used this practice in every one of my businesses. You promise what you're going to do for them and you promise that you can solve their problem, (if of course you can!), but then you go above and beyond. You do that little bit extra; add that extra value. But here is the important part: let them know that you did that for them. This part is really critical. There are a lot of businesses that do extra. They go that little bit above and beyond, but they forget to make sure that their clients know that they have received extra value.

For example, there were a lot of times early in my practice, before I understood the strategies, when someone would come into my office and we would do the basic chiropractic care. But on top of that we would also include some extra therapies. We wouldn't charge them for those and all we would basically say would be, "Have a nice day!" But those extra therapies were valuable. So now what we've trained our staff to say is something like this: "We just wanted to let you know that you had your chiropractic visit, but in addition to that we also did a massage therapy or heat therapy or we've provided you with this appliance. Normally our charges for that would be $300, but for you there is no charge. We just want to make sure that you're comfortable." It's very important to let them know what you've done for them.

Here's another example: I have a friend who is a very high-end carpenter and when he used to go to his clients' homes to do finished carpentry work, he would often do little extra things because he is a very meticulous person. He was really terrific at what he did, but he would do the extra things and the bill would not show that he had given the client added value. Once after he had done work at my house I met with him and shared, "Ray, you know I really appreciate that you've done these extra things but you have given them no extra value. You're not increasing the value of yourself and your company." So I recommended that when he completed his jobs that, even though he is not going to charge for the extras he does, he should let the customers know how much he actually did for them.

So now on Ray's invoices, he lists all the things that they had agreed on at a certain price and then he writes, for example, "In addition to that, we also did this extra chair. We repaired this, we patched that, we laid about 20 extra feet of board on your floor, we made this look right, and I didn't like the way the last guy hung that door so we re-hung it for you. Normally that would have cost you $2,000 but that's all at no extra charge because I wanted to make sure the job got done right". So when you over-deliver, let them know that you over-delivered. Tactfully letting them know that it was done is a very important step in your customer relationship building strategy.

COMMUNICATION

The fourth strategy: Communication. We live in a time of instant gratification. People can go online, type in something on their computer, and the results are up in an instant. Communication is very important but it needs to be done promptly. It is important to get back to people in a reasonable time frame. When people call you, get back to them within a few hours or a day as the latest. If it's an e-mail, absolutely within a day to two days maximum.

People want to know that you're attentive to their needs. People will start to associate your quick response to their communications with your quick response to their needs and that's a great association for them to make; a great reputation to have. That's the kind of communication that you want to have. It's not really a verbal communication per se, but it's going to create the impression that you're in tune with their needs. It is important that you show that you are in tune with their desire for a response and that you are there to deliver to them quickly and efficiently. If you can communicate and connect efficiently and effectively with your clients with an e-mail or with a phone call, then you can show that you are in tune with them and their needs.

CONSUMER RELATIONSHIP SYSTEM IN CRM

Consumer Relationship Systems (CRS) are specialized Customer Relationship Management (CRM) software applications used to handle consumer products and services company's dealings with consumers and customers. Consumer Affairs and Customer Relations contact Centres within these organizations, that are typically Consumer Packaged Goods (CPG) companies providing consumers with packaged items, such as foods and beverages, household consumable products and durable goods, as well as travel services, e.g., passenger airlines and cruise ship lines.

The companies' trained contact Centre representatives handle in-bound contacts from anonymous consumers and customers, replying to inquiries and fulfilling responses. Representatives capture consumer contact information, issues, and verbatim feedback which is stored in the CRM and made available to company stakeholders such as marketing, product management and development, legal, public relations, etc., for input to product and service improvements. The CRS workflow processing and reporting enable issuing of early warning alerts to product problems in the marketplace (e.g., product recalls) and capture of current consumer sentiment ('voice of the customer'). The system has been used to effectively create best-practice actionable voice of the customer (VOC) processes.

The first such CRS was developed in the 1980s. In 1981 Michael Wilke and Robert Thornton founded Wilke/Thornton, Inc. in Columbus, Ohio, to develop new software application systems. By 1983 Wilke/Thornton was creating and implementing a specialized CRM application system for inbound consumer contact call Centres of CPG companies, including Kimberly-Clark, Quaker Oats, and Yokohama Tire. This consumer/customer contact management system was designed to capture and record consumer response (inquiries, reactions, and related issues, such as how-to-use and where-to-buy items) to packaged products and services.

The Consumer Relationship System (CRS) established a niche category—the consumer relationship system—and, because Wilke/Thornton was the earliest developer, become the system became the *de facto* standard for the consumer packaged goods industry niche. Now hundreds of consumer packaged goods companies with global consumer response handling operations now use consumer relationship systems (Consumer Relationship CRM). Some 10,000 contact Centre representatives use these systems daily worldwide. The CRS facilitate the processing of workflow by the representatives who receive the calls, letters, email, and online chat messages from consumers in many locations, across time zones, communicating in many languages, having different postal address formats, and a vast multitude of different product items and issues. These representatives assign item, issue, status and action codes to contacts and carryout the appropriate replies and fulfilment actions.

While the goal of these consumer response handling operations is to increase customer satisfaction, loyalty, and retention, the consumer relationship systems also collect consumer response for early detection of local market product problems and of consumer preference trends to provide detailed response data, including verbatim transcripts, for analysis and insight development reported internally to support product and service improvements. Many of the consumer contact Centre managers who use the CRS are members of the Society of Consumer Affairs Professionals International, a global organization that supports the aims and purposes of these customer care professionals.

Current consumer relationship systems integrate with telephone and call recording systems, with corporate enterprise systems for input and reporting. Consumer response flows from consumer products companies' branded Web sites directly into the response systems.

These systems are popular because they can deliver the 'voice of the consumer' that contributes to product quality improvement and corporate success. The CRS area available by traditional perpetual license and by online subscription service. In recent years Consumer Relationship CRM vendors, like Wilke/Thornton mentioned above, have begun adopting the software-as-a-service business delivery model (SaaS)SaaS which benefits users by reducing up-front capital costs and by being scalable to meet user needs. With the on-demand Web-based CRS subscription service, subscribers pay only for their usage of the system, like traditional utility services.

TRADITIONAL MARKETING THEORY IN CRM

Traditional marketing theory and practice have focused on attracting new customers rather than retaining existing ones. Today, however, although attracting new customers remains an important marketing task, the emphasis has shifted toward relationship marketing—creating, maintaining, and enhancing strong relationships with customers and other stakeholders.

Beyond designing strategies to attract new customers and create transaction with them, companies arc going all out to retain current customers and build profitable, long-term relationship; with them. The new view is that marketing is the science and art of finding, retaining, and growing profitable customers.

Why the new emphasis on retaining and growing customers In the past, many companies took their customers for granted. Facing an expanding economy and rapidly growing markets, companies could practice a "leaky bucket" approach to marketing. Growing markets meant a plentiful supply of new customers. Companies could keep filling the marketing bucket with new customers without worrying about losing old customers through holes in the bottom of the bucket.

However, companies today are facing some new marketing realities. Changing demographics, more sophisticated competitors, and overcapacity in many industries—all of these factors mean that there are fewer customers to go around. Many companies are now fighting for shares of flat or fading markets. Thus, the costs of attracting new consumers are rising, (n fact, it costs five times as much to attract a new customer as it does to keep a current customer satisfied.

Companies are also realizing that losing a customer means losing more than a single sale: It means losing the entire stream of purchases that the customer would make over a lifetime of patronage.

For example, here is a dramatic illustration of customer lifetime value: & Stew Leonard, who operates a highly profitable single-store supermarket, says that he sees $50,000 flying out of his score every rime he sees a sulking customer. Why Because his average customer spends about $100 a week, shops 50 weeks a year, and remains in the area lord about 10 years. If this customer has an unhappy experience and switches to another supermarket, Stew Leonard has lost 550,000 in revenue. The loss can be much greater if the disappointed customer shares the bad experience with other customers and causes them to defect.

Similarly, the customer lifetime value of a Taco Bell customer exceeds $12,000. Lexus estimates that a single satisfied and loyal customer is worth $600,000 in lifetime sales. 3 Thus, working to retain and grow customers makes good economic sense. A company can lose money on a specific transaction but still benefit greatly from a long-term relationship.

ATTRACTING, RETAINING, AND GROWING CUSTOMERS

The key to building lasting relationships is the creation of superior customer value and satisfaction. Satisfied customers are more likely to be loyal customers, and loyal customers are more likely to give the company a larger share of their business. We now look more closely at the concepts of customer value and satisfaction, loyalty and retention, and share of customer.

RELATIONSHIP BUILDING BLOCKS; CUSTOMER VALUE AND SATISFACTION

Attracting and retaining customers can be a difficult cask. Today's customers face a vast array of product and brand choices, prices, and suppliers. The company must j answer a key question: How do customers make their choices The answer is that customers choose the marketing offer that they believe will give them the most value. They are satisfied with and continue to buy offers that consistently meet or I exceed their value expectations. Let's look more closely at customer value and satisfaction.

Customer Value. Consumers buy from the firm that they believe offers the highest customer delivered value—the difference between total customer value and total customer cost. For example, suppose that a large construction firm wants to buy a bulldozer. It will buy the bulldozer from either Caterpillar or Komatsu. The salespeople for the two companies carefully describe their respective offers to the buyer. The construction firm evaluates the two competing bulldozer offers to assess which one delivers the greatest value. It adds all the values from four sources—product, services, personnel, and image. First, it judges that Caterpillar's bulldozer provides higher reliability, durability, and performance. It also decides that Caterpillar has better accompanying services—delivery, training, and maintenance. The customer views Caterpillar personnel as more knowledgeable and responsive. Finally, it places higher value on Caterpillar's reputation. Thus, the customer decides that Caterpillar offers more total customer value than does Komatsu.

Does the construction firm buy the Caterpillar bulldozer Not necessarily. The firm also will examine the total customer cost of buying Caterpillar's bulldozer versus Komatsu's. The total customer cost consists of more than just monetary costs. As Adam Smith observed more than two centuries ago, "The real price of anything is the toil and trouble of acquiring it. "Total customer cost also includes the buyer's anticipated time, energy, and psychic costs. The construction firm evaluates these costs along with monetary costs to form a complete estimate of its costs.

The buying firm now compares total customer value to total customer cost and determines the total delivered value associated with Caterpillar's bulldozer. In the same way, it assesses the total delivered value for the Komatsu bulldozer. The firm then buys from the company that offers the highest delivered value.

Some marketers might rightly argue that this concept of how buyers choose among product alternatives is too rational. They might cite examples in which buyers did not choose the offer with the highest delivered value. For example, suppose that the Caterpillar salesperson convinces the construction firm that Caterpillar's bulldozer offer:, a higher delivered value. Nonetheless, the customer decides to buy the Komatsu bulldozer. Why would the buyer make such a decision There are many possible explanations. Perhaps the construction firm's buyers enjoy a long-term friendship with the Komatsu salesperson. Or the firm's buyers might be under strict orders to buy at the lowest price. Or perhaps the construction firm rewards its buyers for short-term performance, causing them to choose the less expensive Komatsu bulldozer, even though the Caterpillar machine will perform better and be less expensive to operate in the long run.

Clearly, buyers operate under various constraints and sometimes make choices that give more weight to their personal benefit than to company benefit. However, the customer delivered value framework applies to many situations and yields rich insights. It suggests that sellers must first assess the total customer delivered value associated with their own and competing marketing offers to determine how their own offers stack up. If competitors deliver greater value, the firm must act.

How might Caterpillar use this concept of buyer decision making to help it succeed in selling its bulldozer to this buyer It can improve its offer in either of two ways. First, it can increase total customer value by strengthening or augmenting the product, services, personnel, or image benefits of its offer. Second, it can reduce total customer cost by lowering its price or by lessening the buyer's time, energy, and psychic costs. In fact, although Caterpillar products cost more than competing brands, the company claims that its higher quality, superior service, and strong reputation make its products a better value in the long run. Its goal is to provide customers with the lowest total cost per cubic yard of earth moved, ton of coal uncovered, or mile of road graded over the life of the product.

Customer Satisfaction. Thus, consumers form expectations about the value of marketing offers and make buying decisions based on these expectations, Customer satisfaction with a purchase depends on the product's actual performance relative to a buyer's expectations. A customer might experience various degrees of satisfaction. If the product's performance falls short of expectations, the customer is dissatisfied. If performance matches expectations, the customer is satisfied. If performance exceeds expectations, the customer is highly satisfied or delighted.

But how do buyers form their expectations Expectations are based on the customer's past buying experiences, the opinions of friends and associates, and marketer and competitor information and promises. Marketers must be careful to set the right level of expectations. If they set expectations too low, they may satisfy those who buy but fail to attract enough buyers. In contrast, if they raise expectations too high, buyers are likely to be disappointed. For example, Holiday Inn ran a campaign a few years ago called "No Surprises," which promised consistently trouble-free accommodations and service. However, Holiday Inn guests still encountered a host of problems, and the expectations created by the campaign only made customers more dissatisfied. Holiday Inn had to withdraw the campaign.

The American Customer Satisfaction Index, which tracks customer satisfaction in more than two dozen U.S. manufacturing and service industries, shows that overall customer satisfaction has been declining slightly in recent years. It is unclear whether this has resulted from a decrease in product and service quality or from an increase in customer expectations. In either case, it presents an opportunity for companies that can consistently deliver superior customer value and satisfaction.

Today's most successful companies are raising expectations—and delivering performance to match. These companies embrace total customer satisfaction. For example, Honda claims "One reason our customers are so satisfied is that we aren't." Cigna vows "100% Satisfaction. 100% of the Time." Such companies track their customers' expectations, perceived company performance, and customer satisfaction. However, although the customer-centred firm seeks to deliver high customer satisfaction relative to competitors, it does not attempt to maximize customer satisfaction. A company can always increase customer satisfaction by lowering its price or increasing its services, but this may result in lower profits. Thus, the purpose of marketing is to generate customer value profitably. This requires a very delicate balance; The marketer must continue to generate more customer value and satisfaction but not "give away the house."

CUSTOMER LOYALTY AND RETENTION

Highly satisfied customers produce several benefits for the company. Satisfied customers are less price sensitive, talk favourably to others about the company and its products, and remain loyal for a longer period. However, the relationship between customer satisfaction and loyalty varies greatly across industries and competitive situations. The relationship between customer satisfaction and loyally in five different markets. In all cases, as satisfaction increases, so does loyalty. In highly competitive markets, such as those for automobiles and personal computers, there is surprisingly little difference between the loyalty of less satisfied customers and those who are merely satisfied. However, there is a tremendous difference between the loyalty of satisfied customers arid completely satisfied customers. Even a slight drop from complete satisfaction can create an enormous drop in loyalty. For example, one study showed that completely satisfied customers are nearly 42 percent more likely to be loyal than merely satisfied customers. Another study by AT&T showed that 70 percent of customers who say they are satisfied with a product or service are still willing to switch to a competitor; customers who are highly satisfied are much more loyal. Xerox found that its totally satisfied customers are six times more likely to repurchase Xerox products over the next 18 months than its satisfied customers. 9 This means that companies must aim high if they want to hold on to their customers. Customer delight creates an emotional affinity for a product or service, not just a rational preference, and this creates high customer loyalty.

Such as those served by regulated monopolies or those dominated by powerful or patent-protected brands, customers tend to remain loyal no matter how dissatisfied they are. This might seem like an ideal situation for the protected or dominant firm. However, such firms may pay a high price for customer dissatisfaction in the long run.

For example, during the 1960s and 1970s, Xerox flourished under the protection of patents on its revolutionary photocopy process. Customers had no choice but to remain loyal to Xerox, and sales and profits soared despite customer dissatisfaction over machine malfunctions and rising prices. In fact, customer dissatisfaction led to even greats' short-run profits for Xerox: Disgruntled customers were forced to pay for service when machines broke down, and some even leased extra machines as backups.

But as the 1980s dawned, Xerox paid dearly for its failure to keep its customers satisfied. Japanese competitors skirted patents and entered the market with higher quality copiers sold at lower prices. Dissatisfied customers gleefully defected to the new competitors. Xerox's share of the world copier market plunged from, over 80 percent to less than 35 percent in just five years. 10 Thus, even highly successful companies must pay close attention to customer satisfaction and its relationship to customer loyalty. Xerox has now developed industry-leading, customer-driven quality, customer satisfaction, and customer retention programs. As a result, although it has lost its dominance, it is once again a profitable industry leader.

At the same time, a high customer satisfaction rating doesn't guarantee customer loyalty. A major insurance firm learned this when comparing its performance to competitor State Farm:

A study comparing the competitor to State Farm showed only a 6.5 point spread between the percentage of respondents who were totally satisfied with the competitor and the percent totally satisfied with State Farm. So, how can we explain State Farm's consistently higher profitability over the years The answer lies in customer loyalty. By using discounts and guarantees for long-term loyal customers and an agent compensation plan that encourages customer retention, State Farm has created strong customer loyally. Although the study showed fairly minor differences in those totally satisfied, loyalty measures widened the gap between the companies. When customers were asked how strongly they preferred their life insurance company over others, there was an 11 percent spread between the competitor and State Farm, The gulf widened to a 15 percentage point State Farm lead on the statement, "I am very loyal to my company, it would take a lot to get me to switch." Twice as many respondents strongly agreed with the statement, "I would go out of my way to stay with my life insurance company," for State Farm than for the competitor."

Thus, customer satisfaction remains an extremely important component in customer loyalty—a company will find it difficult to earn customer loyalty without first earning high levels of customer satisfaction. However, companies should also carefully examine customer loyalty itself, which often is a better indicator of customer attitudes and behaviour.

GROWING "SHARE OF CUSTOMER"

Beyond simple attracting and retaining good customers, marketers want to constantly increase their share of customer. They want to capture a greater share of the customer's purchasing in their product categories, either by becoming the sole supplier of products the customer is currently buying or by persuading the customer to purchase additional company products. Thus, banks want a greater "share of wallet," supermarkets want to increase their "share of stomach," car companies want a greater "share of garage," and airlines want a greater "share of travel."

Today, the goal isn't to win some business from a lot of customers—its to win all the business of current customers. Feverishly chasing market share is out; trying to maximize share of customers is in. For example, seeking maximum share of Perot System's travel dollars, American Airlines sold the company a program called Airpass. Now, unless a travel schedule demands otherwise, all Perot employees fly American.

It works like this: When Perot employee's book flights, they don't have to bother waiting for tickets; they simply present a card at the ticket counter or gate. Miles are automatically credited to their American frequent flier accounts. Upgrades are readily available and, to complete the package, American allows all Perot employees to use its Ambassadors Clubs for business and leisure travel. For all of this, Perot gets charged at a discounted travel rate against a corporate commitment for a specified number of travel miles. In return, American gets most of Perot's business. It's a winning proposition for everyone—except American's competitors. They just got excluded from a lot of Perot's travel business.

One of the best ways to increase share of customer is through cross-selling. Cross-selling means getting more business from current customers of one product or service by selling them additional offerings. For example, the recent merger between Citibank and Travelers is helping both units of the Citibank Group to cross-sell the company's services. A new Travelers Financial Edge program allows independent Travellers agents to introduce a number of Citibank products to their insurance clients, such as credit cards and student loans, as well as an equipment leasing program for commercial customers.

Similarly, under a new Citibank Partners program, Citibank representatives can offer a fuller slate of financial services to their customers, such as insurance from Travellers and mutual funds from Salomon Smith Barney (another Citibank Group unit). To support the effort to cross-sell a broader range of services for customers, Citibank's personal bankers will be dubbed "client financial analysts" and its branches will be called "Citibank Financial Centres." As a result, Citibank Group will obtain a larger share of each customer's financial services dollars.

BUILDING LASTING CUSTOMER RELATIONSHIPS

We can now see the importance of not just finding customers, but of keeping and growing them as well. Relationship marketing is oriented toward the Song term, Today's smart companies not only want to create customers, they want to "own" them for life. In this section, we discuss several questions about how companies actually build lasting customer relation ships. What levels of relationships can companies build with their customers and what relation ship-building tools do they use Who is responsible for delivering customer value and satisfaction What is the role of total marketing quality.

CUSTOMER RELATIONSHIP LEVELS AND TOOLS

Companies can build customer relationships at many levels—economic, social, technical, and legal—depending on the nature of the target market. At one extreme, a company with many low-margin customers may seek to develop bam relationships with them. For example, Procter & Gamble does not phone all of its Tide customers to get to know them personally and express its appreciation for their business. Instead, P&G creates relationships through brand-building advertising, sales promotions, a 1-800 customer response number, and its Tide Clothesline Web site. At the other extreme, in markets with few customer! and high margins, sellers want to create partnerships with key customers. For example, P&G customer teams work closely with Wal-Mart, Safeway, and other large retailers. Boeing works closely with American Airlines, Delta, and other airlines in designing its airplanes and ensuring that Boeing airplanes fully satisfy their requirements. In between these two extreme situations, other levels of relationship marketing are appropriate.

Today, more and more companies are developing customer loyalty and retention programs. Beyond offering consistently high value and satisfaction, marketers can use a number of specific marketing tools to develop stronger bonds with consumers. First, a company might build value and satisfaction by adding financial benefits to the customer relationship. For example, many companies now offer frequency marketing programs that reward customers who buy frequency or in large amounts. Airlines offer frequent flier programs, hotels give room upgrades to their frequent guests, and supermarkets give patronage refunds.

Other companies sponsor club marketing programs that offer members special discounts and other benefits. For example: Swiss watchmaker, Swatch, uses its club to cater to collectors, who on average buy nine of the company's quirky watches every year. Club members can buy exclusives, such as the "Garden Turf" watch, a clear watch with an Astroturf band. They also receive the World Journal, a magazine filled with Swatch-centric news from the four Corners of the globe-Swatch counts on enthusiastic word of mouth from club members as a boost to business. "Our members are like walking billboards," says the manager of Swatch's club, Trish O'Callaghan. "They love, live, and breathe our product. They are ambassadors for Swatch."

Upon submitting a 525 fee to the Volkswagen Club, members receive the first issue of a club magazine, Volkwagen World, a T-shirt, a road atlas and decal, a phone card, and discount offers on travel and recreation. Members can also take advantage of discounts on parts and service from local dealers, and, as a particularly nifty touch, members can apply for a club Visa card with a picture of their own V W on the front.

Thanks in part to its magic club aimed at children. Spain's Telepizza now claims a 65 percent share of the Spanish pizza market compared to less than 20 percent for Pizza Hut. As the largest membership club in Spain, with 3 million children enrolled, the magic club offers children small prizes, usually simple magic tricks, with every order.

Harley-Davidson sponsors the Harley Owners Group (HOG), which now numbers 330,000 members, about a third of all Harley owners. The first-time buyer of a Harley-Davidson motorcycle gets a free one-year membership with annual renewal costing $40. HOG benefits include a magazine (Hog Tales),a copy of the H. O. C. Touring Handbook, a complete H.O.G. World Alias, an emergency pickup service, a specially designed insurance program, theft reward service, discount hotel rates, and a Fly & Ride program enabling members to rent Harleys while on vacation.

A second approach is to add social benefits as well as financial benefits. Here the company increases its social bonds with customers by learning individual customers' needs and wants and then personalizing its products and services. For example, to build better relationships with its customers, in the summer of 1994 and again in 1999 Saturn invited all of its owners to 3 "Saturn Homecoming" at its manufacturing facility in Spring Hill, Tennessee. The two-day affair included family events, plant tours, entertainment, and physical challenge activities designed to build trust and a team spirit. Says Saturn's manager of corporate communications, "The Homecoming parry is another way of building ....relationships, and it shows that we treat our customers differently than any other car company." More than 60,000 people attended the most recent homecoming, traveling from as far as Alaska and Taiwan, with another 150,000 celebrating the occasion at the dealerships where they bought their cars.

A third approach to building customer relationships is to add structural lies as well as financial and social benefits. For example, a business marketer might supply customers with special equipment or computer linkages that help them manage their orders, payroll, or inventory. McKesson Corporation, a leading pharmaceutical wholesaler, has invested millions of dollars in its electronic data interchange (EDI) system to help small pharmacies manage their inventory, their order entry, and their shelf space. FedEx offers Web links to its customers to keep them from defecting to competitors such as UPS. Customers can use the Web site to link with FedEx's computers, arrange shipments, and check the status of their FedEx packages.

Relationship marketing means that marketers must focus on managing their customers as well as their products. At the same time, they don't want relationships with every customer. In fact, there are undesirable customers for every company. Ultimately, marketing involves attracting, keeping, and growing profitable customers. Thus, in addition to assessing the value that it delivers to customers, a firm should actively measure the value of individual customers to the firm.

Once it has identified profitable customers, it can create attractive offers and special handling to bind these customers to the company for a lifetime. But what should the company do with unprofitable customers If it can't turn them into profitable ones, it may even want to "tire" customers that are too unreasonable or that cost more to serve than they are worth.

A useful type of analysis for assessing the value of a customer to a firm. Customers make up the columns of the figure and products or services make up the rows. Each cell contains a symbol for the profitability of selling a given product or service to a given customer. Customer C1 is very profitable—he or she buys three profit-making products, products P1P2 and P3 Customer C2 yields mixed profitability, buying one profitable product and one unprofitable product.

Customer C3 generates losses by purchasing one profitable product and two unprofitable ones ("loss leaders"). What can the company do about consumers like C3 First, the company should consider raising the prices of its less profitable products or eliminating them. Second, the company also can try to cross-sell its profit-making products to its unprofitable customers. If these actions cause customers like C3 to defect, it may be for the good. In fact, the company might benefit by encouraging its unprofitable customers to switch to competitors.

DELIVERING CUSTOMER VALUE AND SATISFACTION

Marketers alone cannot deliver superior customer value and satisfaction. Although it plays a leading role, marketing can be only a partner in attracting, keeping, and growing customers. Relationship marketing requires that marketers must work closely with other company departments to form an effective value chain that serves the customer. Moreover, the company can be effective only to the extent that it works effectively with its marketing system partners to form a competitively superior value-delivery network. We now take a closer look at the concepts of a company value chain and value-delivery network.

Company Value Chain. Each company department can be thought of as a link in the company's value chain. That is, each department carries out value-creating activities to design, produce, market, deliver, and support the firm's products. The film's success depends not only on how well each department performs its work, but also on how well the activities of various departments are coordinated.

For example, we learned previously that the goal of Ritz-Carlton Hotels is to deliver "a truly memorable experience." Marketers make up an important link in the Ritz-Carlton value chain that creates this experience. They conduct research to learn about customer needs, design services to meet these needs, advertise to inform guests about services and locations, and perform other value-creating activities.

However, other departments must also perform well in order to make the Ritz-Carlton experience a reality. For example, the Ritz-Carlton housekeeping and maintenance staffs make certain that everything at the Ritz-Carlton looks and works just right, meeting customers' exacting standards for room cleanliness and functioning. The human resources department hires people-oriented employees, trains them carefully, and motivates them to ferret out and attend to even the slightest customer want. Ritz-Carlton employees treat customers as individuals, not as nameless, faceless members of a mass market. Whenever possible, they refer to guests by name and give each guest a warm welcome every day. Finally, the information systems department maintains an extensive customer database, which holds more than 500,000 individual customer preferences, accessible by all hotels in the worldwide Ritz chain. A frequent guest who requests a specific type of room at the Ritz in San Francisco will be delighted to find a similar room assigned when he or she checks into the Atlanta Ritz months later, arranged just the way that he or she likes it.

A company's value chain is only as strong as its weakest link. Success depends on how well each department performs its work of adding value for customers and on how well the activities of different departments are coordinated. At Ritz-Carlton, if customer-contact people are poorly selected or trained, or if rooms are anything less than spotless, marketers cannot fulfil their promise of a truly memorable experience. Customer Value-Delivery Network. In its search for competitive advantage, the firm needs to look beyond its own value chain and into the value chains of its suppliers, distributors, and ultimately customers.

Consider McDonald's. People do not swarm to the world's 24,500 McDonald's restaurants only because they love the chains hamburgers. In fact, according to one national survey, consumers rank McDonald's behind Burger King and Wendy's in taste preference." Still, McDonald's commands over a 16 percent share of the nation's fast-food business and over 40 percent of the burger segment. Consumers flock to the McDonald's system, not just to its food products. Throughout the world, McDonald's finely tuned system delivers a high standard of what the company calls QSCV—quality service, cleanliness, and value. McDonald's is effective only to the extent that it successfully partners with its franchisees, suppliers, and others to jointly deliver exceptionally high customer value.

More companies today are "partnering" with the other members of the supply chain to improve the performance of the customer value-delivery network. For example, Honda has designed a program for working closely with its suppliers to help them reduce their costs and improve quality. When Honda chose Donnelly Corporation to supply all of the mirrors for its U.S.-made cars, it sent engineers swarming over Donnelly's plants, looking for ways to improve its products and operations. This helped Donnelly reduce its costs by 2 percent in the first year. As a result of its improved performance, Donnelly's sales to Honda have grown from $5 million annually Co more than $60 million in less than 10 years. In turn, Honda has gained an efficient, low-cost supplier of quality components. As a result of Honda's partnerships with Donnelly and other suppliers, Honda customers receive greater value in the form of lower-cost, higher-quality cars.

Increasingly in today's marketplace, competition no longer takes place between individual competitors. Rather, it takes place between the entire value-delivery networks created by these competitors. Thus, Honda's performance against another automaker —say Toyota—depends on the quality of Honda's overall value-delivery network versus Toyota's. Companies no longer compete—their entire marketing networks do.

2

Customer Service Management

Customer service is the provision of labour and other resources, for the purpose of increasing the value that buyers receive from their purchases and from the processes leading up to the purchase. With the rising dominance of the service sector in the global economy, customer service has grown in importance, as its impact on individuals, households, firms, and societies has become widespread. The modern concept of customer service has its roots in the craftsman economy of the 1800s, when individuals and small groups of manufacturers competed to produce arts and crafts to meet public demand.

In the 1970s, international competition increased, and producers responded by improving the quality of their products and services. The overall quality of customer service - in society and in specific industries - will continue to be determined by the relative balance of power between suppliers and consumers; it will improve as competition becomes more intense, and decline as competition decreases.

Strategic Advantage

A company can outperform rivals only if it can establish a difference that it can preserve. Customer service can be such a difference. It is very difficult to control, and therefore difficult to imitate. It is difficult to control because of its variability. The level of service may vary greatly between two providers in the same organization. It may also vary from one moment to another, even as delivered by the same provider.

The difficulty is compounded in multi-unit operations: in addition to variability within units, there is also variability among units. That is both the challenge and the opportunity. The consistent delivery of superior service requires the careful design and execution of a whole system of activities that includes people, capital, technology, and processes. The few companies that can manage this system do stand out, and are sought out. This is the foundation of their sustainable competitive advantage. For an organization's members to deliver superior service consistently, they must be acculturated, i.e. instilled with the values, traits, patterns, and behaviors associated with a service culture.

The mechanisms of this acculturation include recruitment, training, empowerment, and accountability, within the framework of an organization's ideology of service. An organization's ideology comprises its purpose (Why are we here?) and values (What do we stand for?). Organizations renowned for providing excellent customer service have typically defined their purpose in terms of service – to serve their customers, and to serve their members.

Their values typically include integrity, trustworthiness, reliability, personal responsibility, industriousness, continuous improvement, respect, and consistency. Training is focused on enabling personnel to deliver service in a manner that is beneficial to both the organization's customers, and to itself. Technology has made available a wide range of very powerful customer service tools.

They range from support websites and the ability to have live chats with technical staff to databases tracking individual customers' preferences, pattern of buying, payment methods etc., and tailoring products and service responses based on this advanced data. Specialist software that is designed for the tracking of service levels and for helping recognize areas for improvement are often integrated into other enterprise operational software tools such as ERP software. Whereas outstanding service organizations allow their people to make mistakes and learn from their failures, there is little or no tolerance for violations of its core service values.

People who do not fit into the culture are removed. Delivering customer service begins with understanding what customers want. And this understanding begins with the understanding that they do not always know what they want, or why they want it. Traditional market research assumes that they do. Newer methods recognize that as much as 95% of our decision making is subconscious. Common research methods (e.g., surveys and focus groups) reveal what customers think their motivations are, rather than what their motivations truly are.

When respondents do not comprehend their true motivations, they tend to state how they think they ought to be motivated. Recent progress in neuroscience and in observational technologies have yielded more reliable, less biased results. Companies have Interaction Designers that use User Centred Design methods, among others, to understand what customers need. They often use Personas to represent the research outcomes i.e., to describe the customer they are designing for.

In a competitive environment, however, satisfaction may not be enough. To stay in business, firms must provide at least as much satisfaction as their competitors. Moreover, firms that aim to gain profitable growth must increase the number of their customers while reducing the cost of customer acquisition. This is particularly true of companies that compete in mature industries. The objective then is not merely to satisfy customers, but to convert them into promoters (customers who recommend a company to others). Promoters serve to increase a firm's clientele, without increasing its cost of acquisition – i.e. with no additional marketing or promotional expense.

CUSTOMER RECOVERY

Acquiring the right customers is only the first step in managing customer relationships. A large percentage of new customers—up to 50 percent in some sectors—was found to defect before their third anniversary with an e-commerce site. Once acquired, firms must do everything possible to keep that customer or prevent itself from doing things that force or even allow the customer to switch.

When a customer switches to another firm, not only do you lose the remainder of that customer's lifetime value, but you also incur the costs of attracting a new one to replace the lost customer. The costs of serving a customer are high in the initial stages, as the firm sets up procedures for the new customer and becomes familiar with the needs and situations of that customer.

As time goes by, the costs of serving that customer go down. To replace a lost customer, the firm has to incur all these costs again before costs to serve the customer go down. So adding the cost of attracting new ones and bringing them to the same level of profitability as the old ones doubles the cost of losing a customer.

When you consider the *total cost* to the firm in terms of the opportunity cost of lost customers, it behooves firms to pursue the retaining of customers as a relentless endeavor. The first step in retaining customers is to understand why they would want to switch in the first place. Most firms have established procedures to recover from product failures.

Typically, these customer recovery procedures are a part of customer service, a business function that is generally relegated to the status of a necessary evil. It is typically associated with unpleasant situations like product complaints, product returns and refunds. With the way firms are organized, it might fall upon the customer service department to ensure that these processes are in place and that they work properly. Product-focused firms may be focused on their core product and may view complementary services of the product as customer service. But service is not customer service.

As we saw in Chapter 6, facilitating services such as customer service is just one of the various services that a firm might offer its customers as part of the total solution. The customer service function is a significant factor in the efforts to retain customers. Firms may see it as a function to handle customers' special requests or complaints.

However, customer service from a customer's point of view is more broadly defined than from the firm's point of view. Some scholars have defined customer service as all customer interactions that enhance the core product other than proactive selling. Even in its narrowest definition, customer service as complaint management is very beneficial for the firm. Not only does it provide the mechanism to make amends to the customer for a botched job, it also provides information to the firm for service design improvements.

When the firm goes out of its way to compensate the customer for its failures, it creates an opportunity to obtain a lifelong customer. Traditionally designed for complaint handling and refund/exchange for product returns, customer service as a function serves other important uses. If one takes the perspective that customer service is at the tactical level of customer retention, there is a very important by-product from these customer retention efforts. It can be a powerful research source to obtain information on the customer and on customer value delivered by the firm. This information can be used as input for product and service design improvements. We know that that the customer service process and what many firms struggle to do with it. The customer complaint management process discussed is generalized for any firm. When a customer complaint is received by the front line in any firm, it is important to take the approach that a dissatisfied customer is an opportunity—an opportunity to alleviate the customer distress and compensate for it in such a way that the customer is impressed with the service recovery and is satisfied with the process.

PROCESS OF CUSTOMER SERVICE

A first step in the whole process of customer service is to acknowledge and apologize to the customer. If the customer is in the presence of other customers, it is important to isolate the complaining customer so as not to disrupt the service delivery process for other customers. Let the unhappy customer vent and explain the nature of the product failure. Fully document the customer's complaint and explore the likely actions that the firm and the customer may have committed to cause the unfortunate situation. Customer-focused firms will want to gain as much information as possible about the situation and to indicate to the customer that the firm is taking the problem seriously.

A commitment to customer satisfaction from a customer-focused firm is also evident in the firm asking the customer for suggestions on how the customer may be compensated and how the product and service may be improved for other customers in the future. The firm then initiates remedial action and promises to rectify the situation for the customer and make product and process improvements such that it will not happen again. Finally, it is important that the firm follow through with its promises and follow up with the customer to ensure that the recovery process met with the customer's satisfaction.

It is also a powerful message to the customer if the firm is able to inform the customer about what it has done to prevent such product failures from happening again. Such would be the case when the product failure has indicated a systemic problem with the firm's operation. An important outcome of this whole customer service process is that valuable information has been obtained, recorded, and utilized for permanent product and service improvements to improve customer value created and delivered by the firm. The TARP study concluded that only 4 percent of dissatisfied customers complain; dissatisfied customers share their story with about 9 or 10 other people.

If a complaint is satisfactorily handled, about 70 percent of them will continue to do business with the firm, and if resolved quickly, this figure goes up to 95 percent and they will tell about 5 people about their fair treatment. Thus, it is safe to say that what the firm does in its complaint handling has serious consequences for customer equity. Many firms seem to offer customers avenues to provide feedback. The customer-focused firm will even proactively encourage customers to complain.

The Bank of New Zealand, for example, has complaint procedure brochures available at every teller window that show the customer what to do step-by-step if they need to complain. There are instructions on who to call or write to if the problem is not resolved at the first service encounter. If not resolved by senior management, it lists the address and phone number of the CEO for good measure! Customers will act when they are emotionally charged, either because of the importance of the solution to their need situation or because of the degree of their dissatisfaction.

If the product failure was avoidable, customers are more likely to act. Customer action may be in the form of a customer complaint or defection without complaint. The recovery is likely to be effective if the firm has provided the frontline personnel dealing with the complaint or customer action with the appropriate skills and motivation. Effective recovery requires customer knowledge and freedom to exercise the discretion they require to satisfy the complaining customer and remedy the consequences of the product failure. Customers are likely to forgive the product failure if the firm demonstrated a customer-caring attitude in its handling of the complaint and if the recovery options offered the customer were appropriate. Nevertheless, preventing dissatisfied customers from defecting to a competitor is a challenge.

Why do customers switch? A study of 526 responses covering 45 different service industries, using the critical incident technique to explore the question, found eight main reasons for customer switching behaviour.

These were categorized under price, inconvenience, core product failures, service encounter failures, failed employee responses to service failures, competitive issues, ethical problems, and involuntary factors. The study found that even satisfied customers switch providers for reasons such as price, competitive issues, convenience, or access. The bottom line is that managers need to develop customer retention strategies or customer defection management programs to preempt customer switching, and to minimize or eliminate systemic reasons for customer switching behaviour.

They need to understand why their customers switch. Firms need to be able to identify those customers who are at risk of switching. It is imperative that they set up alerts and remedial mechanisms to reach those customers to prevent them from switching to a competitor. Ensuring a high retention rate must be a treated as a constant endeavor for the customer-focused management. Striving to sustain long-term profitability means ensuring a stable and growing customer base.

Growing the customer base by targeting the right customer is only the start of customer relationship. Enhancing the value of each customer to the firm presumes that the customer is retained by the firm. Retaining the customer base requires a close monitoring of how each customer is feeling and behaving in terms of product purchase and consumption. The defection management system should comprise of a means

- To assess customer value changes so that it can alert the firm about the possibility of customer defections,
- To assess the extent of long-term revenues at risk, and
- To determine and execute the appropriate recovery methods for each type of customer.

CUSTOMER VALUE AND SERVICE ORIENTATION

Understanding the business begins with a clear understanding of customer value. Providing a superior customer value requires an understanding of service orientation. Against this backdrop, the rest proceeds to follow the logic that sound decisions and actions cannot be made and performed without a solid understanding of the customer.

You cannot claim to be customer focused if you don't have the appropriate information on the customer. What kinds of customer data are important and why? How do we collect, interpret, and use this data? Where are the opportunities for gathering customer information? Information on all customer preferences, attitudes, and activities associated with the acquisition and use of the product provides a deeper understanding of the customer. This part develops the various methods and approaches to ensuring that the firm is adequately prepared to make customer-focused decisions.

Customer information should drive the design and delivery of customer value. What is involved in conceiving and designing a customer-focused product offering or service delivery? How would a firm go about tracking whether it is maximizing the returns from its value-creating assets? In this part are about effective and efficient value creation and delivery.

Who are the right customers and how can the firm ensure their loyalty to the firm and its products? This part covers topics such as service quality and guaranteeing quality service. When the product fails the customer, what does the firm need to do to recover from that failure in the context of customer service? What must firms do to proactively manage customer defections?

How does the firm create and maintain a customer-focused culture—a culture that is so focused on the customer that all decisions and actions of all personnel and systems in place create superior value for the customer at a reasonable profit? This final part provides the framework to analyze and manage the firm's value systems to be customer focused.

The principal concepts can be stated as a truism: Businesses cannot succeed in the long term unless they are focused on its customers so as to provide them with superior service. This is how firms attain and maintain a competitive advantage and therefore provide superior customer value at sustainable profits. Thus, the two fundamental and closely related concepts evident here are "customer focus" and "service orientation." After reading this book, you will be able to engage yourself and the firm in a service-oriented mode of designing and delivering customer-focused value to maintain profitable relationships with the right customers. You will appreciate what is required to sustain a competitive advantage for sustainable profits by:

- Adopting a customer-focused and service-oriented frame of mind
- Understanding the business by understanding customer value
- Capitalizing on the opportunities and use of customer information
- Designing and delivering profitable customer value
- Focusing on the right customer and managing that relationship
- Establishing a customer-focused and service-oriented culture in the firm

Customer-focused firms are the product of customer-focused employees and processes. Customer-focused employees are the responsibility of the executives of the firm. As an executive, you will find that when you stop and think of the ideas and concepts, you will have begun to engage in the intellectual exercise leading to a customer-focused and service-oriented frame of mind. You will be able to specify what the firm should actually be doing to be customer focused.

Customer Value and Service Orientation

Customers buy solutions, not products. Every firm needs to understand what it is providing the customer in terms of customer value, not by focusing on the product but by focusing on the customer. In doing so, the firm is able to assess whether it is providing superior customer value and whether it has a sustainable competitive advantage. Competitive advantage cannot be sustained unless it can be protected from competitor matching. Any aspect of the product can be matched by the competition. What is most difficult for the competition to match is how the firm approaches and treats the customer. The firm *serves* the customer by providing product enhancements in the form of service. When other firms can provide the same service, the differentiator is in the service orientation of the firm.

Customer Value

Many firms focus on the product rather than on the customer. When the focus is on the customer, the business is defined in terms of customer value, not in terms of product. The product is viewed as a customer solution and experience. That is, for any firm, the most fundamental definition of its business.

Try this one. What business is Amazon in? That you can buy just about anything on Amazon may not be too much of an exaggeration. The company abandoned or at least cut back on its strategy of buying up companies, as it did with Drugstore.com in 1999. It now handles retail for such established brands as Toys 'R' Us, Target, and Circuit City. Amazon shocked everyone in early 2002, when they announced their first operations profit of $59 million and a net profit of $5 million in the previous quarter. What value does Amazon provide its customer?

Customers don't buy products. They buy solutions. If firms are focused on the customer, they ought to see themselves in the role of providing solutions, not products. The information technology sector has popularized the term "solutions providers, " with labels such as application service providers (ASPs, as they are called) or technology solutions providers. These labels may be appropriate at the very general level and allow people to gloss over and take for granted the real meaning of the term *solutions.* The label has no real meaning as a concept unless it can be translated into customer value terms. Customers buy value in the solutions. Thus, customer value defines the primary purpose of any business.

This presents an approach to conducting a critical analysis of this fundamental question of "defining the business of a firm." In doing so, it defines "customer value" and redefines "products" in the customer-focused perspective. Finally, this briefly indicates the fruits of a customer-focused organization providing superior customer value.

Management guru Peter Drucker said in his 1954 book, *The Practice of Management,* "to know what a business is we have to start with its purpose." He goes on to say: "There is only one valid definition of business purpose: *to create a customer.*" Drucker reiterates this concept in a number of different ways, always emphasizing that "it is the customer who determines what a business is." It is not important what the business thinks it is producing.

The customer determines the value of what the business produces based on what the customer thinks he or she is buying. Such a perspective places the final result in focus—what the product *does* for the customer. Thus, the purpose of a business is what it creates for the customer. The first and foremost question for any firm to ask is, what business are we in? How many firms diligently confront this question? And, when they do encounter this question, whose perspective do they take?

Taking the customer's perspective to answer this fundamental question forces a number of thought processes that benefit the firm in different ways. In fact, businesses will find that approaching the question of *what business are we in?* in so fundamental a manner not only allows the firm to understand its existing customers, but will also help open up new market potential. It forces the analysis of value-creating assets, including the firm's skills and knowledge sets. The question also opens up the analysis of who the competition is. When firms strive to beat rivals, they typically end up competing within the confines of existing business.

Firms sometimes do not realize that they compete with firms in other industries. They are able to see this if they articulate their business from the customer's perspective. When customers consider their options in meeting a need, they don't limit themselves to one industry. Without realizing it as such, their solutions may involve different industries. Firms are forced to redefine their competitive landscape when they take the customer's perspective because they will find themselves competing outside their well-defined spaces. Kim and Mauborgne call it competing in a "market space.

They urge firms to expand their view of their business by looking "across substitute industries, across strategic groups, across buyer groups, across complementary product and service offerings, across the functional-emotional orientation of an industry and even across time." They argue this point with examples of how Home Depot cultivated the do-it-yourself market from homeowners using contractors, how Intuit saw that people managing personal finances using a pencil and paper calculation actually competed with their software, how overnight package delivery firms FedEx and UPS competed with telephones and fax machines, and how Southwest Airlines competed with driving. This argument illustrates the definition of a business from the perspective of the customer. Not only does it underscore the value that the customer places on what the firm delivers, but it also reveals that the customer's perspective redefines the business.

Well-known Harvard scholar Ted Levitt expanded on Drucker's thesis of defining a business from a customer's perspective when he popularized the concept "marketing myopia, " where firms and entire industries (such as buggy-whip makers) could perish when inwardly focused. He used the example of railroads as an industry that suffered from marketing myopia because it did not see itself in the business of transportation, but rather in the railroad business. Contrast this with a firm like the Williams Companies, one of the world's largest pipeline builders. Until a few years ago, it built steel pipes to move oil and natural gas. Today, it also builds fiber-optic pipes for the big cable companies. Clearly, Williams did not see itself as being in the oil and gas business, but as being in the business of serving big companies that needed to move material (or data) through pipes. Would Williams have seen this opportunity if it had been focused on competing within the oil and gas industry?

To expand your opportunities, you need to look beyond the product horizon and into the customer's space. For example, if a family was looking for something to do on a Saturday, consider their options: have some friends over for dinner, go out for dinner, go to a nearby mall, go to the movies, go to a play or a show, go bowling, go to a miniature golf course, go for a drive to the lake or the beach—and many other options. Now, look at these options in terms of all of the different industries that are competing with each other. If you were a firm in any one of these industries, you could be defining your business the same way as any of the other industries, depending on who your typical customer is. The customer's perspective broadens your own view of your product.

Taking the customer's perspective helps firms identify what they are about—their mission and their values. They are better able to understand their strengths and sources of competitive advantage. Firms are better positioned and more effective in allocating resources and efforts, both strategically and operationally. They are better situated to understand what would be considered superior customer value.

Products as Solutions

Where do you even begin when you want to define your business? Let us consider the basics. What *do* businesses sell, at the most general level? In what terms will your response be made? Do you see services and goods as solutions to a customer problem—a need to be met? Customer needs are problems searching for solutions and firms are providers of solutions to customer problems. When seen this way, firms draw focus away from products and orient themselves to the customer with the sole purpose of delivering solutions to problems. The business is defined in terms of customer solutions. Firms suffering from a product focus define their product by its capabilities in terms of product features and promptly lose sight of the customer. The solutions-to-problems approach emphasizes the customer rather than the product. It emphasizes product benefits rather than product features.

Firms must align processes, people, and their entire culture to serving the customer rather than on making and selling products. In customer-focused firms, processes are designed with customers in mind. The output of the processes, the product, is defined by the customer need it serves. In serving the customer, firms offer a combination of benefits or values. Are all products, therefore, a service to the customer? In a sense, yes! The solution represents the value that the firm is providing customers by serving their needs.

Firms' activities produce solutions as value bundles that we call products. All products involve a mix of value producing components—tangibles and intangibles—in value bundles. The proportion of tangibles and intangibles in the entity that the customer takes title to prompts the artificial distinction between services and products. This unfortunate dichotomy detracts from the necessary customer focus in the conception of the product. Regardless of whether the total product is predominantly a packaged good or a service, in a business-to-business (B2B) or business-to-consumers (B2C) context, all solutions to customer problems can be seen as bundles of benefits or value bundles designed to deliver value by meeting customer problems or needs. This book adopts the approach that all products are a mix of physical goods and services in some proportion.

Some solutions employ more tangibles (physical goods) than intangibles (services) in meeting customer needs, while others may provide an intangible (service) involving physical objects. The important question is, what is that total solution from the customer's perspective? It is more important to understand what the value bundle *does* for the customer than what the bundle *is*. To identify the value bundle, one needs to identify and understand the customer.

Identifying the Customer

To understand the customer is to understand your business. To understand the customer's perspective is basic to defining a business. The first obvious question is, who is the customer? If the firm defines the customer too narrowly or without context, any subsequent analysis is flawed. Firms either focus on their end users as packaged-goods firms tend to do, or as in the case of industrial firms, the focus is on the immediate customer. Both cases reflect a narrow view and a lack of understanding of the context. To determine who the customer is, the question to ask is, how does what we produce or provide add value to the client's value creating process?

Most important, what do customers see as the value we are providing to their value creation process? This point is central to what we know as the "value chain" concept. An understanding of customers requires an understanding of the customers' value chain that includes the set of their value consumption activities. If the value created by the immediate customer creates value for a subsequent customer, that customer is also an indirect customer of the firm. We really need to identify the customer as a first step to determine whose perspective we should take and to understand the customer value that we are providing. Performing the analysis of the customer sometimes forces the redefining of the customer. For Bright Horizons, a workplace child care and early education service company, it made a huge difference in how they went about their business when they viewed employers, and not parents, as their primary customers. The company could now tap into the financial and other resources of corporations and gain access to a much wider pool of parents. The value they were providing to the employer became the focus of the company. Chase Manhattan, for example, figured that its child care centre was yielding 110 percent return on investment through reduced absenteeism. Similarly, Merck found that its employee retention rate among those who were young parents went up dramatically.

The customer-focused perspective blurs the boundaries between entities in the value chain. Take the case of Aramark Corp., a firm that caters special events and runs cafeterias for big corporate clients. Nancy Naatz, resident district manager for business services for Aramark, has an office in the premises of her customer, Sears, in Chicago. Since Ms. Naatz is on location at her client's company, she is able to observe and interact with the local vendors Aramark has contracted to supply and serve Sears. Ms. Naatz is able to understand Sears executives' and employees' nutritional needs and interact with the vendors to ensure that the appropriate choices are made available. In this case, Aramark matches the food vendors' solution with the needs of the Sears employees who are the real customers.

So, who is the customer? The perspective of *which* customer I inspect and analyze, so as to help determine the business of my business, is the question. This question also raises the fundamental marketing decision of what or who our target market should be. It is a logical place to start before making any marketing or operations decision. Of all the potential customers that make up the market, which particular type of customer is most appropriate for our solution? The analysis involves segmentation, and the decision involved is one of targeting. We are able then to determine which particular type of customer from the universe of all customers for this product would find most value in what our value-creating assets can produce. We thus segment the market and target those segments for whom our value-creating assets can provide differentiation and a cost advantage. To know who the customer is necessitates an understanding of the typical customer in that segment at a general or aggregate level.

Traditionally, customer profiles have come out of the segmentation exercise. Segmentation variables in the B2C context have included demographic, psychographic, and behavioural variables. For customer-focused management we need information on all of the characteristics of the need or problem or use-situation that the customer is involved in, encompassing all of the activities of the customer that the product is a part of. Consequently, the question, who is the customer? You want to know how the customer purchases and uses the product. Similarly, the profile of the customer in a B2B context involves understanding the business of the organizational customer. For either the B2C or the B2B context, an understanding of the customers requires analysis of their use-situations, and the contexts within which a product helps them in what they do. Of what value are you to them? Now we begin to hint at the notion of what customer value really is. The answers lie in the *consumption* of the product, not in its production.

Customer Value

Customer value is what the customer thinks he or she is getting in return for what the customer has to part with, reflecting an implicit comparison akin to "give and receive." It has been described as the quotient of quality over price. Understanding the customer is about understanding customer value. Customer value is a complex concept and measuring it is complicated. But in the exercise of trying to understand customer value, the manager benefits from a better understanding of the customer and of the opportunities for a superior solution. Here are some characteristics of customer value that any manager should examine in an analysis of the firm and its activities: Customer value

- Is what the customer believes that a product or service provides in a certain use situation.
- Is an implicit comparison between what the customer receives from the provider and what the customer provides in time, effort, and money. The frame of reference is not just the price tag on the product, but also the ease and convenience in the acquisition and use of the product and the whole interactive experience the customer has with the firm.
- Is the customer's rather than the provider's perspective. It has to do with customer perceptions of the product and the firm, and not the provider's perspective of what the firm is delivering.
- Is dynamic, in that it can change over time before, during, and after the purchase, use, over repeated use of the product, and during all the various stages in the relationship with the providing firm.
- Can vary over different use situations. Your automobile may provide less or more value in transporting a group of kids to the ballpark compared to taking the spouse to the boss's house for a party.
- Can be shaped by attitudes, opinions, and behaviours of others, such as friends, family, media, the providing firm, and other competitors in the industry as well as in substitute industries.
- Determines customer satisfaction and the likelihood of brand or firm loyalty. This cause-effect relationship could be affected by comparisons with competitors and other substitutes.
- Is hard to measure and keep track of. Customers may find it hard to articulate all the different dimensions of customer value and firms

may find it a rather onerous task to keep track of all the manifestations of customer value.

Your Value to the Customer

In order to determine what business a firm is in, therefore, the fundamental and imperative exercise is to understand customer value. Let us begin the analysis with the question, what exactly does customer value consist of? It is not easy to determine what the customer is getting as value from a product or service. To understand customer value, you really need to get into the customer's way of thinking about products. In a recent *Harvard Business Review* article, Chase and Dasu urge the use of behavioural science to get into the head of the customer, to understand their total experience with the product or service. Only then can you grasp all the components of customer value.

Examining the components and determinants of customer value is a critical step in the analysis. It requires analysis of the benefits as well as costs to the customer. The benefits seen are evident in the perceptions of the product performance. Perceptions of product performance are framed in the context of customer expectations. The expectations are shaped by past experience with the product and by messages about the product received from a variety of sources such as friends and family as well as from the marketer.

From an analytical perspective, product performance comes from functional (core) benefits and supplemental benefits. Functional benefits arise from the core attributes of the product. For instance, you buy a set of golf clubs. How the golf clubs affect your game is a core and functional benefit, as in the primary benefit from the product. The prestige of the brand image, the product return policy, and other customer service features would translate into supplemental benefits. Every customer value analysis requires that we identify and examine core and supplemental benefits.

Similarly, we need to identify the costs to the customer—both monetary and non-monetary costs. Monetary costs include costs incurred in the acquisition, use, and disposition of the solution. Non-monetary costs could include the time and effort in acquiring and benefiting from the solution and the opportunity costs where the product failed. Tom Wright, Buy.com's vice president of operations called his company's old way of handling returns "almost embarrassing." To return a product that a customer bought from Buy.com, the customer had to telephone Buy.com to generate a return authorization, which led to a shipping label from the package delivery firm (UPS) to be mailed to the customer, who then used that label to send the product back to Buy.com. It was weeks before the customer got credit for the product return! Imagine the non-monetary cost of aggravation to that customer.

Many firms that focus on acquiring customers do not retain customers because of their shallow understanding of customer value. Customer value includes interactions with the firm before, during, and after the consumption of the product. Smart firms are focusing on the whole customer and defining their business in terms of market spaces. The market space is the actual set of customer solutions defined by the consumption activities to which the firm caters.

In recognizing that customer value is dynamic, we need to place this analysis in the context of different use situations and how they are changed over time by various influences. Customers' concepts of what to expect from a provider change with each consumption experience. They learn from their own experiences with the product as well as vicariously from others. Competitor offerings and marketing messages continually shape their expectations. Therefore, implicit in the assessments made by the customer is a comparison with expectations based on the alternative—that is, the competition. Customer value analyses can be performed at a qualitative level and with some difficulty can be quantified as well.

Data-driven representations of monetary worth of what a firm does for a customer are what Anderson and Narus called "customer value models." Such models are useful in assessing the customer value of your product and comparing it with the competition to determine whether you are providing superior customer value or not. The next fundamental question is, Can you provide this superior customer value at a sustainable profit by commanding revenues to cover costs and profits?

Mutual Value of Customer and Firm

Just as the customer value analysis requires an examination of the benefits versus the costs, the firm makes a similar analysis to determine its profit potential. In providing the customer value, what does the firm get in return? How do the monetary and nonmonetary benefits from the customer compare with what it cost the firm to provide that solution to that customer? Can we sustain these profits in the long term? A firm creates value for itself by creating value for the customer. In many ways, the value of a firm is reflected in the profits it provides its investors and the value of the customer to the firm is reflected in the profits that the customer provides the firm. The greater the values of the customer to the firm, the greater are the profits.

This means that the surplus from the revenues after costs is greater if you can attract and retain profitable customers in the long run. Part IV in this book covers the valuation of the customer by the firm. Firms can attract and retain customers if they can provide superior value. It could boil down to, can we command a premium on our solution? If you can, it turns out that the margins are not in the commoditized part of the product, it is in the services provided by the firm. The margins increase when you are able to extend your role in the customer's space. This may come in the form of "cross-selling" or "up-selling."

It may be the case that the total solution provides such value to the customer that the customer is better off with you than with the competition.

As the firm gets more valuable to the customer, the customer gets more valuable to the firm. The value from a customer is derived not only from purchases. Customers can become advocates for the firm, the benefits of which are frequently less understood. The value of the customer in terms of purchases and referrals over the lifetime of the customer should be an imperative calculation for firms who are focused on the customer. It appears that in the final analysis, it is the customer-focused firm that can provide a complete solution through a service orientation that succeeds in providing superior customer value and in return enjoys sustainable profits. So, how is it that a firm is able to provide superior customer value? What gives them a sustainable competitive advantage, such that the firm has sustainable profits?

Delivering Superior Customer Value

What characterizes firms that can provide *superior* customer value? To answer this question, we have ample evidence from research on such firms. Every firm in any industry provides some customer value. The firm that provides superior customer value is the one that has a sustainable competitive advantage. Firms compete with each other on differentiable aspects of the total solution. If we can conceptualize that every product has parts that are commodities and parts that differentiate it from others, superior value is in the augmented product, not in the conceptual core.

For example, all airlines provide transportation from point A to point B. But the total solution includes aspects other than the physical transportation of the person itself, such as amenities on the airplane. A firm must seek opportunities to differentiate itself from the competition in ways that are meaningful and relevant to the customer. How do firms find opportunities to differentiate themselves in a way that it is sustainable?

Consider how CDW creates superior customer value. CDW is the leading B2B e-commerce firm selling technology equipment to small and medium-sized firms. Wall Street analysts claim that the firm uses a “clicks and people” strategy. Supposedly, their competitive advantage is superior customer service and lower customer acquisition costs. The firm’s Web site is tailored to each specific customer as a “custom extranet.” How are they able to sustain this competitive advantage? Their own chief financial officer, Harry Harczak, notes that retaining people is key. In his experience, the productivity difference between an employee who has been at the firm six months versus one there three years is a factor of six. CDW values employee commitment.

What are the generalizable characteristics of firms that create superior customer value? A team of Harvard Business School researchers set out to discover exactly this and concluded that successful firms such as BancOne,

Intuit, Southwest Airlines, ServiceMaster, USAA, Taco Bell, and MCI made employees and customers paramount. These researchers modeled the findings from their case studies into a framework they called "the service profit chain." Their cases provided data to establish powerful relationships between profitability, customer loyalty, and employee satisfaction, loyalty, and productivity. Evident in the whole model is the focus on the customer and the service orientation of satisfied employees, and the implications on investors and other stakeholders of the firm.

As firms focus on customer needs and become service oriented to deliver satisfaction, there are favourable ripple effects throughout the firm. Consistent delivery of customer satisfaction persuades customers to be loyal because perceived risk in buying a product from that firm is substantially reduced. When providers of solutions to customer needs are able to consistently deliver expected value, customers are more likely to be consistently satisfied. By way of their continued patronage, they become more valuable to the firm. When customers are loyal to the provider by choice, it is also in their best interest to support the provider because the prosperity and longevity of the provider is beneficial to the customer. Similarly, with regard to employees, research has shown that when employee satisfaction is high employees are more likely to be loyal to the company. When employee loyalty is high, employees are likely to be more productive and to be providing quality products and service.

Neither employees nor customers are likely to be loyal unless their expectations are met and they are satisfied. Therefore, customer satisfaction and employee satisfaction are inherently tied to each other, in that, when employees are loyal to the firm, they provide superior performances driving customer loyalty. When employees are productive and customer loyalty is high, the firm is successful and can command a premium.

With increased profitability and growth prospects, investors are attracted to the firm, which in turn makes more resources available to the firm. With more resources available to the firm, capital is available to continuously improve value-creating assets (people and processes) and to produce consistently superior customer value in its products and service. This sequence of events, presented as the "loyalty circle", contributes to profitability and growth and requires that people and processes are aligned to deliver superior customer value. Delivering superior value should be a relentless endeavor for the firm.

THE CUSTOMER-FOCUSED ANALYSIS

The analytical frame to understand customer value consists first of identifying the customer and understanding the customer's problem and solution needs. This leads to an understanding of what the solution does for the customer and everything associated with it. The next issue is to focus on the options that the customer would consider appropriate in meeting the need and how the options compare with each other. Are there other options provided by other firms whose value-creating assets have a sustainable competitive advantage? This would dictate whether the firm should be in this business at all; if so, is there the potential for a sustainable competitive advantage? The kinds of questions that need to be asked by the customer-focused firm as it examines its business and how it can provide superior customer value for a sustainable competitive advantage.

THE KEY TO A SUSTAINABLE COMPETITIVE ADVANTAGE

The core of any product is essentially a commodity. Competitive advantage comes from services as product enhancements made to the core. To compete on service, firms need to understand the opportunities and challenges presented by the special nature of services. Sustainable competitive advantage comes from an ability of the firm to compete through service.

A common misconception is to view services as being synonymous with customer service. "Services" are not limited to customer service. Customer service is only one of the services that enhance products. Managers who are product focused and not customer focused usually see services as meaning customer service. They see service as something that is done when a product fails or invoked to prevent it from failing. Others who see service as "freebies" that you toss in with the product are probably sales focused.

Firms with such a product or sales orientation actually do a disservice to the customer in the name of service. Their tendency is to offer a refund or return policy, which is often enough structured to favour the firm rather than the customer. These firms may offer a customer service toll-free telephone number, which is usually set up to be a frustrating encounter for the customer service personnel as well as the customer who may have been calling in for retribution. Such is often the unfortunate consequence in firms that are not customer focused. In customer-focused firms, customer service is not just an add-on, a little something extra to keep the customer happy. Customer service is an integral part of the total product.

Service is not what you *do to the product*, it is what you *do for the customer*. The customer-focused firm looks at the core product as an incomplete solution for customers. These firms supplement the core product with services that help customize or otherwise enhance solutions for customers. Such product enhancements add value for the customer. The Aramark employee being on location at Sears adds value to the core product of catering for Sears. It allows Aramark to be more customer focused by obtaining first-hand customer information and being able to deliver on it. By being on hand, Aramark can be immediately aware and responsive to the customers' needs. Service-based product enhancements are an imperative for the customer-focused firm. This establishes the frame of mind required for the customer-focused firm to be service oriented. You will see what the inherent characteristics of services are, and thus the challenges and opportunities you need to recognize when you incorporate services into the value you create and deliver to the customer.

The Service Orientation Imperative

The traditional view of services is to treat products dichotomously, in two categories—*either* services *or* (physical) goods. Sometimes the term *product* is even used interchangeably with packaged goods but not with service. Not only has this usage caused unnecessary confusion, but it has also encouraged the flawed approach that services and packaged goods are separate and mutually exclusive entities. Scholars have gone as far as to suggest that "most product manufacturers and service providers alike are largely service operations."

They asserted that the role of services is critical for any organization in providing value in the form of "technological improvements, styling features, product image, and other attributes that only services can create." The fact is that all products come with some services. As a matter of degree some products have more services than others and are therefore more intangible than others.

Picture a continuum ranging from products that are most tangible (and least intangible in proportion) at one extreme to products that are most intangible (and least tangible in proportion) at the other extreme. At one end of the continuum, services such as education, consulting, and financial services have very few physical goods that customers take title to. At the other end, packaged goods such as a bar of soap or table salt come with no apparent service unless, for example, the customer initiates a customer service phone call.

In the middle of the continuum are products such as fast food restaurants and custom-made clothing that have an almost equal proportion, with no real predominance of tangibles or intangibles. In products that are predominantly intangible, where the customers don't take title to anything physical, such as in banking services, the service provider might use tangibles such as documentation, statements, and billing. The value for the customer is in the information contained in them.

As a proportion of what the customer is getting in the total product, the predominant source of customer value is from the intangibles in the total product. For physical goods, services enhance the core product and provide opportunities for competitive advantage. Thus, any product has some proportion of services attached to it, and this part of the product has a special nature that needs to be handled differently. If all firms provide some proportion of service components as part of the total product, it behooves them to have an understanding of the nature of services.

Only with such an understanding can we truly get into the service-orientation frame of mind. Take for example, the table salt manufacturer, Morton's. For this firm to look at itself as a packaged goods firm and therefore not concerned with services is a mistake. The fact that Morton's makes the product available at the retail store through the appropriate distribution channels is a service to the customer.

Morton's has essentially outsourced its distribution and retailing to channel intermediaries. To be truly customer focused, Morton's needs to view all the value-added it provides the customer, over and above the product of the production process—the salt—as services it provides to the customer. Morton's cannot manage its service components in the same way that it manages the production of its table salt. Most B2B manufacturing firms intuitively recognize the importance of the service component in enhancing its product. Caterpillar, the earth-moving equipment manufacturer, recognizes that prompt and reliable service is critical to its success and organizes the whole firm around customer locations. You need a service orientation to see such product enhancements as service dimensions that add value to the core product. Service orientation is

- A philosophy or frame of mind reflected in the firm's culture
- An attitude to serve the customer reflected in the firm's treatment of its customers, and
- A view of services as necessary enhancements to any core product to make a complete solution.

To provide complete and competitive solutions to the customer, one needs to understand and adopt the service orientation. The service-oriented frame of mind requires a grasp of the fundamental nature of services (whether as the product or a component of a product). Once the inherent characteristics of services are clear, it becomes apparent that their implications for the customer and the provider offer a number of opportunities and pose a variety of challenges.

As a preface to a discussion of these issues, it would be useful to note the evolution of interest in the concept of service. Prompted by the frustrations of practitioners in the service sector who were finding that marketing practices from the packaged goods world did not make sense for services, scholars began to get interested in the problem. In the late 1970s and early 1980s, for a number of reasons, the academic research community in business disciplines, particularly in marketing, operations, and human resources, began a serious intellectual debate as to whether products that were services, compared to products that were packaged goods, needed to be studied differently.

For example, could you study the marketing of hospitality services the same way as you would the marketing of toothpaste? Some scholars maintained that marketing is marketing regardless of *what* you are marketing. Either way, they argued, one had to go through the tasks of segmenting the market, positioning a product, and making product, pricing, distribution, or promotion decisions. Others argued that although that might be true, one would need to approach these tasks very differently; and they proceeded to offer the rationale for this argument. There was a great deal of interest in this effort, especially among those who recognized the tremendous growth of the services sector. Around the same time there were environmental changes in the economy and in the competitive landscape. Services sectors such as airlines, telecommunications, and, later, banking and insurance were going through deregulation in the United States. Manufacturing was moving to cheaper labour markets in the Far East and in Latin America. Meanwhile, by the late 1980s in the United States, even professional services such as health care and legal services began to recognize the need to employ marketing practices.

Not surprisingly, even manufacturing firms were being forced to add service components to their product offerings. As these changes occurred and services were being established as an integral aspect of doing business, the United States had become a service economy. Ultimately, the debate over whether services were really different from physical products produced the rationale that the skeptics demanded. The evidence and essence of this argument epitomizes the service orientation.

Characteristics of all Services

There are certain fundamental characteristics that are inherent in all service products and in the service components of any product. Let us begin by defining service as *a deed, performance, or action.* Thus, by definition, services are intangible. The product that is a service or that component of the product that is a service cannot be seen, touched, or felt. As a deed, performance or action, a service is consumed as it is produced, such that the acts of production and consumption are inseparable. Thus, services are also perishable, in that they cannot be inventoried or produced and stored for later use. Nor can they be produced without some level of customer interaction.

Since services are produced and consumed in real time, they are inherently variable—from customer to customer, from provider to provider, and from time to time for the same customer and/or the same provider. These statements describe features that are fundamental and are inherent in products or components of products that are deeds, performances, or actions, and may sound very simplistic until you delve into the meanings and consequences of these inherent characteristics to the customer and to the provider.

It is generally accepted that services are different from physical goods along four fundamental characteristics labeled as intangibility, simultaneity or inseparability, perishability, and variability. These characteristics are conceptually inherent in all services or in the service component of any product. Although this framework is more useful as a pedagogical vehicle rather than a framework for research or practice, it is powerful in fully capturing the concept of service orientation and accomplishes the objective of placing the reader in the necessary frame of mind. This mindset is grounded in the appreciation of the fundamental nature of services necessitating appropriate managerial decisions and actions. The fundamental character of services and the associated consequences may play out for the manager. A service orientation requires a thorough understanding of how these inherent characteristics of services are manifested for the customer and the manager.

Intangibility—Services

Services are performances. Services cannot be seen but they can be experienced. The product is a process. As a service provider, you cannot show your product as you could if you were the marketer of a packaged good. Yes, services are the result of value-creating activities, just as physical products are, and may employ tangibles or physical products in producing the service. However, the product being purchased is an experience and not a physical good. Customers cannot take ownership or title to a service. For example, hotels provide the service of overnight stay as their core product. The customer does not take title to the room that is being rented. The hotel provides the use of the room for the duration of the time that the customer has paid for. Similarly, customers don't take title to anything in air travel or in entertainment. When office copiers come with service, there is no ownership involved with the service component unlike with the copier itself. When your automobile comes with free service under warranty, unlike the automobile itself there is no real ownership of the service component.

Now, as a manager, you might say: "All this is well and good, but if it doesn't change the way I manage the product, its production, or its marketing, whether it is a packaged good or service, why should I care? Services are intangible and service components in products are intangible—yes! But so what?" Let us examine this question from the customer's point of view. For customers, one immediate consequence of the intangibility is increased perceived risk. When you cannot see the product or what you are going to get before the purchase, customers have to acknowledge a certain amount of risk they are taking. While there is perceived risk in the purchase of a packaged or physical good, you cannot return a vacation as you can a defective lawn mower.

Thus, you accept a certain amount of risk as unavoidable in the case of a service. When you book your vacation, do you really see the product? If you have previously been to the locations, you may have seen the facility, but your product was the experience. Complicating the perceived risk is the fact that the evaluation of services or the service component of the product is inherently subjective. Compared to packaged goods, customers find it harder to evaluate services before the purchase. In some cases, services are harder to evaluate even during and after their performances.

In the case of health care, for instance, you use several proxy elements, such as the cleanliness of the facility, the medical professional's "bedside manner, " and the process you had to go through. What you are evaluating is a lot more than the core product, the medical treatment itself. Being intangible, services cannot be produced until you have purchased (whether you pay before, during, or after) the service.

Simultaneity—Services

The acts of production and consumption occur simultaneously in services. This is primarily because services are produced and consumed in real time. There is a great deal of interaction before, during, and/or after the service between provider and customer. Some sort of customer interaction is necessary even if customer physical presence is not. At the very least, customers have to specify their needs and their need situations. In most if not all cases, it can be argued that production and consumption cannot be temporally separated. (Thus, this characteristic is also termed "inseparability.") A related complication for services is that in services, the provider is part of the product.

As a customer, the frontline personnel you interact with are a part of the product. In professional services, for instance, the lawyer is part of the (legal service) product, the doctor is part of the (medical care) product, the professor is part of the (education) product.

Comparing this to packaged goods: Do you have to interact with Procter & Gamble and the shop floor employee who made your particular tube of Crest toothpaste? You do interact with the retailer of the toothpaste, but remember that the retail store that makes the toothpaste available to you is a service. What you are consuming from the retailer as it is produced by the retailer is a service. In fact, you interact with the provider of the service component of the packaged good. If you interacted with P&G, it was with customer service.

Once again, let us confront the question: "So what?" To understand what difference it makes for the manager, the customer-focused firm must examine the consequences to the customer from the customer's perspective. The customer has to interact with the provider at some stage or at all stages of the production process. The customer is in the service factory in the case of an amusement park. Sometimes the service factory comes to the customer, as in the case of the landscape contractor. Sometimes the interaction is at arm's length, such as in the case of an online travel agent like Expedia.com. In each case, there is some interaction that the customer usually initiates. Thus, there is some effort on the part of the customer for the product to be produced.

The customer takes on a role in the production process. To perform the expected role, customers have to be educated and sometimes socialized into the process. For example, at a fast food restaurant, the customer needs to get familiar with the process of ordering and picking up the food. When you call your long distance phone company for a question on your bill, you need to have some information ready for the service to be performed. These days you have to be familiar with complex automated voice menus before you can get anything done over the telephone. Since consumption and production are simultaneous, the customer is consuming as the product is being produced. The product cannot be produced ahead of time and then consumed. This means that the product cannot be inventoried.

Perishability—Services

Since services cannot be produced and stored for later use, as physical products can, services are said to be perishable products. What actually perishes? In fact, what perishes is the productive capacity of the service, or more precisely, the opportunity to produce a product. A hairdresser's time is wasted or unproductive when he or she is not serving a customer. The customer service personnel ready to handle customer enquiries is not producing a service unless there is a customer to serve. An empty airline seat perishes without a passenger in it on takeoff. The factors of production such as labour, facilities, equipment, and billable time are the value-creating assets for the service provider.

The opportunity to produce the product from these assets perishes without the adequate number of customers for which the capacity is designed. And the service provider needs to maintain a certain level of capacity that is not easily adjustable. Some services are more capacity-constrained than others. A hotel cannot reduce the number of rooms in its facility when there are not enough guests. A management consulting firm with fulltime employees would be hard pressed to release its staff when there are not enough clients to fill the capacity.

For the customer, service products need to be available and accessible when and where they are needed. When the productive capacity is sometimes not able to meet the demand, customers are likely to have to wait in queues or find another provider. Whether it is on the phone for customer service, at the doctor's office, or in line for a ride in an amusement park, customers will have to get used to waiting. In some services, customers need to plan ahead of time and place reservations. That is how managers instinctively manage the utilization of capacity in the operation.

Conversely, when there is more productive capacity than there are customers to be served, service providers have to look for other customer segment opportunities for their value-creating assets. Service providers have to manage that balance between capacity and demand. They employ methods to anticipate and manage the pattern of demand and to manage the capacity accordingly.

Variability—Services

Service products as experiences vary from one experience to the next, from customer to customer, as well as for the same customer from one occasion to the next. In fact, this variability is compounded with differences among frontline personnel. When there are several steps in the service process where the customer interacts with several different personnel of the service provider, there could be variation from one interaction to another. In some cases, customers will prefer specific frontline personnel with whom they have become familiar and comfortable. Since services are produced and consumed in real time, it is clear that customers will likely see a great degree of variation in product quality.

Customers can receive a different experience each time, even at a standardized operation like McDonald's. Service managers attempt to deliver consistently high quality with frontline training and technology and to customize where possible and standardize where necessary. Customers expect customization even when it is not feasible. Managers have to balance the economics of standardization with the quality issues around customization.

Thus, the fundamental characteristics of services force their implications on the customer. The manager of services and products that involve a significant degree of tangibles are forced to orient themselves to these implications. The complexity of managerial situations as a consequence of these characteristics is manifested as opportunities and challenges. Consequently, the services manager must analyze these consequences, and be prepared to take some actions to address them.

MANAGERIAL OPPORTUNITIES AND CHALLENGES

The implications of the fundamental characteristics of services suggest that managers need to examine how they would adapt their business processes to take advantage of the opportunities and to address the challenges. The following is a discussion of some of the key managerial challenges and opportunities.

REDUCING CUSTOMERS' PERCEIVED RISK

With products that contain a significant proportion of intangibles and where the core product is a service, managers of services need to continuously monitor and understand the risk customers feel when they purchase the service. What is the nature of the risk? How do you lower this risk? Professional services providers such as lawyers and doctors have certifications prominently displayed on their walls. Consulting firms provide lists of clients, mutual funds companies show off their performance charts. What would be most appropriate for you to do to reduce customer perceived risk? To determine this you begin by understanding what those risk levers might be. What is the source of the anxiety that customers feel? To what would you attribute the risk that they feel?

Only when this is clearly understood can you think about the possible ways you might reduce their perceived risk. To understand the risk, you need to break down the service into the features that contribute value toward the total solution. Which service features produce benefits, and how can the risk associated with each feature-benefit connection be reduced? The degree to which the customer feels assured that expectations of these benefits will be met would depend on how you can instill confidence in the customer that you have the ability to deliver on those expectations. Christopher Hart is credited with the concept of service guarantees that works to reduce perceived risk. L.L. Bean's famed "100per cent satisfaction guaranteed" goes back to 1912, when the founder was marketing the Maine hunting shoe. Service providers who understand their customers' perceived risk seek to address it.

Customization versus Standardization

One of the powerful implications of the fundamental characteristics of services is that they are not produced ahead of time. The service is designed, created, and delivered to customer specifications. While customization is possible, some standardized parameters are also necessary to derive economies of scale. There is opportunity to standardize as well as to customize. Where there is low margin from a service component and the volume provides the profits, perhaps ways to standardize the production process would be appropriate. On the other hand, if there is opportunity for high margin, customization and low volume is the way to go.

Consider the difference between automated telephone-based customer service and a fee sometimes charged for customers who want individual attention. Professional or knowledge based services are generally customized and are high-margin, whereas dry cleaning services are low-margin services and require considerable standardization and the required volume. The opportunity is to increase margins by providing customized experiences and the challenge is in standardizing the process to reduce costs and maintain consistent quality.

Quality Consistency

A related issue to the opportunity to customize is the accompanying challenge posed by the variability of the product. Since services are produced in real time, and they have a high degree of variability, the challenge is to ensure a consistent quality in the service. Managers must assess the sources of variation. Sources of the variability are typically associated with the people delivering the service. Every interaction with the customer provides or facilitates some aspect of the product bundle, and therefore the quality of the product is dependent on each and every interaction between the service provider and the customer. Therefore, selecting, training, and motivating frontline personnel become very critical.

For example, service firms such as Walt Disney amusement parks and the Ritz-Carlton hotels have a specific profile in mind when they hire people for the front line. These firms provide extensive service training for their frontline employees, and they motivate employees to provide customer satisfaction. FedEx rewards employees who take care of customers in service failures. Empowered frontline personnel are more likely to deliver quality service.

Demand and Capacity Management

Since services are perishable, productive factors that are in place may be idle at low demand times and stretched to capacity at high demand times. The demand is fluctuating, and it might be impossible or at best a serious challenge to stretch or contract capacity. Therefore, smoothing demand and managing capacity become a constant endeavor for the managers of services. The key to managing this challenge is to understand the demand patterns and to figure out the flexibilities in your capacity. To the extent that the demand patterns can be predicted with a good understanding of customer behaviour, service providers can manage demand as well as capacity. Pricing is commonly used in smoothing demand.

Early bird specials, matinee prices, lower fares if you stay over Saturdays are all different ways by which service firms use pricing to manage demand. Reservations and appointments are another way for service managers to smooth demand. Different segments and markets are served at different times and prices to fill capacity. Hotels depend to a great extent on the lucrative conferences and meetings market to ensure capacity utilization.

Such capacity-constrained services rely more on managing demand than on managing capacity primarily because it is harder to adjust capacity. Product mix adjustments are another way of managing capacity, whereas the more versatile the value-creating assets are in producing different services with the same productive factors, the better the capacity management opportunities. For example, ski resorts turn into hiking or whitewater rafting facilities in the summer. Staffing and scheduling are typical capacity-side management options that the service firm employs. Creative use of value producing assets is critical for efficient and effective management of a firm's capacity.

Managing the Customer

Since the customer is part of the process and some degree of interaction with the customer is necessary and inevitable, managers of services must find ways to educate customers on their roles. If the customer fails in playing the appropriate coproducer role, it could ruin the process and the outcome quality. A clear understanding of the steps in the process and how, where, and when customers interact with the process is a must. Doctors, nurses, and pharmacists provide directions and instructions for patient roles. Banks and other financial institutions have specific protocols for various financial transactions. A key question to ask is how the customer should participate in the process and whether you have the appropriate instructions for your customer. Differences in customer willingness and ability to participate in the production of the process force the issue of segmentation on the service delivery process. Thus, restaurants have self-service, take-out, or drive-through options. Automatic teller machines are an early example of self-service in banking services. Hotels have express check-in and check-out facilities. Airlines have electronic ticketing options. Self-service checkout facilities have become a standard option at grocery stores in the United States and elsewhere.

It is clear as we think about these issues that not all services are alike. While all services face all these challenges to some degree, the challenges manifest themselves differently in different services. In fact, the management solutions presented are more applicable in some and inappropriate or impossible in others. There is a systematic way of addressing these differences among services by examining characteristics that differentiate services from one another. A service that shares characteristics with another service exhibits similar challenges and opportunities.

CATEGORY CHARACTERISTICS OF A SPECIFIC SERVICE

In employing the service orientation, every manager needs to understand that there are different types of services in every product, each with its own manifestations of the fundamental characteristics of services. The nature of these manifestations in different services implies different situations for the customer and the manager. While all services are fundamentally intangible, inseparable, perishable, and variable, services differ from each other along dimensions peculiar to their category. These category characteristics provide the manager with an insight into the specific situations that they have to deal with in their particular service category.

Christopher Lovelock demonstrated that this sort of categorizing is necessary and powerful as a means of understanding the managerial situations specific to each type of service. Service managers should look toward other services that share similar characteristics and expect to find similar challenges and transferable solutions to those challenges. Consider for example that hospitals provide executive-style rooms for the businessperson who is a patient. They learned this from hotels that have executive-style suites for the businessperson. Now consider the service characteristics that are shared between hospitals and hotels.

In both cases, the customer comes to the factory and frequently requires an overnight stay. In both situations, the executive is likely to be away from an office with all its business support for an extended period of time. Both services are similar in the type of customer interactions, even though they are in two completely different service sectors. An analysis represents the benefits of learning from the successes of services that share certain specific service characteristics. Managers of services can understand the specific challenges and opportunities presented by the characteristics of their product and corresponding situations by examining a number of characteristics that profile a service category. Here are a few characteristics to examine:

- Tangible or intangible act
- Person or thing as recipient of the act
- Type of interaction between provider and customer
- Service delivered by people or equipment
- Extent of customization or standardization

What are the tangible and intangible acts involved in the services that you are providing? Is the service act delivered on a person or a thing? For example, if you are an entertainment electronics repair and service provider, you perform tangible acts on a DVD player and intangible acts with the customer as you obtain information on what problems the customer has experienced with the DVD player. Now, examine the nature of the acts and the impact on the customer. When you are working on the DVD player, the customer needs not be present and the process that you employ need not be visible to the customer. However, you do interact with the customer at a number of points, from the initial customer call to the final interaction at delivery or pickup of the DVD player.

Similarly, you might analyze your service about the nature of interaction of with the customer. Is it face-to-face or arm's length, via telephone or the Internet? Do you visit the customer or does the customer visit your premises? How much technology is involved in the interface with the customer? Sometimes the customer does not even interact with a person. How much standardization is built into the service? Are there options provided to customers who require a customized interaction? What benefits does this analysis provide the manager?

The challenges and opportunities discussed earlier as fundamental are common to all service managers. By understanding the characteristics of their specific category of services, the manager can find ways to take advantage of the opportunities and address the challenges of their specific situation. Additionally, in understanding how the fundamental characteristic of intangibility manifests itself in their particular situation, managers can understand customers' perceived risk and use the tangibles in the customer experience to reduce the risk that customers perceive.

By understanding the nature of the interaction, managers are in a better place to manage the roles of customers and recognize opportunities for customization and standardization to improve the customer experience and, therefore, customer value. What is most interesting is that you may find that service businesses in a different industry sharing certain characteristics may offer you innovative ideas to meet these challenges and capitalize on opportunities to better serve customers in your business. In order to understand how the required service-oriented frame of mind needs to be handled in the customer-focused firm, the firm analyzes the various services with which it augments the product. Each service is analyzed from a fundamental and category perspective. The fundamental nature of services requires an analysis of the implications of the intangible, inseparable, perishable, and variable nature of services for managerial action.

The analysis of category characteristics specific to each type of service should deal with how these consequences of these characteristics manifest themselves in that situation. The customer-focused analysis should cover the nature and the recipient of the act, the nature of the interaction, and the fluctuation of the demand.

CUSTOMER DEFECTION MANAGEMENT

Customers switch when the customer value they receive at the individual or segment level is inferior to an alternative. Thus, it is necessary to conduct a continual assessment of customer value as the critical first step. Failpoint data on customer experiences is a metric that could serve as a barometer for customer value changes. Customers who have experienced the service when failpoints have failed are at risk of switching. The firm has failed to deliver the expected customer value for these customers. Customer defection management is proactive—its purpose is to identify customers who are at risk of switching and to initiate an assessment of the status of customer value to the firm, followed by an analysis to determine how to increase customer value to those customers.

One of the functionalities required in a good customer knowledge system is to alert its users when there might be a problem with a customer, and to provide the information necessary to rectify that problem. Customer defection management begins with designing into the customer information system alerts that are triggered by customer switching indicators.

These alerts can be based on thumb rules suggested by the information on successful and unsuccessful customer recovery captured and stored. Thus, any time there is a change in the customer's situation, a thumb rule-based trigger sets off a defection alert that indicates the customer is at risk of switching. As we saw earlier, customers switch for a number of reasons.

CUSTOMER-FOCUSED FIRMS WITH GOOD CUSTOMER INFORMATION SYSTEMS

Customer-focused firms with good customer information systems would have identified reasons for switching behaviour in their customer base. Causes of switching behaviour can be grouped into firm-induced reasons or environmentally induced reasons. Firm-induced reasons are really customer value changes that could be from price changes, product failures, service encounter failures, or problem resolution failures. Environmentally induced reasons can be those that are customer life events. For the individual consumer it could be events such as change in professional or marital status, income changes, relocation, or change in lifestyle—or in other words, change in need situation in general.

For the business customer it could be change in value creation and therefore consumption of productive factors or change in value creation processes, including change in the buying centre, a change in the buying process or criteria, or individuals making the buying decision. Environmentally induced reasons could also include competitor actions that have changed the relative worth of customer value in the firm-such as a price change or a product feature change by a competitor making the firm's own customer value less attractive than the competitor's promise of customer value. Legal, social, or technological factors in the environment could also result in customer switching.

Wherever possible, the firm must attempt to integrate alerts into the customer knowledge for system for when any firm-induced or environmentally induced changes occur portending a negative change in customer value. Once a defection alert is activated, whether related to a specific customer encounter or not, the firm initiates an analysis of whether the customer is in fact at risk of switching.

If the customer is at risk, the firm must now determine if this customer is worth the effort, so to speak. If the loss in customer equity outweighs the retention costs, then the firm must attempt to employ the means necessary to alleviate the switching triggers. Incidentally, this thumb rule could apply at the segment level or to a specific customer.

When the switching triggers are related to a specific encounter with a customer, it usually involves a critical incident, a product failure of some kind. Either the core product has failed or there was a service encounter failure or a failure to resolve a problem for the customer. For any of these reasons, a service recovery procedure needs to be in place to retain the customer. Customer-focused firms should consider it a functional requirement from investments made in any CRM technology that it is able to power a rich recovery database.

The recovery database should yield costs and benefits of the various recovery options for this particular customer either based on segmentspecific information or information related to this specific customer. A recovery database is utilized to determine possible recovery programs, where specific retention options are assessed along with customer input. Once the retention plan is selected and implemented, it needs to be assessed for effectiveness and employed until the point where customer equity does not exceed retention costs.

The recovery database must consist of all the information regarding customer switching behaviour and recovery successes as well as failures.

Customer switching behaviour information should contain the reasons for customer switching obtained from customer satisfaction surveys, from exit interviews, and from customer research in general. All methods of recovery that have been tried need to be recorded for their effectiveness.

A matrix developed to record what recovery procedures worked and didn't work for each switching trigger should determine a recommended retention programme. To accomplish this, retention reports from each customer recovery experience will need to be recorded, analyzed, and stored in the recovery database. The analysis would deal with the costs of the retention programme and the effectiveness assessment of the programme.

Each customer switching trigger needs to be calibrated so that when a segment or customer is at risk the defection alert will move the firm to act with its recovery procedure. A well-planned customer recovery procedure is crucial to a sound customer defection management system. Customer service is considerably enhanced by such a knowledge-based decision support system. Corporate strategy is about core competencies being leveraged to meet corporate goals.

When analyzed into its parts, corporate strategy is about how the core competencies are leveraged in the operations and marketing strategies. Customer service is lost in the shuffle and usually ends up in neither strategy, primarily as a consequence of misplaced definition. Customer service has its unfortunate connotations because of its history and original intent as a business function, and the label does it a tremendous disservice. Customer service is where most of the interactions with the customers occur for a manufacturing firm, whereas for a service firm not all customer interactions need be customer service.

There are interactions whose task is the value creation and delivery of the core product. If firms find that customer service is where most of the customer interactions occur, then customer service should be the most crucial business function for the firm in managing customer relationships. Wherever there is a customer interaction, there is an opportunity to gather information about the customer and how the product meets the customer's needs. The knowledge of the customer's experience with the product in a customer database, if properly utilized, could serve to improve the product. With improved quality and customer value, customer loyalty is nurtured. With the knowledge about specific customers, firms can become intimately familiar with specific preferences of each customer, allowing for customization where possible. Customers can also provide knowledge about how the firm is doing compared to the competition in the customer's eyes. They provide an access to market information not otherwise possible. Firms develop market competence in understanding their competitive advantage and seek the loyalty of the customer by employing this knowledge. As summarized earlier, any manager should be able to look at the good sense in incorporating customer service in the overarching task of managing customer interactions and customer relationships.

Generally, in firms that are not customer focused, customer service has not transcended its image of a necessary evil involving a firm's obligations to take care of the annoyance of product failures. Customer-focused firms elevate customer service to a strategic level by placing it in the context of customer retention and giving it the prominence in the firm that it deserves, alongside customer acquisition, an integral part of customer relationship management.

Elevating the status of customer service function within the firm to a strategic level requires senior managers to practice and perform customer service as well. MBNA requires its senior management to handle four hours of customer service phone calls each month. Folklore in Freeport Maine has it that the founder of L.L. Bean had piped in customer service phone calls to his home! The customer-focused firm makes customer service the responsibility of everyone in the firm. Ritz-Carlton says to its employees, if you are the one to receive a customer complaint, you own it—follow that complaint's resolution process to its conclusion. It is a good practice to regularly involve the backstage personnel in handling customer service. Firms need to construct integrated knowledge management systems that obtain and utilize information from customer service experiences to improve the design and delivery of its value-creating processes. All customer touchpoints in the firm need to be involved in the planning and control functions of the product and service design and delivery.

The customer-focused firm needs to have several things in place to be able to implement a strong retention programme. It needs to have a rich recovery database, the processes to implement the retention programme and the people appropriately trained in recovery procedures. As we will see later, the best-designed processes will not work unless the people involved in the execution of these processes are empowered not only with the knowledge, support, and skills but the motivation and inclination in a customer-focused climate. Operationally, retention programs and the actual customer service activities must prioritize attention for its most valuable (customers) relationships so that all assets of the firm are dedicated at all times to maximum long-term profitability.

The problem is that not all firms are proactive in their management of customer relationships. As a result, customer defections go unnoticed and customer service is the only desk at the firm that handles a customer defect risk. Customer service as an operation of the firm needs to be viewed as within the scope of customer relationship management. It should participate in the firm's retention activities with a much broader scope and higher status. A key consideration is what status the firm has given its customer service function.

Customer-focused quality, when combined with customer-focused productivity, ensures that the firm views operations with a customer focus for an outside-in view of the firm. Productivity is defined differently—not in quantity of customers handled but in quality of their lifetime value. Customer service productivity should not be measured by how many complaints were handled in a certain amount of time, but in terms of how effective it was in retaining customer equity.

Costs and efficiencies are measured in terms of customer lifetime value. A short-term orientation is discarded in favour of acquiring and retaining the more profitable customers for the long term. Short-term losses in a customer relationship are accepted if the long-term relationship with that customer will yield large and sustained profits over the duration of the relationship with that customer.

No customer-focused management decision can be executed without the appropriate customer-focused culture within the firm. The people in a firm, its managers and employees, should be provided with a customer-focused environment. The commitment begins with the CEO. The task of creating and delivering superior customer value must be complemented with the selection of the appropriate employees and the effective management of relationships with those employees. Employee equity, the value of the employee to the firm, should be linked to customer value by valuing an employee based on the individual's contribution to customer value and sustainable profits.

Strategies and tactics that are discussed from the customer-focused perspective are not deliverable unless there is the right kind of environment within the firm. Ultimately, for all of this to work, the people and indeed the corporate culture need to be customer focused and service oriented.

John Chambers runs CISCO Systems, one of the most successful among the largest firms in the world. Rated among the top firms as a "most admired company" and "best company to work for, " by *Fortune* and *Financial Times*, Cisco has grown to over 35,000 employees from about 3,000 when Chambers assumed leadership in 1995. During the same time, sales increased from $2 billion to $22 billion in fiscal 2001. When asked about how he manages growth, Chambers ranked "make your customers the centre of your culture" at the top of his list. To demonstrate the CEO's focus on the customer, Chambers regularly reviews customer satisfaction data and has a daily critical list of customers for whom the firm's products are in jeopardy of failure. He has access to a customer knowledge system that allows him, as he says, to explode critical information on each customer. Chambers focuses on recruiting, developing, and retaining the leadership team that can implement his customer-focused strategy. He ties manager and employee compensation to customer satisfaction.

Over and over again, it is very clear that the successful firm focuses on its people and ensures that new hires fit its corporate culture. Southwest Airlines' director of field employment says: "We hire for attitude and train for skill." Candidates are put through a rigorous interview process, taking as much as six weeks sometimes. After that, the training period rejects 20 percent of the new hires because they don't fit into the corporate culture. Like CISCO, Southwest has a culture of teamwork and cooperation. This final chapter is about the glue that keeps the entire firm collectively focused on the customer and on delivering a service-oriented customer value that is superior to the competition.

Each chapter in this book thus far has outlined and discussed the critical business decisions and processes in the customer-focused firm. The success of the firm in executing and delivering on the goal is predicated upon the ability of its people, managers and workers, to make it happen. Without the employees, workers, and managers, individually and collectively sharing and believing in a cohesive culture or climate conducive to performing as a customer-focused firm, none of what has been covered in this book would have any meaning.

The CEO sets the tone for the climate within a firm. Senior managers take their cue from the CEO. You can tell how strong the culture is by observing how senior managers refer to their CEO. If you have had the opportunity to hear or watch Jeff Bezos, CEO of Amazon, you will have noted his playful nature and "we can make it" attitude. This attitude is also evident in how the people in his firm approach their tasks. Another CEO credited for his firm's customer-focused culture is Fred Smith, of FedEx, who says: "Customer satisfaction begins with employee satisfaction."

Lou Gerstner talked about changing IBM's culture as critical to competing in the information age. By most accounts, he appears to have succeeded. GE's Jack Welch, one of the great CEOs of our time, talked about shared values as critical to realizing his vision. If the culture is not customer focused, the firm cannot be customer focused.

The German ERP software company SAP almost disappeared into oblivion until its CEO, Hasso Plattner, who founded the company around an engineering-focused corporate culture, began to heed customers who had been asking for changes in the way its product was configured and were demanding a Web-enabled interface for the product. When CEOs who have been successful in getting a firm to the top or keeping the firm at the top of their industry are asked about how they did it, there is always some mention of the attention they gave to the culture of the firm. The importance of culture in the performance of a firm comes to the fore following mergers and acquisitions.

In a survey of 1,200 adults, Andersen Consulting (now called Accenture) reported that customers of recently merged firms compared to other customers in the three telecom sector players—cable companies, Internet service providers, and phone companies—felt that service was worsening. The telecom industry had been and is still going through some pretty significant series of takeovers, mergers, and consolidations, causing the customers, even the goldplated and special ones, to suffer from lack of customer focus. CEOs who have been successful in leading a firm through a merger are likely very good at also shaping cultures. Such CEOs are much sought after and financially well rewarded by firms going through dissolution, turnaround, consolidation, acquisition, a merger, or some other form of asset reorganization.

The clash of cultures is perhaps the most important challenge for this CEO.It takes a capable CEO who understands the importance of corporate culture and renders it prominent attention to successfully lead and shape the culture of the firm. To ensure a customer-focused culture, the CEO must commit his attention to it. Fleet bank CEO Chad Gifford pledged $75 million in 2002 "to improve the overall customer experience, " recognizing the severity of the customer service problems it had after its merger with BankBoston. Through a number of mergers, Bank of America's CEO, Kenneth Lewis, said he has been insistent on "one culture" and feels that he has succeeded in bringing the previously disparate entities with their respective cultures into one single culture.

A major cornerstone of his efforts was the six-sigma programme and the "Spirit to Serve" customer service training at the bank. As of this writing the jury is still out on how successful Carly Fiorina, CEO of Hewlett Packard, is with her reorganization and change, involving everything from strategy, structure, and culture to compensation, following their controversial merger with Compaq in 2002. It had only been a few short years since Compaq itself had acquired Digital Equipment Corp.

Even Wall Street has not been kind to its darling, HP. The challenge is tremendous and the rewards are huge. The task of shaping culture is perhaps the most important and fundamental challenge for any CEO. For a successful corporate culture that emphasizes a focus on the customer, the commitment has to begin at the top and be reflected in how the CEO runs the shop.

How an organization behaves depends on what Peter Drucker calls its "theory of the business." He says that the assumptions that a firm makes about its markets, about its technology, and about the strengths and weaknesses of the firm are what define its behaviour. He draws evidence from IBM creating the computer industry in the 1950s, Apple bringing personal computers to the household in the 1980s, and GM inventing lifestyle segmentation in the 1990s. These companies had the right theory of their business because the assumptions they made about the world around them were the right ones.

The characteristics that define a customer-focused firm align closely with the assumptions that Drucker is talking about. Drucker's three assumptions centre around markets, technology, and firm. In customer-focused management terms, these relate directly to customers and to the firm's value-creating assets. Firms must understand their customers and be open-minded about the technology of the value creation and delivery in their business to leverage its core competencies toward superior customer value. The strategic decision making process begins with assessments of markets and firm to determine the customer value that can be created profitably from its productive assets. These assessments serve to define the customer in terms of consumption activities and to define the solution or value bundle it will provide the customer through the core and supplementary product. Value-creating and delivery processes are designed according to these definitions of customer and product. What follows from the definition and analysis of the customer is the estimate of the lifetime value of all customers or more appropriately the long-term profits of the firm. In parallel, the product definition will guide the asset and resource allocation toward the more profitable products. Firms seek to maximize the value to the firm by serving the most profitable customers with the most profitable value bundle that can be produced with its assets.

The strategic decision-making process incorporates a customer focus to guide value creation and delivery decisions. As developed and emphasized throughout this book, the principles of customer-focused management are the following:

- Obtaining and utilizing information about customers, especially with respect to their consumption cycle
- Designing value creation and delivery strategy and processes that are based on that customer knowledge
- Implementing the strategy and processes that provide superior value to customers so as to meet the firm's goals

To make any of this work, the entire firm has to get behind believing in these principles of customer-focused management. To become customer focused, the firm must really change the way it thinks and behaves, such that the customer is always the centre of the value creation and delivery. The firm must have in place the appropriate people with the appropriate attitude. When the goals, structures, processes, and rewards are also in place, the culture and climate should follow for the firm to become customer focused. Two underlying fundamental concepts defining organizational behaviour become evident here in the processes and people requirement: organizational structure and corporate culture. *Organizational structure* refers to how firms define the roles and relationships between the various functions or processes and the individuals responsible for and given the authority to fulfill them. *Corporate culture* refers to the values and beliefs held in the firm that dictate how the firm operates.

Value creating and delivering processes may be designed so that firms can be customer focused. But if the culture does not provide the climate, the firm cannot be customer focused. Just about everything in the firm from the office and building design to social hours can affect the culture of the firm. Nokia, the wireless devices giant from Finland, went so far as to instruct its building designers to design and construct an environment where individuals are immersed in the corporate culture and can interact with the company and fellow employees on a variety of levels. Notice the company's slogan: "Connecting

People." Citibank has "pulse lunches" at its banks where managers have a weekly lunch with employees and listen to their concerns and then act on them. These are two examples of how climate can be created for the firm to be customer focused.

VALUE CREATING AND DELIVERING PROCESS

For the value creating and delivering process to be customer focused as intended, the organization design should follow the way that people who execute the processes need to relate to each other.

Traditional organizational structure may not be designed for a customer-focused operation. McKinsey introduced the notion of the "horizontal corporation" in 1996, citing examples of firms that had reorganized around natural workflows rather than conventional functional areas. What is interesting about the principles behind their horizontal organization model is that most of them would translate very well to the customer-focused firm.

Among other things, such firms, they say, must focus externally on the customer and realign organizational roles and resources around the processes that deliver customer value. They offered the following as evidence of the benefits of reorganizing into a horizontal corporation.

- A division within Motorola reduced cycle time by 80 percent and late supplier deliveries by 30 percent.
- A GE production facility improved productivity by 50 percent, reduced manufacturing cycle from three weeks to three days, and customer complaints from 2 to 0.2 percent.
- Ford's customer service division increased productivity by 20 percent and improved customer satisfaction performance by 20 percent to 60 percent.
- Saab Aircraft reduced lead times by 50 percent, value-added costs by 20 percent, and customer complaints by 70 percent.

The point to be made with these examples is that the benefits from an organizational structure that is designed to focus on the customer can be very powerful. A structure that integrates both suppliers and customers and is conducive to a focus on creating and delivering customer value is a prerequisite for customer-focused strategies to work.

An interesting support to the logic of making radical changes to the traditional functional, geographic, or product-based forms of organizational structure can be drawn from the following example. The manufacturing chief at Rowe Furniture in Salem, Virginia, disassembled the assembly line and allowed the factory workers to figure out their own processes to get the furniture built.

The result? The shop floor seemed to be crazed, but productivity and quality went up dramatically! Organizational structure and design including such things as hierarchy, power structure, and decision making and hiring, training, and rewarding are critical to ensure that the firm is customer-focused. Organizational design can take various forms depending on the value creation and delivery process.

With the recent revolutionary advances in information technology, newer forms are becoming evident. In what is also referred to as the knowledge economy, virtual organizations are commonplace today. A new model has emerged where organizations draw knowledge-based assets from entities outside the firm to create and deliver value to the customer. Clearly, information technology plays the crucial pivotal role in making this possible. Scholars have suggested that in such a virtual organization, three vectors—customer interaction, asset sourcing, and knowledge leverage—are the key components in the strategy and structure of the successful business model. The organization structure must be designed so as to perform its value creation and delivery processes in a customer-focused culture.

UNDERSTANDING THE CUSTOMER-FOCUSED CULTURE

To understand what customer-focused culture is, it is important to first understand what "culture" means in the context of organizations. One commonly accepted definition of corporate culture among scholars studying organizational behaviour is: the pattern of shared beliefs and values that guide the way the firm behaves. Mrs. Fields would say, "It's the way we do things around here."

Culture is deeply rooted in values and translates to "climate" in a day-to-day "feel" of the place. Climate is a manifestation of culture. Schneider and Bowen, two wellknown scholars from the fields of psychology and organizational behaviour who have done a great deal of research on customer-focused culture and service climate, view climate as the "tangible layer on top of the organization's underlying culture." Culture, along with mission and strategy, is also seen as an important piece for the vision of a firm to work.

Corporate culture has been proven to be predictive of the performance of an organization. For example, in a sample of 102 companies, it was found that corporate culture was strongly linked to innovativeness. In this study, investment in technology was found to be influenced by corporate culture when firms provided the climate that fostered innovations. When Snapple, the beverage industry's surprise breakthrough firm, fell on hard times, Michael Weinstein of Triarc Companies, who took over the firm, focused on corporate values to turn the firm around.

Cultures are relatively stable, and it takes a long time to shift core values of a firm. The resistance to change has led to the demise of such former giants such as Polaroid. Polaroid's I-Zone instant pocket camera zoomed to number one status in less than three months after its introduction. This product almost didn't happen. During its development at the firm, the marketers who brought this idea to the table faced powerful resistance from old-line scientists and engineers at the firm who could not imagine what the founder of the firm, Edwin Land, would say about moving away from creating elegant products based on high technology. At one of the design meetings, the chief engineer was said to have asked, "Have we lost our minds?"

He wondered why the same firm that Land had founded would produce something that was small, clunky, with a cheap lens, to produce fuzzy, thumbnail-size photographs! The culture of a firm is its soul, and it resides in its employees and managers. Home Depot founder Bernard Marcus is known for his reliance on employee empowerment to make his vision a success. But, how many firms show a real caring for their employees? The statistical analysis software company SAS is often cited as one of the few information technology companies to have weathered the technology sector-led recession in the last couple of years because of its strong culture and caring for its employees. The firm has won several "best places to work" awards over its 25-year history. The CEO of SAS, Jim Goodnight, says, "I think our history has shown that taking care of employees has made the difference in how employees take care of our customers. With that as our vision, the rest takes care of itself." Unfortunately, it is the exception when a firm is able to say this and execute those sentiments in any meaningful way. The result is that employees are left to fend for themselves and leave unhappy. The Creative Group, a firm that specializes in recruiting creative talent, reported that in their survey, two-thirds of their sample of advertising and marketing executives from the nation's largest companies said the creative professional changed jobs every other year.

It is not only important to attract the right employee, it is even more important to retain customer-focused employees. It shouldn't come as a surprise that firms that are customer-focused are also ones that take care of their employees. When firms minimize their efforts in developing employee dedication to creating and delivering customer value they face high employee turnover. Harvard researchers Schlesinger and Heskett called this unfortunate but common attitude among senior managers, the self-perpetuating "cycle of failure."

Among the reasons they offered to explain why firms fall into this cycle is an inability to measure the costs of employee dissatisfaction. They cite firms such as Wells-Fargo, ServiceMaster, Dayton Hudson, Au Bon Pain, and Fidelity Bank of Philadelphia, who have broken the cycle of failure by paying attention to their frontline employees. Recruiting, training, and rewarding practices of frontline employees at these firms are remarkably simple but different from those of the "average" firm. They pay more and reward their employees and managers who are productive and customer focused. The results in the form of employee and customer satisfaction are very compelling. The direct correlation between employee satisfaction and customer satisfaction is often underestimated. Researchers Schneider and Bowen have shown through a series of studies of bank tellers that satisfied employees deliver satisfying customer encounters that result in employee and customer satisfaction feeding off each other. The key prerequisite is to create an atmosphere that fosters a focus on creating and delivering superior customer value. Such an atmosphere or climate comes from a firm that has a customer-focused culture and instills in its employees the values of customer-focused behaviour. Almost all top researchers in the field of services marketing, operations, and management have called for increasing attention to the culture that promotes satisfying service encounters. A firm cannot hope to satisfy its customers if the employees are not happy themselves. If the employees are not happy they leave. Guess who leaves first? The ones whose skills are most in demand are the ones who are most mobile—usually the best employees.

CUSTOMER-FOCUSED EMPLOYEE

Turnover at Dallas-based The Container Store is 20 percent compared to the industry average in retail operations, which generally ranges from 80 percent to 120 percent. Full-time employees at the company get 235 hours of training in their first year and are constantly asked what they need to do their job well.

The company won *Fortune* magazine's "America's best workplace" honor in 2000. Similarly, at the 60-employee sports apparel company, Athleta Corp., employees set their own schedules and handle personal matters during the workday, backed by a CEO who believes that they will make up the time. To break the cycle of failure, firms have to value their employees.

They ought to rethink the way they hire and groom their employees and managers. To do this, firms should be asking, what kind of employee do we need to attract and retain so that we can create and deliver a customer-focused solution? Managers from the functional areas of human resources, operations, and marketing management should jointly help determine the ideal employee for any position that is directly involved in creating and delivering value to the customer. Human resource decisions centre on hiring and training and are critical to acquiring the appropriate human capital in the firm. Study firms such as Disney, Nordstrom, Southwest Airlines, Ritz-Carlton, and American Express, which are known for their customer-focused culture, and you will see that all of them are very careful in how they select and hire their employees.

They have in mind specific profiles that characterize the desired skills and personality traits that are necessary for the customer-focused employee in their business. Some of them use quite sophisticated ways of assessing the service orientation of the recruit. With the training and education these companies have in place, new employees are socialized into the corporate culture, whatever that culture might be. In a study within a large firm of five strategic business units (SBUs), 3,500 managers responding to a survey confirmed that the degree of market orientation in the processes of recruiting, training, and reward/compensation were found to strongly correlate with job satisfaction and trust in management. A very revealing and useful exercise would be to investigate the hiring practices of the firm and check for how well the requirements for a customer-focused employee are reflected in the hiring and training practices.

Does the firm have customer-focused criteria in their employee selection process? Do the job requirements and ideal candidate description reflect a customer focus? If the firm is well coordinated and integrated, customer knowledge is likely to be well utilized by the human resources department as well as the operations functions. Knowledge of the consumption activities of the customer should guide the practice of attracting and retaining human capital. If this is in place then the training and education is also likely to be designed to develop the employee for operational excellence contributing to creating and delivering the desired customer value. The operational excellence assumes the appropriate knowledge and attitude of the value creating and delivering role of the employee.

Many firms now complement operations skills training with training on customer interaction skills or other customer-focused skills for the frontline employee. Previously, for example, banks would provide operations training for tellers but not customer skills training. Once hired and trained, the operations and marketing functions take over the direct allocation, motivation, and supervision of the employee. Employees must be able to enjoy their work and find it rewarding not just financially but emotionally as well. How well these functions value the employee will have a major effect on the efforts of the firm to create and deliver the desired customer value.

The customer-focused firm ought to be very interested in the welfare of its employees. Otherwise, employees tend to disconnect from the firm and are not committed to their jobs. For example, Dupont began a programme to "re-engage" with employees by helping employees design their career paths in an attempt to win back employee loyalty.

Northeast Delta Dental is one of the major dental care insurance providers in New England. CEO Tom Raffio expresses his main challenge as "how to retain the customer-focused culture that has given us success as we continue to grow." He succeeds by being very close to his employees. He goes to the extent of meeting the families of his employees so that he has an intimate knowledge of his employees' lives. His office is in the middle of the busiest floor of the corporate office. He likes being accessible and close to his employees. Tom brings customer feedback directly to his employees and asks them what they thought the firm ought to be doing. He is genuinely interested in the growth and development of the employee. The employee is empowered with the operational skills and with customer knowledge. The customer-focused firm is proactive in rewarding employees for being customer focused. As we saw earlier, Commerce Bancorp of New Jersey gives its employees $50 to come up with any practice of the bank's that is not customer-focused. The company almost instantly rewards an employee for specific customer-focused actions in a customer experience or incident. Whoever has wowed the customer gets a "Wow" award hand-delivered the next day from head office. The customer-focused firm ensures that the workplace is a place where people can grow, where they are comfortable at what they are doing.

Several firms have begun to include a measure of customer satisfaction in the compensation and bonus criteria for employees. Here is an interesting example of a culture spillover from a merger that benefits the bigger company. PTC, formerly Parametric Technology, which acquired Computervision, found that their own salespeople were not concerned with managing the customer relationship after the sale while those who came from Computervision emphasized customer service. Today, all salespeople in the company are evaluated on customer satisfaction scores as well, and PTC is focusing on solutions rather than the software product. More than a decade ago, GE began a customer education programme at its Management Development Institute, where customers and employees are educated on the firms' goals and processes. The idea was to get the customers and employees together and explain the goals and strategies of the firm.

In this new economy, knowledge-based employees are very mobile with their expertise. Firms would be well advised to assess each employee's worth, including replacement cost, similar to the analysis in managing customer relationships, to determine the firm's need to retain the individual. Retention efforts should be prioritized according to that worth of the employee. When firms reluctantly started laying off workers during the recent recession, employers were also offering enticements with bonuses so that they would return to the firm when it was ready to rehire workers. Charles Schwab was offering bonuses and $20,000 worth of college tuition money, hoping that these workers would come back to Schwab when the company started to hire again.

Treacy and Wiersema argued that a firm has to have at least one of the three value disciplines they organize their thesis around—operational excellence, customer intimacy, and product leadership. Either firms have to be very good at the customer value that they create and deliver, their values should be built around intimate customer knowledge, or they should be at the forefront of product innovation. The argument that these are separate value disciplines is often commonly accepted. However, in a discussion of the customer-focused firm, the distinction appears to be irrelevant. The customer-focused firm assumes that it has to be good at all these three value disciplines simply because they are interrelated. A customer-focused firm derives its competitive advantage from its service orientation. With its intimate knowledge of the customer (customer intimacy), the firm excels in creating and providing superior customer value (operational excellence), and by anticipating and responding to evolving customer needs it continues to improve its customer value (product leadership).

In the new economy, a firm with a customer-focused culture leverages its people and its information technology to be close to the customer so that it can create and deliver superior customer value. Its people and information technology, as the primary productive factors, have to be employed in such a way as to ensure the firm's ability to understand the customer and to use that knowledge in its value creation and delivery. Thus, the importance of customer intimacy and operations excellence is taken as a guiding element in corporate strategy and performance. This approach requires a culture that is customer focused as a prerequisite to derive a sustainable competitive advantage.

CUSTOMER EXPECTATION OF SERVICE MANAGEMENT

As the consumer market segment of the Internet economy continues to grow, the role of customer service in the emerging logistics supply chain systems will continue to change. Therefore, the need to improve logistics customer service (LCS) to consumers is greater than ever before. Finding meaningful ways to meet consumer service expectations requires LCS programmes that strategically blend website service activities (e.g., online ordering procedures) with offline logistics supply chain activities (e.g., order delivery). This balance may be a key strategy in satisfying and maintaining loyalty relationships with online consumers. Yet very little is understood about the nature of website-enabled LCS and the impact on online customer loyalty, although the level of e-logistics service expectations is often thought to be higher than that demanded by customers in brick-and-mortar environments.

The purpose of this study is to examine:

- The factors that determine the level of perceived LCS quality in the Internet-enabled logistics supply chain, and
- The impact of LCS quality on customer loyalty towards online retailers'websites.

Internet-enabled logistics supply chain refers to the total logistics system of transportation, warehousing, inventory, order processing, information flow, and website-enabled order processing procedures that drive the level of perceived quality of LCS in this system. Perceived LCS quality is defined as the level of expectation-minus performance gap and customer intended loyalty is defined as the tendency of online consumers to repurchase from the same website, as reflected in repurchase intentions or intention to recommend a website to peers. Following conventional practice, LCS was defined as the total output of the logistics system, but with emphasis on cognitive impact: perceived service speed and consistency of service speed, perceived availability of merchandise on the retailer's website and in the supply chain, and perceived responsiveness of the retailer. This study contributes to the literature on two levels. At the conceptual level, the study provides an empirical validation of the logistics customer service-customer loyalty linkage in the online environment. While this linkage has been widely established in traditional business-to-business markets, it remains to be established in the online environment where the impersonal and self-service nature of customer service may raise doubts about the validity of the LCS-customer linkage.

At the managerial level, the study suggests ways to create a consumer-oriented online logistics customer service strategy by identifying the relevant web-based and traditional supply chain logistics activities that are important in creating and maintaining loyalty relationships with online consumers. As with all service activities, not all website features are likely to be relevant to consumer perception of online LCS quality. Moreover, different website features are likely to play different roles in consumer perception of LCS quality. Thus, this study provides insight into which website features should be emphasized in the different phases of the Internet-enabled logistics supply chain.

The following discussion presents an overview of the influence of website design strategy on LCS quality assessment among online consumers. Using the consumer disconfirmation theory as a theoretical foundation, a conceptual framework is proposed including the hypotheses isolating influences of key website design features on LCS quality, followed by the field study that was conducted to specifically examine the service encounter evaluation of 373 online transactions. Finally, analysis and findings are discussed followed by a discussion of the managerial implications and suggestions for future research.

VALUES AND ATTITUDES DIFFER ACROSS CULTURES

Values and attitudes help to determine what members of a culture think is right, important, and/or desirable. Because behaviours, including consumer behaviours, flow from values and attitudes, services marketers who want their services adopted across, cultures must understand these differences While American brands often have an "exotic" appeal to other cultures, U.S. firms should not count on this as a long-term strategy.

In the late 1990s, Wal-Mart found that the cachet of U.S. brands was falling in Mexico. The Mexican news media alerted consumers to shoddy foreign goods and some Wal- Mart customers turned to a spirit of nationalism. The retailer responded with an "Hecho en Mexico" programme similar to the "Made in the U.S.A." programme that was successful in the United States. In some situations it is more than a case of nationalism: Brand attitudes are negatively influenced by specific prejudices toward "dominating" cultures. The Korean ban on Japanese movies and the French phobia about Euro Disney are good examples of the latter.

STRATEGIES MANAGEMENT IN CUSTOMER SERVICE

The customer service study revealed that no specific tactic, technology, or mission statement is the key to effective customer service delivery. In fact, what is clear is that effective customer service delivery is organization specific, since services are designed around the targeted customers' desires and the frontline employees delivering the services.

The components of the process for producing effective customer service delivery include appropriately identifying and targeting the ideal customer, establishing a customer-focused vision that is consistent with the prioritized desires of the target customers, establishing the operational procedures and internal infrastructure that support customer service, continuously measuring customer and employee satisfaction, embracing change, and striving persistently to improve.

The customer service literature clearly demonstrates that both profit-seeking and public agencies that implement effective customer service strategies realise financial benefits, either through increased profits or through reduced costs associated with long-term, informed customers; customer referrals; employee retention; improved information exchange; and streamlined service delivery.

Child support enforcement, in this case, is like any other business. In order to implement effective customer service strategies and reap the benefits of good customer service, the Office of Child Support Enforcement (OCSE) agencies will need to implement the process of developing effective customer service.

In an effort to become "more results-oriented and responsive to customers," the Office of Child Support Enforcement (OCSE) contracted with Circle Solutions, Inc. to undertake a study of public and private sector practices and outcomes in customer service. The study included a review of customer service literature, a review of the annual reports and Web sites of 40 companies mentioned in the literature, telephone interviews with companies sited as leaders in customer service in the literature, and site visits to three agencies—two private and one child support agency.

Throughout the study, an advisory group of four State child support enforcement directors provided input and feedback. As a final product of the study, this report summarizes the literature on effective approaches to customer service delivery, highlights four promising practice case studies, conjectures about the transferability of these concepts to child support, and offers future research recommendations. Child support enforcement agencies can refer to this report as a guide for improving customer service, as a resource to learn the costs and benefits of effective customer service delivery, and to inspire future inquiries into effective customer service delivery. In the 1990s, IBM conducted global research on the question, "What will keep CEOs and senior management awake at night as we begin the twenty-first century?" The study found that, regardless of the industry or geographic location, the most common response was a desire to generate a more customer-oriented culture or business vision.

Customer service is not merely customer relations or how nice frontline workers are to customers. Rather, satisfying or even delighting customers is the goal of excellent customer service. Because customers for different types of services have different needs, customer service strategies will differ and must be tailored to the target customer.

It improves trust and information exchange: In the public sector, including child support offices, good customer service generates satisfied or delighted customers. Satisfied customers lead to increased compliance, improved information exchange, improved relationships, increased trust, and, potentially, decreased workloads or costs. For instance, police departments across the Nation have embraced the concept of community policing. Through community policing, police departments incorporate a customer focus as well as an attitude of partnership with customers, to increase satisfaction and trust and even reduce fear of crime in the community. Customers actually participate in addressing crime and disorder problems, thus reducing the workload on patrol officers.

It saves money and increases profit: In the private sector, good customer service leads to satisfied or delighted customers, which generates customer loyalty, which produces increased revenues and reduced costs. For example, during the early 1990s, IBM transformed itself into a customer-driven organization. From 1994–1999, customer satisfaction increased by 5.5 per cent, revenue increased from $63 billion to over $80 billion, cost and expense savings equaled $7 billion, and stock prices improved over 1,000 per cent.

Upon becoming CEO of Greater Southeast Hospital, a private, nonprofit community hospital, Tom Chapman refocused customer service strategy to save the faltering hospital. Instead of trying to attract more clientele outside the community or turning away the uninsured in the community it served, under Chapman's leadership, Greater Southeast sought to provide better customer service—improving the quality of life and creating community-specific services. The emphasis shifted to treating people when it was cheapest—not in the emergency room but rather when their problems were minor—and to instituting preventative care.

He opened a clinic in the high school to address minor health issues and provide health education resources to teach students about prevention. Additionally, Mr. Chapman improved coordination with the local health clinic and obtained the specific technology from which patients served by the hospital would benefit. Before his arrival, Greater Southeast spent only $20,000–$30,000 a year on a blood pressure programme, although a single stroke victim could cost $30,000 to treat.

The public and private sector customer service literature concurs on the process for delivering great customer service, even if outcomes differ. The current literature supports an outside-in strategy of customer service, rather than the traditional inside-out model for providing services. In the private sector, profit and growth are the *outcomes,* not goals.

Profit and growth are generated by customer loyalty. Loyalty is generated by customer satisfaction. Customer satisfaction is the *goal* that companies should seek and focus on, because high customer satisfaction, as a matter of course, produces customer loyalty and subsequently profit and growth. At this point, the public and private sectors converge—customer satisfaction is the *goal.* Customer satisfaction is achieved by providing valued services and products, where value is the positive difference between customers' actual experiences and their service delivery expectations. Productive employees also create value.

Employee productivity stems from employee loyalty, and loyalty is a product of employee satisfaction. Satisfaction is generated by high-quality support services (people, information, and technology) and by being empowered to provide value and resolve customer complaints. This customer service culture must be supported by leadership that emphasizes the importance of each customer and employee. These leaders must be creative and energetic (not lofty or conservative), participatory and caring (not removed or elitist), that is, one who can be a coach, teacher, or listener (not just a supervisor or manager).

Such a leader demonstrates company values (rather than simply institutionalizing policies) and motivates by mission (rather than by fear). Some components of this model are cyclical. A 1991 study of property and casualty insurance companies found that employees who felt that they were meeting customer needs had twice the job satisfaction level of employees who did not believe they were meeting customer needs. In that study, when a frontline service worker left the company, customer satisfaction levels dropped from 75 to 55 per cent.

In the customer service literature, five guiding principles are adopted by public as well as private agencies delivering excellent customer service:

- Embrace change and persistently strive to improve (be a learning organization).
- Continually ask the target customers what they want and then give it to them.
- Empower, support, and reward frontline personnel.
- Harness the power of information.
- Establish an enabling infrastructure.
- Identify the Target Customer.
  - Begin by identifying the target customers and by considering the point of purchase, point of service delivery or receipt, and point of consumption.

- Cluster or segment target customers based on their common behaviours, knowing that targeting the wrong customers can have adverse effects on the organization.
- Determine the priorities of various clusters of customers, knowing that the capabilities of the organization are crucial in addressing these priorities.
- When possible, focus on customers with high current or future value. (Perhaps in child support this is a custodial parent with many children in the system.) This does not mean that other customers will not receive service, but it may mean that they will receive a different level of service. Consider the frequent flier programmes that airlines and hotels offer to their customers with high current and future value. This does not mean that other passengers will not receive services, but services may not be at the same level.
- Discourage non-target customers, those who are not likely to be satisfied by the services, and those to whom it is expensive to provide services, which is a necessary part of a customer focus. A simple example is offered as an illustration. A fire department could discourage residents from contacting the department to remove cats from trees by charging a $20 fee for performing the service and by advertising their busy emergency call load. The equipment and time investment of sending a ladder truck and several firefighters may reduce the effectiveness of the department at responding to an emergency and may not be the most prompt means of accomplishing the task for the customer.

• Determine What Customers Want..
  - Determine what target customers want (not just what they need right now) by asking them in person or as part of a mail or telephone survey or by using other mechanisms (e.g., electronic tracking and researching marketing trends) to determine what they want. Be aware that advertising, word of mouth, and public relations influence customers'expectations. Meeting customers'basic needs or expectations does not always bring high levels of satisfaction. Exceeding expectations produces high satisfaction-therefore, determine customers'ideal desires.
  - Determine how the target customers prioritize their"wants."Generally, customers want convenience, quality products and services, variety or selection, low prices, and protection or security. However, each organization must identify what is most important to its customers.

  - Weigh how important the customer-identified"wants"are to the organization. Are the services something that the organization does, is capable of doing, or wants to pursue?
  - Determine how well the organization can meet the customers'"wants"in comparison with competitors. The success of other companies at meeting and exceeding customer expectations changes a customer's frame of reference and increases a customer's expectations.
  - Determine which"wants,"if performance delivery were to be improved, would most impact the organization's bottom line (profit, cost, loyalty, trust, or compliance).
- Establish an Organizational Culture Supportive of Customer Service.
  - Utilizing the information gathered, establish the company's customer-focused vision. The vision statement should be simple and may also identify what the company does not want to be. Some examples of simple vision statements include"Absolutely, Positively Overnight"by Federal Express and L.L. Bean's promise "Guaranteed. Period."
  - Live up to what is promised by concurrently developing and applying externally and internally oriented strategic service concepts that reflect the vision. If the organization does not implement both internally and externally oriented service strategies consistent with the vision, the organization will have good intentions but poor customer service (Thompson).
  - Continually reflect on the vision and goals and the way services are delivered to customers. Be creative about the mechanisms used to create and deliver new services. Be willing to change existing practices to integrate improvements.
- Implement an Externally Oriented Strategic Service Concept. The externally oriented strategic service concept establishes how the organization's service is designed, marketed, and delivered to target customers.
  - Take into account the costs of providing services and ways to minimize those costs while implementing quality control. The service concept must be developed with the frontline worker at its centre. Determine the necessary financial, human, and technological resources necessary, as well as how the organizational structure and flow can enable the frontline worker to delight the customer and deliver the promised vision.
  - Use advertising/educational strategies to set appropriate customer expectations.

- When planning, realise that control of information can take the place of assets. For instance, the Rural/Metro Fire Department in Scottsdale (AZ) has reduced the size of its crew and trucks because of technology that allows crews to view microfiche floor plans on the way to a fire. The added knowledge of the building layout allows fewer fire fighters to accomplish the same task that requires more firefighters when they do not have this advance knowledge.
- Provide a feedback loop for incorporating customer comments and complaints into the planning processes. Customer complaints are an invaluable resource and source of information without which organizations cannot be successful. Complaints brought to the organization are one of the most efficient and least expensive ways to obtain information about customer expectations of products and services. Complaints are a more direct means of obtaining information than conducting research studies of customer expectations, conducting transaction studies, or reviewing customer expectations in parallel industries. Another means of soliciting customer feedback that has been implemented by a number of service leaders is to interview lost customers-those who have switched service providers. (Perhaps in child support these customers were custodial parents who had been making timely payments but who stopped doing so.) Still other options are holding customer meetings, hosting social events, and attending seminars or conferences where customers are present. Ensure that the complaint resolution strategy supports the customer-focused vision. Most research shows, "...if customers believe their complaints are welcomed and responded to, they will more likely repurchase." British Airways found that 67 per cent of its complaining passengers fly again if their complaints are handled well. British Airways even implemented a creative and convenient way to allow customers to complain by installing video booths at Heathrow Airport so that customers could immediately go into a booth and state a complaint, even during non-business hours. The videotapes are reviewed and addressed during business hours.
- One final element of an externally oriented service strategy is to regularly measure customer satisfaction or delight in the products and services.

• Implement an Internally Oriented Strategic Service Concept.

The internally oriented strategic service concept establishes how the organization's internal processes will support the customer-focused vision. The premise behind the internally oriented strategic service concept is "...capable workers who are well trained and fairly compensated provide better service, need less supervision, and are much more likely to stay on the job. As a result, their customers are likely to be more satisfied...". A study by Sears in 1989 found that "employee turnover and customer satisfaction are directly correlated." Stores with high customer service ratings had a 54 per cent sales force turnover versus 83 per cent in stores with low customer service ratings. This is supported by examples throughout the literature. Taco Bell found that the 20 per cent of stores with the lowest employee turnover rates have 55 per cent higher profits (an outcome of customer satisfaction) than the 20 per cent of stores with the highest turnover rates.

A number of other studies provide convincing evidence as to why companies should avoid employee turnover. Merck and Co. found in 1990 that turnover costs were 1.5 times an employee's annual salary. Clearly this varies based on a number of cost factors (e.g., workers compensation claims, hiring process costs, training costs, and lost business), but it is commonly noted that employee turnover is an expensive problem. Abt Associates studied an automobile dealer's sales and determined that it cost $36,000 to replace a salesperson with 5–8 years of experience with a salesperson with less than 1 year of experience. The economic costs of excessive employee turnover in one trucking company were analysed, and it was determined that the company could increase profits by 50 per cent by cutting driver turnover in half.

- Ensure that leaders of the learning organization exhibit the company values. Leaders must foster the creation and testing of new ideas and be unabashedly willing to change existing practices to integrate improvements.
- Identify employee groups important to implementing the externally oriented service concept. Frontline workers are of central importance.
  - Identify the characteristics and needs of the employee group(s) and how well those needs are met. This may include resources needed to successfully perform the job or needs can refer to compensation, work environmental factors, or personal needs. Understanding employee needs helps an organization to develop successful processes as well as employee retention policies. Learn how targeted employees perceive the proposed customer services. An organization cannot change without the participation of its employees.
- Focus on recruiting employees who support the customer service vision. The costs of employing people who do not support the customer service vision are considerable. Forum Corporation research in the service industry showed, "...only 14% [per cent] of customers who stop patronizing service businesses do so because they are

dissatisfied with what they bought. More than two-thirds defect because they find service people indifferent or unhelpful." Oftentimes, the right employees are those that fit in with the corporate culture's customer service vision, not necessarily those with the most experience in the industry. Additionally, develop career paths that allow successful customer-oriented employees to remain on the frontline.

- Focus on training and employee development throughout employment. A study by Ryder Truck from 1988 through 1989 found that increased training meant lower employee turnover.
- Empower frontline employees to do what it takes to satisfy the customer. Management must support employee empowerment by clearly defining the parametres of the empowerment, while remaining flexible within the parametres. This will encourage creativity. Rules should be simple and few—Continental Airlines actually had an employee handbook burning party to signify the change from a procedural environment to one of empowered customer service. Also, in support of internal customers, the Department of Defence reduced its 230 pages of travel regulations to 17 pages.
- Ensure that management supports employee decisions and judgment calls, even if this means that the cost of satisfying customers initially increases. In positions of high customer contact, quality control is not met by increased supervision, but by the use of incentives to emphasize quality, making service providers highly visible to customers, and by building a peer group to instill a sense of pride and teamwork.
- In addition to skills and empowerment, equip frontline personnel with the technology, information, and internal resources to do what it takes to satisfy the customer. The literature is replete with examples of how incorporating the latest information technology can improve employee productivity. For example, Charles Schwab developed IWIN, a system that allows an agent to identify and view electronically Charles Schwab literature to respond to customer questions received by telephone. Before this system was implemented, agents who were unfamiliar with the literature in question could not provide immediate and succinct answers to customer questions.
- Ensure that divisions and individuals within the organization communicate. Frontline employees and other employees need information and a support network. A customer should never have to tell one employee what another employee already knows.
- Develop cross-functional teams for operations and improvement tasks. First ask those who are doing the work for suggestions to improve

productivity. The Social Security Administration nearly doubled its telephone-answering capacity by implementing automated features, utilizing additional technology to change the way employers' reports of wages are recorded, and cross training its employees to work outside their normal areas of responsibility during peak periods.

- Link all employees' compensation to (and offer rewards for) good customer service performance. Rewards can be money, status, praise, acknowledgement, or perks such as trips or special events. While Charles Schwab does provide monetary incentives based on the amount of money a broker team brings into the company, if the customer service survey for the quarter does not show strong customer service by the team, the reward is reduced or even eliminated for the quarter. This policy in a profit-seeking environment leaves no doubt that customer satisfaction is the primary goal.
- Finally, measure employee satisfaction regularly. Leaders in the service industry have employed such methods as toll-free numbers, periodic roundtable meetings, and surveys to collect employee satisfaction information.

DETERMINE WHAT CUSTOMERS SERVICE

Want and Give It to Them

A number of child support agencies, including those in Texas and California, have implemented customer surveys. Customer surveys can and should be used to determine what child support customers most want from child support services and to seek input on improving services, collect baseline information by which to measure results of improvements to the system, and to reinforce a customer focus. The Urban Institute prepared a sample customer survey for OCSE from which questions could be gleaned, and child support agencies also may use one another as a resource for samples.

Implement an Externally Oriented Strategic Service Culture

Establishing an externally oriented strategic service culture in child support follows the same process as similar procedures in the private sector. In this culture, management places an emphasis on minimizing costs, increasing quality control measures, educating customers, establishing a customer complaint mechanism and resolution strategy, and measuring customer satisfaction.

Both First Interstate Bank and Cherner Automotive Group offer creative quality control procedures. At Cherner and FIB, frontline supervisors serve as coaches or mentors and are trained to serve in this capacity. FIB has a policy to"inspect what they expect."In child support services, rather than relying only on statistics or monthly reports about the quality of services at field offices, central office management could regularly visit child support field offices. The visit would include discussions with field office managers regarding operations, observations of customer interactions with staff, auditing and reviewing measures identified as important to customer service, addressing patterns of complaints, brainstorming on improvement opportunities, and rewarding excellent customer service practices.

A creative customer education tool used by FIB is the I-Beetle. Employees of FIB drive a Volkswagen Beetle painted with an advertisement for FIB's Web site. This takes the message to the customers-during traffic jams, on trips to the supermarket, while shopping at the mall, etc. Opportunistic marketing may be something worth considering in child support. Messages about responsible parenting or a new child support Web site or call centre telephone number could be distributed where child support customers are already going-whether at the supermarket, on downtown streets, at shopping malls, at job placement centres, or at the town ball field.

California Child Support Services has automated its complaint tracking and established an Interagency Agreement with the Department of Social Services, State Hearing Office, to conduct State hearings when appropriate.

Implement an Internally Oriented Strategic Service Culture: Implementing an internally oriented strategic service culture in child support means hiring the right people; continually training employees in customer service; seeking input from employees; empowering, rewarding, and supporting frontline personnel; utilizing technology to reduce the workload on CSOs and other frontline personnel and to provide easy access to information; creating an enabling environment where discretion is clearly defined and frontline judgment calls are supported by management; utilizing cross-functional teams; and measuring employee satisfaction.

©This may mean hiring staff with an aptitude and attitude for customer service, even if child support skills must subsequently be learned. Such a culture may also be actualized through software that categorizes and automatically queues cases for attention by CSOs, based on the status of the case. This means instituting incentives for providing great customer service, whether perks, recognition, or merit raises.

It also means that divisions or departments within child support services must communicate and cooperate with one another. It includes proactively attempting to deter burnout of CSOs and call takers by encouraging staff to take appropriate breaks and eat lunch away from work, use vacation time, and modify the work that a person does. What Recommendations or Lessons Learned Do the Model Agencies Interviewed Offer to OCSE?

- Understand that good customer service takes time, patience, persistence, consistency in message at all levels, accountability, courtesy, respect, and emphasis on team players.
- Make sure upper management and executives at the top are sold on a customer service culture.
- Put a human face on customers—treat them with a personal touch, rather than as a collective.
- Make it easy for customers to do business with the service.
- Listen to customers to learn what they need and want.
- Address the immediate needs of the customer.
- Hire the right people by hiring on attitude and training on the skill.
- Mentor new employees.
- Manage by staying close to the frontline.
- Train the frontline on how to address customer problems.
- "Inspect" what you "expect."
- Don't focus energies on the bad apples—put energies and resources into those employees that want to work in customer service.
- Ensure that management/executives listen to their employees' complaints (without interruption) and have trust in their employees.
- Ask open-ended questions.
- Have uniform expectations of the customers.
- Establish uniform processes, policies, and procedures to collect payments. Customers must be able to expect the same expertise, collection efforts, production, recovery, and professional delivery regardless of which branch or individual is working.
- Develop working relationships with other partners (e.g., courts, credit card companies, vendors, or other banks) that play a role in debt collection.
- When working with a customer complaint, try to understand the customer as well as those available to help address the problem.
- Frontline employees should mentally separate themselves from problems in an effort to address the issue so that the outcome is positive for all involved.
- Maintain an orderly work atmosphere.

The results of this study provide a glimpse of how child support agencies may be able to strategically plan and implement a customer-focused culture and the benefits that child support agencies should expect from successfully implementing excellent customer service. The study also suggests several possible areas for future study:

- OCSE may consider selecting one or several elements of the process for further study. For example, what specific performance measures may be appropriately implemented for child support officers when the agency has a customer focus? Circle Solutions, Inc. (Circle) has recently received a contract from the Department of Justice to conduct a school resource officer performance measures study and pilot programme with four police agencies that are implementing community policing in schools. Under this programme, customers and stakeholders in school safety are participating in the development of the performance measures. A similar pilot programme could be adapted and utilized for child support agencies.

- OCSE may consider studying the effectiveness of specific customer service strategies in child support enforcement in pilot states that implement the customer service process outlined in this study.
- OCSE may wish to highlight many more promising customer service practices in child support across the Nation. Case examples or a compilation of examples within the structure of the customer service process could offer States a point from which to brainstorm.
- OCSE may wish to create a toolkit for developing a customer-focused culture. Circle Solutions recently completed a"Collaboration Toolkit"for the Department of Justice. The Toolkit is a nuts-and-bolts guide for law enforcement and their partners to develop, fix, and sustain productive law enforcement-community partnerships to support the advancement of community policing. The Toolkit offers worksheets and exercises for working through pitfalls and organizing these efforts, and it refers the reader to resources to learn more. A similar toolkit presentation of the customer service process may be useful for State child support agencies.
- OCSE may also wish to explore in more detail some creative strategies of serving customers related to co-location of child support with other offices or businesses, payment choices, call management, training strategies, etc.

Certainly, this study lends itself to a great deal of further exploration. The study revealed that no specific tactic, technology, or mission statement is the key to effective customer service delivery. In fact, what is clear is that effective customer service delivery is organization specific, since services are designed around the targeted customers' desires and the frontline employees delivering them. The components of the process for producing effective customer service delivery include appropriately identifying and targeting the ideal customer, establishing a customer-focused vision that is consistent with the prioritized desires of the target customers, establishing operational procedures and internal infrastructure that support customer service, continuously measuring customer and employee satisfaction, embracing change, and striving persistently to improve.

The customer service literature clearly demonstrates that both profit-seeking and public agencies that implement effective customer service strategies realise financial benefits, either through increased profits or through reduced costs associated with long-term, informed customers, customer referrals, employee retention, improved information exchange, and streamlined service delivery. In this case, child support enforcement is like any other business. In order to implement effective customer service strategies and reap the benefits of good customer service, child support agencies will need to implement the process of developing effective customer service.

3

Customer Experience Management

But customers do not make recommendations lightly. When they make a recommendation, they put their own reputations on the line. Firms must earn that recommendation through the consistent delivery of outstanding customer service. Customer experience management (CEM) is "the process of strategically managing a customer's entire experience with a product or a company".

Marketing research has shown that about 70 to 80% of all products are perceived as commodities, that is, seen as being more-or-less the same as competing products. This makes marketing the product difficult. Marketers have taken various approaches to this problem including: branding, product differentiation, market segmentation, and relationship marketing. Relationship marketing, (also called loyalty marketing) focuses on establishing and building a long term relationship between a company and a customer. There are several approaches that have been espoused including customer experience management, customer relationship management, loyalty programs, and database marketing.

The development of customer experience management originally started with a critique of three existing marketing concepts. It concluded that the following three concepts do not go far enough:

- Marketing concept—Since the 1970s there has been a gradual shift from a product-, technology-, and sales-focused orientation towards a customer- and market-oriented approach by determining the wants and needs of customers and satisfying them more efficiently or effectively as compared to competitors. However, the approach is still mostly functional, with similarities and differences between competitors being defined mostly by product features and customer benefits. In addition, the customer is perceived as being rational, which is in most cases not the case, as e.g. Kahneman and Tversky's Prospect theory has proven. Also, it is asserted that market research is mostly analytical leaving little room for qualitative assessments of customer relationships towards products, services, or brands. It is claimed (by Shultz) that traditional marketing, in practice, takes an inside-out approach (starting with internal variables like production capabilities and available capital then moving to external variables like customer needs), rather than taking an outside-in approach as marketing theory requires.

- Customer relationship management is claimed to be deficient because it primarily consists of database and software programs used in call centers and thus, focuses too much on quantitative data. By doing this, it is led by transactions rather than a desire to build lasting relationships with customers.
- Customer satisfaction is an outcome-oriented attitude deriving from customers who compare the performance or value of the product with their expectations of it. It is claimed that the customer satisfaction approach depends too heavily on outcome oriented measures like satisfaction and too superficially on direct experiential measures. A customer is said to be satisfied when a product's performance is above the customer's expectations. Thus, traditional customer satisfaction techniques are deficient if they don't help firms to understand and manage customers' experiences, experiences that lead to the following equation: good experience = satisfaction.

CEM recognizes, as does all of marketing since the early 1970s, that customers are a company's most valuable asset. What makes CEM different from traditional marketing is that it claims that marketing theory has seldom been implemented adequately. CEM is a methodology that tries to overcome the gap between theory and practice by reformulating basic marketing principles. The result is that CEM stresses four aspects of marketing management :

- CEM focuses on all sorts of customer-related issues
- CEM combines the analytical and the creative
- CEM considers both, strategy and implementation
- CEM operates internally and externally

Although all marketing management and strategic management does all of these, CEM supporters claim that they have a methodology that will yield better results.

Being convinced that the marketing concept is too product-centered, Customer relationship management too focused on quantitative data, and customer satisfaction too functional, CEM looks for another perspective on the relationship of a consumer with a product or service. And what's key? The experience linked to it is the key.

This enables companies to strategically manage a customer's experience with a brand and by doing so, achieve a truly customer focused management concept. To accomplish this, a framework is required based on clearly defined company objectives. Schmitt's book "Customer Experience Management" offers the following five step framework that should help managers understand and manage the "customer experience":

Step 1: Analyzing the Experiential world of the customer

- Analyze sociocultural context of the customer (needs/wants/lifestyle)
- Analyze business concept (requirements/solutions)

Step 2: Building the Experiential platform

- Connection between strategy and implementation
- Specifies the value that the customer can expect from the product (EVP = experiential value promise)

Whereas steps 1 (Analysis) and 2 (Strategy) form the basis for CEM, steps 3, 4, and 5 are focusing on Implementation.

Step 3: Designing the Brand experience

- Experiential features, product aesthetics, "look and feel", e.g. logos

Step 4: Structuring the Customer interface

- All sorts of dynamic exchanges and contract points with customers
- Intangible elements (i.e. value, attitude, behaviour)

Step 5: Engaging in Continuous Experiential innovation

- Anything that improves end customers' personal lives and business customers' working lives

And finally, to bring all pieces together, a holistic approach is required that provides a linkage between the different steps and connects them with the organization.

Organizing for CEM includes three tasks:

- Financial planning of CEM in terms of customers - CEM's ultimate goal is a fair and mutually beneficial long-term business relationship between a company and its customers. Customers will reward the company financially by doing business with it. The value of the customer to the firm, referred to as customer equity, will increase, and the company will grow and be profitable.
- Allocation of organizational resources - Improving the customer experience, and thus increasing customer equity, requires internal resources. The company needs to ask what financial, structural, and personnel resources it needs to engage in CEM to deliver an ongoing desirable experience to customers. Resources must be allocated to the brand experience, the customer interface, and innovation.
- Enhancement of the employee experience - The concept of experience applies also to the internal customers, the company's employees. What all employees, across all levels, get from an experience-oriented organization is a more rewarding employee experience that includes a new form of professional and personal development. Employees of such an organization live a more experiential and thus more satisfying

and productive life. They are also more motivated and capable of delivering a great experience to customers.

METHODS AND TECHNOLOGIES OF CUSTOMER RELATIONSHIP MANAGEMENT

Customer relationship management (CRM) covers methods and technologies used by companies to manage their relationships with clients. Information stored on existing customers (and potential customers) is analyzed and used to this end. Automated CRM processes are often used to generate automatic personalized marketing based on the customer information stored in the system. Customer relationship management is a corporate level strategy, focusing on creating and maintaining relationships with customers.

Several commercial CRM software packages are available which vary in their approach to CRM. However, CRM is not a technology itself, but rather a holistic approach to an organisation's philosophy, placing the emphasis firmly on the customer. CRM governs an organization's philosophy at all levels, including policies and processes, front-of-house customer service, employee training, marketing, systems and information management. CRM systems are integrated end-to-end across marketing, sales, and customer service.

A CRM system should:

- Identify factors important to clients.
- Promote a customer-oriented philosophy
- Adopt customer-based measures
- Develop end-to-end processes to serve customers
- Provide successful customer support
- Handle customer complaints
- Track all aspects of sales
- Create a holistic view of customers' sales & services information

There are three fundamental components in CRM:

- Operational - automation of basic business processes (marketing, sales, service)
- Analytical - analysis of customer data and behaviour using business intelligence
- Collaborative - communicating with clients

Operational CRM provides automated support to "front office" business processes (sales, marketing and service).

Each interaction with a customer is generally added to a customer's history, and staff can retrieve information on customers from the database as necessary. According to Gartner Group, operational CRM typically involves three general areas:

Sales Force Management Systems

These automate some of a company's critical sales and sales force management tasks, such as forecasting, sales administration, tracking customer preferences and demographics, performance management, lead management, account management, contact management and quote management.

Customer Service and Support (CSS)

CSS automates certain service requests, complaints, product returns and enquiries.

Enterprise Marketing Automation (EMA)

EMA provides information about the business environment, including information on competitors, industry trends, and macroenvironmental variables. EMA applications are used to improve marketing efficiency. Integrated CRM software is often known as a "front office solution", as it deals directly with customers. Many call centers use CRM software to store customer information. When a call is received, the system displays the associated customer information (determined from the number of the caller). During and following the call, the call center agent dealing with the customer can add further information. Some customer services can be fully automated, such as allowing customers to access their bank account details online or via a WAP phone.

Analytical CRM analyses data (gathered as part of operational CRM, or from other sources) in an attempt to identify means to enhance a company's relationship with its clients. The results of an analysis can be used to design targeted marketing campaigns, for example:

- Acquisition: Cross-selling, up-selling
- Retention: Retaining existing customers (antonym: customer attrition)
- Information: Providing timely and regular information to customers

Other examples of the applications of analyses include:

- Contact optimization
- Evaluating and improving customer satisfaction
- Optimizing sales coverage
- Fraud detection
- Financial forecasts
- Price optimization
- Product development
- Programme evaluation
- Risk assessment and management
- Strategic Marketing
- Operational marketing

Data collection and analysis is viewed as a continuing and iterative process. Ideally, business decisions are refined over time, based on feedback from earlier analyses and decisions. Most analytical CRM projects use a data warehouse to manage data. Collaborative CRM focuses on the interaction with customers (personal interaction, letter, fax, phone, Internet, e-mail etc.)

Collaborative CRM includes:

- Providing efficient communication with customers across a variety of communications channels
- Providing online services to reduce customer service costs
- Providing access to customer information while interacting with customers

Driven by authors from the Harvard Business School (Kracklauer/Mills/Seifert), Collaborative CRM also seems to be the new paradigma to succeed the leading Efficient Consumer Response and Category Management concept in the industry/ trade relationship. In its broadest sense, CRM covers all interaction and business with customers. A good CRM programme allows a business to acquire customers, provide customer services and retain valued customers.

Customer services can be improved by:

- Providing online access to product information and technical assistance around the clock
- Identifying what customers value and devising appropriate service strategies for each customer
- Providing mechanisms for managing and scheduling follow-up sales calls
- Tracking all contacts with a customer
- Identifying potential problems before they occur
- Providing a user-friendly mechanism for registering customer complaints
- Providing a mechanism for handling problems and complaints
- Providing a mechanism for correcting service deficiencies
- Storing customer interests in order to target customers selectively
- Providing mechanisms for managing and scheduling maintenance, repair, and on-going support

The following factors need to be considered:

- Scalability: The system should be highly scalable, as the volume of data stored in the system grows over time
- Communication channels: CRM can interface with a variety of different channels (phone, WAP, Internet etc.)
- Workflow - A company's business processes need to be represented by the system with the ability to track the individual stages and transfer information between steps
- Assignment - The ability to assign requests, such as service requests, to a person or group.

- Database - the means of storing customer data and histories (in a data warehouse)
- Customer privacy Considerations, such as data encryption and legislation.

CRM applications often track customer interests and requirements, as well as their buying habits. This information can be used to target customers selectively. Furthermore, the products a customer has purchased can be tracked throughout the product's life cycle, allowing customers to receive information concerning a product or to target customers with information on alternative products once a product begins to be phased out. Repeat purchases rely on customer satisfaction, which in turn comes from a deeper understanding of each customer and their individual needs.

DRIVES THE RELATIONSHIP WITH THE CUSTOMER

THE MECHANICS AND MANAGEMENT

The model presented here is based on Parasuraman, Zeithaml, and Berry's work on service quality. It uses the same logic to incorporate more directly the notion of costs to the customer. *Quality* may not fully convey the point that it is customer value that drives the relationship with the customer. Analysis of quality without the associated costs will not completely capture the customer's frame of reference. The crux of the model is that there are an ideal and an actual for both the customer and the firm:

- The customer's ideal—expected customer value
- The customer's actual—experienced customer value
- The firm's ideal—product concept
- The firm's actual—operations design

The ideal and the actual of the customer's expectations and perceptions and the firm's product concept and operations design are placed in the context of the competition, the technology, the economy, and the legal and social environment within which they operate. For example, competitive forces and the social environment can shape customer expectations and affect their comparative evaluation of customer value.

The firm's ability to hire the appropriate personnel to deliver the product as conceived and designed can also be affected. Firms design a product concept based on their understanding of the customer's expectations, and then configure their value-creating assets accordingly in an operations design, which for the most part determines what they actually deliver as customer experience. Thus, customer expectations, product concept, operations design, and customer experience are all linked. Customer value is dependent on this *expectations* link, the *design* link, and the *execution* link. The product concept needs to be closely aligned with customer expectations—the expectations link into the firm. The firm interprets and converts the customer's ideal—expected customer value—into what becomes the firm's ideal—product concept. The firm's actual—the operations design—is the firm's implementation of the firm's ideal—the product concept. The design link is how well the firm has been able to implement the firm's concept of customer expectations with its productive assets.

The design or configuration of a firm's assets executes the product concept, which is what the customer experiences. The execution link reflects how well the customer's actual experience is aligned to the intent of the operations design. Thus, firms must align the customer's ideal expectations to the product concept with a strong expectations link, which in turn is linked to the operations design by a strong design link, followed by an execution link, which determines the customer's experience.

Customer expectations management, studied with a sample of about 100 managers at the leading service firms in the U.K., was found to be composed of three key dimensions: keeping promises, marketing orientation, and employee skills. Another study in a small electric utility company in the United States found that frontline employees had a good understanding of customer expectations. If we assume that customer's expectations were perfectly understood, reflected in the product concept and translated into operations design and therefore customer experience, we should find that customer value is high.

However, in practice this is an invalid assumption. Customer expectations play a very critical role in shaping customers' perceptions of quality. When customer expectations are met, we find perceived quality is high, and when not met, we find perceived quality is low.

A closer look at the model will reveal that it is a good vehicle to frame all that can be done to improve customer value by increasing benefits and decreasing costs to the customer. It is a safe assumption to make that improving quality will improve customer value. Creators of the University of Michigan's American Customer Satisfaction Index have shown that customer expectations are linked to perceived value and customer satisfaction over time. Improving quality relative to costs to the customer requires strengthening all the links in the model. Tracking the logic from expectations to product concept, to operations design, to customer experience are a number of management actions that must be taken to ensure the desired customer value.

As, firms can make several check to ensure that the customer-focus and service orientation helps keep the value created and delivered closely aligned with customer expectations. Firms devote most of their attention to the value creation and delivery that affect the perceptions of the customer. However, if service quality is defined as the comparison between expectations and perceptions, shouldn't firms be focusing attention on shaping customer expectations as well?

Managing the Expectations Link

How closely the firm's conception of the product resembles the customer's expectations is a key conceptual link. This link is a function of how well the firm understands customer expectations and how well that understanding is translated into product concept and design. Evaluating the quality of products, especially that of services and service components of products, is difficult for the customer. To understand the implications of this difficulty, think of services as being dependent on search, experience, and credence dimensions. Some services are higher in search qualities that can be evaluated before the purchase.

Experience qualities are those that can only be assessed during or after consumption, whereas credence qualities are hard to evaluate even after the service. Similarly, customer expectations are just as complicated as customer evaluations. Research has shown that there is a zone of tolerance in customer expectations. The zone of tolerance is the range of expectations on any of the attributes that are important to the customer. The low end of the range is the minimum level of service that determines what is adequate. The high end of the range is the maximum level of service, referred to as what is desired. Customers will accept anything below the desired, as long it is above the adequate level.

To be able to manage expectations, firms need to understand how customer expectations are shaped. Firms need not only to understand customer expectations but to help shape them so that they are realistic. Customers form expectations from their own past experience with the firm's product as well as with similar products from competitors. In the absence of such experience, customers draw from their experience with the firm's other products or from similar products in general. The firm's own communications, both explicit and implicit, shape customer expectations.

Explicit communications come from all overt marketing messages. Implicitly, all visible actions and evidence of the firm—its prices, its location, its culture reflected in the way it conducts business—could communicate something about the firm. Customers are also influenced by others regarding consumption need situations and the solutions appropriate for those needs. This product-related information can come from messages they receive from the media, family, and friends. Firms are generally focused on their own overt communications and ignore the effect that other sources have on customers and their expectations.

It should become clear now that customer knowledge management is a critical starting point for any firm. The firm's effective use of CRM technology can enable the firm to have a more thorough understanding of customer expectations. Based on customer knowledge, we can see that a failure in this regard could be the result of ineffective use of available sources of information on the market segment and individual customer information. Are all the touchpoints set up to capture and record customer information? Is there a process for sharing customer information across the firm?

For example, is there bottom-up communication from frontline employees to managers who participate in product design? Recognizing that customer expectations are dynamic, market research and customer research should be a continuous exercise. Instruments used to gather customer information should be evaluated for validity and reliability and should be easy to use. Inappropriate or inaccurate market research could result in management designing the product concept based on poor information from the marketplace about expected customer value.

An effective customer information system is critical in designing a product concept that would deliver the expected customer value. Management could perceive market needs and customer expectations inaccurately or make poor use of information in defining the service concept. How good is the information on the customer? How complete is it? How well has the information been analyzed, interpreted, and assessed by the product designers? Information regarding the market needs to be disseminated and shared among individuals who are responsible for the service design. Is the information current, and is there adequate indication of how these expectations are likely to change in the near and long-term future? Corresponding changes in product design should be prompt and responsive.

Linking the product concept to the needs/expectations of the customer is dependent on how well information has been obtained on customer expectations and how well they have been utilized in the product concept. The irony is that sometimes the information is about the wrong customer! The value and validity of the information for product design depends on whose expectations are obtained and used in developing the product concept. The heaviest users or, more precisely, the ones with the most lifetime value should be the priority. In other words, the weight given to the information should be prioritized by the lifetime value of the customer. There is also the possibility that the customer not being the right customer could simply be a result of poor segmentation methods or targeting the inappropriate segment(s) or customer(s).

As we have seen, it is important that the right customer be drawn to the firm. Marketing communications could be attracting customers who are not intended for the service. This might be manifested in poor media or message strategy, setting up inappropriate customer expectations for the product concept. The question here, of course, is whose expectations were obtained and who is actually using the product.

Thus, if the firm has not attracted the customer whose needs it can best satisfy at sustainable profits, then at the outset, the firm is at a disadvantage. Customer expectations are hard to measure. As we saw on customer knowledge management, firms may not have good information on the critical aspects of what customers expect. Research can be flawed and the data not valid, or the means of ascertaining the information is not reliable. Frequently the information is stale and customer expectations, being dynamic, have changed. If you have an inappropriate or inaccurate account of customer expectations, the product concept is not going to be aligned with what customers actually expect.

The Execution Link

If the product concept is not supported by the appropriate corporate culture, frontline employees are at a disadvantage in executing the product concept. Backroom employees should see frontline employees as internal customers and the entire corporate culture focused on customer satisfaction. A number of things must happen for the firm to ensure that the product concept can be delivered. All productive factors must execute the design to deliver the product as conceived.

Employees need to be selected, hired, trained, and motivated to execute the design. They need to be empowered so that they have the ability and the inclination to provide the service as designed. Employees need to be allowed the discretion to accommodate and customize to each customer as far as possible. With the right kind of training, frontline employees in services other than just professional services can also make the right decisions.

What was actually delivered and the customer's perception of the product experience need to be continually monitored by the firm, so that the firm understands whether customer expectations were met. Perhaps, during customer interactions, the provider was ineffective in obtaining customer-specific information or in interpreting and using it in customizing the experience for each customer. In many services, customization is a key determinant in how well each customer is satisfied with the product experience.

For example, customers use tangibles (service provider's smile and other nonverbal cues) differently. Some customers need more assurance regarding the product than others. Some customers' information needs are different from others, and their evaluation of the service provider's responsiveness depends on how well the service provider is able to accommodate them. The service provider's ability to empathize with the customer reflects the ability of the service provider to understand the individual customer so that the actual delivery is closer to the individual customer.

Customer perceptions are just as critical as customer expectations. Customer experience may in reality be different from the intial concept. One way firms reduce the disparity between perceptions and reality is to encourage or require managers to work in the front line. By the same token, an argument can be made for allowing the frontline to work backstage, so that they are knowledgeable about how the backstage works to support the frontline. Another way is to empower the frontline employees so that they have the flexibility and authority to accommodate specific customer preferences that standard operating procedures preclude. This is an effective customer relationship management practice as long as the front line is also appropriately trained to make informed judgments as to when and where such accommodations are reasonable and beneficial to the firm. Such a policy is especially useful to handle disgruntled customers following a product failure.

The Design Link

The link in the chain between what is conceived and what is designed into the firm and its value-creating processes depends on how effectively the firm's resources (people, raw materials, supplies, and systems) have been configured to create and deliver the product as per the product concept. The link could be broken with inaccurate configuration of a firm's resources, for instance, in poor selection of employees. In other words, the fit between job description (responsibility and tasks) and employee profile (skills, education, experience, and personality) represents a significant factor in how well the design is linked with the concept.

Poor empowerment of the frontline employee could fail the product concept in design. This could result from inadequate technical and customer service training, information systems, backroom efficiency, and other support structures. To be able to deliver the product as conceived or designed, internal marketing should be effective. For example, lack of clear communication of such things as the product concept, customer expectations, the marketing strategy, etc., to the frontline employee reflects poor internal marketing—and similarly in reverse, when the product concept decisions have not incorporated the frontline employee, the product is not conceived and operations not designed with that valuable input from the frontline.

In any firm, there is an inevitable disconnect between what the customers expect and what the frontline perceives that the customer wants or what the managers think that the customer wants. For the frontline personnel to be empowered, they require the knowledge and the tools as well as the authority and motivation to use them. If not, the firm will find a disconnect between product concept and execution.

Promise only what you can Guarantee

Whatever resides in the minds of the managers as product concept is what is promised in advertising messages from the firm to the customer. And whatever resides in the minds of the frontline or sales people as product concept is promised during direct interactions with the customer. These promises are conceptual manifestations of the product. A useful diagnostic exercise is to check the customer experience as articulated in customer surveys and other methods of customer feedback against the product as imagined by managers and all customer contact personnel. Similarly, the design of the operation in terms of the configuration of the productive factors can be checked agaisnt whatever resides in the minds of the customers as customer expectations. Is the firm's operation set up to deliver on those customer expectations? Customer expectations and the firm's promises must be delivered. Customer-focused firms should be able to guarantee what can be delivered. That which cannot be delivered must not be promised. Promise what can be delivered and deliver what is promised.

This means providing product performance such that customer perceptions are that expectations will be met. As we have also seen, every customer feels a certain amount of risk prior to purchase and during consumption. Even loyal customers know there is a risk of nonperformance and simply place confidence in the provider and are comfortable with taking that risk with that provider.

Helping with risk perception is a task of managing customers. Service guarantees are a powerful mechanism to manage customer's perceived risk in having their expectations met. A service guarantee is simply a promise to compensate the customer if service delivery fails established standards.

Expectations and Perceptions

For all the reasons inherent in the characteristics of services, intangibles in a product are bound to fail. There is no opportunity to "recall" a service, as is possible with the physical component of the value bundle. Therefore, guarantees are a meaningful and powerful technique to reduce the customer's perceived risk. The most important precondition is of course to ensure that the firm is able to deliver as promised, or in other words ensuring that you can deliver what you guarantee.

For example, Amtrak recently scrapped its service guarantee because it couldn't meet the goal of unconditional customer satisfaction or a complete refund of fare. They found the refunds were getting too expensive because of their frequency, about 4 per 1,000 passengers, which was four times what they had hoped for. In designing service guarantees, firms must consider the scope of the guarantee, the specific risks that the guarantees are aimed to alleviate, the ease of invoking a guarantee, etc. To make these decisions in a customer-focused manner requires an analysis of the customer's context.

What is it that needs to be guaranteed and from what? To get at this, one needs to understand the key customer concerns and what the perceived risk levers are. It is useful to examine this along the RATER dimensions since by definition these are the dimensions that customers use to evaluate quality. With this analysis, it is possible to determine what the scope of the guarantee should be. It is useful to think of the consumption activity cycle and the process blueprint to help with deciding the scope of what should be guaranteed. Xerox and others in the copier business, for example, provide a guaranteed response time for service calls, or an "up-time" guarantee to relieve the risk of failure. Once the scope of the guarantee is decided, it now makes sense to think about under what conditions the guarantee is offered. This is a litmus test of sorts; if you cannot deliver something that you are guaranteeing, you tend to start putting conditions on the guarantee. The problem then is that the guarantee becomes meaningless. Conditional guarantees violate the spirit of a guarantee.

The fear of abuse of guarantees prompts firms to render guarantees worthless with numerous disclaimers and other conditions. The reality is that customer abuse of guarantees is minimal compared to the incremental benefits accrued by the firm from a guarantee. Customers who invoked guarantees cost Embassy Suites $3.94 million in 1996, while the hotel gained $23.14 million in incremental revenue from guests who said they stayed at the hotel only because of its guarantee.

At Hampton Inn it was $3.98 million in costs offset by $31.7 in incremental revenue. Following a significant loss of market share from poor quality, in the early 1980s Holiday Inn improved its standards and launched its successful satisfaction guaranteed programme: "Your room will be right when you check in and if not we will make it right or your stay is free." The conscientious firm will ensure that the quality is in place before promises are made in guarantees.

The benefits of service guarantees to the customer are obvious. The interesting thing about service guarantees is that there are benefits to employees as well. Team Xerox found that the employees knew what they were working toward and the service guarantees put the internal goals in perspective. The firm won its Malcolm Baldrige award because it was able to engage the whole firm in its quest for improving customer satisfaction by focusing on what customers were telling them about their firm and everything they did.

IMPORTANT TO NON-PROFIT ORGANIZATIONS IN CUSTOMER RELATION MANAGEMENT

CRM is an alternative to the "one size fits all" approach. In industrial markets, the technology can be used to coordinate the conflicting and changing purchase criteria of the sector. The data gathered as part of CRM raises concerns over customer privacy and enables persuasive sales techniques. However, CRM does not necessarily involve gathering new data, but also includes making better use of customer information gathered as a result of routine customer interaction. The privacy debate generally focuses on the customer information stored in the centralized database itself, and fears over a company's handling of this information. For example, there is virtually no way a consumer can determine if the company shares private (personally identifiable) data with third parties. Furthermore, companies may not always accurately declare to the consumer the types of information collected by CRM systems and the specific purposes for which the information is used.

CRM is also important to non-profit organizations, which sometimes use the terms "constituent relationship management", "contact relationship management" or "community relationship management" to describe their information systems for managing donors, volunteers and other supporters. salesforce.com, a popular CRM service that is on demand, offers its products for free to nonprofit organizations. Price and quality of service have become negligible differentiators for companies in the communications, media and entertainment industries (e.g., wireline, wireless, broadband cable, and satellite service providers). The customer experience is emerging as the primary way service providers can stand apart from competitors. This new differentiation requires a new way of doing business: integrated customer management. Integrated customer management, or ICM for short, was conceived as a business strategy that helps service providers create and, more importantly, deliver an intentional customer experience. Why intentional? Because the customer experience is too valuable to be an unintended, often haphazard by-product of internal business processes. ICM enables service providers to deliver an on-purpose experience that is consistently simple, uniquely personal and immediately valuable for customers at every point of service. The desired end result is stronger, more profitable customer relationships.

ICM can be achieved through three operational fundamentals: Alignment: All people, processes and systems must be aligned to meet both business goals and customers desires. For example, bundling products is a good example of an initiative that crosses lines of business and/or departments. The product development, marketing and sales departments for local and long distance, wireless and data services must work in conjunction to enable the company to assemble and sell bundled services. Beyond this, customer service, accounting and other functions must also align support resources to shield customers from the complexity of all behind-the-scene operations that make these and all offers possible. Alignment allows customers to perceive and interact with their service providers as one company, not as disparate lines of business.

Agility: In industries where the pace of change has greatly accelerated, service providers must be able to quickly and efficiently react to changing market conditions and customer demands. Entering new businesses or bringing new products to market quickly and cost-effectively is critical and is often a key differentiator between large organizations and their newer, more nimble niche players (e.g., a former utility, wireline service company versus VoIP provider; a traditional financial institution versus a credit card company). Agile organizations can change direction when it makes sense for them to do so—or when their customers demand it—without being hampered by organizational stovepipes, or by inflexible business processes or IT infrastructure. Customer-centricity: In the past, ostensibly due to the original utility status of many communication service providers, the customer experience was not a primary concern. Providers sought only to make their products and services available, not necessarily easy to access or use. Therefore, the customer experience was primarily a by-product of internally focused processes designed to achieve the desired result (market or activate a service, generate a bill, enable customer service) efficiently and cost-effectively. Today, consumers have more authority and less patience with a slow, frustrating or otherwise unfulfilling customer experience. Whether they're interacting with a customer service representative, responding to an advertised offer, downloading content or paying their bill, customers demand that their experience be simple and, optimally, create value for them. Therefore, service providers must put the customer at the center of their business. Customer-centricity means making the business easier for customers to do business with. It also involves understanding customers' needs and desires and mapping processes and resources to meet them.

The phrase, "integrated customer management," was coined by Amdocs in 2004. Even though Amdocs pioneered it, ICM has become an accepted concept in the communication industry. For example, reporting on the 3GSM World Congress in Barcelona February 14, 2005, Financial Times printed the headline: "Vendors unveil systems for the real world; Integrated customer management and boosting revenues are the main issues for operators."

RELATIONSHIP AND VALUE OF CUSTOMER SERVICES MARKETING

A Services marketing is marketing based on relationship and value. It may be used to market a service or a product. "Managing the evidence" refers to the act of informing customers that the service encounter has been performed successfully. It is best done in subtle ways like providing examples or descriptions of good and poor service that can be used as a basis of comparison. The underlying rationale is that a customer might not appreciate the full worth of the service if they do not have a good benchmark for comparisons.

However, it is worth remembering that many of the concepts, as well as many of the specific techniques, will work equally well whether they are directed at products or services. In particular, developing a marketing strategy is much the same for products and services, in that it involves selecting target markets and formulating a marketing mix. Thus, Theodore Levitt suggested that "instead of talking of 'goods' and of 'services', it is better to talk of 'tangibles' and 'intangibles'". Levitt also went on to suggest that marketing a physical product is often more concerned with intangible aspects (frequently the `product service' elements of the total package) than with its physical properties. Charles Revson made a famous comment regarding the business of Revlon Inc.: `In the factory we make cosmetics. In the store we sell hope.' Arguably, service industry marketing merely approaches the problems from the opposite end of the same spectrum.

4

Customer Information Management

Firms cannot claim a customer focus or attempt to satisfy customers unless they have customer knowledge—that is, a deep understanding of the needs of the customer. With all the brouhaha regarding the growing importance of customer relationship management (CRM), too many hotel companies are still vexed when it comes down to delivering on a service promise.

For hotel companies looking to differentiate themselves from the competition, exceeding guest expectations is paramount since it leads to building loyalty. In this complex era, it is crucial to truly understand and anticipate guest desires in order to fulfill that service promise. But just how to do it effectively has been an elusive and vague notion not fully grasped by many hoteliers.

Customer-focused firms really understand their customers by proactively acquiring information on the entire consumption process, especially the consumption activities of the customer. Such information must be processed and used to guide each and every interaction with that customer. This information can be used not only to make changes and improvements in the value-creation and delivery processes of a firm but also in managing relationships with the right customers. Managerial decisions and actions cannot be customer oriented when customer data is lacking.

Do we know enough about the customer's consumption activities to enable us to create and deliver customer-focused value and manage relationships with the customer? Hotel companies need to be in the customer intimacy business. They have to focus on delivering what the customer wants. You have to have some product leadership to deliver on customer intimacy but you have to focus on the relationship above all else. All goals should be focused on customers rather than the product or operations. And getting those loyal relationships are paramount to the property or brand's success. 10 percent of all hotel guests account for 44 percent of all hotel nights. To get those loyal customers, it's crucial a hotel employ a culture of managing the "total customer experience" and also embrace a culture of managing "moments of truth" when that experience is on the line. Also, property leadership should demand a culture that puts the customer at the "centre of your world."

While a hotelier doesn't have direct control over what someone says after they walk out, it's very possible to control the guest experience in such a way that they leave with only positive thoughts. Customer intimacy is essential for success in today's world. "If people don't feel welcome and have an emotional connection, their loyalty will be in question."

It's also a matter of creating emotional loyalty rather than functional loyalty. Whereas functional loyalty comes into play if a hotel is conveniently located near an airport, for example, emotional loyalty transcends pure need and promotes frequent stays because the experience moves beyond the brand attributes to an attachment to the guest's psyche.

As Lew Platt, former CEO of Hewlett Packard, is widely quoted as saying: "If HP knew what HP knows, we would be three times as profitable." With the increasing ubiquity of information technology, there is an increasing focus on information—in a way, simply because it is there. Most managers understand the crucial role that good information plays in decision making. And here is a seemingly radical proposition: most data is underutilized in business. If you don't know what data is important, you may not recognize it when you see it. When there is an opportunity to obtain what may be valuable data, you will not access or gather, process, or utilize it.

Careful observation would reveal that as a norm, firms don't capitalize on opportunities to gather critical customer data. One reason may be that firms focus on the sort of data that is needed for a specific decision, such as in the development of a new product or an advertising campaign, especially in the B2C context, where there are no direct interactions with the customer. In the B2B context, where there is direct interaction with the customer, there is a greater amount of customer information being utilized for decision making. This is partly because formalized systems are in place to document customer information.

The customer being a business is very likely to have formalized purchasing procedures. Information-age technology has very naturally developed in the B2B case earlier and faster than in the B2C case. In the B2C business, where there is direct interaction with the customer, this technology is opening new thinking about customer data. A basic question is, what information is needed and for what purpose? To manage the customer relationship, it's crucial to have deeper customer intelligence and then use that information to make each stay more memorable. For example, it is better to match up what your hotel does with each individual's lifestyle and give them something unique based on that lifestyle to reinforce the relationship. One suggestion made is to give, for example, a customer who stays 20 times a year and uses the gym regularly, a gym membership in their home town. That way, every time they go to the gym they will think of that hotel. It is a much better way to build loyalty then just giving them more points on their loyalty programme.

The Total Customer Experience. Customers want:

- A positive, enjoyable and unique experience from the beginning until the end of their experience
- They desire an emotional connection that, once made, often ensures long-term loyalty
- They must be valued for a lifelong contribution versus a one-time contribution to revenues
- Customers desire the perception that they are in control - ensure your customer-facing processes are engineered for how customers buy, when they buy and what they buy
- Customers want choice
- And they want this across all channels

The convergence of numerous information technologies in the gathering, storing, processing, disseminating, accessing, and using data has revolutionized the most generic of all business tasks—making informed business decisions. Communication, storage, and computational technologies have made this possible. Firms have found ways to deploy these technologies toward of increasing productivity. When the promise of technology is not delivered, as in many CRM and ERP projects, the focus has turned to how and why this data is useful for a business to support the investment in information technology.

One of the primary information systems of a firm is the customer information system. Customer-focused firms have used their information technology to develop smart customer information systems and broaden the scope of this business function. The role of the Chief Knowledge Officer, a title that was unheard of just a few years ago, is to manage the creation, discovery, and dissemination of knowledge in firms.

In the context of managing the knowledge resident with the firm about its business, customer information is one of the key pieces of the knowledge this person manages. The status given to this function is reflected in the seniority of the position and indicates the commitment of the firm to managing customer information that can be used to improve the value created and delivered by the firm.

The key issues discussed are: what kinds of customer information are needed to perform as a customer-focused firm, what information is required to usefully profile a customer, and how such a customer profile helps a firm understand the customer.

CUSTOMER INFORMATION IN SERVICE UNIFORMITY

The customer's desire to be known, confidence in service consistency, convenience, a feeling of welcoming and belonging and a comfort level where they know if there is a problem it will get handled right away. Of course, true loyalty goes beyond the physical hotel. These days loyalty is built with every single customer communication as well. One way hotel companies communicate to customers is via emails. However, many companies are not communicating to their guests based on established preferences. For example, hotel brands will still offer ski vacations to die hard sun worshippers. At the hotel, many hotels are at the point where they are collecting information but are simply not tapping into that information to improve a guest stay.

This can actually disenfranchise the guest since they have gone tot her trouble of providing their desires which are not being executed. It's better to not gather the information, or say when it will actually be used. "It is more harmful to ask for that information and then not use it,In earlier, we saw that delivering superior customer value is a prerequisite for sustainable competitive advantage and that to be able to deliver superior customer value, a firm requires a good understanding of what customers value. A good understanding of customer value presupposes good customer information.

You cannot claim a customer focus, or seriously attempt to satisfy your customers, unless you understand their needs. An effective customer information system ensures that the appropriate knowledge of the customer is available for customer-focused decisions and actions. Without customer information, for example, it would be impossible to customize customer experiences, let alone manage customer relationships. Knowledge of the customer is about being intimate with the customer.

Customer intimacy is not just a cliché. Customer intimacy is a value discipline for firms that value and use an intimate knowledge of their customers to determine precisely which types of customers to serve and then align all their value-creation processes to create and deliver solutions to their specific type of customer. In a competitive landscape where competing products with little defensible product differentiation are becoming commodities, customization is one very powerful way to de-commoditize a product and build customer relationships.

Customization, as a term, is used broadly here to denote making changes in value creation and delivery such that the customer value is adjusted to each customer when and where appropriate. To know when and where customization is appropriate, you need to know your customer. Customer-focused firms pay attention to their customers. They listen to their customers. They really know their customers. The more knowledge the firm has about its customers, the more poised and able the firm is to deliver superior customer value.

Ritz-Carlton is known for its ability to personalize its service encounters with its frequent guests by maintaining a detailed preference profile at the individual customer level. With smart customer information systems, Ritz-Carlton's frontline employees are empowered to address guests by their first names and with knowledge of the guest's specific preferences. CLASS (Customer Loyalty Anticipation and Satisfaction) is an example of the information technology backbone to the Ritz-Carlton's guest relationships management programme.

Nadia Kyzer knows that having a database system is not enough, saying: "If our employees didn't put the information to real concrete use, the system would be worthless." Many firms use their knowledge of the customer to tailor their products and messages, or to promote new services to their customers.

For example, on the Internet, firms use knowledge gained from cookies to model patterns of customer behaviour on their Web sites so as to target promotions deemed appropriate for that customer.

But good customer information management goes beyond targeting messages and promotions. QVC, the television-based retailer, uses a "daily activity report" to capture, monitor, and respond to customer perceptions of quality. Indeed, customer information should drive all business processes of the firm, including anticipating and meeting customer needs, creating and delivering services, and anticipating and recovering from service failure. Customer-focused firms must have good customer information to support the decisions and activities of the firm.

Customer-focused decisions affecting customer value require information on customers' needs, their product preference criteria leading to brand choice or loyalty and their perceptions and behaviour with regard to the product. This is true not only in the acquisition and use, but also in the disposition of products. Since service firms interact with the customer during consumption of the product there is ample opportunity to obtain and respond to customer information.

For example, New England's largest bank, FleetBoston, recently instituted the "customer experience crusade." The firm hired new staff to be stationed in the lobbies of its large-volume banks to serve as "meeter-greeters" assisting customers with their banking problems. Ostensibly, the attempt was to reverse the lousy service reputation FleetBoston had acquired due to its preoccupation with challenges following its merger with BankBoston.

With the knowledge gained from the activities of these customer service agents, the bank could be learning a lot about customer experiences and about how its customers actually use a number of the bank's services. This knowledge could then be used to drive all decisions about structuring and delivering the bank's services.

Good customer information is an asset of the firm. Logically, anything that contributes to sustainable competitive advantage is an asset to the firm. Since information on customers is useful in better matching a firm's products as solutions to customer needs, customer information is an asset that contributes to sustainable competitive advantage. For example, retailing has become so fiercely competitive that customer information assets are now seen as a competitive advantage. Customer loyalty programmes in retailing are an attempt to link customer information to transaction data. Customer databases with purchase histories showing shopping preferences can be used in customercentric business decisions. Customer information is so valuable that firms who share customer information have to be careful about ownership of the database. At the end of a joint project, for example, Wells Fargo bank and Microsoft went to court to determine who owned a customer database that was created as part of that joint venture.

A good example of the power of customer information is on the Internet. Personalized Web pages use customer information "on-thefly" to customize the online customer experience. It is common knowledge now that firms have data that tells them who is visiting, how long they are staying on the site, and where on the site visitors are spending their time. Firms have knowledge of customer behaviour on their Web site with information on where visitors were entering the Web site (beyond the home page) and leaving the Web site, what keywords or links brought them to the site, and so on. All this is possible with data-warehousing and data-mining techniques.

In the Internet age, entire new services, such as online investment brokerage firms, have sprung up with value propositions enabled by technology-powered databases of customer information. In the brave new investment world, such new business models have forced traditional investment brokerage houses to incorporate these added value propositions to their existing businesses.

Other new financial service models have emerged. For example, a number of online firms offer instant mortgage or credit application and approval. Much of this is possible because rules-based algorithms created from studying databases allow firms first to offer conditional approval then then to be able to verify the credit risk because financial institutions have well-developed databases of an individual's financial history with them.

While the technology is available to do more with information, it is unfortunate that the kinds of information that most firms obtain on a regular basis are usually limited to transactional data—such as what was purchased, when, and for how much. With this information, firms are able to use recency, frequency, and monetary data and conduct what is called RFM analysis. Patterns of relationships between the variables are used to determine the best prospects among the customers in the database—those that might be high-propensity targets for a promotion. Transactional data is important, but not adequate to make customer-focused decisions.

In addition to being able to individualize interactions with the customer, with customer information that goes beyond transactional data a firm can derive knowledge to guide anything from cost-saving measures in operations to new product decisions. To really understand the customer, firms need information on a multitude of dimensions other than just transactions around their other actual consumption activities.

Kinds of Customer Information

Customer-focused decisions and actions require customer information at two levels. At the aggregate level, customer information is about the market—or more specifically, about the typical customer in the segment(s)—and at the individual level, it is about a specific customer. When the number of customers for a firm is large and there is no opportunity to directly interact with the customer, it does not make economic sense to get down to the level of individual customer-specific profiles.

For example, Procter & Gamble may not be able to interact with each and every Crest toothpaste user. In such a situation, the customer profile is aggregated and constructed at the market segment level. On the other hand, for firms that directly interact with the customer, it makes sense to profile specific individual customers. For example, General Electric interacts with individual customers of kitchen appliances who contract customer service agreements. GE can use their knowledge of each individual customer to target service contract renewal offers or offers for replacement products when the normal life of the appliance has passed.

In general, it should become apparent that the more the aggregation, the less specific and accurate the information on individual customers. The level of aggregation of the information will also determine whether that information is useful for individualized or segment-level decisions, processes, and activities. As the level of aggregation of customer information increases, the level of aggregation of the customer solution increases and the firm is working at the segment level. With lower levels of aggregation, the firm is working at the individual customer level.

Customer information, whether at the market segment level and/or at the individual level, provides a profile of the customer that guides a customer-focused firm's decisions and actions. A customer profile should be based on two broad categories of information: *Background profile* is general customer information not directly related to the product and is not product-specific; and *consumption profile* is directly related to the product and is product-specific, in that it is about behaviour related to the consumption of the specific product.

UNDERSTAND THE CUSTOMER'S PRODUCT

The background profile helps to identify the customer and to understand the customer's product-related behaviour. Firms have been diligent about gathering demographic and psychographic data to establish the background profiles of customers in the B2C market.

Customer-focused firms use this background profile to understand product-related consumption behaviour. Such information is managed on an ongoing basis. In the B2C context, "who the customer is" can be profiled along the dimensions of demographic, psychographic, and consumption behaviour. Of these three dimensions, the demographic and psychographic dimensions provide the background profile. Similarly, the background profile of the B2B customer needs to be in terms of their size, type of industry, their corporate culture, and other characteristics used to identify the firm. In the B2C context, customers purchase and consume solutions for individual or household use.

Consumers' consumption of products are determined to a great deal by their backgrounds. Their personality, family, economic, social, ethnic, and cultural profile influence the way they think, feel, and behave at home, with their friends and social circles and in society in general. This background profile helps us understand their consumption profile and the customer value they seek in specific product solutions for their needs in the context of their activities.

Similarly, in the B2B context, the background profile of customers helps us understand their consumption profile and the customer value they seek in product solutions in the context of their value chain activities. Business customers purchase and consume solutions for their own business activities.

The type of industry they operate in, what value they create, their size, the skills and knowledge sets of their employees, and the "personality" of their firm (their corporate culture) affect the way firms think, feel, and behave in the marketplace with all their stakeholders, especially with their suppliers and their customers.

The Consumption Profile

Whereas the background profile serves to identify the customer, to truly understand customer value one needs systematic information on the purchase and use of the product by the customer. This information is crucial to get a complete picture of benefits and costs to the customer.

A consumption profile comprises information that provides a comprehensive view of the customer's knowledge, attitude, and behaviour with respect to a specific need and associated solutions. The consumption profile containing information on product-related behaviour helps profile a customer in terms of the how the product is acquired, consumed, and disposed. Such a framework allows the provider of the solution to get into the "customer activity cycle, " as Sandra Vandermerwe calls it. Consumer behaviour models frequently divide a customer's consumption experience or customer activity cycle into the three stages of preconsumption, consumption, and postconsumption.

In essence, when the customer recognizes a need to be filled, the customer

1. Processes the options and selects a solution to meet that need,
2. Engages in procuring and utilizing that solution, and
3. Evaluates the effectiveness of that solution.

The valence of the evaluation of the experience with the solution provider then determines the predisposition of the customer toward that solution provider for subsequent consumption cycles. A positive predisposition may materialize in the form of repurchase, brand loyalty, and favourable word-of-mouth behaviour. All of the customer activities in each of the three stages of consumption should be the focus of the firm's attention.

In some consumption contexts, these stages are not as distinct as in others. For example, in most B2B and high-involvement contexts, the three stages and their respective decisions and activities are quite pronounced, while in low-involvement consumption contexts these stages are not as pronounced and deliberate.

Regardless of whether the customer is highly involved with the consumption context or not, the information available to the firm regarding the customer's behaviour (purchase, use, and disposition) should help align the firm's decisions and actions in all three stages of consumption. It is important to note here the differences in the consumption of tangible-dominant products and intangible-dominant products vis-àvis the firm's production activities.

In the case of tangible-dominant products, the firm produces the product and then the customer consumes, or purchases and uses it. Whereas, with intangible-dominant products, the consumption process is temporally overlaid on the production process.

The Preconsumption Stage

Customer behaviour during this stage of the consumption cycle falls into three broad and sequential sets of activities: experiencing the need for a solution to a problem, identifying and analyzing the options to the problem, and deciding on a specific solution or way of meeting the need. For interactions with the customer during the preconsumption stage to be customer-focused, firms need to understand the perceptions, attitudes, and activities of customers as they go through their purchase decisions. Firms need to understand what customers expect from the solutions provider during this phase. Since a product is a means to an end, to really know how the firm is doing with its products it is necessary to understand what the ends are.

It becomes necessary to find out what role the firm's product plays in its use for the customer. It is also important to understand what those product roles might be in different usage situations. Often the customer's preferred solution can vary from one situation to another and yet the provider may not pay attention to that important change in the value that the customer is expecting from each customer experience. The customer engages in accessing and assessing the relevant information on the ways in which a need can be met.

Based on the information available to them, customers identify the various options and sort through information to determine the merits of each option. A number of complex issues about the customer experience in this stage are relevant for the firm.

Where do customers get the information on the options—from what channels and in what form is the information sought? What are the firms, brands, or solution providers that are evoked in the customer's mind? What are the criteria that the customer uses to evaluate the choice of providers of solutions? What are their expectations from the solution? How do customers benefit from the products and services? When Nike introduced its slip-on sneaker Presto, teens could select designs for their shoes, attach matching music to them, and email them as music videos to friends.

Nike was engaging itself in the preconsumption activities of the teen shopper. The firm acted on its understanding of how teens make and follow fads and fashion to introduce a new and innovative footwear design. If you can understand and reach into the customer's preconsumption activities, you can identify and attract the most appropriate customer for your firm's solution. Customer acquisition efforts can be more precise.

Customers make their choice after weighing all options against their criteria. Firms must learn how they make these vendor decisions. Who is involved in the purchase decision making? Who influences the customer's preferences and biases? Household (B2C) and organizational (B2B) consumption activities can involve several different individuals in a purchase decision. Individuals play roles of users, buyers, influencers, decision makers, and so on, in what are called "buying centres."

What are the various perspectives of each of these individuals and units engaged in the process? What are their respective roles in the decision? How is the purchase decision made, and what process do the customers follow? When and how often is the decision made? What are the preferences on the method of payment? How do these customers evaluate you and your products before purchase? Who is involved in that evaluation? This kind of detail in the purchasing activities of the customer, if gathered and utilized, can improve the effectiveness of the firm's customer acquisition efforts.

When the firm can interact directly with the customer, as in the case of services, there is the opportunity to obtain answers to these questions and respond immediately. Where there is an intermediary involved, the firm has to rely on the intermediary to represent the firm during this stage because the customer interactions are with the intermediary, not the firm. In the hand-held ("pocket PC" or "PDA") market, the competition is so fierce that companies are constantly monitoring the retailer to ensure that their products and promotions are well displayed and that the salespeople are well informed about them. The personal digital assistant maker Palm sends its agents as mystery shoppers to retailers carrying their products. Microsoft, for example, gave a free Casio EM500 Pocket PC device to salespeople who completed a Pocket PC training. In first-time experiences with a service provider, customers may want to obtain information from the provider; thus that interaction is required prior to the consumption of the product. In situations where prices and terms of sale are negotiated, quite often the case in services, there is a significant amount of interaction. In most cases of intangible-dominant products, there is some customer involvement at least in the specification of the needs of the customer so that the specific solution can be configured for each customer.

Every firm should explore the opportunities it has for customer information to help in its acquisition efforts. The total solution includes the firm's contribution to the customer's preconsumption activities. Rich Hanks, Marriott's executive vice president of sales, recalls the early days of Marriott's Web presence. He says they did not even know that they had to put reservations on the first page. The way to design Web pages is to think like the customer and ask what the customer would like to do on the Web. Whatever prepurchase decision-making process the customer will be using should be used in Web site design. For example, at what stage of the consumption activity cycle should a Web site charge a visitor for a service? Some visitors balk when they are asked to pay up front for a service they haven't used—they mightn't want to pay member fees when they only want one transaction, for example.

The Postconsumption Stage

Here, customer evaluations and their disposition to be loyal to your firm is the main feature of the customer's experience. When the product is predominantly a service product, the customer might be in a formal membership relationship with the service provider, such as in the case of banking or financial services, or enrolled in an educational programme, or a fitness club, or a contractual obligation, as in a B2B context. At the end of each interaction in the case of service products, customers may assess their experience and determine their inclination toward the solution provider. In such cases, it would be important to collect customer reactions and impressions after each consumption experience so that the relationship is intact. With packaged goods, on the other hand, where there is no interaction during the use of the product, customer assessment of the provider is made during and after the use of the product.

What is the level of satisfaction with the features of your product and with the interactions they have had with your firm? They may be pointing out systematic failures in how you are creating and delivering customer solutions. Are there fail points in your value-creation processes that need more attention? It is possible to get some very critical process-improvement suggestions from the customer. How can the benefits to the customer be improved and costs to the customer reduced so that the net customer value is improved? Which aspects of your product are most and least useful for the customer? This information would be useful in conducting a cost-benefit analysis of the service enhancements to your product. What is the value of each customer to your firm, by transaction and in the long-run? Can the value of the customer to the firm be increased? Are there opportunities to increase the role you are playing in meeting customer needs by providing a more complete solution either by adding products or adding features to the product? Are there ways to reduce the costs of serving the customer?

Although strictly speaking not part of the consumption profile, customers may have valuable information on how well your frontline personnel are providing value to the customer. Customers can provide you with an assessment of how well your intermediaries and resellers are representing you. For example, travel agents who represent hotels, airlines, and other travel-related services might need more information, attention or encouragement to represent you appropriately. All things being equal, retailers have no incentive to sell a particular brand in a nonexclusive retail store.

As long as the customer purchases the item from their store, the retailer does not care which particular brand is purchased. Customers are the best judge of your suppliers and vendors as well. If there are aspects of your value-creation processes that are subcontracted out, customer feedback is critical in assessing whether these contracts are working as desired and whether there need to be any changes in how these processes are structured.

How will the customer want to convey feedback? Have you provided the avenues that customers are most likely to use to tell you what they think about the solution and your performance? Are your touchpoints able to solicit, record, and report customer information? The next develops these issues around customer information management.

Understanding customer value is a prerequisite for being able to create and deliver superior customer solutions. Firms need to study customers' consumption profiles to understand their needs and what they seek in the best solution. The background profile of the customer is a useful context in which to analyze the information on the consumption activities of the customer. The consumption activity framework attempts to frame the information on the customer in the three stages of consumption activities. The types of information that would be required to help understand customer value.

Companies focus attention on attracting and acquiring customers so that data collection is generally geared toward the preconsumption phase. Existing customers' transaction data is used to guide attempts to generate more sales from them. When data on consumption and postconsumption activities are gathered, a great deal more can be done to inform the entire range of the firm's decisions and activities in creating and delivering the product.

The Consumption Stage

Firms that are not customer focused are focused on product and sales. They typically pay a great deal of attention to the sales and purchase process—

the preconsumption stage, but not the consumption process. During the consumption stage, it is important to understand how the customer uses the product or service and what kinds of customer activities are associated with the value that your firm's product provides. To truly understand customer value, the firm needs to dig deeper into the consumption activities of its customers. Who is involved in the use of the product? How do they use the product?

Does the customer have all of the information it needs on your firm's product to fully benefit from its use? Will the customer want to interact with the firm during the consumption stage? Will customers need customer service assistance, and if so, what kinds of usage assistance would they need? What kinds of issues dictate the effectiveness of the solution from the perspective of a consumption process?

Understanding when, where, and how a product is used is often a powerful piece of information if used effectively. Consider the following examples of firms using the context of the consumption activities as they relate to their products: Starbucks gives out free Frappuccino samples on a hot day at a busy square in Manhattan.

Unilever hands out free Lever 2000 handwipes at a food court in a shopping mall and body wash and deodorant to fitness class students at a Bally's Fitness Club. Schering-Plough provides blister treatment cushions to runners at a marathon. These firms are obtaining and using their knowledge of how their products are used at the point-of-use of the product. They are in a position to determine what customer education is necessary and what customer value improvement opportunities there may be.

Product-focused firms remain focused on the product and its sale and on not much after that. To these firms, most likely, a complaining customer is the cost of doing business and a necessary evil, and is frequently cast to the unwilling hands of a customer service person. Consider the example of the "easy to assemble yourself" products that come in a box with some assembly required by the consumer. The unsuspecting customer is frequently confronted by a confusing set of directions written by someone who doesn't need directions to assemble the product.

Procter & Gamble has been actively collecting first-hand information on how consumers use their packaged household products, just to understand how the customer uses the product—rather than depend on the pencil-and-paper survey method or focus group discussions. Those methods are fine for demographics and psychographics information, but are fraught with misinformation since they rely on the accuracy of memory and communication by the consumer as well as the interpretation and visualization on the part of the firm's researcher.

In fact, P&G goes as far as to send ethnographer filmmakers who spend full days—from the time a family wakes up until bedtime—for several days, just to understand how the firm can create value for the lives of families—a way to look for new product opportunities. In the case of service-dominant products, since production and consumption are simultaneous, the consumption phase involves the firm's production activities as well. There could be a significant degree of customer interaction and participation in the production of the solution. The customer is part of the production process, and the information regarding each interaction needs to be carefully documented and utilized to deliver customer-focused experiences.

Customer roles need to be scripted and customer performances in these roles need to be monitored and managed. This information about customer interactions is critical in improving the processes involved in service delivery. Consider what package delivery staff have to do at some of their destinations. "Please place boxes in barrel. If they (it) don't fit, put on top of barrel—Dogs will rip up if left on ground, " is a set of instructions given to Land's End by a catalog customer for package delivery by a courier. Customer data must be collected, and the value creation and delivery system should be designed to obtain and use that information appropriately.

REVOLUTIONIZED CUSTOMER INFORMATION MANAGEMENT

Technology has revolutionized customer information management. Information technologies allow firms to gather, store, and interpret demographic and behavioural data so that each subsequent interaction with the customer is customized, based on historical data gathered from each customer interaction.

Digitized purchase transactions in commerce have enabled numerous opportunities to track customer interactions. Chip technology has progressed so rapidly that soon there could be a computer chip in just about any product that would enable mindboggling links to improve customer value and the customer-firm relationship. For example, take the Internet and e-commerce.

Most Web sites will ask simple unobtrusive questions of customers when they browse the site. This information identifies the customer and tracks the customer's activities or "clickstreams" on the Web site. Subsequently, software can use this information to personalize the Web site and the experience for the customer. A number of firms have emerged that provide customer information management software.

Such software can customize Web pages for each customer depending on the customer's profile, which is created based on the customer's previous interactions with the firm and the Web site. Vignette's software allows Web sites to dynamically generate pages that are custom-made for each customer. Silknet's virtual sales assistant guides customers through a series of questions about their need situations and then makes product recommendations. Marriott has an enterprise-wide software that integrates information on customers from different departments so that its sales reps can anticipate and respond more quickly to customer needs. Similarly, H&R Block uses software from Clarify to combine and coordinate customer records from its tax offices, discount brokerages, its customer service centre, and its Web site so that customer interaction personnel in each department have access to all of the information on the customer. There are a variety of methods for analyzing data.

Data mining techniques attempt to discern patterns in the data where one set of characteristics affects another set in a certain way. SAS Enterprise Dataminer software helps detect patterns in databases and construct models to predict customer response to the firm's actions. Software from iMarket looks at customers' most recent or most frequent purchase decisions and the monetary value of these purchases for the firm and helps decision makers select a subset of customers for targeting specific promotions or new product introductions.

Epiphany and Digimine are examples of firms that use a set of their own proprietary algorithms to analyze customer data for their clients. Early clients of Epiphany included Charles Schwab and Hewlett Packard, and for Digimine include Nordstrom. Edify has software that will link customer feedback such as survey responses to individual customer profiles for anlaysis. There is also software such as Nudist available for the analysis of qualitative data. When firms are able to sort through their customer databases and group customers by the relevant characteristics with such datamining software, the power of segmentation and targeting is fully realized with such datamining software.

In general, data is useless for decision making unless it is organized for interpretation. When organized appropriately, data can be contextualized so as to be transformed into information. Displaying and disseminating information is critical to the firm's success. Without proper reporting procedures, decision makers do not benefit from the information that the firm has.

For example, ESRI has a programme called Arcview that allows the user to spatially display numerical data. The user can view the data in his or her preferred format to match individual cognitive styles. As Peter Drucker notes, no two executives organize the same information in the same way. Therefore, software that allows the users to display information in their own preferred formats is valuable in customer information management.

The task of the customer information management system is to generate intelligence on the customer so that firm can be more customer-focused in its serving the customer. Intelligence generation capability has been shown to be positively correlated to superior customer value. In a study that involved hour-long in-depth interviews and surveys of sixty-six of the largest one thousand electronic firms by scholars interested in the characteristics of the market-oriented firm, firms are urged to treat learning about the customer as an investment. Ultimately, customer information is useless unless it is available to the user. Scholars researching the value of information have called this the "value in use" metric. The more the information is used, the more value it has! Customer information management, therefore, involves determining how the information needs to be made available, to whom, when, and in what form. The focus here is on who needs the information.

In the spirit of customer focus, the information system serves an internal customer—the decision maker. What will the user need the information for? What specific information is needed for the firm's decisions and activities? Is the user of the information able to enhance customer value with the information?

At what level of aggregation is the information used: policy level and customer level, segment level, and individual level? Such decisions need to be made so as to prioritize the customer information according to its impact on customer value. In making judgments about committing resources to managing and leveraging customer information, the firm should consider the worth of the information in terms of how it would help the firm provide superior customer value at a reasonable profit.

Customer information must drive any business process and activity. Customer-focused management requires a customer-focused analysis of the information necessary for designing processes and making decisions regarding value creation in the firm. These run the gamut of decisions regarding creating and delivering customer solutions, product improvements, attracting and retaining customers, customer service, recovering from product failures, hiring and motivating employees, and ensuring a customer-oriented climate and culture.

FIRMS CREATE AND DELIVER CUSTOMER VALUE

Firms create and deliver customer value as a bundle of benefits contained in a core and supplementary product. Since the core of any product is a commodity, the competitive advantage comes from the supplementary product.

Designing and delivering superior customer value is all about adding value to the customer's value chain and doing it better than the competition. Paying careful attention to the details in each and every encounter with the customer ensures a customer-focused delivery of the value created by the firm. Since the customer-focused firm competes on service, it also faces the classic challenge of any service firm—matching demand and supply.

In order to maximize the profitability from its value-creating assets, firms have to determine the most profitable mix of segments for its customer portfolio.

Designing and Developing Superior Customer Value

How do you design customer-focused solutions that compete on service? Let customer information drive the decision on how best to leverage the productive assets of the firm. Market-based as well as asset-based assessments are necessary to configure value-creating assets into core and supplementary product benefits that provide a sustainable competitive advantage. How does a small startup bank beat the big boys of the banking industry in their own backyard? Commerce Bancorp in New Jersey is not your standard bank. You will find their branches open at 8:00 AM and at 8:00 PM, and for most of the day on weekends. Vernon Hill, founding CEO of the bank, who also owns Burger King franchises, has embraced retailing practices in successful firms such as Walmart, Home Depot, and Starbuck's. The core product at Commerce Bancorp is the business of banking, of course. But the total solution includes access and convenience benefits for the customer that most definitely distinguish it from other banks.

There are even bathrooms for patrons in each branch at Commerce Bancorp. The total solution for any product includes a core product with supplementary features that in combination present a resultant value to the customer. Product differentiation and superior customer value is not in its core product, but in that total solution. The total solution for Commerce Bancorp is not just banking delivered by human or automated tellers in physical branches, it is banking at the customer's convenience when, where, and how the customer wants it.

Indeed, the difference in a customer-oriented firm is very evident at any Commerce Bancorp branch. Commerce bank has found powerful ways of differentiating itself by being customer focused and then it has been able to execute its customer-focused value creation and delivery.

Firms create and deliver value from their assets. Firms must determine how they might be able to create customer value that is superior to the alternatives available to the customer. With a customer focus, the firm seeks to design a superior solution that will provide the firm with sustainable profits. This covers issues and decisions involved in conceiving, designing, and delivering the customer-focused product offering. What must happen to ensure that the productive assets of the firm, facilities, processes, and people, are set up to create and deliver customer-focused value?

CAPTURING THE VOICE OF THE CUSTOMER

A company doesn't blindly respond to customer needs and opportunities. A business strategy which defines customers and markets to be served, competitors, and competitive strengths provides a framework from which to evaluate potential opportunities.

The interface with the customer should not be the exclusive responsibility of the sales, marketing or customer service organization. Many of the functional disciplines involved in product development should be exposed to customers and establish relationships to facilitate communication. This insures a wide variety of perspectives on customer needs, develops greater empathy on the part of product development personnel, minimizes hidden knowledge, and overcomes technical arrogance. This direct contact with customers can be accomplished by sending development personnel into the field to meet with customer personnel, by observing customers use the company's products, or by rotating development personnel through marketing, sales, or customer support functions. These practices have resulted in fundamental insights such as engineers of highly technical products recognizing the importance to customers of ease of use and durability rather than the latest technology.

Where a company has a direct relationship with a very small number of customers, it is desirable to have a customer representative(s) on the product development team. Alternately, mechanisms such as focus groups should be used where there are a larger number of customers to insure on-going feedback over the development cycle. Current customers as well as potential customers should be considered and included. During customer discussions, identify the basic customer needs. Frequently, customers will try to express their needs in terms of "how" the need can be satisfied and not in terms of "what" the need is. This limits consideration of development alternatives. Development and marketing personnel should ask "why" until they truly understand what the root need is. Breakdown general requirements into more specific requirements by probing what is needed. Once customer needs are gathered, they then have to be organized. The mass of interview notes, requirements documents, market research, and customer data needs to be distilled into a handful of statements that express key customer needs. Affinity diagramming is a useful tool to assist with this effort.

Brief statements which capture key customer requirements are transcribed onto cards. A data dictionary which describes these statements of need are prepared to avoid any mis-interpretation. These cards are organized into logical groupings or related needs. This will make it easier to identify any redundancy and serves as a basis for organizing the customer needs for the first QFD matrix. In addition to "stated" or "spoken" customer needs, "unstated" or "unspoken" needs or opportunities should be identified. Needs that are assumed by customers and, therefore not verbalized, can be identified through preparation of a function tree. These needs normally are not included in the QFD matrix, unless it is important to maintain focus on one or more of these needs. Excitement opportunities (new capabilities or unspoken needs that will cause customer excitement) are identified through the voice of the engineer, marketing, or customer support representative. These can also be identified by observing customers use or maintain products and recognizing opportunities for improvement.

CUSTOMER NEEDS TO PRODUCT CONCEPT

The assessment must be done both at the aggregate, segment level and at the individual, customer level, where appropriate. The aggregate, segment-level assessment orients the firm's thinking about overall product strategy. When a firm directly interacts with its customer, the individual, customer-level assessment helps the firm configure the product within that strategy to the individual customer. In keeping with the view that a product is really a bundle of benefits, the core value in any product for any firm is the primary benefit that the firm provides.

The supplementary product includes as parts of the solution additional benefits that augment the core product. Typically, a large part of the supplementary product is comprised of services. For the most part, the core product is a commodity, as in the example of Commerce Bancorp. All banks offer deposits, withdrawals, and investments and banking products such as checking and savings accounts, and fixed and variable income securities, and today most banks offer mutual funds. These products comprise the core product for banks. How these products are different from bank to bank is represented in the supplementary components of the total product. Commerce Bancorp offers free checking and money orders and does not compete on its lower interest on its savings accounts and CDs. Thus, Commerce Bancorp differentiates itself on a number of different supplementary benefits to the customer, ranging from the quality of its customer interactions to a number of facilitating services such as bathrooms in its branches. Similarly, most if not all banks have an online presence, but customers at banks like Allfirst Financial can talk with bank personnel via their home personal computer.

The hotel industry is one that grew out of its room-and-board days to a total product offering that today includes a multitude of facilitating services. "Room and board" was the commodity. As all hotels in a certain level, competitors in the same segment, began offering the same set of supplementary services, such as room service, meeting and conference rooms, a swimming pool, a gift shop, personal grooming salon service, business services, cable, or Internet service in each room, these became commodity and part of the core product.

By March 2001, 78 precent of all Ritz-Carlton hotels offered highspeed Internet. While only two hotel chains—Omni and Westin hotels—have laptops available for guests, most hotels in that class offer two phone lines. Thus, over time, as competing firms add supplementary services, these previously differentiating value components become a commodity and lose their differentiating ability. Consider the recent "advances" in the form of supplementary services in the hotel industry. Electronic kiosks can not only check you in with your room key and print your bill at checkout, but can also be an electronic concierge providing a guest with directions or maps to locations of interest. Human butlers are back in the hotel industry. A growing number of hotels at the top end will provide a bath butler to prepare your luxury bath, a technology butler to solve your gadget problems, a private butler to pack your clothes or make your plans. If you are traveling with a baby or young child, you can find a hotel that offers a room for a nanny and kiddie perks such as baby-sitting, some one to read a bedtime story with live actors, or toys and activities for the child.

If you are bringing a pet along, some hotels will even offer you special pet services for a fee! Over time, hotels in the premium category will all be offering some or all of these supplementary features. These features become part of the standard offering and reduce themselves into a commodity for that category of hotels. You can expect that the "technology butler" service will be adopted by hotels for the business traveller segment, briefly providing a differentiating feature only very quickly to become standard fare. In designing superior customer value, a firm must translate customer needs to the specifications of a solution in terms of core and supplementary benefits. All hotels need not have the same core product. That statement might seem confusing. Consider the Station Inn, in Pennsylvania, between Pittsburgh, and Harrisburg. It sits 125 feet from the railroad tracks. Railroading buffs sleep at the hotel just to see the freight trains, about 60 of them in a space of 24 hours. Same industry as hotels—but a somewhat different core product. Precise definition of a product can only emerge from deep inspection of the "What business are we in?" analysis.

The Supplementary Product

If product differentiation is derived from the enhancement that the supplementary product provides the core benefit, what constitutes supplementary product? Starting with the familiar: customer service is a common supplementary product (sometimes mistaken as the only element in the supplementary product). There are elements of the supplementary product, such as billing and payment, that are also common to all firms. They are required to facilitate the core product. These must also be viewed as part of the supplementary product to the extent that they affect customer value.

A firm can add to the customer value when its billing and payment process is customer focused or can detract from customer value if it is unpleasant in the customer's experience. Thus, there are some supplementary features that are found in all products that may not necessarily be recognized as such. Services marketing scholar Christopher Lovelock visualized this concept as a flower with petals. Think of the supplementary product as composed of elements of the total value bundle that facilitate and enhance (or detract from) the primary benefit sought in a product. Visualize these elements in three broad categories: facilitating services, quality of customer experience, and brand image.

Facilitating Services

Facilitating services are all those features of the product and activities of the firm that serve to facilitate the consumption of the core product. All firms have to provide some of these services at some level. Large retailers such as Sears, Walmart, and Lowe's will provide assembly and installation services for a fee and sometimes for no charge. The four broad categories of facilitating services—complementary services, customer education, customer access, and customer service. Customer-focused firms differentiate themselves by excelling in these facilitating services.

Complementary services are those related to the consumption of the core product. Some are almost necessary, like the waiting area in a physician's clinic or parking facilities at a hotel. Passengers on long international flights enjoy a wide range of inflight entertainment activities such as films, TV channels, and even casino-style gambling or electronic shopping and services such as being able to rent a car or book hotel rooms from the technology at their seats. Some complementary services are product differentiators.

For example, recognizing that some of its customers were coming in to the bank to conduct their business bringing little children with them, some Wells Fargo branches have a play area with television cartoons, Nintendo, and the like—and even sells toys to children. Washington Mutual offers calculators, pens, and piggy banks for a small fee.

To compete for advertising within its *Mutual Funds* magazine for instance, the publisher, Time, Inc. offers its advertising customers anything from primary research and use of its subscriber list to assistance in customizing gifts and promotions to readers or sponsorship featured on special cover-wraps. These are examples of complementary services that help differentiate value created by different providers.

Only with an intimate understanding of the customer's value chain consumption (and creation) activities can firms begin to see what opportunities there might be to facilitate the consumption of the core product. Sometimes complementary products are outsourced and provided directly to the customer by the supplier, as Wells Fargo did when it invited Starbuck's to open locations at some of its branches.

Ultimately, these complementary products ought to be consistent with the positioning strategy for the product. When a complementary feature is offered by all competitors in a particular product category, it becomes a commodity and part of the core product for that category and ceases to be a product differentiator.

Customer education is a form of facilitating service in that it provides information to the customer about the firm or the product in such a way that it facilitates the acquisition and consumption of the product. Instruction manuals and product support via telephone, fax, or the Internet are examples of customer education. Consider what some banks are doing to be more accessible for customers looking for assistance. Tellers and managers are dressed in khakis and casual shirts to appear approachable and friendly. Bank of America has tested concierges in their lobby to help direct customer questions. Home Depot provides free classes on home improvement projects. Once again, the service feature might be a necessary component of the total product, but how it is designed and delivered may be a source of product differentiation.

Customer access has to do with everything that the firm does to make its products available to the customer and to facilitate the acquisition and consumption of the product. The hours of operation and location are a simple example of customer access for a service. The various touch points that are available to the customer to access the services of the firm or to reach someone within the firm would be a measure of the customer access. The methods of billing and payment for the product would relate to access to the product and can be a product differentiator.

For example, the convenience of payment by credit card was once a source of competitive advantage. Convenience and ease of use is a critical component of customer value for any product. Services such as financing options are also related to this idea of customer access. If these are not customer-focused, they will fail the customer and the firm.

Customer service is a key facilitating service and includes the commonly understood activity of businesses related to product complaints or failures, product returns, refunds, and such. The accommodation of special requests or adapting to unusual or irregular customer situations would be an example of customer service as well. Poor customer service reduces customer value and risks losing the customer.

QUALITY OF CUSTOMER EXPERIENCE

When the total product provided by all firms contains the same set of facilitating services, the product is not necessarily a commodity. The quality of the service offered remains a source of differentiation and therefore a supplementary feature of the product. Perceived quality enhances, and lack thereof reduces, the value of the core product. For example, even when Internet service is offered by all hotels, the quality of the customer experience with the Internet service is still a differentiator.

One hotel may require you to get into a closet, fish out the cables and force you to shape yourself into a yoga pose to hook up those cables to your laptop, while another hotel may offer wireless Internet access from anywhere on the property.

All airlines provide seating and, depending on distance and class, also provide meals and entertainment while transporting you from point A to point B. Differentiation in seating can come in legroom and comfort. First-class services can offer six and a half feet of seat length, single seats, pajamas, and privacy partitions between seats. The quality of the entire customer experience is most definitely a source of differentiation.

Brand Image

Brand image is a supplementary feature of the product in that it adds to customer value. Brand image is the sum total of all the perceptions and attitudes about a brand. The image of the firm in the general media as well as for each individual customer provides a measure of the perceived quality of the product. The reputation of a firm is usually a result of the firm's product and actions.

Where there is very little tangible evidence of the product, as in the case of Web-based services, an entire industry of so-called "reputation managers" has emerged. These reputation managers are Web sites that rate the reputation of others! A firm's image is an implicit source of differentiation in the market. Brand image is the ultimate differentiator. When all else can be seen as equal, the brand image captures the essence of the difference in customer value among the alternatives available to the customer.

Firms have to determine what their total product offering is and what it should be. The value bundle of core and supplementary product needs to be designed based on what the customers expect as standard from all providers of a solution in a product category. The supplementary product might also contain features that are sources of differentiation among solution providers reflecting the positioning strategy of the firm. Firms must constantly watch the various solutions that are being offered. Sometimes the threat of competition comes from newer business models.

For example, online broker ETrade surprised the banking business when it began to open ATMs with new services. A deep and broad analysis of customer needs could reveal value-creating opportunities.

Matching Product to Customer Value Chain

To determine how best to match the total product as the superior solution to fit customer need, the firm must understand the customer's value chain. This is an integral part of the product concept development of the customer-focused firm. A thorough understanding of the customer needs and the customer value chain will help the firm conceive its product from the customer's point of view. Firms that best relate their own value chain to the buyer's value chain, said Michael Porter, will enjoy a sustainable differentiation strategy.

The value chain is essentially a chain of value-creating and value-consuming activities, where the value created as output from one activity becomes the input to another value-creating activity that in turn creates value as input for another activity, and so on. Thus, any activity can be assessed by the value it creates versus the value it consumes. This is why activity-based costing practices make a lot of sense. As, the value creating activities *within a firm* are those that contribute to the creation of either the core product or the supplementary product. The value created by these activities is derived by the processing of the productive factors of the firm—its people, facilities, and equipment. There may be assets or value components sourced from external suppliers or intermediaries that contribute toward producing either the core or the supplementary product. Some outsourced services may even be delivered directly to the customer.

When any value component of the total product is outsourced, as in the case of a retailer offering customers outsourced financing options for purchases, or airlines outsourcing catering services, there is the obvious issue of quality assurance in the value creation that is outside the control of the firm. Externally (to the firm) when you relate other firms' value-creation activities into a value chain, you see that the value created by one entity contributes to the value created by the next entity in the value chain.

The same idea is referred to by economists, in the context of forecasting, as "derived demand." The demand for a product is dependent on the market for another product, such as aluminum and aircraft sales for example. A homeowner who gets a home improvement job done receives (customer) value from the home contractor who in turn is receiving value from the retailer who in turn receives value in the form of products and services from the supplier or manufacturer.

ROLE IN CUSTOMER VALUE OPPORTUNITIES

An understanding of the role that the firm's product plays in the customer's value chain could open up value-creating opportunities. A customer-focused firm has a detailed picture of the customer's consumption domain. When a firm views value consumption activities, it can see if there are other value creating opportunities that it can leverage from its assets.

The watchmaker Swatch, for example, offers wrist watches with the technology that allows them to function as electronic passes at ski resorts in Switzerland or for public transportation in Finland. Wrist gadgets can now serve not only the function of telling time, but also making phone calls, playing music and videos, browsing the Internet, or sending email. This example defies categorization of product. What is the product? It is a wallet or a pocketbook, as well as a telephone, a personal stereo, a personal VCR, and an Internet communications device! The exercise of determining what revenue opportunities Swatch's value-creating assets would offer forces a complete redefinition of the product. The (product) solution is conceived to take advantage of opportunities to meet the needs in the customer's life with the assets that the firm has.

Swatch has found a way to provide value to a recreational activity—skiing—and a functional activity—public transportation. It is contributing to the "customer access" components of the ski resort's and public transportation's product. By enabling customer access, information technology provides a whole range of supplementary benefits to a variety of products. Contrast this with the example of a firm that does not understand the value of complementary product components and the customer's value chain.

A customer came out of a movie theater in Kendall Square, Cambridge, and experienced a 40-minute ordeal trying to leave the theater's parking lot. She spent 30 minutes standing in line in frigid weather to pay the $2.50 parking fee and a further 15 minutes to exit the parking lot. When complaining to the management of the movie theater, she asked if she could pay the parking fee as she bought the movie ticket. She was told that the parking lot was owned by a different company and the theater would not take responsibility for the customer's bad experience at the parking lot. In contrast, the airline SAS has been known to provide an annual dinner to taxicab drivers in Stockholm because the SAS management wants the drivers to treat passengers on the way to and from the airport with professional courtesy and respect.

Clearly, firms that are customer-focused conceive their product differently from other firms, because of their intimate knowledge of the customer's consumption activities. Information about the customer's consumption cycle, therefore, is a key prerequisite to exploring the opportunities that might be tapped.

An understanding of how the customer actually benefits from the solution and the information of how, when, where, and with whom the customer consumes the product should provide some interesting revelations of what the firm is doing and can be doing in the composition of the total product solution for customers.

Thus, Procter & Gamble sends its researchers to homes to observe how people actually use laundry detergent. When Samsung was trying to break into the microwave business in the late 1970s and early 1980s, their design engineers observed homemakers shopping for microwaves at the retail store. You can stay ahead of the curve by offering value through supplementary product that your customer information tells you customers will be willing to pay for. Even if the value-producing feature or activity cannot be priced separately, you may be able to command a premium for your superior customer value. Being customer-focused is critical in identifying opportunities for establishing superiority in customer value.

Conceiving and Designing

All decisions about the product and, therefore, the value-creating activities of the firm are based on an understanding of the value-consumption activities of its customers. What are the decisions and what are the issues to be considered in determining the total product by a firm? The three major decisions constituting the product strategy are: the product concept, the operations design, and the value creation and delivery process. The *product concept* defines the customer to be served and what value is to be provided. The *operations design* defines the productive assets of the firm required to create and deliver that value for that customer.

Together, the product concept and the operations design define the scope and configuration of the productive assets that can be leveraged to produce the specific customer value that maximizes profits to the firm. The *value creation and delivery process* executes the product concept with the operations design. In developing the product strategy, the firm makes a fundamental decision in answering the question of how the product will be positioned among all potential solutions to the customer's need.

This positioning question poses an asset- and market-based decision that comprises two perspectives.

- The *market-based perspective* looks outward at the market and asks what customer needs can be most profitably served by the firm.
- The *asset-based perspective* looks inward, at the firm's assets, and asks what assets of the firm can be most profitably leveraged by the firm.

The market-based perspective drives the product concept and the asset-based perspective drives the operations design. Thus, the initial step in developing product strategy involves two critical analyses. The product concept requires analyses of the various segments in the marketspace, while the operations design requires analyses of the firm's productive factors. These two sets of analyses are essential to determining what value-creating activities the firm should engage in to generate the maximum revenue from its assets.

The Market-Based Perspective

A market analysis to determine what would be the most profitable segment mix for a configuration of the productive assets of the firm is the foundation for product strategy. First you need to identify the segments and the solutions that are currently available to the segments. The target market selection or the selected market segments to be served can be based on the profitability and size of each segment that the firm's assets are best positioned to serve.

Here, a formal comparison of all the current solutions from the customer's perspective is necessary. Based on this analysis, the firm is able to determine what it can provide better than the alternative available to the appropriate target market, thus framing the firm's competitive advantage. Only after such customer needs analysis is it possible to specify what would be the desired customer value in the product offering.

The intended customer value in the product offering can now be translated into a detailed picture of the product concept—what the core and supplementary product ought to be.

Remember that the customer value also reflects the customer's implicit assessment of the firm's solution compared to competitive offerings and, indeed, all solutions that are available to customers in the segment. To ensure that the product concept can effectively be superior customer value, the core product should combine the imperatives that have become commodities in the product category with the appropriate features in the supplementary product to reflect superiority in customer value. Thus, the product concept embodies the product differentiation and the superiority in customer value.

The Asset-Based Perspective

The operations design decision rests on how best the assets of the firm can be most profitably leveraged and follows a sequence of questions that pertain to the productive assets and capabilities of the firm and how they should be deployed: What people, facilities, equipment assets are needed to create and deliver the product? Which employees' skills and knowledge would be needed? When and where would specific human capital be needed and for how much time? Similar questions are asked about the facilities and equipment of the firm. Of course, when the asset or resource is not available within the firm, it seeks suppliers or outsources that part of the value creation. Ultimately, the question is what competitive advantage the firm is capable of and how the assets needed should be configured.

VALUE CREATION AND DELIVERY PROCESS

The process decisions are about determining the specific activities of the value creation and delivery. The process of making the product and delivering it to the customer must be detailed. The value creation and delivery activities required are set in a specific sequence. The firm must deliberate on the structure, content, and process of creating and delivering the product to the customer.

No product differentiation from supplementary product can be seen in isolation. If the total benefits from the product are not worth the costs that the customer incurs in acquiring and using the product, the product is likely to fail. The more carefully the firm designs the process with the customer in mind, the more likely the process ensures ease, convenience and quality for the customer. Thus, the customer-focused firm designs the creation and delivery process with the customer's perception of benefits and costs in the value consumption process.

MANAGING CUSTOMER INTERACTIONS

The process of delivering value is a tricky and detail-rich exercise; it requires careful planning, using techniques such as blueprinting to visualize the entire customer experience. From the customer perspective, some service encounters are critical incidents requiring more attention than others. All service encounters must be staged for a customer-focused experience just as in the production of theater.

Why does Kimberly-Clark manage the discount retailer Costco's inventory of its diapers? The firm has a salesperson live near the Costco headquarters, and a data analyst responsible for overseeing stock at 155 Costco stores in the western United States. Similarly, Procter & Gamble stations 250 people near Wal-mart's headquarters in Bentonville, Arkansas. Large retailers are asking suppliers to more actively manage the movement of products from factory to retail store shelves. P&G estimates that stock-outs amount to 11 percent of an average retailer's annual sales.

When firms like Kimberly-Clark pay more attention to how its immediate customers—the retailers—create value to their customers, they demonstrate that they are being customer focused. In fact, the Kimberly-Clark salesperson passed on information on how customers place packages in their shopping cart that played into package design for diapers. Wayne Sanders, chairman and CEO of Kimberly-Clark, attributes this change to the information age.

Prior to the industrial revolution, a service orientation and the individual-to-individual interaction was the predominant mode of competitiveness. Assembly-line production distanced the firm from the customer due to the sheer number of customers and the physical distance between the customers and the firm brought about by the wonders of modern transportation. Manufacturing goods became the engine of individual and collective (national) economic growth.

Mechanization far outpaced services and replaced producer-customer interaction, relying instead on intermediary institutions to provide a specialized set of competencies that the producing firm lacked. Businesses lost sight of the customer. Now, information technology has brought this full circle, back to the customer.

We call it the information age because what has changed in our time is that new technology has revolutionized the way information is handled. Another equally significant revolution is the change in the customer's domain. Customers not only have access to more information on products and service offerings, they also have the ability to interact with the providers of products and services in ways not previously possible. Providers can also present enhancements to customer experiences from the functionalities presented by technology. Service providers must, however, also manage customer participation when they utilize technology.

When firms take advantage of online marketplaces, it might be necessary to make changes in organizational structure so that value creation and delivery processes are adjusted to the addition of the online delivery. Two key technologies underlie this information age technology phenomenon: the Internet and wireless communications. What customer access to these technologies has done is to bring customer interactions to a new level and to the front and centre in how a firm deals with the customer. These interactions are essentially service encounters with the customer.

Much has been said about the service encounter—customer interactions with the firm. In a way, all customer relationship management (CRM) solutions are basically technology support to ensure that the firm maximizes returns from customers by enabling customer-focused interactions. The service encounter is truly "where the rubber hits the road"—where the prospects of customer loyalty are materialized or lost. It is where promises made in advertising are honored or reneged on, and where expectations of customers are disappointed or met. It is where all the assets of the firm need to be brought to bear.

Service encounters with the customers are also laden with the challenges of a product that is produced and consumed in real time, where failures are bound to happen. When the firm designs the value creation process with the customer in mind, it will be prepared for all predictable eventualities. When the service fails, smart firms have smart processes, that recover and learn from the failure. They have service recovery and knowledge management processes in place.

As firms compete more and more on services, the management of the customer interaction becomes critical to ensure superiority in customer value. As the core product is a commodity, and most facilitating services approach the commodity state, the competitiveness comes from how the customer is treated by the firm at each and every encounter.

This discusses a method for designing the value delivery process with special attention paid to the service encounter and the critical incidents in the value creation and delivery process. A framework for designing the service encounter based on the theatrical metaphor is offered as a way to examine the customer focus of value creation and delivery.

The Ingredients of Customer Interactions

Analyzing customer interactions can be very rewarding. Amazon constantly tracks the reasons for every customer contact. It has made numerous changes to its value creation and delivery process based on customer input. The customer service function at Amazon is considered a research lab for ways to improve the Amazon customer experience. We can turn to the unique characteristics of services to obtain a clear understanding of what is involved in a customer interaction. Something intangible is always exchanged in the interaction (intangibility). Without a customer, there is no interaction and the separation of production and consumption is irrelevant (inseparability).

To conduct the interaction, the firm has the resources and infrastructure in place that "perish" when not utilized (perishability). Each interaction is unique (variability). From these characteristics, emerge situations that are challenges and opportunities typical to the service firm. We need to keep these in mind as we design the process of creating and delivering customer value. At the most general level, all customer interactions occur in a certain place (or space), at a certain time, for a certain duration, between certain entities, in a certain manner for a certain purpose.

Consider these as ingredients in a customer interaction and categorize them into elements of structure, content, and process. When the customer interaction is mapped onto the consumption activity cycle, the objective of the interaction becomes the driving force behind the design of the interaction in terms of its structure, content, and process.

- *Structure* relates to who or what entities are involved in the interaction.
- *Content* relates to the subject, the task, and its significance in the interaction.
- *Process* relates to the sequence of steps in the interaction.

The primary decisions that would configure the structure of the interaction involve the nature of the interaction—what entity should represent the firm, should the interaction be face-to-face or not, what technology can be utilized, where should it occur, and so forth. As a complementary question about the customer: What entities from the customer's domain are involved in the interaction? Similarly, decisions determining the content of the interaction should centre around the task and include what information should be required in the interaction, what should transpire between the parties, and what value should be created and consumed in the interaction.

Decisions about process would include a script of the interaction and the roles of both parties in the interaction. Any of these decisions must be based on the information that the firm has about the customer's consumption cycle and on preferences regarding these dimensions of the interaction. For example, technology may provide the firm with scale economies, but the customer may want to disengage from the script and interact with a person instead. Ultimately, the important question is what value is being created in the interaction.

ENSURING CUSTOMER-FOCUSED VALUE CREATION

Firms must also recognize that since customer value is dynamic, they need to continually monitor and improve this customer value. Ignorance of the need to innovate to sustain competitive advantage is a common mistake committed by the complacent firm. The argument is sometimes made that the firm's priority of customer focus minimizes the attention to innovation. Customer focus and innovation are not contradictory, an either/or strategic decision. Indeed, to be customer-focused would mean that the firm is continually looking for new ways and solutions to meet customer needs—and to be aware that customer needs evolve as well.

Visualize what the firm needs to do to ensure that it is creating and delivering customer-focused value that can be sustained. To sustain superiority in customer value the firm must ensure that management continually assess its market and its assets to ensure that the choice of customer and the value being created and delivered by the firm maximizes the profit goals of the firm.

How well is the customer value in the product concept translated to the operations design and the value creation and delivery process? Is the superiority in customer value being executed. The answer lies in the customer's judgment. Customer-focused firms will let the customer decide whether the firm's value creation and delivery is customer-focused.

Continual customer satisfaction assessment information needs to be available for the customer-focused firm to improve by changing the product concept, the operations design, and the value creation and delivery process, or to continually reassess whether its assets and capabilities are being leveraged to realize the maximum profit potential. To ensure customer-focused value creation and delivery, firms must assess customers' perceptions of the benefits they receive as well as the costs incurred by them.

As an ongoing assessment of customer value, firms must continually assess customer needs and customer satisfaction. As customer needs change, the value bundle needs to be reviewed in terms of its product concept, operations design and delivery. An assessment of customer satisfaction presents an opportunity to improve customer value. The smart firm will continually monitor customer satisfaction to understand what customers perceive as the benefits they are getting from product compared to the costs that they incur.

Based on customer satisfaction, does the value bundle need to be modified and redesigned? Are the assets and capabilities of the firm being leveraged for maximum sustainable profits? If the expected customer value cannot be delivered with the existing value-creating assets, then the firm has two choices. Either it acquires or outsources the required value-creating assets and capabilities, or it determines that the target market decision needs revisiting. These questions are posed as a frame for a customer-focused analysis of the value creation and delivery of the firm.

THE VALUE CREATION AND DELIVERY PROCESS IN PRODUCT

As, the execution of the product concept as the delivery of the product involves a process, a sequence of activities. Therefore, designing the product must necessarily include a design of the delivery process. Lynn Shostack proposed a technique called "blueprinting" to detail the process design in the delivery of services. The service blueprint is a map or flowchart as a visual representation of the process of service delivery. Essentially, the blueprint design is diagramed in three steps.

In the first step, all types of customer interactions with the firm are listed. Next, these interactions are arranged in sequence of occurrence. In the final step, processes within the firm that are required to create and provide each customer interaction are mapped. How and what information, materials, facilities and equipment, and people are processed must be included in the service blueprint. The customer-focused blueprint is one that is designed with the customer in mind.

With the activities in the customer's consumption cycle in mind, processes within the firm need to be designed in such a way that the desired value added in the solution is reflected at each and every encounter with the customer. Commerce Bancorp, for example, encourages its employees to make suggestions in streamlining the service delivery process. Commerce Bancorp employees receive a fifty-dollar reward for finding something about a process that does not contribute to customer value and instead is an impediment to serving the customer; the bank immediately adjusts its operations. Even as a simple representation of the value creation and delivery process, the service blueprint has a variety of important strategic, analytical, and diagnostic uses.

In designing the delivery of the product, it can be used to determine the uniqueness of the service process. When compared with competitive blueprints, where and at which points in the process the firm derives its competitive advantage and superiority in customer value become evident.

Thus, the service blueprint can be used in a strategic analysis of the differentiating features and benefits of the service delivered by the firm. Only with such comparative analysis of the service blueprint is it possible to ensure that the value creation and delivery processes are commensurate with the superior customer value planned in the product concept and operations design.

The service blueprint has two major dimensions that characterize the nature and scope of the service delivery process: complexity and divergence. The complexity dimension reflects the number of steps or activities in the process. A highly complex service process has a great variety of activities during the series of customer interactions. Some of these activities occur in the front stage and some in the back stage, away from the customer's view.

A so-called line of visibility determines what the customer sees or does not see. The customer-focused firm will need to examine everything that the customer sees and experiences to determine whether the service delivery at the service encounter is contributing to or detracting from customer value.

The divergence dimension reflects the degree of flexibility at each customer interaction. The greater the divergence, the greater the customization built into the service—the greater the number of options the customer is given to choose from at each interaction. Therefore, supplementary product benefits such as customization must be mapped into the service delivery process.

Complexity and divergence decisions will determine the position of the firm's offering compared to competitive offerings. Competitive blueprints can be compared to determine how competitive value bundles differ from each other. It becomes clear that the positioning of each competitive offering is reflected in the service blueprints. The patient experience is very carefully orchestrated to support the entire concept of the "Shouldice Method." The surgical procedure itself is probably the least sophisticated element of the whole process. The recovery process is more important than the surgery. Every step in the blueprint is designed for a speedy recovery and an overall "enjoyable" experience—despite the anxiety and pain of the surgery. The method is known for a very low recurrence rate and high customer satisfaction. The hospital even has patient reunion parties each year that are sometimes attended by as many as a thousand former patients. For this service, its critical steps are not in the surgical procedure but in in the recovery process and the total customer experience.

All customer interactions depicted in the blueprint are not of equal importance in terms of criticality toward customer value—some are more important to the customer than others. It is imperative that the firm employ its knowledge of customer expectations so that the critical interactions are highlighted for priority when allocating resources of the firm. This is the primary application of the blueprint technique.

Jan Carlson, CEO of the SAS airline, popularized the notion of the "moment of truth" in services. While each customer interaction is a moment of truth, those product features and customer encounters with the firm that are considered critical to the satisfaction of the customer are considered *critical incidents.*

The critical incident technique has been applied in the managing of services to understand what can make or break the customer's experience. The method was initially developed for the U.S. Air Force in simulations to help in cockpit design and pilot training. A simple question to the customer soliciting a verbal description ofmct is stocked and well displayed and that the floor salespeople are presenting the product to the customer in the way Handspring had instructed them to do.

Microsoft hands out a free Casio pocketPC to every sales rep who completes its training. These examples show an awareness that customer interactions at these intermediaries are failpoints and need to be monitored. Critical incidents help in assigning the appropriate level of resources within the firm.

Thus, the service blueprint is useful from a quality control perspective. Customer evaluations of a firm's service can be linked to specific customer encounters in the blueprints and all processes directly affecting or affected by the critical incidents must be monitored for quality. Customer-focused quality control efforts can be focused on critical variables that can be controlled. Service recovery procedures must be designed into the process at these points. Interactive technologies provided by the information age revolution are now an integral part of the design of the value creation and delivery process. These technologies work through the three primary productive components of customer value—the people, the infrastructure in facilities and equipment, and processes and systems of value creation and delivery. Consider all the ways in which the customer can interact with a firm. Each touch-point can be made by the converging technologies of today. For example, in some interactions the location of either buyer or seller becomes irrelevant. Customers can interact by wireless or wired means, which can be by voice, video, or text, initiated by either party; they are constantly getting cheaper and better in features and functionality.

The basic difficulty with any of this newer interactive technology is that the objective and role of the technology can be lost sight of and the technology itself become the focus. The final measure is whether the technology is contributing toward sustainable profits for the firm by improving customer value. The benefits of interactive technology come in the form of efficiency and efficacy.

Efficiency is reflected in increasing productivity and efficacy is reflected in improved customer value. Both of these outcomes contribute to the bottom line of the firm. For a firm competing on service, interactive technology is critical to sustain profits because of what it can do to customer value. Maximize the return from interactive technologies by deploying it at the critical points; prioritized by its customer value-creating power. For example, a common source of dissatisfaction and irritation to the customer is the length of waiting time before being served. Any point in the process where there is likely to be a wait is a potential critical incident requiring the firm's express attention. If there are interactive technologies that can be used to effectively manage the customer in these situations, customer value is not threatened.

The Problem of Waiting Time

All the service components in the total product, being susceptible to the inherent characteristic of being produced and consumed in real time, force customers to the experience of "wait." As, demand and supply need to be matched as closely as possible. To avoid idle capacity, services adopt the queuing (and scheduling) approach to processing customers, resulting in a certain amount of wait before the process begins. In multi-stage processes, which many services are, in-process waits are common as well. The problem of course is that no one wants to wait. Customers will wait for a certain amount of time that is reasonable to them as per their expectations. What is reasonable is a very subjective judgment, of course—one that requires analysis of the factors that determine the perception of waits.

Maister's work on the psychological cause and effects of wait suggests a way to reduce the negative consequences where wait is a given.

- Preprocess waits feel longer than in-process waits. Allow the customer to begin the process by completing the first step in the value delivery process.

- Unoccupied waits feel longer. Keep the customer in wait occupied with activities, preferably related to the product or service.
- Uncertain waits feel longer. Keep the customer informed about how long the expected wait is to likely to be.
- Unexplained waits feel longer. Keep the customer informed about why they are having to wait.
- Inequitable waits feel longer. Serve customer based on priority, determined by what is considered just in the ambient society.
- Value of the service. Ensure that the customer value you are providing is clearly superior to any alternative.

The most important common thread through all of these suggestions is that they all have to do with managing the customer perceptions. The firm is better placed if the customer perceptions can be influenced favourably by managing customer role and expectations in the value creation and delivery.

THE CUSTOMER-FOCUSED FIRM

To varying degrees, customers play a role in the production of products and not just in the consumption. Firms that realize this have paid serious attention to how the customer fits in the organization. In services, the role of the customer is abundantly evident. Customers engage in a coproduction role. In services or in the service component of the product, customers are coproducers in self-service configurations.

All services as we saw earlier involve some kind of customer participation, as in the case of providing required information to the tax preparer, for example. Even when placing the order with the provider, the customer is essentially contributing to the production of the product by providing input into product specifications.

When the customer is interacting with the firm and this interaction has some relevance to the production of the product, by definition we have the customer engaging in coproducing the product. Service firms instinctively manage the role of the customers in their participation in the service. Restaurants have menus, professors have syllabi, airlines have their method of emplaning passengers according to a certain priority, etc.

Sometimes managing customer roles may be in the form of a complementary service. For example, Universal is experimenting with a calming zone adjunct to its roller-coaster rides, for people who need help with coaster-phobia before they get on the ride. UPS and other package delivery firms instinctively accommodate special customer requests as to where their packages should be deposited if the customer is not at the location of delivery.

It is a matter of perspective. If we take the notion of value creation a step further, we could argue that even in the case of packaged goods, the value hasn't really been created to the customer until the customer actually begins to use the product. Value creation and value consumption are both inextricably interwoven into a continuous and overlapping set of activities.

This is an important issue in a service orientation. In the case of services, customer interaction is a given. And the firm must include the customer in the design of its operations. The customer-focused firm by always keeping the customer in central view manages the role of the customer in the value creation and the value consumption activities. For example, providing excellent product assembly instructions improves the value created for the customer in an "easy to assemble yourself" product.

Conversely, even with a well-engineered product, poor instructions reduce customer value. Recent product innovation studies have shown that some firms are equipping customers with the tools to design and develop their own products, ranging from minor modifications to major new innovations. PTC (formerly Parametric Technology) is a world leader in computer-assisted-design (CAD) technology, whose software solutions bring suppliers and customers together so that a client can use the software during product development to virtually interface with upstream and downstream players.

Ultimately, anything that the firm can do to manage the customer's role in the value creation as well as value consumption process is an imperative for the customer-focused firm. As mentioned earlier, Procter & Gamble is recruiting families to allow a team of their ethnographer-filmmakers to observe their daily routines to get a better sense for how their customers use household products.

The actual use situation says a lot about how a product should be designed. It would also be a way to learn how the customers should be instructed in the appropriate use of the product. How does a firm take a systematic approach to managing the customer? First, the firm identifies all the activities that the customer enacts in the value creation as well as value consumption blueprint.

Next, the firm scripts the role for the customer at each activity. Firms then have to determine how best to communicate and educate the customer in playing the appropriate role. Customers' performance of their roles will depend on their ability and inclination to perform those roles. The consumer's ability will depend on consumption skills that the customer's past experience may have provided.

The customer's inclination will depend on the personal characteristics of the customer. Familiarity with the service and service provider could affect the ability and the inclination of the customer in the role performance. In the case of services and the service components of a product, customer role is managed by the service provider. The service provider's production skills and motivation could affect the way in which the service provider manages the customer's role. The service provider's familiarity with the segment and the specific customer will influence the service provider's skills and motivation in managing the customer's role performance. The service provider's production skills are reflected in its operations and customer interaction skills. The personal characteristics of the service provider can affect the service provider's motivation. When designing the service delivery process, it is important that the firm incorporate these factors on the customer's role performance.

STAGING THE CUSTOMER INTERACTION

The essence of customer-focused design of the value delivery process is in the design of the customer interactions that make up the blueprint. Customer interactions have gone by various names in research on services—service encounters and moments of truth, for example.

Designing the customer interaction requires analysis and decisions regarding three of the structural dimensions of the value delivery process: the process itself, the participants, and the physical facilities and equipment. Customer roles have to be defined so that customer participation can be designed into the delivery process as appropriate. One useful framework that has utility in managing customer interactions is to view service encounters metaphorically as "drama."

When firms and customers interact, firms try to put on the best performance—like theater. The firm's *actors* perform their roles for the *audience*, the customer. In any service, there are actors and audiences involved in producing *performances* in a *setting*. For example, restaurant customers are audiences with hosts and waitstaff as actors in the physical setting of the restaurant.

Just as in theatrical production, there is a stage (the dining area) and a backstage (the kitchen); there are acts (welcome and seating, appetizers, main course, and dessert), scripts (menu and specials), props (menu card and table setting), and costumes. Each element is carefully choreographed to produce the intended impression on the audience.

Any service provider can examine each of these elements and determine the exact impression that would be appropriate for each customer segment. The "drive-thru" or take-out type of fast-food restaurant confronts different impression management challenges compared to the sit-down type of restaurant. Different types of services would require a different combination of these theatrical elements for the desired impression.

Services rendered at arm's length over the telephone or by mail, such as in investment brokerage services or credit card services, would see these elements differently from the face-to-face setting of hotels or airlines. Internet "clicks" retailers would find a different set of issues compared to the "bricks" retailers. Hybrid retailers have to approach the issues differently for the two different settings. In some cases, the performance is shared by a number of customers, as in a restaurant or a hotel or airline where customers share many aspects of the firm's productive factors—employees, facilities, and equipment. The setting dictates a shared product, and some aspects of the setting are visible (onstage) to the customer and some are invisible (backstage). Performers or actors (frontline employees) utilize scripts, costumes, and props in their performances. Every feature or theatrical element is carefully choreographed for the intended impression.

Therefore, just as in theater, managers can focus on impression management for customer-focused business activities. World-class service firms like Disney employ a service orientation profile (personality and skills) in their hiring; they call their employees the cast and carefully train them in both operations and customer interaction skills. Disney's "guests" are treated in a customer-focused manner evident in the culture, in the way the cast is empowered and motivated to provide customer-focused performances.

What is the type of setting where the customer value is delivered? There could be no interaction necessary with the value provider at certain phases in the consumption cycle, and there could be phases of physical, face-to-face interaction, or electronics-mediated interactions. At each interaction, the value provider must determine the line of visibility between onstage and backstage, what is or should be visible to the customer.

What is the process and duration of the various steps in the interaction, and what kinds of orientation must there be for the participants? What is the customer role in each setting, and are there other customers in shared experience?

Ultimately, all of the theatrical elements need to be carefully directed and choreographed to provide the appropriate impression. *Servicescape* is a term that refers to the immediate physical and social environments containing a service experience, transaction, or event.

The servicescape plays a number of different roles such as packaging the value bundle, facilitating the value delivery activities, socializing the employee and the customer, and differentiating the product. Managers must understand which servicescape elements can be controlled for the desired behaviours from both employees and customers.

5

Database Management in Customer Relationship Management

DBMS FUNDAMENTALS

A database management system is a set of software programmes that allows users to create, edit and update data in database files, and store and retrieve data from those database files. Data in a database can be added, deleted, changed, sorted or searched all using a DBMS. If you were an employee in a large organisation, the information about you would likely be stored in different files that are linked together. One file about you would pertain to your skills and abilities, another file to your income tax status, another to your home and office address and telephone number, and another to your annual performance ratings. By cross-referencing these files, someone could change a person's address in one file and it would automatically be reflected in all the other files. DBMSs are commonly used to manage:

DBMSs and File Management Systems

Computerised file management systems (sometimes called file managers) are not considered true database management systems because files cannot be easily linked to each other. However, they can serve as useful data management functions by providing a system for storing information in files. For example, a file management system might be used to store a mailing list or a personal address book. When files need to be linked, a relational database should be created using database application software such as Oracle, Microsoft Access, IBM DB2, or FileMaker Pro.

The Advantages of a DBMS

Improved availability: One of the principle advantages of a DBMS is that the same information can be made available to different users.

Minimized redundancy: The data in a DBMS is more concise because, as a general rule, the information in it appears just once. This reduces data redundancy, or in other words, the need to repeat the same data over and over again. Minimizing redundancy can therefore significantly reduce the cost of storing information on hard drives and other storage devices. In contrast, data fields are commonly repeated in multiple files when a file management system is used.

Accuracy: Accurate, consistent, and up-to-date data is a sign of data integrity. DBMSs foster data integrity because updates and changes to the data only have to be made in one place. The chances of making a mistake are higher if you are required to change the same data in several different places than if you only have to make the change in one place.

Programme and file consistency: Using a database management system, file formats and system programmes are standardised. This makes the data files easier to maintain because the same rules and guidelines apply across all types of data. The level of consistency across files and programmes also makes it easier to manage data when multiple programmers are involved.

User-friendly: Data is easier to access and manipulate with a DBMS than without it. In most cases, DBMSs also reduce the reliance of individual users on computer specialists to meet their data needs.

Improved security: As stated earlier, DBMSs allow multiple users to access the same data resources. This capability is generally viewed as a benefit, but there are potential risks for the organisation. Some sources of information should be protected or secured and only viewed by select individuals. Through the use of passwords, database management systems can be used to restrict data access to only those who should see it.

The Disadvantages of a DBMS

There are basically two major downsides to using DBMSs. One of these is cost, and the other the threat to data security. *Cost*: Implementing a DBMS system can be expensive and time-consuming, especially in large organisations. Training requirements alone can be quite costly. *Security*: Even with safeguards in place, it may be possible for some unauthorised users to access the database. In general, database access is an all or nothing proposition. Once an unauthorised user gets into the database, they have access to all the files, not just a few. Depending on the nature of the data involved, these breaches in security can also pose a threat to individual privacy. Steps should also be taken to regularly make backup copies of the database files and store them because of the possibility of fires and earthquakes that might destroy the system.

COMPONENTS OF A DBMS

If we take an architectural look into a DBMS, as suggested, find a number of components, that inter-operate in order to offer the DBMS services. We can illustrate these components and their interrelations by the following picture:

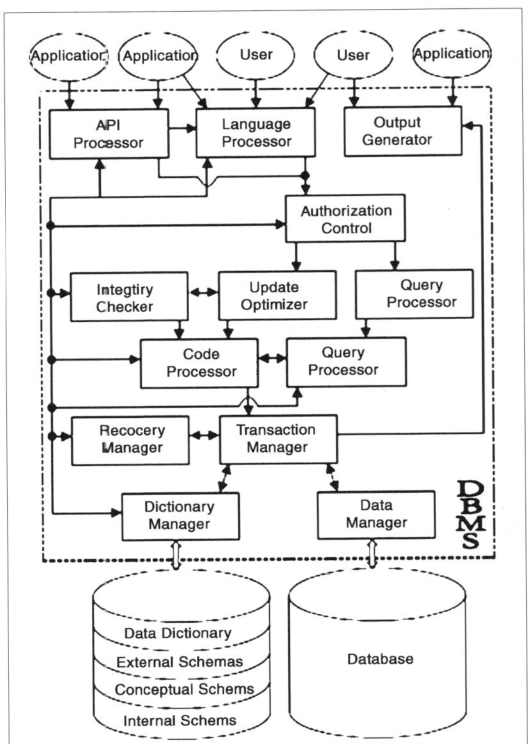

Fig. Components of a DBMS.

We find here a number of components, that we have discussed before: the physical database, the meta database with the schemas, the users, and the database applications.

But we also find a number of other important components:

- *API processor:* The API processor is essentially just the public interface to the DBMS made available through an API. In this way, database applications may be written directly in the host language making use of the DBMS services by invoking the functions in the API. In some cases, the API allows the database application to contain embedded DDL or DML statements. These statements are handled by the API through the language processor.
- *Language processor:* The language processor is the pre-processor, parser, and compiler for the DDL and DML languages. Both the API processor and the language processor uses the meta database to verify the legality of the operations requested. Following this initial legality check, control is passed over to the authorisation control.
- *Authorisation control:* The authorisation controls is the central security agency. All manipulations of the database must pass this component

that checks that these manipulations are legal according to the user and application credentials. The authorisation control will also check the manipulations against the available schemas. After the authorisation control, there are two possibilities. Either we are dealing with a database query, or we are dealing with a database update.

- *Query processor:* If we are dealing with a database query, control is passed to the query processor. The query processor will usually convert the query to an internal format, which is more suitable for the next step, the query optimisation.
- *Query optimiser:* The query optimiser is a very central component in most database systems, and often the cornerstone to the efficient workings of the DBMS. The optimiser will, based on information on the conceptual schema, and especially information in the physical schema. The purpose is to find the most optimal way to execute the manipulations, both taking the logical and physical properties of the physical database. Especially in the relational database model, the query optimiser is able to make massive optimisation, based on the mathematical properties of the relational algebra, which is the foundation of relational DML.
- *Update optimiser:* If, on the other hand, we are dealing with an database update, control is passed to the update optimiser. Essentially, this component function like the query processor and optimiser. Database updates needs to be verified in order to ensure the integrity of the database.
- *Integrity checker:* The integrity checker is responsible for ensuring that no manipulations bring the database into an inconsistent state. This is done by analyse the update requests against the integrity rules in the meta database. After either the query or the update request have been analysed and optimised, these components generate internal code to be executed by the central database engine.
- *Code processor:* The code processor is given code to be executed from the query or the update optimisers, and possibly the integrity checker. It is the responsibility of the code processor to execute this code to fulfil the query or update request. However, the code processor needs some assistance in order for the database system to be able to support multiple, concurrent users, and in order to protect the database against failures in hardware and software. This help is given through the transaction manager.
- *Transaction manager:* The transaction manager is responsible for controlling the different activities that are conducted in parallel in the DBMS, especially due to multiple users using the same DBMS. The transaction manager cooperates with three other components,

namely the recovery manager, the dictionary manager, and the data manager.

- *Recovery manager:* The recovery manager is used for the purpose of supporting transactions, but equally importantly to support the protection of the DBMS against hardware and software failure. As suggested, not deal in more details with failure protection in this report.
- *Dictionary manager:* The dictionary is the only component in the DBMS that is allowed to access the meta database.
- *Data manager:* The data manager is the only component in the DBMS that is allowed to access the physical database. *Output processor:* The last component worth mentioning is the output processor. All DBMS has facilities (more or less advanced) for producing printed reports, etc. These facilities are all parts of the output processor.

TRANSACTIONS

A *transaction* is a (finite) sequence of database query or update operations. A transaction is an abstraction of a sequence of operations, that the application programmer considers a high-level operation. The purpose of making the sequence of actions into a transaction is to have the DBMS ensure ACID on the transaction as a whole.

Acid

As already described, a DBMS must offer services for protecting the data against multiple users, failure in hardware and software, and ensure integrity of the data. Fundamental for offering these services is, that the DBMS is able to ensure the so-called ACID property for transactions.

ACID is an acronym for the following:

- A— *Atomicity:* The operations in a transaction on the database is atomic, implying that either they are fully executed, or no trace of their partial execution can be observed.
- C—*Consistency:* the sequence of operations in a transaction must bring the database from one consistent state to another consistent state. However, special to the execution of transactions, the database is allowed to be in an inconsistent state between the individual operations during the execution of the transaction.
- I—*Isolation:* If two transactions are executed in parallel on the date base, they are executed independently if each other, and there is no way that the one transaction can gain access to partial or intermediate results from the other transactions during its execution.
- D—*Durability:* The results of the transaction (*e.g.*, manipulations of the data in the database) must be stored in the database at the completion of the transaction. Durability.

Any DBMS must support the ACID property. However, just supporting ACID for each individual query or update operation is not sufficient. In many cases, the queries or updates involve several different data sets in the database, and cannot therefore be expressed in one single request, but needs to be expressed as a series of requests. Only supporting ACID at the level of individual database operations is thus obviously too simple a model. Most DBMS therefore implement what is called transactions.

Now, one possible way, that the transaction manager can fulfil the ACID property is naturally:

- By executing all transactions sequentially; and
- Make all updates to the database in some local storage, and only move these changes to the physical storage, if the transaction succeeds.

However, this naive implementation is not satisfactory since it implies that no two users can work simultaneously on the database, even if they are working on totally separate data sets, and for realistic database applications (such as banking applications) this is obviously not satisfactory. The purpose of the transaction manager is therefore to analyse the transactions, that are to be executed in parallel, and to control their execution in such a way, that they are executed using the most optimal concurrency, and at the same time ensuring that the ACID property is maintained for them. This in done by a component inside the transaction manager: the *scheduler*.

This is a highly complex task but the principle is that the scheduler takes the operation sequences from the transactions, and creates what is called a *serial schedule*.

A serial schedule is a sequential sequence of the operations from the original transactions that, when executed, will fulfil the requirements of the original transactions, but at the same time preserve ACID, and maximize the parallel execution of the transactions. Until now, we have assumed, that a transaction is a sequence of database operations.

However, there are three important operations directly related to transactions, namely abort, commit, and checkpoint:

1. *Abort:* During the execution of a transaction, the logic of the transaction code may realise that the transaction cannot be completed. This may be due to the transaction realising some inconsistency, or lacking information, etc. The logic of the transaction may in this case choose to terminate the transaction prematurely by issuing an *abort*. When a transaction aborts, it is the responsibility of the transaction manager to ensure that all traces of the execution are removed such that the atomic and isolation properties are maintained. Due to the concurrent execution of transactions, this may involve the transaction manager having to abort other transactions.

2. *Commit:* The transaction may also realise, that it have fulfilled its functionality. In this case the transaction issues a *commit*. When a transaction commits, it first of all terminates, but it is then the responsibility of the transaction manager to finalise the transaction by making the results of the transaction persistent, such that other transactions may benefit from the results. In some transaction systems, merely terminating a transaction implicitly issues a commit of the transaction.
3. *Checkpoint:* In some cases, a transaction may take relatively long time, and the transaction may at certain times realise, that it is in a consistent state, and that this internal state is of some value to other transactions. Instead of merely dividing the transaction into a number of smaller transactions, being executed sequentially, the application programmer may choose to issue a *checkpoint*. When a checkpoint is issued in a transaction, it is similar to issuing a commit, except that the transaction is not terminated. That is, the changes are made persistent and thereby available to other transactions. When the transaction continues after a checkpoint, it may later issue abort, commit, and further checkpoint commands. However, if the transaction later issues an abort, only changes made since last checkpoint will be made void.

Nested Transactions

Now, since the transaction concept implements an abstraction mechanism, in which a sequence of database operations can be grouped together to a single operation, it is natural to expect, that a transaction can be executed as part of another transaction. This is called a *nested transaction*. Not all DBMS offer nested transactions, since they are more complex to implement (*e.g.*, if the outer transaction aborts, the inner transaction needs to be aborted too). Nested transactions are important since without nested transactions, reuse of transactions become very difficult, and also reuse of application code may be hampered, since the caller of an application function does not always know, if this function internally uses a transaction.

If the application programmer then wants to invoke this function as part of his own transaction, this will be hindered by the lack of nested transactions. Nested transactions are also a solution to two often arising problems with transactions, namely recursive invocation of transactions, and problems related to cascade deletion. If a transaction invokes itself, a notion of reentrant transactions is needed, and nested transactions is one possibility.

Cascade deletion (especially in normalised tables in the relational data model) is when the deletion of a tuple in a relation triggers deletions of other tuples in other relations, etc. In some cases, this cascade deletion ends up making additional deletions in the originating relation, which then will trigger a new cascade deletion transaction on that relation. These cascade deletions therefore often also requires nested transactions to make them possible to implement.

Cooperative Transactions

Another problem with the definition of transactions, originates from the independence property of ACID: underlying this is the assumption, that the database should to the individual user appears as if he or she is the only user of the DBMS at the given time. That is, the DBMS is designed to protect users against knowledge about each others with respect to the DBMS services. This basic assumption is fairly valid for some types of database applications, such at front desk applications in a banking environment where the work with the data elements are usually limited to very short time periods (from a few seconds to 1-2 minutes), but in many other application areas, this transaction definition is a problem.

If we are dealing with an application area, where the users are working for extended periods of time with the data in the database. Using the concept of transactions will not be useful. Actually, already the definition takes a little step in the direction of ignoring the Independence property, since making use of checkpoints are one way in which traditional transactions can make partial results available to other transactions during their execution. A *cooperative transaction* is a transaction that is expected to take long time (sometimes also referred to as a *long transaction*), and possibly involve more that one user. Cooperative transactions impose several new demands on the transaction manager.

As the transaction takes long time, there needs to be ways to checkpoint the transaction, or to transfer the transaction from one user to another user. The difference between using checkpoints and transferring the transaction is, that using checkpoints will make the changes available for all users, whereas transferring the transaction only will make the changes available to the user receiving the transaction. A *group transaction* is a transaction that is expected to take long time, and involve more than one user. As more than one user is involved, some kind of decision process is needed in order to agree on when to commit the transaction.

One way to realise group transactions is to impose a group concept on top of cooperation transactions. Transactions within the group can cooperate in ways not permitted for transactions outside the group (or among groups). A final interesting new development within modern database systems is the multidatabase transactions which deals with transactions involving more than one database system.

RULE-BASED TRIGGERS

Conventional database systems are passive: They only execute queries or transactions explicitly submitted by a user or a database application. For many date models it is however important to monitor situations of interest and to trigger a timely response when the situation occur. An *active database system* is a database system than include facilities for monitoring situations of interest and, when they occur, triggers an appropriate response.

The desired behaviour is expressed in *production rules* (also called *event-condition-action rules*), which are defined and stored in the database. This has the benefit that the rules can be shared by many database applications, and the database system can optimise their behaviour. The events of an event-condition-rule can be events like insert, delete and update operations in the relational data model, but can also include events related to transactions, such as commit, abort, or prepare-to-commit.

In some rule systems, events can be temporal, implying that they are triggered be time (*e.g.*, at 8pm). In objectoriented data models, there are possibilities for more elaborate events, such as typespecific events (method invocations), object creation, object deletion, etc.

CONCURRENCY

To support concurrent execution of transaction, and especially, mutual exclusion between parallel transactions manipulating the same data, most DBMSs allows users to put locks on the data they are using. In some DBMSs, these locks are automatically put on data, when it is manipulated. There are in principle two groups of locks, *read locks* and *write locks*. A read lock specifies that the user is intending to read from the data, and a write lock specifies that the user is intending to update the data. In most DBMSs, multiple real locks on the same data are legal, whereas there can only be one write lock on a piece of data (and no read locks, if there is a write lock on the data).

In some DBMSs, the locking structure is more advanced, including a hierarchy of locks, but as suggested, not discuss this here). The handling of locks influence the transaction mechanism since the locks naturally interfere with the possibilities of the scheduler for scheduling the transactions. Locks have given rise to a number of different scheduling strategies, including locking protocols like two-phased-locking, and scheduling protocols like pessimistic and optimistic protocols.

An interestingly different strategy for handling concurrency control is semantic locking based on the notion of *atomic data types*. This semantic model is especially interesting in relation with object-oriented data models. One interesting lock type is shared locks, which implies that more than one transaction may share the same lock (*e.g.*, the transactions are in the same group). When a lock is shared, both transactions may manipulate the locked data (naturally still under the control of the transaction scheduler). Locks may also in a cooperative setting be transferred from one transaction to another to allow the other transaction to continue the work of the initial transaction. Finally, in some cooperative settings, it may be allowed for a transaction to force access to a given data, knowing that it may be changed shortly after. All these possibilities for breaking the original locking protocols must be seen as necessary facilities in a cooperative environment, where a given information structure (*e.g.*, a CAD drawing) may be locked by a user for extended periods of time (days, weeks), and it would be a huge hindrance to cooperation if more than one person could not cooperate on the information; if one could not pass a partial work to somebody else to complete the work; or is some else could not gain access to it, *e.g.*, just to review the current state of the work.

RECOVERY

One of the very fundamental properties of DBMSs is to protect against hardware and software failures. And the DBMS architecture specified a responsible component: the recovery manager.

We can divide the possible failures into three categories:

1. *Transaction failures:* This category of failures is tightly related to the *abort* facility of transactions.
2. *System failures:* This category of failures is related to software errors in the DBMS code, in the operating system, hardware failures in the CPU, or power failures.
3. *Media failures:* This category of failures is related to the physical storage media for the meta and physical database.

Recovery after transaction failures are an intrinsic part of the database application since the consequences of a transaction failure is semantically dependent on the application semantics. The basic recovery involved in cleaning up after the transaction as a result or the abort is the responsibility of the transaction manager. Recovery after media failures is very similar to systems failures, and will therefore not be discussed. The following discussion will therefore focus on system failures.

The recovery manager communicates, through the transaction manager with the data manager during the entire operation of the DBMS. During transactions, the transaction manager communicates with the recovery manager to inform about newly started transactions, etc. The recovery manager will, through the data manager, ensure, that only consistent data is actually made persistent by the data manager. This is done by working with temporal data buffers, partial database copies, and other techniques, that implies that transactions essentially works in isolation until they commit.

The recovery manager often also maintains a so-called log buffer of resent activities, such as active transactions, active buffers, etc.). If a system failure occurs, and the DBMS initiates recovery (either partial, or after a full system restart), the recovery manager will examine the log buffer (maintained on special stable storage), and informs the data manager to destroy active data buffers, etc., and informs the transaction manager, that some transactions needs to be restarted.

DISTRIBUTION

A *distributed database* consists of a collection of *nodes* or *sites*, each of which represents one computer and its associated secondary storage devices. Some pairs of nodes are connected by links, allowing data or messages to be transmitted from one of the pair of nodes to the other, in either direction.

For example, a bank might have a computer at each branch, and that computer would store the information about accounts at that branch. The connections among nodes might be low-capacity connections, making communication between the nodes slow and costly, implying that the distributed database system must be designed to reduce communication to a minimum while executing transactions, managing locks, and committing transactions.

Distributed databases gives rise to a number of new problems:

- *Resilience of Networks:* The network is voluntary to failures of nodes and links, and the distributed database system must be designed to be able to function even in the case of node or link failures. Especially problematic is however failures that might result in the network being partitioned into disconnected sub-nets. Especially important is her how to recover when the disconnected sub-nets become connected again.
- *Local and Global data:* A given information structure may be partitioned in different ways across the network:
- It may be available is several copies on different nodes (to protect against failures of one particular node).
- It may be physically partitioned across the network (*e.g.*, the relation containing all accounts of the bank is distributed out in every branches, holding its own accounts.
- Including the possibilities for the information to migrate around in the network, possibly controlled by the usage patterns, such that the information is moved to be as close to the users of the information at any time.

This implies that the distributed database will have a very powerful data manager to be able to control the information being spread across the network:

- *Distributed Locking:* That data is spread across the network naturally gives rise to changes in the locking strategies, since locks now are becoming distributed. This will often give rise to new lock types that takes the distributed nature of the database into account, including

Write-Locks-All, and Majority Locks. It should also be noted, that the so-called Two-phased Locking protocol is available in a distributed version.

- *Data Distribution:* In order to speed up the database, distributed databases can use a number for different strategies for distributing information across the network. Essentially all these methods deals with copies of the information being spread out onto multiple nodes in the network:
- *Primary Copy Protocol:* In the primary copy protocol, one single site is responsible for controlling the data element (locks, etc.). However, the actual manipulation of the data element is usually done at the remote nodes (updates naturally mapped back onto the primary copy, and from their onto the copies).
- *Central Node Method:* Like the Primary Copy Protocol, except that one node is controlling all data elements being spread across the network.
- *Migrating Protocol:* Here the data elements are moving around the network to try to have the data element as close to the heavy usages of the data as possible. Usually this is implemented such that the data element is assigned a home node. The home node will at any time know where the data element is actually residing currently, and therefore divert all data access to that node.
- *Distributed commitment:* Transactions may be initiated a one site and spawned nested transactions at several other sites. Special commit protocols needs to be available for this distributed transaction to be able to do a commit, especially complex is the situation if the network at the time of the commit is hit by a failure, making the network become disconnected.
- *Distributed recovery:* Again due to the possibilities of the network being disconnected, special protocols needs to be implemented to enable distributed recovery. This includes that each node needs to maintain own, local lob buffers, and special recovery protocols between the nodes to ensure, that the recovery is conducted such that the distributed database ends in a consistent state.

RELATIONAL DATABASES

Before looking at SQL itself it's worth looking more closely at what is meant by a database. Although some people talk about SQL databases, there is in fact no such thing. SQL itself makes no references to the underlying databases which it can access, which means that it is possible to have a SQL engine which can address relational databases, non-relational (flat) databases, even spreadsheets. However, SQL is most often used to address a relational database, which is what some people refer to as a SQL database. The relational model of a database was first defined by Dr E Codd in 1970, working at the IBM Research Labs at San Jose, and it describes a way of structuring data which is mathematically consistent and abstracted away from the physical implementation of the database.

The key concept of the relational model is that data sits in tables, and that data elements within different tables can be related in some way to provide meaningful information rather than just lists of data. Each table in the database has a number of fields which define the content and a number of instances of that field - think of the fields as columns in a table and the instances as rows.

For example if we had a table of LAN users, then it might have fields of first name, surname and userID. The rows in such a table would contain the values which define each instance of user, for example the entry to define user John Smith might be: John, Smith, JSmith. A single table of LAN users does not provide very much, even though it is more useful than no table at all. However the user table becomes immediately more useful when there are other tables to which it can be linked dynamically.

Imagine that there is also a table of software products, with fields of Product, Version, User Licence and Product Code. Again this is useful information, especially for inventory purposes, but its value is magnified when there is a relationship between the user table and the software table.

For example a link between these tables could be used to record which users are licensed for which software products. From this it would be possible to find out how many users are licensed to use product X, or which products user Y is using.

Add fields of department to the user table, for example, and it's possible to derive the relationship between departmental software requirements and the software that is licensed and so on. Obviously there is much more to the relational model then this, but as far as SQL is concerned it is the concept of tables, fields and relationships which is important.

DESIGNING A DATABASE

Finally, we're almost ready to start looking at some SQL code. The first place to start is in the creation of our sample database. In every kind of database project, the first step is to design the database on paper rather than jumping straight in with the code. One of the aims of this example database is to record the software that is installed on a network and to link this to users and to their departments. Additionally, building on the inventory side of things, it will also keep track of the PC hardware we have installed.

Based on these requirements four tables are required:

- *User*: To record users
- *Software*: Table for the installed software products

- *UserSoftware*: To record the Software used by each user (more on why we need this table later)
- *PC*: Table to record the PC details of each user

Designing each table is a fairly straightforward process of deciding what information is required for each element in the table. For the User we obviously need First Name, Last Name and Department, but we have to beware of having two users with the same name, so we need to be able to differentiate between them. One way to do this would be to use some kind of unique UserID, an email address or network login, for example. An alternative would be to either create a unique code for each user, or else to use some pre-existing unique identifier, such as an ID from a payroll application. In this example a field called EmpNo will be used to contain this unique identifier, which we shall also assume is an integer rather than a mix of alphanumerics. Finally, we want to record the type of PC for each user, so we'll add a field called PCType.

Our User table therefore looks like this:

- First Name - First Name - a text string
- Last Name - Last Name - a text string
- User ID - Network User ID - a text string
- Dept - Department - a text string
- Emp No - Employee Number from Payroll system - an integer
- PC Type - Unique identifier for type of PC - a text string

The Software table has the following fields:

- Product Name - Name of Product - a text string
- Vers - Product Version - a text string
- Product ID - Unique identifier for product - a text string
- Licenses - Number of users licensed - an integer
- DateOfPurchase - Purchase data from invoicing system - a date
- Cost - PPersecutors of product -a currency code

Our table of software used by each user we'll call UserSoftware. In the case of the User table a code for this was included for the PCType, why not do the same with the Software? Because each user is likely to have many pieces of software, and each piece of software is likely to have many different users. It therefore makes sense to create a separate table to record this many-to-many relationship. For this simple table we need fields only for EmpNo - to uniquely identify the user - and ProductID to uniquely identify the software. Our final table stores the data for the different PCs, and provides the value to enter into the PCType field of the User table.

- PC Type Name - A text string
- Processor - CPU Processor - A text string
- OpSys - Operating system name - A text string
- RAM - Mb of RAM - An integer
- Disk - Gb of hard disk - An floating point number

- ScreenSize - Screen size in inches - A text string
- Date Of Purchase - Purchase date from invoicing system - a date code
- Cost - Cost of purchase -a currency code

WORD ABOUT DATA TYPES

Many kinds of data can be stored in a database, from simple text to various types of number to Boolean flags to binary objects and graphics. This is one area where there are differences between different products. Not just in the formats of data that can be stored, but also in how these formats are named. Boolean fields, for example, are called Yes/No fields in Microsoft Access, and Bookean in the later releases of MySQL. This is one of the areas where you have to refer to the documentation of whatever database platform you are using. In this tutorial datatypes (or column types as they are also known), will conform as closely as possible to those which are most commonly supported on the majority of platforms.

CREATING A DATABASE

Many database systems have graphical interfaces which allow developers (and users) to create, modify and otherwise interact with the underlying database management system (DBMS). However, for the purposes of this tutorial all interactions with the DBMS will be via SQL commands rather than via menus, wizards or any of the other tools which sit between the developer and the database. This is, after all, a SQL tutorial...It is assumed, therefore, that you have access to a DBMS system that allows the use of SQL commands directly. SQL commands follow a number of basic rules.

SQL keywords are not normally case sensitive, though this in this tutorial all commands (SELECT, UPDATE etc) are upper-cased. Variable and parameter names are displayed here as lower-case. New-line characters are ignored in SQL, so a command may be all on one line or broken up across a number of lines for the sake of clarity. Many DBMS systems expect to have SQL commands terminated with a semi-colon character, a practice that is followed in this tutorial. Finally, although there is a SQL standard, actual implementaions vary by vendor/system, so if in doubt always refer to the documentation that comes with your DBMS.

Creating a database is remarkably straightforward. The SQL command is just:

```
Create DataBase dbname;
```

In this example we'll call the database AssetReg, so the command is:

```
Create DataBase AssetReg;
```

Once the database is created it, is possible to start implementing the design sketched out previously.

DATABASE STRUCTURE SYSTEM

A collection of interrelated data together with a set of Programmes to access the data, also called database system, or simply database. The primary goal of such a system is to provide an environment that is both convenient and efficient to use in retrieving and storing information.

A database management system (DBMS) is designed to manage a large body of information. Data management involves both defining structures for storing information and providing mechanisms for manipulating the information. In addition, the database system must provide for the safety of the stored information, despite system crashes or attempts at unauthorized access. If data are to be shared among several users, the system must avoid possible anomalous results due to multiple users concurrently accessing the same data.

Examples of the use of database systems include airline reservation systems, company payroll and employee information systems, banking systems, credit card processing systems, and sales and order tracking systems.

A major purpose of a database system is to provide users with an abstract view of the data. That is, the system hides certain details of how the data are stored and maintained. Thereby, data can be stored in complex data structures that permit efficient retrieval, yet users see a simplified and easy-to-use view of the data. The lowest level of abstraction, the physical level, describes how the data are actually stored and details the data structures. The next-higher level of abstraction, the logical level, describes what data are stored, and what relationships exist among those data. The highest level of abstraction, the view level, describes parts of the database that are relevant to each user; application Programmes used to access a database form part of the view level.

The overall structure of the database is called the database schema. The scheme specifies data, data relationships, data semantics, and consistency constraints on the data. Underlying the structure of a database is the logical data model: a collection of conceptual tools for describing the schema.

The entity-relationship data model is based on a collection of basic objects, called entities, and of relationships among these objects. An entity is a "thing" or "object" in the real world that is distinguishable from other objects. For example, each person is an entity, and bank accounts can be considered entities. Entities are described in a database by a set of attributes. For example, the attributes account-number and balance describe one particular account in a bank. A relationship is an association among several entities. For example, a depositor relationship associates a customer with each of her accounts. The set of all entities of the same type and the set of all relationships of the same type are termed an entity set and a relationship set, respectively.

Like the entity-relationship model, the object-oriented model is based on a collection of objects. An object contains values stored in instance variables within the object. An object also contains bodies of code that operate on the object. These bodies of code are called methods. The only way in which one object can access the data of another object is by invoking a method of that other object.

This action is called sending a message to the object. Thus, the call interface of the methods of an object defines that object's externally visible part. The internal part of the object-the instance variables and method code-are not visible externally. The result is two levels of data abstraction, which are important to abstract away (hide) internal details of objects. Object-oriented data models also provide object references which can be used to identify (refer to) objects.

In record-based models, the database is structured in fixed-format records of several types. Each record has a fixed set of fields. The three most widely accepted record-based data models are the relational, network, and hierarchical models. The latter two were widely used once, but are of declining importance. The relational model is very widely used. Databases based on the relational model are called relational databases.

The relational model uses a collection of tables (called relations) to represent both data and the relationships among those data. Each table has multiple columns, and each column has a unique name. Each row of the table is called a tuple, and each column represents the value of an attribute of the tuple. The size of a database can vary widely, from a few megabytes for personal databases, to gigabytes (a gigabyte is 1000 megabytes) or even terabytes (a terabyte is 1000 gigabytes) for large corporate databases.

The information in a database is stored on a nonvolatile medium that can accommodate large amounts of data; the most commonly used such media are magnetic disks. Magnetic disks can store significantly larger amounts of data than main memory, at much lower costs per unit of data.

To improve reliability in mission-critical systems, disks can be organized into structures generically called redundant arrays of independent disks (RAID). In a RAID system, data are organized with some amount of redundancy (such as replication) across several disks. Even if one of the disks in the RAID system were to be damaged and lose data, the lost data can be reconstructed from the other disks in the RAID system. *See* Computer storage technology

Logically, data in a relational database are organized as a set of relations, each relation consisting of a set of records. This is the view given to database users. The underlying implementation on disk (hidden from the user) consists of a set of files. Each file consists of a set of fixed-size pieces of disk storage, called blocks. Records of a relation are stored within blocks. Each relation is associated with one or more files. Generally a file contains records from only one relation, but organizations where a file contains records from more than one relation are also used for performance reasons.

One way to retrieve a desired record in a relational database is to perform a scan on the corresponding relation; a scan fetches all the records from the relation, one at a time. Accessing desired records from a large relation using a scan on the relation can be very expensive. Indices are data structures that permit more efficient access of records. An index is built on one or more attributes of a relation; such attributes constitute the search key. Given a value for each of the search-key attributes, the index structure can be used to retrieve records with the specified search-key values quickly. Indices may also support other operations, such as fetching all records whose search-key values fall in a specified range of values.

A database schema is specified by a set of definitions expressed by a data-definition language. The result of execution of data-definition language statements is a set of information stored in a special file called a data dictionary. The data dictionary contains metadata, that is, data about data. This file is consulted before actual data are read or modified in the database system. The data-definition language is also used to specify storage structures and access methods.

Data manipulation is the retrieval, insertion, deletion, and modification of information stored in the database. A data-manipulation language enables users to access or manipulate data as organized by the appropriate data model.

There are basically two types of data-manipulation languages: Procedural data-manipulation languages require a user to specify what data are needed and how to get those data; nonprocedural data-manipulation languages require a user to specify what data are needed without specifying how to get those data. A query is a statement requesting the retrieval of information. The portion of a data-manipulation language that involves information retrieval is called a query language. Although technically incorrect, it is common practice to use the terms query language and data-manipulation language synonymously.

Database languages support both data-definition and data-manipulation functions. Although many database languages have been proposed and implemented, SQL has become a standard language supported by most relational database systems. Databases based on the object-oriented model also support declarative query languages that are similar to SQL.

SQL provides a complete data-definition language, including the ability to create relations with specified attribute types, and the ability to define integrity constraints on the data. Query By Example (QBE) is a graphical language for specifying queries. It is widely used in personal database systems, since it is much simpler than SQL for nonexpert users.

Forms interfaces present a screen view that looks like a form, with fields to be filled in by users. Some of the fields may be filled automatically by the forms system. Report writers permit report formats to be defined, along with queries to fetch data from the database; the results of the queries are shown formatted in the report. These tools in effect provide a new language for building database interfaces and are often referred to as fourth-generation languages

(4GLs). Often, several operations on the database form a single logical unit of work, called a transaction. An example of a transaction is the transfer of funds from one account to another. Transactions in databases mirror the corresponding transactions in the commercial world.

Traditionally database systems have been designed to support commercial data, consisting mainly of structured alphanumeric data. In recent years, database systems have added support for a number of nontraditional data types such as text documents, images, and maps and other spatial data. The goal is to make databases universal servers, which can store all types of data. Rather than add support for all such data types into the core database, vendors offer add-on packages that integrate with the database to provide such functionality.

A suite of Programmes which typically manage large structured sets of persistent data, offering ad hoc query facilities to many users. They are widely used in business applications. A database management system (DBMS) can be an extremely complex set of software Programmes that controls the organisation, storage and retrieval of data (fields, records and files) in a database.

It also controls the security and integrity of the database. The DBMS accepts requests for data from the application programme and instructs the operating system to transfer the appropriate data.

When a DBMS is used, information systems can be changed much more easily as the organisation's information requirements change. New categories of data can be added to the database without disruption to the existing system.

Data security prevents unauthorised users from viewing or updating the database. Using passwords, users are allowed access to the entire database or subsets of the database, called subschemas (pronounced "sub-skeema"). For example, an employee database can contain all the data about an individual employee, but one group of users may be authorised to view only payroll data, while others are allowed access to only work history and medical data.

The DBMS can maintain the integrity of the database by not allowing more than one user to update the same record at the same time. The DBMS can keep duplicate records out of the database; for example, no two customers with the same customer numbers (key fields) can be entered into the database. Query languages and report writers allow users to interactively interrogate the database and analyse its data.

If the DBMS provides a way to interactively enter and update the database, as well as interrogate it, this capability allows for managing personal databases. However, it may not leave an audit trail of actions or provide the kinds of controls necessary in a multi-user organisation. These controls are only available when a set of application Programmes are customised for each data entry and updating function.

A business information system is made up of subjects (customers, employees, vendors, etc.) and activities (orders, payments, purchases, etc.).

Database design is the process of deciding how to organize this data into record types and how the record types will relate to each other. The DBMS should mirror the organization's data structure and process transactions efficiently.

Organizations may use one kind of DBMS for daily transaction processing and then move the detail onto another computer that uses another DBMS better suited for random inquiries and analysis. Overall systems design decisions are performed by data administrators and systems analysts. Detailed database design is performed by database administrators.

The three most common organizations are the hierarchical database, network database and relational database. A database management system may provide one, two or all three methods. Inverted lists and other methods are also used. The most suitable structure depends on the application and on the transaction rate and the number of inquiries that will be made.

Database machines are specially designed computers that hold the actual databases and run only the DBMS and related software. Connected to one or more mainframes via a high-speed channel, database machines are used in large volume transaction processing environments. Database machines have a large number of DBMS functions built into the hardware and also provide special techniques for accessing the disks containing the databases, such as using multiple processors concurrently for high-speed searches.

The world of information is made up of data, text, pictures and voice. Many DBMSs manage text as well as data, but very few manage both with equal proficiency. Throughout the 1990s, as storage capacities continue to increase, DBMSs will begin to integrate all forms of information.

Eventually, it will be common for a database to handle data, text, graphics, voice and video with the same ease as today's systems handle data. A database management system provides the ability for many different users to share data and process resources. But as there can be many different users, there are many different database needs. The question now is: How can a single, unified database meet the differing requirement of so many users?

A DBMS minimizes these problems by providing two views of the database data: a logical (external) view and physical (internal) view. The logical view/ user's view, of a database programme represents data in a format that is meaningful to a user and to the software Programmes that process those data. That is, the logical view tells the user, in user terms, what is in the database. The physical view deals with the actual, physical arrangement and location of data in the direct access storage devices(DASDs). Database specialists use the physical view to make efficient use of storage and processing resources. With the logical view users can see data differently from how they are stored, and they do not want to know all the technical details of physical storage. After all, a business user is primarily interested in using the information, not in how it is stored.

One strength of a DBMS is that while there is typically only one physical view of the data, there can be an endless number of different logical views. This feature allows users to see database information in a more business-related way rather than from a technical, processing viewpoint. Thus the logical view refers to the way user views data, and the physical view to the way the data are physically stored and processed...

DBMS FEATURES AND CAPABILITIES

Alternatively, and especially in connection with the relational model of database management, the relation between attributes drawn from a specified set of domains can be seen as being primary. For instance, the database might indicate that a car that was originally "red" might fade to "pink" in time, provided it was of some particular "make" with an inferior paint job. Such higher arity relationships provide information on all of the underlying domains at the same time, with none of them being privileged above the others.

Throughout recent history specialized databases have existed for scientific, geospatial, imaging, document storage and like uses. Functionality drawn from such applications has lately begun appearing in mainstream DBMSs as well. However, the main focus there, at least when aimed at the commercial data processing market, is still on descriptive attributes on repetitive record structures. Thus, the DBMSs of today roll together frequently-needed services or features of attribute management. By externalizing such functionality to the DBMS, applications effectively share code with each other and are relieved of much internal complexity. Features commonly offered by database management systems include:

Query Ability

Querying is the process of requesting attribute information from various perspectives and combinations of factors. Example: "How many 2-door cars in Texas are green?" A database query language and report writer allow users to interactively interrogate the database, analyse its data and update it according to the users privileges on data.

Backup and Replication

Copies of attributes need to be made regularly in case primary disks or other equipment fails. A periodic copy of attributes may also be created for a distant organization that cannot readily access the original. DBMS usually provide utilities to facilitate the process of extracting and disseminating attribute sets. When data is replicated between database servers, so that the information remains consistent throughout the database system and users cannot tell or even know which server in the DBMS they are using, the system is said to exhibit replication transparency.

Rule Enforcement

Often one wants to apply rules to attributes so that the attributes are clean and reliable. For example, we may have a rule that says each car can have only one engine associated with it (identified by Engine Number). If somebody tries to associate a second engine with a given car, we want the DBMS to deny such a request and display an error message. However, with changes in the model specification such as, in this example, hybrid gas-electric cars, rules may need to change. Ideally such rules should be able to be added and removed as needed without significant data layout redesign.

Security

Often it is desirable to limit who can see or change which attributes or groups of attributes. This may be managed directly by individual, or by the assignment of individuals and privileges to groups, or (in the most elaborate models) through the assignment of individuals and groups to roles which are then granted entitlements.

Computation

There are common computations requested on attributes such as counting, summing, averaging, sorting, grouping, cross-referencing, etc. Rather than have each computer application implement these from scratch, they can rely on the DBMS to supply such calculations.

Change and Access Logging

Often one wants to know who accessed what attributes, what was changed, and when it was changed. Logging services allow this by keeping a record of access occurrences and changes.

Automated Optimization

If there are frequently occurring usage patterns or requests, some DBMS can adjust themselves to improve the speed of those interactions. In some cases the DBMS will merely provide tools to monitor performance, allowing a human expert to make the necessary adjustments after reviewing the statistics collected.

DATA INDEPENDENCE

Data independence is a form of database management that keeps data separated from all Programmes that make use of the data. As a cornerstone for the idea of a DBMS or database management system, data independence ensures that the data cannot be redefined or reorganized by any of the Programmes that make use of the data. In this manner, the data remains accessible, but is also stable and cannot be corrupted by the applications using it. Database management within the environment of a centralized DBMS relies on the process of data independence. While data transparency still exists as far as the ability of different applications to access and use the data for completing tasks, no programme or application can read and then begin to make changes to the data itself. The consistency of the data makes the overall process of maintaining and managing a single database or multiple databases within a single environment much easier.

The concept of data independence is different from another approach referred to as data dependence. With this approach, the data used to run an application is actually represented in the source code for the programme. The ability of the data to be modified by the programme, and vice versa, means that the data is not considered constant and may be changed either by initiating the change through modifications to the source code or through using the programme in other ways to adapt the core data.

One of the functions of data independence is to restrict access to the storage structure of the data by the user applications. By effectively hiding the specifics of the structure from the applications, the potential for any one application to alter the nature of the data becomes impossible. Thus, the essential data retains its integrity and remains consistent no matter how many databases or database applications access the core data.

Data independence is normally thought of in terms of two levels or types. Logical data independence makes it possible to change the structure of the data independently of modifying the applications or Programmes that make use of the data. There is no need to rewrite current applications as part of the process of adding to or removing data from then system. The second type or level of data independence is known as physical data independence. This approach has to do with altering the organization or storage procedures related to the data, rather than modifying the data itself.

Accomplishing this shift in file organization or the indexing strategy used for the data does not require any modification to the external structure of the applications, meaning that users of the applications are not likely to notice any difference at all in the function of their Programmes.

DATABASE LANGUAGE

A generic term referring to a class of languages used for defining and accessing databases. A particular database language will be associated with a particular database management system. There are two distinct classes of database language: those that do not provide complete programming facilities and are designed to be used in association with some general-purpose programming language (the *host language*), and those that do provide complete programming facilities (*database programming languages*). Some products adopting the former approach seek to minimize host-language programming by the provision of fourth-generation language (4GL) facilities. A database language must provide for both logical-schema specification and modification (*data description*) and for retrieval and update (*data manipulation*). In some cases, particularly products derived from the CODASYL network database standard, these aspects are treated distinctly as the *data description language* (DDL) and the *data manipulation language* (DML). Modification to the storage is also generally separately provided.

DATA INTERFACE

Using a foreign language is challenging for most of us. Clearly there are many benefits of knowing languages for when we travel, but finding the time to learn them seems elusive. The situation with relational databases is seemingly similar. We know that so much information is now stored in databases in an organization, that it is tempting to think that we could do our jobs better if only we had the computer skills to work more directly with them.

Unfortunately, getting better database querying skills can involve a significant investment of time. Most databases now are based on relational database technology. The idea behind a relational database is very simple: It is just composed of tables of information, and so absorbing information from a small database is often easy. Each row is an example on which we have information, and the information is given in the entry for each column.

In this way, a table in a relational database is no different to a table we might draw on a piece of A4 paper. Whilst using simple relational databases is straightforward, problems arise when we have larger tables – ie. tables that do not fit on a manageable number of pages.

Consider a telephone directory. We might consider this as a table. Each subscriber is a row in the table, and the columns are for name, address, area, and telephone number. In a sense such a big table is manageable because the rows are sorted according to the alphabetical order of the names. Having such an order allows us to quickly find the number of someone in the books.

But consider trying to find a particular number in a telephone book, or trying to find all the people who live in particular road. And these are relatively simple queries you could ask. The formal language for querying relational database is usually SQL.

There are simpler querying facilities for querying and manipulating data in many databases packages such as "query by example" and the ability to select a column and then order all the items in the table according to the ordering in that column.

That would solve our problem of finding a person by their telephone number in the previous paragraph. But it is only part of the answer. SQL provides the most expressive way of querying and manipulating data in a database. Obviously English (or indeed any natural language) is more expressive than SQL. But the problem with English is that it is too expressive. There are many ways of saying the same thing using different words, abbreviations, phraseology, and grammatical constructions.

Furthermore, in using English there are many ways of saying things in indirect ways. For example, using metaphor, analogy, euphemisms, and humour. Yet it seems very appealing to be able to query a relational database using natural language.

If we accept that we need to use relatively restricted subset of English, then it is possible to develop useful natural language interfaces with some degree of flexibility and robustness. A natural language interface for a database needs to incorporate both syntactic knowledge and semantic knowledge. The syntactic knowledge is relatively well-established for this kind of task and includes grammar of the language, conjugations, declensions, rules of agreement and rules of word order.

It is normally knowledge that is common to all database interfaces, and so is relatively stable knowledge. It can be built into the software tools by the software developers, and normally doesn't need amending.

In contrast, most semantic knowledge is dependent on the application. Simple examples are the ability to deal with synonyms in a context sensitive way. For example, in a database on names and addresses, we don't want to treat the uses of *bank* in *Barclays Bank and Kew Gardens Seed Bank* as symonymous in questions like "Give me the names of banks and building societies that have branches in the Borough of Richmond".

Whilst handling semantic knowledge is a complex and open-ended problem. There have been plenty of promising experimental natural langauge database interfaces developed that combine syntactic and semantic knowledge. Unfortunately these developments have not led to overwhelming commercial success so far.

As long ago as 1985, Ovum (an independent IT consultancy) published a report predicting that "By 1987 a natural language interface should be a standard option for users of database management systems and 'Information Centre' type software, and there will be a reasonable choice of alternatives". With hindsight this prediction appears incorrect because the advantages of graphical and form-based query techniques were under-estimated.

However, as the limits of these other approaches are reached, it is likely there will be increased interest in natural language querying. Currently, there are products on the market for building natural language interfaces for pc-based relational databases. Though it is still very much a niche market with suppliers being very small companies such as Elf with its Access ELF product for Microsoft.

The Access ELF software incorporates syntactic knowledge together with a general-purpose lexicon. When configuring the software for a particular database, the lexical knowledge is updated. Some is by the system analysing the entries in the tables and analysing queries to the database, and some is by the users directly updating the lexical knowledge. Using this knowledge, the software is able to understand and process quite complex queries. For example, for a typical customer orders database it can handle the following types of query.

- Which customers have placed more orders than average?"
- Which customers have placed fewer than 10 orders?"
- Which customers have ordered tofu but not Longlife tofu?"
- Make a list of the clients that use Federal Shipping exclusively"
- Which customers ordered tofu in the week of 5 April?"

In general getting software to handle such queries can be very useful. But it is not difficult to find queries that can confound an interface. As a result natural language interfaces for databases are still regarded as a niche technology. But it is likely that this will change rapidly over the next few years with developments in artificial intelligence and computational linguistics providing more intelligent and more robust solutions. In particular, there has been much research into developing semantic knowledge using techniques such as semantic networks and automated learning technology. Currently, much of this new technology is being directed at natural language search engines such as Ask Jeeves (www.askjeeves.co.uk), and given the current economics of the web, it is not surprising that some technology start ups, such as Easy Ask, have shifted their focus from selling natural language interfaces to selling natural language search engines. But as the web drives information technology forward, it likely natural language interfaces to databases will become better and more widely used.

What is a Relational Database?

Relational databases are the most commonly used kind of database. In a relational database, information is stored in tables. Each table has one or more columns, and one or more rows. We can consider each row as an example and each entry in a column in the row gives details about the example.

For example, we can have a customer database where each row represents an individual customer, and each entry in the row gives details about that customer such as name, address, and telephone number. The basic idea is simple and yet so much business information easily falls into this format. This largely explains the ubiquity of relational databases in commercial information systems.

What is SQL?

SQL stands for Structured Query Language. To illustrate SQL, let us consider a table of customers that has columns Name, House number, Road, Town, County, Postcode, Telephone Number, Fax number, and Email. We call this table Customers. Now consider the following SQL. This will retrieve all rows from the Customers table.

Select

From Customers

Now consider the following SQL query. This will retrieve all rows where the entry for the County column is East Sussex.

Select

From Customers

Where County = East Sussex

So far so good. But the language does quickly get much more complicated. This is not a criticism of SQL. Indeed the language is very clear if you are prepared to invest the time to learn it. However it is by necessity very precise so as to avoid the ambiguities that arise in natural language. Furthermore, it does not directly handle synonyms and common-sense abbreviations. For example, consider the following query which many would regard as equivalent to the query above.

Select

From Customers

Where County = E Sussex

Here, common-sense would dictate that East Sussex and E Sussex are equivalent. But in SQL this equivalence needs to be made explicit. Making all the desirable semantic knowledge explicit can be challenging.

Kind of Natural Language

Within the focused domain of an SQL database, natural language interfaces can be constructed that can understand and respond correctly to a wide range of queries. To illustrate, let us consider the Customer table:

We start with the simplest query:

Select *

From Customers

Even trying to handle a simple query such as this could be posed in many different ways such as:

What customers do we have?

List all customers?

Please give me all customers?

Who are our customers?

I want a list of all our customers?

Can I have list of all customers?

SYSTEMS OF CUSTOMER MANAGEMENT

Companies need a method for viewing all customer and marketing-related information in an integrated way. Often marketing organizations maintain multiple databases for each business and marketing activity with data that is not easily integrated for strategic or operational purposes. A new generation of software that is Internet based gathers information from customer service, Web sites, direct mail operations, telemarketing, field sales, customer service, distributors, retailers and suppliers for the purpose of managing marketing, sales and customer service activities.

The major applications families are commonly referred to as sales force automation (SFA) and customer relationship management (CRM) systems.

Some CRM systems are fully integrated with SFA applications and some are standalone. The worldwide market for such systems is projected to grow five times faster than the overall software market, from $5 billion in 1999 to more than $22 billion in 2003.

Sales Force Automation

SFA is a customer management tool that is one of the fastest growing elements of the MkIS. SFA applications are often integrated with the CRM system. SFA involves the application of information technology to the sales function or, more appropriately, to the activities leading to a sale. These activities include acquiring sales leads, managing the sales opportunity, closing the sale and managing the customer relationship. The historic role of personal selling has been to move the product—to generate transactions.

As selling has become increasingly more professional, sales people emphasize building relationships with customers that will generate loyalty-based repeat transactions over time. Relationship building often necessitates that the sales person has consultative and advisory skills in addition to product knowledge and sales abilities. Team-based selling places emphasis on role specialization, collaboration and coordination. Customers have become more sophisticated as well.

Requirements for customised solutions, rapid response times and the need for concurrent and post-sale service have greatly increased the need for information technology in the sales process. The goals of SFA are to increase the effectiveness of the sales organization, improve its efficiency and to create superior value for the customer. Sales effectiveness focuses on getting the sale by improving lead generation, qualifying prospects, coordinating sales efforts, and tracking commitments.

Effectiveness is a function of improving the sales process. Sales efficiency is evaluated by measuring the return on sales efforts. SFA can improve sales efficiency by reducing sales cycle time, by managing workflow, and tracking the current status of critical activities related to the sale.

Proposal generation, opportunity management, fulfillment, and follow up are facilitated by SFA. Superior customer value is achieved when the customer expectations are exceeded. It is a primary determinant of customer satisfaction. SFA enables better understanding of customer expectations and management of the customer account.

The Sales Process

The typical field sales process consists of a series of steps that are designed to lead to a sale. The typical role of the MkIS is to support the sales process steps of lead generation, sales process management, and account management.

- *Lead generation*: Leads represent potential customers. The identification of a lead is the beginning of the sales cycle. After leads are identified, they must be qualified. This process involves gathering information about the lead and comparing the result against qualifying criteria. The lead generation process is becoming more automated with regard to obtaining more pre-qualifying information directly from the lead and augmenting it from commercial and other databases such as credit bureaus. The advent of Web-based technologies is driving this trend. Qualified leads are then distributed to the sales force.
- *Sales Process Management*: This process starts when the sales person receives the lead information. The primary information system need is for a convenient method to track the process and store data the data generated at each stage. There are a number of sub-steps to this stage of the process.
  - *Verification of the opportunity*: The sales person usually contacts the lead and attempts to verify the existence and nature of an opportunity including its size, timing, and appropriateness of the products and services of the selling company. Sales people will also desire to verify the lead's ability to purchase, identify the names of key decision-makers and influencers, and the level of budget authority. This information is entered into the sales database.
  - *The Sales Call*: If the lead is amenable and the opportunity justifies it, a sales call is scheduled. Information may be sent to the prospect and a custom presentation may be created. The SFA system is used to provide a single point of interface for the sales person to coordinate the activities leading up to the sales call. After the call, the SFA system is updated with customer requirements, new information and commitments made by the sales person.
  - *Opportunity Management*: If the sales person is successful, the next step is typically the receipt of a request for proposal (RFP) from the prospective customer. The RFP will generally state the customer's requirements and the date for the final submission. Follow-on visits may be necessary to clear up or identify new requirements. The prospect may want to visit the seller's manufacturing site. The final product of this stage is the creation of a proposal and price quote to be presented to the prospect.

This document should build a sound economic case for the purchase. All these interactions, requirements, commitments, and competitor information are tracked by the SFA system that provides the database, tools and templates to generate the proposal.

- *Closing the Sale*: The presentation of the proposal and the price quote is the start of the closing process. Even if the sales person has done a good job of presenting the business case, further negotiations may be necessary to close the sale. If all objections are met and the proposal is accepted the close is successful. If not, the sales team will need to debrief the sessions learned to determine why the proposal was not accepted. The outcomes are recorded in the SFA system.

- *Account Management*: The automation of the sales process may result in a standalone system that is not integrated with other management systems. However, SFA is increasingly being integrated with the overall CRM system. This is especially true of the account management function. Since the primary goal of the CRM system is to manage the customer relationship in order to generate repeat sales, a good sales person will want to keep track of the status of a new account and how well the customer is being served. This is especially true if the account is to become "referenceable" to other prospects. The account management function of the CRM system enables the sales person to track order entry, order processing, shipment, and installation. The sales person may need to ensure that post-sales service is delivered or monitor the results of and installation and track the customer's satisfaction. The ability to track outcomes and interact with the customer in order to reassess needs and create new opportunities is a major benefit that flows from effective account management.

Sales Force Automation Tools

SFA tools consist of software applications that enable the salesperson to better target sales opportunities and manage the sales cycle. The tools are increasingly available bundled as integrated suites that are Internet enabled, accessible through a browser and linked to the CRM system.

The software applications may be categorized as:

- *Document management tools*: These tools support all stages of the sales process. They include word processors, graphics programmes, spreadsheets, e-mail, expense reports, proposal generators, and "product configurators." A Web-accessible sales library or encyclopedia of previously developed product information, brochures, product demonstrations, presentations, financial information, price lists, white documents, and public relations materials is a key resource for sales force productivity.

- *Personal management tools*: These tools focus on increasing the efficiency and effectiveness of the sales teams efforts. They typically include calendar and scheduling programmes, contact management systems, and call reporting capabilities.
- *Process management tools:* These tools are used to keep track of customer requirements and sales commitments. They include opportunity management systems, project management systems, account management systems, order-entry systems, telemarketing systems, team-selling systems.

Increasingly, with the rise of Web-based hosting and the application service provider (ASP) industry, SFA applications and databases are being hosted by third-party specialists and accessed remotely on the Internet. With the ASP model, client companies are essentially outsourcing all or part of there IS function. Remote hosting raises issues of security and scalability. The advantages of an ASP approach are its browser-based simplicity, rapid implementation, and lower cost of deployment. Most ASP applications use a subscription-based pricing model. Some vendors are proposing that renting the application or paying by the transaction may become the pricing model of the future.

Customer Relationship Management

The Internet has facilitated a fundamental shift in market power from sellers to buyers. Customers, newly endowed with the power of market information, have much different expectations than before. Customers can easily move their business to another vendor with the click of a mouse. They have access to the same cost data as their suppliers and they demand 24x7 customer service.

Customers now have almost unlimited ability for interactions with organizations through the Web in addition to the traditional phone and mail methods. Company web sites facilitate information search, shopping and customer support. E-mail communication can target specific offers on a one-to-one basis. Understanding and meeting demanding expectations has placed a renewed emphasis on managing customer relationships. The primary goal of CRM systems is to increase the return on marketing expenditures by enabling the understanding of the complete history of a firm's interactions with its customers.

CRM applications can deliver targeted solutions that promote customer loyalty as measured by increased response to promotions, purchase frequencies and volume, and minimizes the time between orders. CRM systems are able to target marketing communications to likely buyers, facilitate sales efforts and deliver customer service. CRM systems increase revenue, lower costs and optimize customer lifetime value.

Customer Relationship Management Design Principles

The CRM field is rapidly evolving into an integrated discipline that manages all of a company's touches with the customer.

Accordingly, several design principles have evolved as the foundation for CRM development:

- The CRM system should offer the customer multiple channels for communication such as the telephone, e-mail, fax, on-line or some combination. Each channel should lead to an interaction that satisfies customer expectations. Customers must be able to choose the method that best meets their needs on each occasion.
- Each CRM interaction should deliver value to the customer. The CRM system must be able to determine what value is required and deliver it quickly whether it is a product or service transaction or a customer service request.
- The CRM system integrates the customer throughout the firm's value chain. Customers should be able to reach into all necessary functions of the organization not just to the sales organization, or customer service, but to manufacturing and even the CEO. Better integration of the customer into the process can lead to higher levels of trust, loyalty and repeat purchases. The cost of acquiring a new customer often far exceeds that of retaining existing ones.
- Knowledge is captured during each CRM interaction. The CRM system should capture knowledge about the customer and the customer's relationship with the company over time. Sales and customer support histories should be analysed for indications of how well the vendor is doing in meeting customers' needs and how valuable the customer is to the marketer.

Customer Relationship Management Functions

CRM applications provide the customer-related information that is necessary to drive a firm's ebusiness activities. Better customer information enables more effective demand forecasting, product launches and marketing campaigns. CRM functions are sometimes referred to as the company's "front office."

CRM functionality includes:

- E-commerce support
- Sales force automation
- Telesales and call centre automation

- Direct mail and catalog sales
- E-mail and e-newsletter response
- Web sales and personalization
- Analysis of Web generated data
- Traditional customer support and service
- On-line support and customer service
- Mobile support through laptops, handheld devices.
- Training

Modern CRM systems are fully integrated with the "back office" elements of the enterprise resource planning (ERP) system such as accounting, manufacturing, project management, and human resources. This integration enables the sharing of customer information that can impact the operations of the enterprise and vice versa. Common customer definitions, price lists, employee definitions, service requests, call histories, order histories, contracts, service level agreements are accessible by all who need them. Correspondingly, marketing can access information on items such as new product development, product costs, order status, delivery dates and backorders.

6

Business Performance of Customer

Every company must be able to satisfy and retain customers. That is the key to its business performance. Your job—as an executive in charge of improving quality, customer satisfaction, or loyalty—may be to enable others to act through training and support. Alternatively, if you're in the quality, customer assessment, or development areas of your company, your job may be to do the work directly—to collect, analyse, or use customer data to improve quality, satisfaction, and retention.

Whether you are an enabler or a doer, customer satisfaction and retention are your responsibility. Providing high-quality products and services builds strong relationships with customers and ensures future revenue streams. Even though you may agree about the importance of customers in driving performance, an important question remains. Does your company align its activities to satisfy and retain customers? Too often the answer is either "no" or "not so well." To help understand the problem, consider how a customer focus has evolved in recent decades.

In the 1970s, quality gurus argued that "quality is free." That is, a tireless pursuit of improvement should not only increase efficiency but also increase customer satisfaction in the process, saving enough on costs and bringing in enough new and repeat business to more than cover any expenditures on quality. This was an underlying concept in the success of many Japanese companies. In the 1980s the experts began to focus more directly on increasing customer satisfaction as an explicit goal. Satisfying and keeping customers, it was argued, is simply less expensive than constantly replacing them. More recently, quality and satisfaction have been viewed as not sufficient by themselves. Companies boast of moving "beyond" quality and satisfaction to focus directly on customer loyalty as the key to profitability.

Yet to argue that quality, or satisfaction, or loyalty is what matters misses the point. These factors form a chain of cause and effect, building on each other so that they cannot be treated separately. They represent a system that must be measured and managed as a whole if you want to maximize results. An example from our teaching experiences underscores the nature of the problem and why companies need to take a systems approach to customer measurement and management. Back in 1993 an executive seminar participant from a Fortune 100 company introduced himself as the "customer satisfaction manager" for his organization.

This prompted one of the authors to ask, "What happened to the quality manager?" The participant replied that quality was passé, and that customer satisfaction had become the hot topic in his organization. In fact, being the quality manager had become the "kiss of death" from a career standpoint—a dead-end job! Five years later, a seminar participant from the same company introduced himself as the "customer loyalty manager" for the organization.

Again the natural question arose, "What happened to the customer satisfaction manager?" "Oh, him?" It turned out that the satisfaction manager was now the one with the dead-end job. Many business organizations are beginning to recognize the need to avoid this "Book of the Month Club" mentality and to view customers from a systems perspective.

They want explicit linkages that extend from internal processes to customer perceptions to customer satisfaction to loyalty—and ultimately to bottom-line performance. The framework in this book will give executives hard numbers and not just persuasive theories to show that the connection is real and that improving satisfaction and loyalty really does improve profits. And those on the front lines—the quality engineers and service providers—will get specific guidance on what to improve and how to improve it to get the optimal response from customers. This book will show you how to create an integrated customer measurement and management system that will help you allocate resources and increase profits.

To create such a system, you must first understand your company's entire system for generating profit, from internal quality through to business performance. A systems approach acts on the basis of collected and interpreted customer data—but then you have to use the data to allocate resources and create change in the system or else you merely waste time and money. With an effective customer measurement and management system, you can build organizational value.

To do so, you will continually pursue three key activities that underlie a customer orientation: (1) gather customer information, (2) spread that information throughout the organization, and (3) use the information to maintain, improve, or innovate in products and processes. You need solid information about the concrete product and service attributes or features that customers value, the more abstract consequences and benefits these attributes provide, and ultimately the personal values they serve.

The purpose is to understand what your customers want not only in today's products and services but in tomorrow's as well. When you understand your customers at the various levels that motivate their behaviour, you can see their present needs and predict their future needs as well. To maintain a customer orientation throughout your organization, you need to make sure that customer information gets to everyone who is involved—either directly or indirectly—in improving quality and value and satisfying customers.

This both prepares the entire organization for change and provides benchmarks by which to monitor its performance. Finally, you need to prime the organization to act on the customer information to improve product and service offerings so as to increase satisfaction, loyalty, and profitability. This makes it essential to clarify the links among these three factors and understand how your company delivers a compelling product to its customers. Creating a customer measurement and management system is central to the pursuit of all three of these activities. With such a system in place, you have your customer information in a form that can serve as a basis for both incremental and more revolutionary product and service improvements.

The system also makes it easier to share customer information throughout an organization, enhancing its ability to follow through on that information to make product and process changes. It is essential to view customer measurement from a systems perspective that encompasses multiple areas of measurement and expertise (from engineering and design through market research and strategy to finance and accounting) so that you pick up both concrete and abstract details— both what the customers like and dislike and why they react that way—and develop information that will be genuinely useful.

Now you may well be saying, "But we already do a good job of gathering customer information, spreading it, and acting on the voice of the customer." The question is whether you really adopt the "lens of the customer" in this process or fall into the trap of relying on the "lens of the organization." The lens of the customer shows you your products and services—and the benefits they provide—from your customers' perspective.

You see them as they really are in the marketplace, rather than the different and potentially misleading picture you're likely to get from the lens of your own organization. For example, if you run a convenience store chain you may be inclined to view the chain's stores as providing customers with people (service), products (from soft drinks to gasoline), and operations (such as opening hours), each under the management of a different department or business function. The problem is that customers may not share this perspective. Customers view products and services from the standpoint of the benefits they provide and problems they solve, which may not align well with individual business process areas. In this case, customers are looking for safety, convenience, and cleanliness, which are benefits that are not uniquely provided by specific business process areas. Rather, they cut across the people, products, and operating policies of the stores. Aside from providing a more accurate picture of the drivers of satisfaction and loyalty, adopting the lens of the customer has other advantages. It blurs functional boundaries and provides a common basis and language for communication.

The forging of concrete links from area to area within a company is also a key to effective implementation. When an organization reaches a consensus on the importance of customer benefits that are not defined along functional or business process lines, it finds it much easier to engage in the cross-functional activities required to truly innovate and implement change. We emphasize the word *framework* here. Our aim is to show just what links and models are possible.The actual elements and links in any model vary tremendously from company to company and context to context.

After describing the framework, as suggested, show this point using two very different cases in which companies (Volvo and Sears) have developed models to become more customer focused. The framework includes four general areas: internal quality, external quality and satisfaction, customer loyalty and retention, and financial performance. *Internal quality* encompasses various production and maintenance processes.

In the case of a manufactured product, it includes everything from manufacturing processes to the physical characteristics and attributes that describe the product. In a service and retailing context, it includes the service offer, the physical surroundings, and the satisfaction of employees and the resulting service quality they provide.

External quality and satisfaction encompasses what customers see in the purchase and consumption experience: the attributes and benefits that products and services provide and the costs they impose, and the conclusions the customers draw about the company. In the area of customer loyalty and retention, *loyalty* is a customer's intention or predisposition to buy, while *retention* is the behaviour itself (as when a customer returns to a restaurant, comes back to buy the same brand of car, or purchases another financial instrument from the same institution).

Although as suggested, use the term *loyalty* at times to encompass both intended loyalty and actual retention, it is important to understand the distinction. When actual retention information is available, it proves extremely valuable in sorting out the drivers of financial performance.

When it is unavailable, as it often is, you can use loyalty measures as a proxy for retention. Quality, satisfaction, and loyalty ultimately affect financial performance, both directly and indirectly. The framework shows this point and highlights the possibility that there may be a tension between direct and indirect effects. Consider first the impact of internal quality. Producing a high-quality product or service at an attractive price indirectly affects financial performance through its effect on external customer perceptions of the purchase-consumption experience. But internal quality may also have a direct effect on costs and revenues.

EXTERNAL QUALITY, VALUE, AND CUSTOMER SATISFACTION

The "quality is free" argument, improvements in internal quality can increase productivity and lower internal costs and thus directly increase profitability. Recent research suggests, however, that this link is likely to be more positive for products and less positive or even negative for services. Why the difference? Services are produced and delivered at a time and place that is typically dictated by the customer. Thus improving service quality often requires an increase in personnel and operating or contact hours, which raises operating costs.

The external quality, value, and customer satisfaction component of the framework also has both direct and indirect effects on costs and revenues. Indirectly, a positive overall experience predisposes customers to stay loyal towards a product, service, or provider, which generates future sales. Satisfaction thus contributes to financial performance through its effect on loyalty and retention. But satisfaction also has direct effects, independent of loyalty. The cost of maintaining a customer account—or fixing a product—is a direct function of how happy the customer is. Satisfied customers are less likely to demand expensive product repairs or replacements or to invoke service guarantees. Also—even outside the world of TV commercials—people do talk about the products and services they buy, and your company's entry into that stream of word-of-mouth publicity is through perceived quality and satisfaction rather than through loyalty. Satisfaction is *news*—something to talk about—while loyalty is a background state that goes without saying unless something happens to damage it.

The direct effects of loyalty and retention on performance include revenues from repeat purchases, reduction in costs of finding new customers (to replace lost customers), and revenues generated through cross-selling. Another direct effect is the price premium that loyal customers often pay. Because loyal customers are not actively shopping for alternatives, they tend to be insulated from price incentives and offers such as coupons, price cuts, and free merchandise. The recent turnaround at Volvo Car Company provides a good example of how a durable goods manufacturer views the links described in our framework.

In 1991, Volvo was performing poorly in the global automotive market. It ranked as low as twenty-sixth out of thirty-four brands in the J. D. Power Initial Quality Study in the United States, and sales and profitability were suffering. In its comeback effort, Volvo began to develop a customer orientation from a total quality management foundation. Formerly, Volvo had emphasized changing internal quality to improve productivity and reduce costs.

Its management realised, however, that just focusing on internal quality was insufficient. Internal improvements had to matter to the customers before they could create improved external quality, customer satisfaction, and loyalty.

Volvo's approach is just one example of the variety of tailored models that are consistent with the framework. Like Volvo, Sears has attempted to radically transform itself into a more customer-focused organization. But since Sears is a retailer that competes primarily on service, its model has evolved quite differently. Internal quality at Sears is primarily about its people and the service they provide. The Sears model draws directly on a service-profit chain that links internal quality (including employee satisfaction and loyalty) to service quality, and the satisfaction generated by service quality to loyalty and financial performance. In developing its model, Sears has discovered both direct effects of satisfaction on financial performance and indirect effects through loyalty, which is consistent with our framework.

A quantitative employee-customer-profit model at Sears has helped the company to establish very specific links that have enabled it to improve financial performance. The model shows, for example, that a 5-point improvement in employee attitudes (on a 0 to 100 scale) drives a 1.3-point improvement in customer satisfaction, which in turn drives a 0.5 per cent improvement in revenue growth. The Volvo and Sears models share a common logic, but each model is uniquely tailored to the organization's own situation. Both models link internal quality through to profitability.

At the same time, each reflects the nature of a specific company, its customers and offerings, and the contexts involved. When you look at your own company, you will see that the same logic will work for you when you develop a similar understanding of your own customers and what you can offer them. The best measurement system can only provide information— it can't make decisions for you. People make decisions, whether it is the convenience store executive who sets corporate priorities, the front-line service manager who translates these priorities into policies and procedures, or the service worker who translates policies and procedures into concrete actions.

At all three levels, decision makers are much more likely to choose to do something that will help the store chain succeed if they understand what matters to customers and how the job at hand can enhance that value. The process of moving from information to decisions draws heavily on *importance-performance analysis.* The most cost-effective areas of product and service performance to improve are those that are important to customers *and* on which, at the same time, the company is performing poorly. Executives and managers must identify these priority areas of high importance and low performance. As an output of this selection process, they can categorize and display the drivers of satisfaction and loyalty using a strategic satisfaction matrix.

The matrix identifies four categories of performance drivers with different market action implications. Again, the aspects to improve first are those where impact or importance is high and performance is weak. This focuses resources and quality improvement efforts likely to have the greatest impact on satisfaction and thus on loyalty and profitability. Those aspects where performance and impact are both high reflect a firm's competitive advantage.

It is essential to maintain if not improve performance on these drivers. When impact and performance are both weak, on the other hand, there is no need to waste resources on improvement. More interesting is the low impact–strong performance category. This may be an area where resources have been wasted in the past because the benefits and attributes are not important to customers. Alternatively, this category may contain drivers of satisfaction that customers see as basic and necessary—so much a part of the product or service that they ignore it as long as it's there when they want it, like electric power or water on tap.

Although such drivers are important in an absolute sense, they have little to no impact on satisfaction because there is little variance in their performance. The danger is that a reduction in performance quality would increase the impact on satisfaction (this danger is often referred to as a "slippery slope"). Another possibility here is to find a new target market segment for the product or service.

For example, if the quality of an electrical system is so constant that it has no impact on satisfaction in one application, the system might be used in applications where minor fluctuations in this quality are more important and therefore likely to have a real impact on satisfaction. There is also a danger that something in this category may become important in the future. For example, few customers considered "environmental friendliness" to be an important factor until recently, but more and more people are beginning to pay attention to this aspect of the goods and services they buy. In a growing variety of fields, companies that predicted the importance of this area and prepared their business accordingly clearly have an advantage over those that did not. The circular nature of the process reflects the continuous nature of a customer orientation.

Customer needs, competitive offerings, and business technologies change constantly, so customer focus is an ideal of constant growth rather than static achievement. The cycle in is thus a continuous process of planning, researching, analysing, deciding, implementing, and learning. This includes identifying the system's purpose or goals within a more balanced set of corporate performance measures (including financial goals, employee satisfaction goals, process improvement goals, knowledge and learning goals, and so forth). The key customer and market segmentation issues upon which the system is based, including the distinction between internal and external customers.

Conducting interviews and focus groups and observing customers provides you with the lens through which customers view products and services. This lens is the basis for your quality-satisfactionloyalty modeling. It discusses ways to develop and administer surveys that assess the attributes and benefits your products and services provide and the overall levels of customer satisfaction and loyalty that result. The goal is to customise the measurement of quality, value, satisfaction, and loyalty for a particular customer segment, company, and context.

Again, the purpose is to identify both the relative importance and performance of key satisfaction and loyalty drivers. It provides guidelines for identifying the area or areas where importance is high and performance is low, which offer the most potential return on quality improvement efforts. We develop a statistical approach to help you estimate your system or model linking quality to loyalty and financial performance. We also provide concrete examples. As emphasized earlier, management must take part in categorizing the output of a customer analysis into a strategic satisfaction matrix. Just where boundaries are set between highversus low-impact drivers and strong versus weak performance depends on a variety of factors, including what you can achieve in the time available, your cost structure, and your overall strategy. Interpreting model outputs also requires appropriate bench for evaluating both performance and importance.

Who should collect your customer data, analyse it, and use it to set priorities and allocate resources? It often seems logical to delegate the satisfaction and loyalty measurement operation to outside research firms and consultants. This is especially true early in the process of becoming a customer-oriented organization, because outside specialists offer specific skills related to collecting and analysing customer data that you do not have. Unfortunately, if you delegate the system, your company does not take ownership of it, and you and your people may fail to learn or acquire the skills necessary to measure and manage customer data on your own.

The consultant's bills, heavy as they are likely to be, are only a small part of the cost of handing off a customer information system. Bear in mind that when customer information is the key to strategy, it should reside within the company. Your best teachers about what is right and wrong with your products and services are your own customers. Direct contact with customers and customer data is a critical part of learning what it takes to satisfy customer needs.

No matter how good the consultants are, they will always function as filters. An important part of establishing a customer orientation as a core competency is creating, over time, internal specialists to measure, model, and manage quality, satisfaction, and loyalty. Early in the process, external experts are apt to be a necessity. They can provide the interviewing, surveying, data warehousing, statistical analysis, and interpretation skills that you may lack or not yet want (or be able) to invest in. Over time, however, continued reliance on external specialists becomes costly and also fails to develop customer measurement and management as a core competency. Internalization of the process allows you to adapt to changing market needs and competitive environments in a cost-effective fashion. More important, your organization accepts ownership of the process and the data—and the decisions that emerge. This is not to say that all parts of the process should be brought in-house in all cases.

BUSINESS ORGANIZATIONS

You may not want to try to run a survey that involves computer-aided telephone interviews or a Web-based system with highly specialized personnel (such as trained interviewers) and potential economies of scale. Even in the most customer-savvy organization, it may be best to outsource certain parts of the process. At the same time, a truly customer-oriented firm should own rather than rent the ability to observe and to talk to customers, formalize survey instruments, analyse and interpret customer data, and use the output to make resource allocation decisions.

Over the last three decades business organizations have evolved from a focus on quality to a focus on customer satisfaction, and onward to a focus on loyalty as a means of creating value. A customer measurement and management system views each of these areas as an indispensable link in a chain of causes and effects that runs from internal quality through to profitability. The goal of this book is to help you and your organization create an integrated customer measurement and management system for making effective resource allocation decisions and increasing profitability. In the process of building a system, organizations develop internal specialists capable of gathering, analysing, and interpreting customer data.

Truly customer-oriented companies should, over time, add these skills to their core competencies. A systems approach to customer measurement and management also requires that you tailor the system to your unique purpose, customers, and contexts. As an illustration, Volvo's model incorporates the positive effects of improving internal quality on both productivity and customer perceptions of quality, satisfaction, and loyalty. In contrast, a major retailer such as Sears incorporates the central role that satisfied employees play in delivering quality and value to customers. These measurement systems and models are not substitutes for decision making. Rather, they provide the information you need to make resource allocation decisions and manage the process.

The system provides information on how the company and its competitors are performing in different areas and how important the areas are to customers. When combined with cost and strategy considerations, the system allows both enablers and doers to create organizational value through a continuous focus on customers. To maximize the value generated by the system, make sure your company's own staff perform the bulk of the work of collecting and interpreting customer data, so that you get the full benefit of the insights generated by the effort. Before you dive in and start conducting customer interviews or surveys, you must know how your measurement system will be used. Since a customer orientation builds on internal quality, we'll start with a brief overview of quality management and its role in driving company strategy and customer measures. We'll then discuss two related approaches to translating strategy into action: policy deployment and balanced performance measures.

Then we'll focus on the process of getting started on developing a customer measurement and management system—or improving an existing one—which involves taking a look at the breadth and depth of the proposed system and the role of market segmentation in it. In our customer satisfaction framework, internal quality is the first in the chain of events that drives financial performance.

It's important not to underestimate the role of *total quality management* (or TQM, also known as *company-wide quality management,* CWQM, and as *total quality control,* TQC)—nor to exaggerate it. For longterm survival, businesses have been forced to improve their abilities to change and innovate. But internal quality management is not in itself sufficient to assure success. Internal quality improvements must be linked to improvements in external quality, satisfaction, loyalty, and financial performance. And the links must be established in an environment of constantly evolving customer preferences, markets, competitors, and technologies. The broad principles and methods of quality management apply directly to the development of a customer measurement system.

The concept of quality should unify all of a company's activities. After all, only your customers can ultimately define quality for you! In the end, it doesn't matter how well the production system works, how well marketing functions are performed, or how good the company's strategy is. If no one buys, there will be no revenues.

Quality experts emphasize three basic strategies for successful quality management: use reference models or benchmarks, set priorities for quality improvement, and focus your resources. Do not try to do things completely on your own. Instead, make use of reference models or benchmarks when they're available. Benchmarking is particularly important in developing a customer measurement and management system. Process benchmarking—finding out how things are done— works as well in developing a customer measurement and management system as in any other area of business.

When you can manage it, arrange visits to firms with strong reputations to gauge their practices and learn what they are doing, see how they are doing it, and understand what is possible. Devote some time to reverse engineering their products as well. And don't limit the benchmarking to competitors—in a general area such as customer measurement, you'll find individuals or organizations in many fields who excel in areas that you are interested in improving. Benchmarking on their processes can help you to learn how to conduct better customer interviews, develop and administer more effective surveys, and analyse customer data in more productive ways—and they're likely to be much more willing to share information with you if you're not trying to sell the same offering to the same customers. For *output* or *performance benchmarking,* you will measure your product or service against direct or indirect competitors on various dimensions such as internal or technical quality, external or perceived quality and value, and overall customer satisfaction, loyalty, and retention. The external benchmarks will help you interpret your findings regarding your own customers and decide just where to devote your resources to get the most mileage from your improvement efforts.

SALES PROMOTION OF CONSUMER

Consumer sales promotions encompass a variety of short-term promotional techniques designed to induce customers to respond in some way. The most popular consumer sales promotions are directly associated with product purchasing. These promotions are intended to enhance the value of a product purchase by either reducing the overall cost of the product (i.e., get same product but for less money) or by adding more benefit to the regular purchase price (i.e., get more for the money).

While tying a promotion to an immediate purchase is a major use of consumer sales promotion, it is not the only one. As we noted above, promotion techniques can be used to achieve other objectives such as building brand loyalty or creating product awareness. Consequently, a marketer's promotional toolbox contains a large variety of consumer promotions.

The following 11 types of consumer sales promotions:

- Coupons
- Rebates
- Promotional Pricing
- Trade-In
- Loyalty Programs
- Sampling and Free Trials
- Free Product
- Premiums
- Contests and Sweepstakes
- Demonstrations
- Personal Appearances

Coupons

Most consumers are quite familiar with this form of sales promotion, which offers purchasers price savings or other incentives when the coupon is redeemed at the time of purchase. Coupons are short-term in nature since most (but not all) carry an expiration date after which the value may not be received. Also, coupons require consumer involvement in order for value to be realized. In most cases involvement consists of the consumer making an effort to obtain the coupon (e.g., clip from newspaper) and then presenting it at the time of purchase.

Coupons are used widely by marketers across many retail industries and reach consumers in a number of different delivery formats including:

- *Free-Standing Inserts (FSI)*: Here coupon placement occurs loosely (i.e., inserted) within media, such as newspapers and direct mail, and may or may not require the customer to cut away from other material in order to use.
- *Cross-Product:* These consist of coupons placed within or on other products. Often a marketer will use this method to promote one product by placing the coupon inside another major selling product. For example, a pharmaceutical company may imprint a coupon for a cough remedy on the box of a pain medication. Also, this delivery approach is used when two marketers have struck a cross promotion arrangement where each agrees to undertake certain marketing activity for the other.
- *Printout:* A delivery method that is common in many food stores is to present coupons to a customer at the conclusion of the purchasing process. These coupons, which are often printed on the spot, are intended to be used for a future purchase and not for the current purchase which triggered the printing.
- *Product Display:* Some coupons are nearly impossible for customers to miss as they are located in close proximity to the product. In some instances coupons may be contained within a coupon dispenser fastened to the shelf holding the product while in other cases coupons may be attached to a special display where customers can remove them (e.g., tear off).
- *Internet:* Several specialized websites, such as HotCoupons.com, and even some manufacturer's sites, allow customers to print out coupons. These coupons are often the same ones appearing in other media, such as newspapers or direct mail. In other cases, coupons may be sent via email, though to be effective the customer's email programme must be able to receive HTML email (and not text only) in order to maintain required design elements (e.g., bar code).
- *Electronic:* The Internet is also seeing the emergence of new non-printable coupons redeemable through website purchases. These electronic coupons are redeemed when the customer enters a designated coupon code during the purchase process.

Rebates

Rebates, like coupons, offer value to purchasers typically by lowering the customer's final cost for acquiring the product. While rebates share some similarities with coupons, they differ in several keys aspects. First, rebates are generally handed or offered (e.g., accessible on the Internet) to customers after a purchase is made and cannot be used to obtain immediate savings in the way coupons are used. (So called "instant rebates", where customers receive price reductions at the time of purchase, have elements of both coupons and rebates, but for our purposes we will classify these as coupons due to the timing of the reward to the customer.)

Second, rebates often request the purchaser to submit personal data in order to obtain the rebate. For instance, customer identification, including name, address and contact information, is generally required to obtain a rebate. Also, the marketer may ask those seeking a rebate to provide additional data such as indicating the reason for making the purchase.

Third, unlike coupons that always offer value when used in a purchase (assuming it is accepted by the retailer), receiving a rebate only guarantees value if the customer takes actions. Marketers know that not all customers will respond to a rebate. Some will misplace or forget to submit the rebate while others may submit after a required deadline.

Marketers factor in the non-redemption rate as they attempt to calculate the cost of the rebate promotion. Finally, rebates tend to be used as a value enhancement in higher priced products compared to coupons. For instance, rebates are a popular promotion for automobiles and computer software where large amounts of money may be returned to the customer.

Promotional Pricing

One of the most powerful sales promotion techniques is the short-term price reduction or, as known in some areas, "on sale" pricing. Lowering a product's selling price can have an immediate impact on demand, though marketers must exercise caution since the frequent use of this technique can lead customers to anticipate the reduction and, consequently, withhold purchase until the price reduction occurs again. Promotional pricing is also considered within the framework of the Price marketing mix component.

Trade-In

Trade-in promotions allow consumers to obtain lower prices by exchanging something the customer possess, such as an older product that the new purchase will replace. While the idea of gaining price breaks for trading in another product is most frequently seen with automobile sales, such promotions are used in other industries, such as computers and golf equipment, where the customer's exchanged product can be resold by the marketer in order to extract value.

Loyalty Programs

Promotions that offer customers a reward, such as price discounts and free products, for frequent purchasing or other activity are called loyalty programs. These promotions have been around for many years but grew rapidly in popularity when introduced in the airline industry as part of frequent-filer programs.

Loyalty programs are also found in numerous other industries, including grocery, pizza purchasing and online book purchases, where they may also be known as club card programs since members often must use a verification card as evidence of enrollment in the programme.

Many loyalty programs have become ingrained as part of the value offered by a marketer. That is, a retailer or marketing organization may offer loyalty programs as general business practice. Under this condition loyalty programme does not qualify as a sales promotion since it does not fit the requirement of offering a short-term value (i.e., it is always offered). However, even within a loyalty programme that is part of a general business practice, a sales promotion can be offered such as special short-term offer that lowers the number of points needed to acquire a free product.

Samples and Free Trials

Enticing members of a target market to try a product is often easy when the trial comes at little or no cost to the customer. The use of samples and free trials may be the oldest of all sales promotion techniques dating back to when society advanced from a culture of self-subsistence to a culture of trade.

Sampling and free trials give customers the opportunity to experience products, often in small quantities or for a short duration, without purchasing the product. Today, these methods are used in almost all industries and are especially useful for getting customers to try a product for the first time.

Free Product

Some promotional methods offer free products but with the condition that a purchase be made. The free product may be in the form of additional quantities of the same purchased product (e.g., buy one, get one free) or specialty packages (e.g., value pack) that offer more quantity for the same price as regular packaging.

Premiums

Another form of sales promotion involving free merchandise is premium or "give-away" items. Premiums differ from samples and free product in that these often do not consist of the actual product, though there is often some connection. For example, a cellphone manufacturer may offer access to free downloadable ringtones for those purchasing a cellphone.

Contests and Sweepstakes

Consumers are often attracted to promotions where the potential value obtained is very high. In these promotions only a few lucky consumers receive the value offered in the promotion. Two types of promotions that offer high value are contests and sweepstakes.

Contests are special promotions awarding value to winners based on skills they demonstrate compared to others. For instance, a baking company may offer free vacations to winners of a baking contest. Contest award winners are often determined by a panel of judges.

Sweepstakes or drawings are not skill based but rather based on luck. Winners are determined by random selection. In some cases the chances of winning may be higher for those who make a purchase if entry into the sweepstake occurs automatically when a purchase is made. But in most cases, anyone is free to enter without the requirement to make a purchase.

A sub-set of both contests and sweepstakes are games, which come in a variety of formats such as scratch-off cards and collection of game pieces. Unlike contests and sweepstakes, which may not require purchase, to participate in a game customers may be required to make a purchase. In the United States and other countries, where eligibility is based on purchase, games may be subjected to rigid legal controls and may actually fall under that category of lotteries, which are tightly controlled.

Demonstrations

Many products benefit from customers being shown how products are used through a demonstration. Whether the demonstration is experienced in-person or via video form, such as over the Internet, this promotional technique can produce highly effective results. Unfortunately, demonstrations are very expensive to produce. Costs involved in demonstrations include paying for the expense of the demonstrator, which can be high if the demonstrator is well-known (e.g., nationally known chef), and also paying for the space where the demonstration is given.

Personal Appearances

An in-person appearance by someone of interest to the target market, such as an author, sports figure or celebrity, is another form of sales promotion capable of generating customer traffic to a physical location. However, as with demonstrations, personal appearance promotion can be expensive since the marketer normally must pay a fee for the person to appear.

TRADE SALES PROMOTIONS

A trade promotion aimed at retailers may encourage retailers to instruct their employees to promote a marketer's brand over competitors' offerings.

With thousands of products competing for limited shelf space, spending on trade promotion is nearly equal that spent on consumer promotions.

Many sales promotions aimed at building relationships with channel partners follow similar designs as those directed to consumers including promotional pricing, contests and free product. In addition to these, several other promotional approaches are specifically designed to appeal to trade partners. These approaches include:

- Point-of-Purchase Displays
- Advertising Support Programs
- Short Term Allowances
- Sales Incentives or Push Money
- Promotional Products
- Trade Shows

Point-of-Purchase Displays

Point of purchase (POP) displays are specially designed materials intended for placement in retail stores. These displays allow products to be prominently presented, often in high traffic areas, and thereby increase the probability the product will standout. POP displays come in many styles, though the most popular are ones allowing a product to stand alone, such as in the middle of a store aisle or sit at the end of an aisle (i.e., end-cap) where it will be exposed to heavy customer traffic.

For channel partners, POP displays can result in significant sales increases compared to sales levels in a normal shelf position. Also, many marketers will lower the per-unit cost of products in the POP display as an incentive for retailers to agree to include the display in their stores.

Advertising Support Programs

In addition to offering promotional support in the form of physical displays, marketers can attract channel members' interest by offering financial assistance in the form of advertising money. These funds are often directed to retailers who then include the company's products in their advertising. In certain cases the marketer will offer to pay the entire cost of advertising, but more often, the marketer offers partial support known as co-op advertising funds.

Short Term Trade Allowances

This promotion offers channel partners price breaks for agreeing to stock the product. In most cases the allowance is not only given as encouragement to purchase the product but also as an inducement to promote the product in other ways such as by offering attractive shelf space or store location, highlighting the product in company-produced advertising or website display, or by agreeing to have the retailer's sales personnel "talk-up" the product to customers. Allowances can be in the form price reductions (a.k.a. off-invoice promotion) and buy-back guarantees if the product does not sell in certain period of time.

Sales Incentives or Push Money

Since sales promotions are intended to stimulate activity that leads to meeting promotional objectives, it makes sense that these can also apply to those in a channel member's organization who also affect sales. Thus, a marketer may offer sales promotions to their reseller's sales force and customer service staff where they are used as incentives to help sell more of the marketer's product. Sometimes called push money, these promotions typically offer employees cash or prizes, such as trips, for those that meet sales requirements.

Promotional Products

Among the most widely used methods of sales promotions is the promotional product; products labeled with the brand or company name that serve as reminders of the actual product. For instance, companies often hand out free calendars, coffee cups and pens that contain the product logo.

Trade Shows

One final type of trade promotion is the industry trade show (a.k.a. exhibitions, conventions). Trade shows are organized events that bring both industry buyers and sellers together in one central location. Spending on trade shows is one of the highest of all sales promotions. In fact, the Promotion Marketing Association estimates that over (US) $20 billion is spent annually by marketers to participate in trade shows.

Marketers are attracted to trade shows since these offer the opportunity to reach a large number of potential buyers in one convenient setting. At these events most sellers attempt to capture the attention of buyers by setting up a display area to present their product offerings and meet with potential customers. These displays can range from a single table covering a small area to erecting specially built display booths that dominate the trade show floor.

7

Customer Relationship Management in Marketing

CUSTOMER SERVICE CULTURE

FMC stresses the importance of creating a holistic customer service culture by beginning with upper-level management and actualizing this goal among all staff including frontline personnel. The framework for the customer service culture at FMC includes learning what the customers want; implementing steps to provide for those wants for which a business case can be made; equipping frontline employees with training, information, empowerment, and motivation; and monitoring success through customer and employee feedback mechanisms.

When the U.S. call centres were being developed, the director researched other call centres to find a model for their design. In favour of economies of scale (related to technology, resources, and personnel), FMC implemented call centre access on a national scale at four sites. Even with this consolidated design, FMC is committed to providing personalized service.

Call centre management utilizes customer telephone and mail survey results as well as focus group findings to guide implementation. Once analysed, this information is provided to the areas within the call centre for which it applies. (For example, customer feedback about loan rates goes to employees responsible for making policy decisions about rates. Customer input about experiences and interactions with personnel are provided to staff in training and human resources.)

Call centre managers are expected to coach and mentor call takers, based on performance during quality control checks. FMC management utilizes formal feedback initiatives to ensure that communication between the frontline and management remains open. One of these programmes is the Voice of the Customer Committee. On this committee, frontline workers meet with management during a monthly meeting at which staff relay what customers want, based on their interactions with customers that month and over time. Another mechanism, the Ideas Programme, offers an opportunity for frontline personnel to submit a proposal to management on how to improve customer service. Employees are rewarded for submitting proposals, and when ideas are implemented, a gift card is provided.

Frontline employees, especially through the Voice of the Customer Committee, have made important contributions to improving customer service at FMC. For example, frontline staff identified necessary changes in the voice menu wording, suggested options that should be added and some to omit from the phone tree menu, and identified customers' information needs. Frontline personnel are encouraged not only to report to management any processes that are not working, but to offer potential solutions.

The key to hiring someone on the front line, according to FMC management, is to hire staff with a passion for customer service. Training for FMC staff includes training on teams, as well as learning how to give and receive feedback, how to be a good team member, and how to improve telephone communication skills.

One important motivator for employees is the policy within the company that includes customer satisfaction as a determining factor in employee compensation. Quarterly, customer telephone survey results are tabulated, and employees receive bonuses that are tied directly to their scores. Also, prizes are offered for customer letters or phone calls of praise. Lunches are offered to teams who perform well in customer service.

In an effort to make the payment process as convenient as possible for customers, FMC piloted a phone pay system through Western Union. Currently, this programme produces 350,000 transactions each month. Other pay options include direct electronic payments from a bank account or payroll deduction and Internet-based payment processing. Twenty-two per cent of FMC payments are processed electronically. At the time of this report, they are also considering whether to permit credit card payments.

During a month when the customer simply cannot pay, FMC works with customers who struggle to make full and timely payments. For example, a customer may be permitted to skip a payment and add that payment to the end of the loan. Another option is reducing the amount of the monthly payment and extending the length of the loan. Accountability is enforced through late payment charges and reports made to the credit bureau.

Customer service is key to the day-to-day operation of Cherner Automotive Group (Cherner). This sentiment is echoed from the frontline employee to the upper-level executive. The Cherner philosophy of customer service delivery is customer satisfaction through continued friendly communication and interaction, coupled with accessibility and responsiveness. Cherner's approach is very individualized, and they believe that customer service is relative to the customer being served. In no case did a Cherner employee claim to be in the business of selling vehicles; rather, employees view themselves as"in the people business."Building customer relationships is underscored. Cherner employees realise that exemplary customer service brings in new customers, as well as repeat customers. This is accomplished by reputation or referral.

Cherner operates two dealerships, both of which are located in the Northern Virginia technology corridor. Cherner has a wide customer base that includes retired persons, business professionals, members of Congress, and community residents. Many Cherner customers are repeat customers or referrals.

Cherner is a family-owned and -operated business. The corporate culture embraces change; strives to learn what customers want and gives it to them; and seeks both customer and employee loyalty. Cherner considers customers'first impressions to be important and strives to create a warm and inviting environment. Cherner employees attempt to make customers feel welcome and to provide individualized attention.

The only"formal"policies for making this occur include the"10-foot rule,"whereby employees who are in the area should acknowledge customers within this range and ask to be of assistance, and a policy that all customers who enter the dealership are acknowledged within 30 seconds. Cherner employees understand the value of smiling and being pleasant to all customers.

According to Cherner staff at all levels of the company, customers deserve responsiveness. The ability to individualize service is, in their opinion, what sets them apart in customer service delivery. There are no written guidelines, but employees have a degree of autonomy in making decisions.

For example, the service advisor has the latitude to refund money or to adjust a charge ticket. The core ideology is that each employee is encouraged to do whatever it takes within reason-based on the situation-to serve a customer immediately. Employees are discouraged from having a"this is my job or that is not my job"attitude. Rather, all employees work for the same company and every employee is responsible for serving customers and making them happy.

Integral to Cherner's customer service delivery is the need to understand customer expectations. Cherner listens to their customers and provides convenient forums for customer feedback. The most widely used method is their customer satisfaction survey. Each customer who purchases an automobile receives a questionnaire from Ford Motor Company. The results are shared with the dealer. Also, Cherner hires an outside company to phone a sample of their service customers to collect data on customer satisfaction. These findings are presented in the monthly report"Viewpoint."The service area also has a customer feedback/suggestion box, posted beside the cash register.

Staff at all levels of the organization articulated their customer service orientation as:

- Being pleasant and smiling at customers.
- Being a good listener (and being empathetic to customers'situations).
- Doing the job right the first time.

- Being accountable.
- Building trusting relationships with customers.
- Treating people fairly.
- Making customers fully happy.
- Being willing to apologize.

Cherner's owners and managers set the tone for the company. Managers are expected to"lead by example."The general manager adheres to a policy of"Management by Walking Around."In other words, he and other managers try to stay connected with employees throughout the organization by working side-by-side with them. Senior-level executives have an open-door policy and solicit employee input during staff meetings. Calls are not screened, so customers also can contact managers directly.

Managers attempt to empower employees by providing a supportive environment in which employees are encouraged to make decisions. Managers are expected to coach frontline staff. During interviews, frontline personnel indicated that if a frontline employee were experiencing difficulties, managers would speak with that individual and coach him/her. However, frontline staff felt that improvement would be expected and that the employee would be held accountable for improving, or the employee would be terminated. As an employee's experience increases, so does the amount of discretion allotted to the employee.

Cherner frontline personnel perceive that they are supported by management in that whatever they feel they cannot handle can be turned over to management, with frontline staff confident that the situation will be addressed. Management also listens and responds to the needs of the employees. This is handled in different ways. For example, when employees in service determine that they need some training or equipment to do the job better, they can write the request on a white board designed for this purpose, and a member of management will address the request (and keep the notation on the board until the request is resolved). The white board is also an information-sharing tool for frontline employees. Employee meetings are an another forum for raising and addressing issues.

Most of the dealership's employees have longevity with the company. During each discussion with Cherner employees, regardless of organizational level, the interviewee acknowledged that to deliver great customer service, a company must hire and retain the right people. Managers added that "the right person" is one who can get along with others, possesses good judgment, can work on a team, is motivated, and possesses the desire to grow and learn. Cherner wants to hire sales personnel who are motivated not by money, but rather by the desire to help people.

Cherner offers multifaceted, ongoing training for employees. In order to continually provide effective customer service, employees are trained both in-house and by the manufacturers. Ford Star Satellite training, Ford's training facility in Centreville (VA) and printed training materials from KIA and ISUZU are designed to keep employees current on various features and aspects of the products being sold and serviced. Other training offered is designed to enhance selling techniques and customer service and to update technicians on vehicle and repair technology. In the past, employees received gender sensitivity training that was offered to improve customer service for female customers.

Among the most creative training strategies is Cherner's frontline mentoring system, whereby a senior salesperson mentors a new salesperson for 90 days. The senior salesperson is responsible for teaching sales basics, orienting the new employee to Cherner culture and attitude, describing Cherner products, and detailing processes. One frontline employee stated that this type of mentoring is a key component to great customer service that is transferable to other organizations.

At all levels of the organization, employees reported being very self-motivated—driven by personal pride and the desire to do a great job. This may be a result of Cherner's hiring policies as well as employees' positive perceptions of their work environment.

Most of those that were interviewed commented that separate and distinct from the actual family ownership of the dealership, the working environment feels like a family environment. Employees know and talk with one another, even across departments; employees support one another; employee picnics and gatherings allow families to get to know each other; and employees simply "get along." This family environment proves to be a strong motivator for Cherner employees at all levels.

Another motivator that was mentioned comes directly from individual customers. Employees reported receiving Christmas cards, gifts, notes, and personal appreciation and friendship from satisfied customers. Cherner, as well as the vehicle manufacturers, offers incentives to foster and sustain employee motivation. Cherner sponsors contests, and the winners are given free tickets to sporting events or dinner coupons, monetary awards, and other "per's" (e.g., use of a vehicle, recognition, etc.) Rewards are also offered based on customer survey scores, reported by Ford. At times, there are luncheons or dinners.

Rather than a point-in-time formalized evaluation process, employees are continuously recognized for good service. Similarly, management addresses negative behaviour as it is observed or identified via customer surveys or complaints and seeks to correct this behaviour through mentoring and coaching.

Technology is a resource primarily used for training and in the service area. Service employees are linked to each of the manufacturer's databases and have access to sophisticated on-line reference manuals. They are connected to nationwide databases that have background information on the history of the car, as well as customer history. This allows for a more detailed, efficient, and expedient service call and better customer service. Ford Star is a satellite training initiative that allows employees to remain at the dealership while receiving training. Employees can even take the required tests and receive their scores via the Internet. This lends convenience for employees being trained.

The attitude of customer responsiveness holds true for complaints. Employees echoed the same sentiment: "If you receive it, handle it. If you can't handle it, find someone who can until the problem is solved." Employees explained that complaints are an information resource for them, and that they utilize the information to improve services.

Cherner boasts a low turnover rate, estimated at approximately 10 per cent. In fact, an average employee will remain with Cherner for 10 years. The General Manager has been with Cherner for 29 years. This low turnover is attributed to the family-oriented atmosphere, competitive wages, and knowledge that the jobs at Cherner are secure (as Cherner does not have a history of layoffs).

One challenge to this positive environment has been a recent decision to respond to customer and manufacturer desires to operate on Saturdays. As such, employees who used to be off each weekend now find themselves working on some Saturdays. In an effort to reduce employee burnout or turnover that such a change may produce, Cherner offers special incentives to these employees. For example, an employee who works on Saturday may choose to take the following Monday off (service advisors can take Friday) or to be paid for an extra day of work at overtime rates. Management also provides lunch for employees who work on Saturday.

Cherner focuses on outcomes rather than the process. Cherner offers its vehicle repair customers a shuttle back to work, within a reasonable distance, or to the transit station. However, Cherner recognizes that because of local traffic conditions, offering this service during evening rush hour is counterproductive. Therefore, customers are reimbursed for cab fare back to Cherner when traveling from the transit station to Cherner to pick up a vehicle during evening rush hour. While Cherner could have told customers that the shuttle does not run during rush hour and that transportation would have to be arranged on their own or during non-rush hours, Cherner went the extra mile with customers and found a mutually beneficial way of providing this service.

Cherner aims to exceed customer expectations. When customers have their vehicles at Cherner to be serviced, they are provided with complementary car washes. Cherner proclaims that the benefits of customer service delivery are happier customers, high employee morale, employee and customer loyalty, free advertising (word of mouth), and sales generation. "If you do it right the first time, you won't have to do it again." This is the premise from which they operate. Satisfaction the first time results in not having to spend more labour hours rectifying a situation. This, in turn, makes daily business operations more fluid and service more efficient. Satisfaction the first time also enhances the dealership's community reputation as that of a professional, people-oriented business. This business stance generates a larger customer base. High employee morale is also a benefit of good customer service. Employees take pride in their work.

The costs to Cherner for delivering great customer service include employee incentive costs, salaries, and bonuses; training costs; car wash expenses; shuttle service expenses; and write-off costs for services performed but not charged to the customer.

As part of its external customer service strategy, the Child Support Division in Texas has developed a programme called *Compact with Texans,* which outlines the vision, guiding principles, and goals of the division and explains how external customers can continue to provide feedback on child support.

The guiding principles are:

- Always do what is best for the child, by putting children first.
- Treat everyone with dignity, respect, honesty, and courtesy.
- Walk in the customer's shoes—have empathy.
- Be a leader in doing the right thing, not just in doing things right.
- Participate and contribute in finding solutions—work as a team.
- Maintain objectivity and be nonjudgmental.
- Respect customer' privacy.
- Bear in mind that the customers' perceptions of reality are their reality.

These principles are designed as the framework for action at the agency and individual levels when serving both internal and external customers. Everyone in the division is provided with a copy of these principles to hang on their office walls, and these principles are also posted in conference rooms and hallways throughout the office. To advance these principles, the customer service action plan addresses:

- Improving access to services and staff by implementing regional call centres; expanding and publicizing the Office of the Attorney General (OAG) Child Support Web site—including online application for services; publicizing the complaint process on posters and the Internet; considering a plan to increase office hours; and putting computers in six office lobbies, on which customers may access some case information as well as conduct job searches.
- Ensuring comprehensive, accurate, and easily accessible information that is easy to understand by recording information about billing and interest, credit bureau reporting, and license suspension laws on a toll-free line; providing telephone access to information about mail-out dates; providing call takers with screen pops; providing parents

with an information packet and video (and also including it on the Web site) about customer expectations, services, procedures, and timeframes when they first enter the system; providing presentations in public forums or for selected groups regarding child support; comprehensively training new employees; and providing staff with information online.

- Ensuring prompt action on new case information and responses to customer requests and inquiries by instituting several policies, including: the service delivery process must begin within 20 days of receiving an application for services; telephone messages must be addressed within 2 business days, and action must be taken within 2 business days of information receipt; actions taken on a case or information received must immediately be documented; responses must be made to written inquiries within 10 days; follow-up efforts to telephone inquiries must be undertaken within 15 business days; automated wage withholdings must be acted upon within 2 business days of receiving information about a new employer; either customers are seen when they walk in or appointments must be scheduled to occur within 10 days of the customer's request. Additionally, prompt action is actualized by improving the automated computer system and allowing parents to make address changes on an automated toll free line.
- Improving accuracy and quality by revising forms, standardized letters, and publications as necessary to ensure that they are clear and current and that they use plain language; training all central office staff in writing techniques; training managers in leadership development; creating a compliment-tracking system; establishing an employee recognition programme (including revising performance plans and defining merit raise criteria); providing automated management reports; conducting a workload study; sharing best practices; and creating a customer service advisory team.
- Treating customers professionally, courteously, and respectfully by pilot testing privacy measures in waiting rooms, providing customer service and other professional training to all staff, creating individual staff training plans, attaching information about court procedures to court notices (including expected wait time), and instituting a regular customer feedback process.

The Child Support Division of the Texas OAG works with mothers, fathers, and legal guardians of children to locate absent parents; establish paternity; establish, enforce, and adjust child and medical support orders; and collect and distribute the money associated with these orders. They have over 1 million active cases.

In 1997, the Texas legislature mandated the Sunset Advisory Commission to review the OAG Child Support Division to determine whether the OAG should continue to administer the State's child support programme. Legislators were receiving too many complaints about the Division from constituents. The Sunset Commission conducted its review in 1998 and recommended that the OAG continue to administer the programme for a 2-year probationary period. The Commission made a number of recommendations for improving the programme. The highest priority was improving customer service and, in particular, accessibility. Too often, customers needing information about their cases could not get through to staff for information. Of the 1.5 million calls a month that child support received, only 14 per cent of those who wished to speak with staff could do so. Thousands of calls each day were abandoned. A customer service survey revealed that 48 per cent of customers were dissatisfied.

Shortly after the Commission issued its report, a new Attorney General took office. He hired a new Deputy Assistant Attorney General for child support, and they both made customer service a top priority, with answering the phones as the number one objective. A full-time staff person was hired to develop the customer service strategy and action plan. The process included focus groups with internal and external customers, a customer satisfaction survey, and an employee satisfaction survey, as well as and soliciting input from various special interest groups.

Customers said that they were most concerned with obtaining timely and accurate information, preserving their personal dignity, and being respected. Employees wanted empowerment and discretion.

To make the plan "stick," the administration realised that they needed to communicate, improve staff development, measure performance, and increase employee accountability and recognition. Quarterly, the regions report on their progress through action plans.

In the quarter from March through May 2001, regional progress reports revealed that regions:

- Maintained telephone answer rates at approximately 95 per cent.
- Implemented external customer surveys and suggestion boxes.
- Sought employee input through surveys, suggestion boxes, and staff meetings.
- Rewarded employees with merit increases, promotions, donated food, gift certificates, tickets, and special events, as well as via a recognition board or e-mail commendations.
- Implemented flex and optional work schedules.
- Focused on improving relationships with other agencies/individuals within the system, especially court personnel (one region instituted court greeters).

- Instituted a job pool to reduce hiring delays.
- Implemented quality control procedures such as "mystery callers."
- Maintained on-the-job training efforts.
- Improved office appearance.

Overall, after the first year of implementation, a general customer satisfaction survey revealed a statewide increase in customer satisfaction to 63 per cent (up from 52 per cent in 1999). Furthermore, in Spring 2001, a survey of custodial parents who had recently had an establishment performed reported an 82 per cent satisfaction rate. Intuitively, management claims that staff stress levels are down and that morale and job satisfaction are on the rise.

Efforts to improve customer service are continuing through the undertaking of the "e-degree" project (in which employees use educational leave and agency computers to take up to 3 hours of online college-level courses per semester) and the WorkSMART model office-reengineering project. The WorkSMART project is in the planning stages. WorkSMART embodies an ideal for service in which customers gain empowerment over their cases through increased access to online information online.

Customers will be able to electronically enter their case into the child support system via a streamlined application process, use a graphical roadmap to know the status of their case, and review frequently asked questions and answers while experiencing shorter processing times. Much of the detailed development of these action plans has been pushed down to the regional level (e.g., training strategies, measurement strategies, reward systems, and customer input mechanisms). Texas is working on maintaining consistency in these procedures while allowing each region some discretion. This strategy was designed to increase buy-in and ownership at the regional level. As a result of this autonomy, different offices may vary in their customer service strategies and levels of success. While executive management has found this autonomic setup effective, the downside is that its varied measurement strategies do not lend themselves to easy statewide assessment.

At the beginning of the customer service implementation, the Director closed the central call centre and created regional call centres. At the regional level, managers focus on getting the phones answered and supporting employees—through training and cross-training, by clearly outlining expectations, through consistent management, by serving as role models, by rewarding good work and good customer service, and by encouraging open communication.

A regional call centre manager stressed the importance of his own attitude (attitude filters from the top down, according to this manager) as a means of setting the tone of the office and keeping employees productive and willing to provide the best services possible. In support of this belief, every day he walks around the office and greets each employee, offers assistance, provides answers to questions, and maintains an open-door policy. He emphasizes results and delivering a consistent message. As long as the center's goals are being met, he offers flexibility (e.g., in scheduling lunch breaks and requests for time off). He has instituted strategies to cope with the unit when it is not fully staffed, by flexing lunch schedules and by having management serve as backup. He tries to handle most problems by talking with all of the staff instead of isolating an individual. However, individual accountability does play an important part in the management strategy. This particular call centre succeeds both in meeting its telephone answering goals (staff and managers answer 96 per cent of all incoming calls) and in maintaining low employee turnover (approximately 22 per cent in the region, but of those who have left, every person still works within the Texas Child Support Division via transfer or promotion).

Call centre management has trained employees that their role is to accurately handle as many incoming phone calls as possible. The purpose is to free up time child support officers (CSOs) to be able to process cases. Brief interviews with frontline call centre staff suggested that call centre employees and managers share a rapport and can rely on one another for help or answers to questions. Two people said that the best part of their job is the feeling of helping someone. Another person took pride in thoroughly addressing all of the callers' issues so as to deflect calls for CSOs. One call taker even assigns "ticklers" on his calendar so that he knows to check the system to make certain that appropriate action has been taken on a call he has received.

Call takers reported some challenges, including balancing the target talk time (about 4 minutes) with providing thorough information to the caller, dealing with callers who are not truthful, and handling concerns that caseworkers may not be able to perform requested follow-up. However, the call centre statistics show that 95 per cent of calls are answered, the average wait time since inception of the regional call centres is approximately 30 seconds, and that call takers spend an average of 3 minutes of talk time per call.

Management places the same emphasis on hiring call centre staff as they do in hiring CSOs. Call centre staff are paid at the CSO level. Some call centre staff were hired from field offices, as well as from county child support offices, and others were hired with customer service backgrounds but with no child support experience. Management for the six call centres includes personnel from the central office, some of whom had worked in field offices and others from general hiring pools.

All child support staff receive 2 days of basic training in customer service, even those personnel serving internal customers only. New staff also receive this training. During this training, instructors stress that the Division's guiding principles apply to both internal and external customer service. Managers receive advanced customer service training on how to support staff to deliver great customer service. Training is offered regionally, and therefore staff from all levels train together. In addition to customer service training, staff are trained in how to deal with hostile customers. The next initiative is to design and implement a follow-up course in customer service.

Motivation is addressed on a number of levels:

- Staff participated in the internal focus groups that led to the Compact with Texans. This participation generated introspection, and executive personnel believe that this introspection may be a positive motivation.
- Additionally, some regions cross train and cross work. For example, personnel in Dallas train on both call centre and field office tasks and then, depending on the workload, staff can assist in either location. This additional knowledge helps the employees in one location understand the impact of their actions on their coworkers.
- The call centre manager sets high expectations of staff and strives to provide employees with the training, information, and resources needed to meet them.
- The customer service culture has clearly been established as a permanent priority. Executive staff stress the importance of adhering to the customer service philosophy and individual accountability, and staff are aware that they can be dismissed for a lack of customer service.
- Performance plans include customer service measures and clearly outline performance expectations and standards.
- Staff are rewarded with merit increases, promotions, food, gift certificates, tickets, and special events, as well as via a recognition board or e-mail commendations. (Worth noting: during one office recognition celebration, staff from another field office came to offer phone support so that everyone could attend the event.)

According to Texas Child Support Division executives, one of the keys to the improvement of customer service in Texas child support is technology. In particular, six regional call centres were established and were equipped with technology and systems to improve efficiency, information availability, and information exchange. The call centres handle approximately 25 per cent of all customer service contacts.

First, a model- the Erlang C Formula-was used to understand the relationship between the amount of incoming calls, time taken to handle those calls, wait time for callers, and number of call centre staff. With this formula, executive personnel determined the number of staff needed given call volume, target maximum wait times, and handling times for calls. Initially, the number of required staff calculated by this method was higher than that of actual staff available for the effort. As a result, Texas had to address another factor in the formula-handle time.

Efficiencies in call handling have been gained through a number of innovations:

- Calls are automatically disseminated to call takers based on availability of their lines. Once a call taker hangs up, the call taker has a pre-set amount of time to perform call wrap up activities, and then the line automatically becomes part of the call queue once again. (Previously, call takers had to proactively re-set their "ready" buttons.) The system includes a way to put a line on "break" as necessary.
- Screen pops were designed to utilize the incoming phone number to pull up a case, rather than requiring the call taker to obtain a case or social security number upon answering the call. This feature saves an average of 15 seconds per call.
- A Graphical User Interface ("GUI") screen was developed to contain the core information used on typical calls to child support. This feature was created so that call takers spend less time flipping from screen to screen. This feature also can save an average of 76 seconds per call. Additionally, data entry options on GUI save additional data entry time-about 92 seconds per call.

The database of cases (TXCSES) includes a diary function that permits staff members, whether in a call centre or field office, to make a notation on the case so that anyone who opens the case will be current on action taken or contact made on the case. It also allows staff to e-mail one another directly. Another useful feature allows call centre staff to mark the correspondence or case so that the call taker receives a reminder notice to perform follow-up.

Still other call centre technology allows call centre staff to be acutely aware of the number of calls coming in and the length of wait time. First, a digital light board posted in the office provides this real-time information. Additionally, a computer tracking system provides aggregate statistics on the calls and is located in the break room.

Intellicenter software is used by call centre managers to provide quality control by periodically screening calls and coaching staff, as appropriate. At the call centre, everyone agreed that technology has made their jobs easier.

Another technological improvement for customer service has been the interactive Web site. On the site, customers can provide information, obtain payment information, and make complaints. Customers are using the site for all of these things. The Web site was designed to reduce the number of phone calls, while increasing information access for customers. Web site use has been increasing since inception. In August 2001, there were 196,403 transactions from individuals who had entered their pin number and were actually accessing case information. On average, the site receives 3,967 hits daily. Ten per cent of all customer service contacts are over the Web site. The Web site won an award from Computer World Magazine.

SPECIFIC GOOD OR SERVICE IN MARKETING

The consumer market is composed of individuals who buy a specific good or service. Rarely does one product interest the entire population. This statement applies even to staples, such as sugar, flour, and salt. A small percentage of households do not eat these products, so even if a company did target the entire population, not everyone would be a potential consumer. The same statistical truth applies to cultural products. However, because of the extremely fragmented nature of the cultural sector, some distinctions are in order. For example, looking at this sector as a whole, it can be said that nearly 100% of the population consumes one type of cultural product or another. Indeed, in its broadest sense, the cultural sector encompasses everything from the performing arts to heritage, compact disks, movies, book and magazine publishing, and radio and television, with each of these disciplines appropriating a more or less important share of global demand.

In Canada, for example, statistics1 show that 37.0% of families attend a performing arts event at least once a year: movies 62.2%, museums and art galleries 32.9%. In the United States the figures for cultural consumption are: classical music 15.6%, opera 4.7%, musicals 24.5%, plays 15.8%, ballet 5.8%, art museums 34.5%, and historical parks 46.9%.2 In Australia3 the figures are: musical theatre 19.3%, classical music 7.7%, festivals 21.9%, concerts 23%, and museums 27.8%. Of course, within each of these sectors, consumers cluster just as to specific poles of interest.

This leads to sharper market segmentation. The consumer makes a discriminating choice among various cultural products to acquire or consume the type of product desired. The distribution of consumers just as to various market segments differs in both time and space. Markets undergo and reflect the influence of opinion leaders, trends, tastes, and societal characteristics.

Markets also vary from country to country just as to different social structures. Over the past 40 years, various surveys focusing on the sociodemographic profile of consumers of cultural products have been carried out in nearly every European country as well as in Canada, the United States, Australia, and Japan.4 It is fascinating to note that, regardless of whether the surveys were conducted in the 1970s, 1980s, or 1990s, they all obtained the same attendance rates and the same sociodemographic profiles.

Differences in the measuring tools used can sometimes make it difficult to compare countries; nonetheless, these studies have consistently and systematically revealed strong polarization of audiences between high art and popular culture across all countries over the past four decades. They show, for example, that cultural products catering to high art attract educated consumers, whereas those catering to popular culture draw on all segments of the population, in accordance with the relative weight of each. The proportion of university graduates making up Canadian audiences, for example, ranges between 50% and 70% for high art, compared with 10% to 25% for popular culture. By way of comparison, the overall percentage of university graduates in Canada is 25%. Similar results have been found in other countries, most notably in France5 but also in Russia, where university graduates make up 50% of performing arts audiences but only 7% of the general population. Other sociodemographic variables are also linked to attendance, including average income and type of occupation. It should be pointed out once again that this profile is based on averages. Less-educated individuals with lower income may be great consumers of culture, as is the case for students and those specialized or working in the cultural milieu.

Indeed, it is well known that, as a rule many people active in the arts are highly educated yet so ill paid that they struggle to stay above the poverty line. On the other hand, there are people with both very high salaries and very high educational levels who are not interested in the arts and gladly keep their distance. Four factors are known to influence an individual's penchant for complex cultural products: family values that encourage or discourage high art; the educational milieu and the value it places on high art; the fact of having attended performances or visited museums as a child; and amateur art practice.

A more detailed analysis of the typical cultural consumer's traits reveals other nuances based on the different disciplines. For example, dance audiences are relatively younger and even more female in composition than those of the other performing arts; similarly, more women than men read novels, although a larger proportion of men read daily newspapers. In the film sector, there are two very different segments of avid cinema-goers; one of these segments is dominated by a young clientele, while the other is made up of educated people. The majority of consumers in the film sector belong to one or the other of these two segments.

BUSINESS BUYING BEHAVIOUR

The business market is comprised of organizations that, in some form, are involved in the manufacturer, distribution or support of products or services sold or otherwise provided to other organizations. The amount of purchasing undertaken in the business market easily dwarfs the total spending by consumers. Because the business market is so large it draws the interest of millions of companies worldwide that market exclusively to business customers.

For these marketers understanding how businesses make purchase decisions is critical to their organizations' marketing efforts. In some ways understanding the business market is not as complicated as understanding the consumer market.

For example, in certain business markets purchase decisions hinge on the outcome of a bidding process between competitors offering similar products and services. In these cases the decision to buy is often whittled down to one concern–who has the lowest price. Thus, unlike consumer markets, where building a recognizable brand is very important, for many purchase situations in the business market this is not the case.

However, in many other ways business buying is much more complicated. For instance, the demand by businesses for products and services is affected by consumer purchases and because so many organizations may have a part in creating consumer purchases, a small swing in consumer demand can create big changes in business purchasing.

Automobile purchases are a good example. If consumer demand for cars increases many companies connected with the automobile industry will also see demand for their products and services increase. Under these conditions companies will ratchet up their operations to ensure demand is met, which invariably will lead to new purchases by a large number of companies. In fact, it is conceivable that an increase of just one or two per cent for consumer demand can increase business demand for products and services by five or more per cent. Unfortunately, the opposite is true if demand declines. Trying to predict these swings requires businesses to not only understand their immediate customers but also the end user, which as suggested, discuss, may be well down the supply chain from where the business operates.

Principles of Marketing Tutorials discusses the unique characteristics of the business market. As suggested, see that marketers must appeal to business customers in ways that are distinct from how they would approach consumers. While marketers selling to other businesses operate with most of the same marketing tools used by marketers of consumer products, how they employ these tools to reach their marketing objectives may be quite different.

SUPPLY CHAIN MARKET

The supply chain consists of mostly for-profit companies engaged in activities involving product creation and delivery. Essentially the chain represents major steps needed to manufacture a product that will eventually be sold as a final product.

Each member of the supply chain purchases products and services enabling them to carry out its business objectives. When making purchase decisions supply chain members may be motivated by such factors as: product cost, return on investment, assurance of consistent supply, reciprocity with supplying firm, and much more. Examples of purchasing occurring in the supply chain include: manufacturing and plant equipment, information technology, office supplies, professional business services, etc.

In the table we arbitrarily identify five main categories of supply chain members primarily based on the stage at which they contribute to the manufacturing process. However, it is conceivable that these categories can be further divided in order to flush out more specific activities.

Supply Chain Member	What They Do	Example
Raw Material Suppliers	These companies are generally considered the first stage in the supply chain and provide basic products through mining, harvesting, fishing, etc., that are key ingredients in the production of higher-order products.	Copper is mined and extracted from copper ore. Copper is then refined to remove impurities.
Processed Materials or Basic Component Manufacturers	Firms at this level use raw materials to produce more advanced materials or products contained within more advanced components.	Copper is purchased by electrical wire manufacturers.
Advanced Component Manufacturers	These companies use basic components to produce products that offer a significant function needed within a larger product.	Electrical wire is purchased by a manufacturer of electrical power supplies.
Product Manufacturers	This market consists of companies that purchase both basic and advanced components and then assemble these components into a final product designated for a user. These products may or may not be sold as stand-alone products. Some may be included within larger products.	Power supplies are purchased by manufacturers of desktop computers.
Support Service Firms	These companies offer services at almost any point in the supply chain and also to the business user market. Some services are directly related to the product while others focus on areas of the business not directly related to production.	Distribution companies, such as truck firms and storage facilities, assist in moving products from one supply chain member to another. However, in most cases they do not take ownership of products that pass through the supply chain.

BUSINESS USER MARKETS

Besides selling final products and services to supply chain companies, several additional user markets also make purchases either for their own consumption or they buy with the intention of redistributing to others.

Market	What They Do	Considerations When Buying	What They Buy
Government	Made up of Federal, State, Local and International governments. They use purchases to assist with the functioning of the government that may include redistributing to others.	Mostly require suppliers to be approved, meet specifications and to bid for purchases.	Defense equipment, heavy equipment for public works projects, office supplies, pharmaceuticals, etc.
Not-For-Profit	Organizations whose tax structure precludes earning profits from operations and whose missions tend to be oriented to assisting others.	Look for purchases that will fit within tight budgetary restrictions and also within the mission of the organization.	Office equipment and supplies, office rental, professional services, etc.
Reseller	Also called distributors, these companies operate in both the consumer and the business markets. Their function involves purchasing large volumes of products from manufacturers and selling these products in smaller quantities. Includes wholesalers, retailers and industrial distributors.	Seek products that are of interest to the reseller's customers. Other issues include how delivery is handled and whether the supplier offers incentives to help the reseller promote the product.	Consumer and industrial products to be redistributed to other businesses and co

In these purchase situations the buyer generally does not radically change the product from its form when it was purchased from a Product Manufacturer. While technically these markets are also part of the supply chain, members of the business user market do not, in most cases, engage or directly assist in production activities.

BUSINESS VS CONSUMER MARKETS

For marketers, the selling environment of business markets present uniquely different circumstances when compared to selling to consumers.

At the beginning of this tutorial we saw two ways in which consumer and business markets differ:

- Business markets are more likely to be price driven than brand driven, and
- Demand in business markets tends to be more volatile than consumer markets.

However, the two markets are dissimilar in other ways requiring marketers to take a different approach when selling to business customers than to consumers.

These differences include:

- How Decisions Are Made
- Existence of Experienced Purchasers
- Time Needed to Make Buying Decision
- Size of Purchases
- Number of Buyers
- Type of Promotional Effort Needed to Reach Buyer

BUYING DIFFERENCES

Buying Centre Decisions

In the consumer market a very large percentage of purchase decisions are made by a single person.

As we discussed in the Consumer Buying Behaviour tutorial, there are situations in which multiple people may be involved in a consumer purchase decision, such as a child influencing a parent to choose a certain brand of cereal or a husband and wife deciding together to buy a house, but most of the time purchases are individual decisions. The business market is significantly different.

While single person purchasing is not unusual, especially within a small company, a significant percentage of business buying, especially within larger organizations, requires the input of many.

In the marketing literature those associated with the purchase decision are known to be part of a Buying Centre, which consists of individuals within an organization that perform one or more of the following roles:

- *Buyer*: Responsible for dealing with suppliers and placing orders
- *Decider*: Has the power to make the final purchase decision
- *Influencer*: Has the ability to affect what is ordered such as setting order specifications
- *User*: Those who will actually use the product when it is received

- *Initiator*: Any Buying Centre member who is the first to determine that a need exists
- *Gatekeeper*: Anyone who controls access to other Buying Centre members

For marketers confronting a Buying Centre it is important to first identify who plays what role. Once identified the marketer must address the needs of each member, which may differ significantly. For instance, the Decider, who may be the company president wants to make sure the purchase will not negatively affect the company's bottom line while the Buyer wants to be assured the product will be delivered on time. Thus, the way each Buying Centre member is approached and marketed to requires careful planning in order to address the unique needs of each member.

Experienced Purchasers

As noted in the discussion of the Buying Centre, organizations often employ purchasing agents or professional buyers whose job is to negotiate the best deals for their company. Unlike consumers, who often lack information when making purchase decisions, professional buyers are generally as knowledgeable about the product and the industry as the marketer who is selling to them.

Decision Making Time

Depending on the product, business purchase decisions can drag on for an extensive period. Unlike consumer markets where impulse purchasing is rampant, the number of people involved in business purchase decisions results in decisions taking weeks, months or even years.

Size of Purchases

For products that are regularly used and frequently purchased, businesses will often buy a larger volume at one time compared to consumer purchases. Because of this business purchasers often demand price breaks for higher order levels.

Type of Promotions

Companies who primarily target consumers often use mass advertising methods to reach an often widely dispersed market. For business-to-business marketers the size of individual orders, along with a smaller number of buyers, makes person-to-person contact by sales representatives a more effective means of promotion.

TYPES OF BUSINESS PURCHASE DECISIONS

While it would appear business customers face the same four purchase situations faced by consumers, the nature of the business market has led many marketing academics to group business purchase situations into only three categories. The reason is that the idea of a minor order may not hold as well in the business market, where buyers tend to place larger orders and where suppliers' marketing efforts are directed toward the most profitable buyers.

- *Straight Re-Purchase*: These purchase situations involve routine ordering. In most cases buyers simply reorder the same products or services that were previously purchased. In fact, many larger companies have programmed re-purchases into an automated ordering system that initiates electronic orders when inventory falls a certain pre-determined level. For the supplier benefiting from the re-purchase this situation is ideal since the purchaser is not looking to evaluate other products. For competitors who are not getting the order it may require extensive marketing efforts to persuade the buyer to consider other product or service options.
- *Modified Re-Purchase*: These purchases occur when products or services previously considered a straight re-purchase are for some reason now under a re-evaluation process. There are many reasons why a product is moved to the status of a modified re-purchase. Some of these reasons include: end of purchase contract period, change in who is involved in making the purchase, supplier is removed from an approved suppliers list, mandate from top level of organization to re-evaluate all purchasing, or strong marketing effort by competitors. In this circumstance the incumbent supplier faces the same challenges they may have faced when they initially convinced the buyer to make the purchase. For competitors the door is now open and they must work hard to make sure their message is heard by those in charge of the purchase decision.
- *New Task Purchase*: As the name suggests, these purchases are ones the buyer has never or rarely made before. In some ways new task purchases can be considered as either minor or major depending on the total cost or overall importance of the purchase. In either case the buyer will spend considerably more time evaluating alternatives. For example, if faced with a major new task purchase, which often involves complex items, such as computer systems, buildings, robotic assembly lines, etc., the purchase cycle from first recognizing the need to placement of the order may be months or even years.

DISTRIBUTION PACKAGING AND CUSTOMER MANAGEMENT

This relates to the package the final customer receives in exchange for their payment. When the final customer makes a purchase he or she is initially exposed to the Primary Package – the outermost container that is seen and touched by the final customer. This primary package can be further divided into the following:

- *First-Level Package:* This is packaging that holds the actual product (e.g., Tylenol Bottle). In some cases this packaging is minimal since it only serves to protect the product. For instance, certain frozen food products are sold to consumers in a cardboard box with the product itself contained in a plastic bag found inside the box. This plastic bag represents the first-level package. In other cases frozen food products are sold in the plastic bag that contains the product. In these cases the plastic bag is both first-level package and the primary package for convey product information.
- *Second-Level Package:* In some cases the first-level package is surrounded by one or more outer packages (e.g., box holding the Tylenol Bottle). This second-level package may act as the primary package for the product.
- *Package Inserts*: Marketers use a variety of other methods to communicate with customers after they open the product package. These methods are often inserted within, or sometimes on, the product's package. Insertions include information such as instruction manuals and warranty cards, promotional incentives such as coupons, and items that add value such as recipes and software.

This packaging is used to transport the customer package through the supply chain. It generally holds multiple customer packages and also offers a higher level of damage protection than that of customer packaging.

Factors to Consider

Packaging decisions are important for several reasons including:

- *Protection:* Packaging is used to protect the product from damage during shipping and handling, and to lessen spoilage if the protect is exposed to air or other elements.
- *Visibility*: Packaging design is used to capture customers' attention as they are shopping or glancing through a catalog or website. This is particularly important for customers who are not familiar with the product and in situations, such as those found in grocery stores, where a product must stand out among thousands of other products. Packaging designs that standout are more likely to be remembered on future shopping trips.
- *Added Value:* Packaging design and structure can add value to a product. For instance, benefits can be obtained from package structures that make the product easier to use while stylistic designs can make the product more attractive to display in the customer's home.
- *Distributor Acceptance:* Packaging decisions must not only be accepted by the final customer, they may also have to be accepted by distributors

who sell the product for the supplier. For instance, a retailer may not accept packages unless they conform to requirements they have for storing products on their shelves.

- *Cost:* Packaging can represent a significant portion of a product's selling price. For example, it is estimated that in the cosmetics industry the packaging cost of some products may be as high as 40% of a product's selling price. Smart packaging decisions can help reduce costs and possibly lead to higher profits.
- *Expensive to Create:* Developing new packaging can be extremely expensive. The costs involved in creating new packaging include: graphic and structural design, production, customer testing, possible destruction of leftover old packaging, and possible advertising to inform customer of the new packaging.
- *Long Term Decision:* When companies create a new package it is most often with the intention of having the design on the market for an extended period of time. In fact, changing a product's packaging too frequently can have negative effects since customers become conditioned to locate the product based on its package and may be confused if the design is altered.
- *Environmental or Legal Issues:* Packaging decisions must also include an assessment of its environmental impact especially for products with packages that are frequently discarded. Packages that are not easily bio-degradable could draw customer and possibly governmental concern. Also, caution must be exercised in order to create packages that do not infringe on intellectual property, such as copyrights, trademarks or patents, held by others.

Labelling

Most packages, whether final customer packaging or distribution packaging, are imprinted with information intended to assist the customer. For consumer products, labelling decisions are extremely important for the following reasons.

- Labels serve to capture the attention of shoppers. The use of catchy words may cause strolling customers to stop and evaluate the product.
- The label is likely to be the first thing a new customer sees and thus offers their first impression of the product.
- The label provides customers with product information to aid their purchase decision or help improve the customer's experience when using the product (e.g., recipes).
- Labels generally include a universal product codes (UPC) and, in some cases, radio frequency identification (RFID) tags, that make it easy for resellers, such as retailers, to checkout customers and manage inventory.

- For companies serving international markets or diverse cultures within a single country, bilingual or multilingual labels may be needed.
- In some countries many products, including food and pharmaceuticals, are required by law to contain certain labels such as listing ingredients, providing nutritional information or including usage warning information.

CATEGORIES OF CONSUMER PRODUCTS

In addition to categorizing by type of offering, most products intended for consumer use can be further categorized by how frequently and where they are purchased.

- *Convenience Products:* These are products that appeal to a very large market segment. They are generally consumed regularly and purchased frequently. Examples include most household items such as food, cleaning products, and personal care products. Because of the high purchase volume, pricing per item tends to be relatively low and consumers often see little value in shopping around since additional effort yields minimal savings. From the marketer's perspective the low price of convenience products means that profit per unit sold is very low. In order to make high profits marketers must sell in large volume. Consequently, marketers attempt to distribute these products in mass through as many retail outlets as possible.
- *Shopping Products:* These are products consumers purchase and consume on a less frequent schedule compared to convenience products. Consumers are willing to spend more time locating these products since they are relatively more expensive than convenience products and because these may possess additional psychological benefits for the purchaser, such as raising their perceived status level within their social group. Examples include many clothing products, personal services, electronic products, and household furnishings. Because consumers are purchasing less frequently and are willing to shop to locate these products, the target market is much smaller than that of convenience goods. Consequently, marketers often are more selective when choosing distribution outlets to sell their products.
- *Specialty Products:* These are products that tend to carry a high price tag relative to convenience and shopping products. Consumption may occur at about the same rate as shopping products but consumers are much more selective. In fact, in many cases consumers know in advance which product they prefer and will not shop to compare

products. But they may shop at retailers that provide the best value. Examples include high-end luxury automobiles, expensive champagne, and celebrity hair care experts. The target markets are generally very small and outlets selling the products are very limited to the point of being exclusive.

In addition to the three main categories above, products are classified in at least two additional ways:

- *Emergency Products*: These are products a customer seeks due to sudden events and for which pre-purchase planning is not considered. Often the decision is one of convenience (e.g., whatever works to fix a problem) or personal fulfilment (e.g., perceived to improve purchaser's image).
- *Unsought Products:* These are products whose purchase is unplanned by the consumer but occur as a result of marketer's actions. Such purchase decisions are made when the customer is exposed to promotional activity, such as a salesperson's persuasion or purchase incentives like special discounts offered to certain online shoppers. These promotional activities often lead customers to engage in Impulse Purchasing.

CATEGORIES OF BUSINESS PRODUCTS

The amount spent on business purchasing far exceeds consumer purchasing. Products sold within the b-to-b market fall into one of the following categories:

- *Raw Materials:* These are products obtained through mining, harvesting, fishing, etc., that are key ingredients in the production of higher-order products.
- *Processed Materials:* These are products created through the processing of basic raw materials. In some cases the processing refines original raw materials while in other cases the process combines different raw materials to create something new. For instance, several crops including corn and sugar cane can be processed to create ethanol which has many uses including as a fuel to power car and truck engines.
- *Equipment:* These are products used to help with production or operations activities. Examples range from conveyor belts used on an assembly line to large buildings used to house the headquarters staff of a multi-national company.
- *Basic Components:* These are products used within more advanced components. These are often built with raw material or processed material. Electrical wire is an example.
- *Advanced Components:* These are products that use basic components

to produce products that offer a significant function needed within a larger product. Yet by itself an advanced component does not stand alone as a final product. In computers the motherboard would be an example since it contains many basic components but without the inclusion of other products (e.g., memory chips, microprocessor, etc.) would have little value.

- *Product Component*: These are products used in the assembly of a final product though these could also function as stand alone products. Dice included as part of a children's board game would be an example.
- *MRO (Maintenance, Repair and Operating) Products*: These are products used to assist with the operation of the organization but are not directly used in producing goods or services. Office supplies, parts for a truck fleet and natural gas to heat a factory would fall into this category.

COMPONENTS OF A PRODUCT

On the surface it seems a product is simply a marketing offering, whether tangible or intangible, that someone wants to purchase and consume. In which case one might believe product decisions are focused exclusively on designing and building the consumable elements of goods, services or ideas.

For instance, one might think the key product decision for a manufacturer of floor cleaners is to focus on creating a formula that cleans more effectively. In actuality, while decisions related to the consumable parts of the product are extremely important, the Total Product consists of more than what is consumed. The total product offering and the decisions facing the marketer can be broken down into three key parts:

Core Benefits

Consider what we have talked about many times in this tutorial; people make buying decisions that satisfy their needs. While many needs are addressed by the consumption of a product or service, some needs are not. For instance, customers may need to be perceived highly by other members of their group or need a product that is easy to use or need a risk-free purchase. In each of these cases, and many more, the core product itself is the benefit the customer receives from using the product.

In some cases these core benefits are offered by the product itself (e.g., floor cleaner) while in other cases the benefit is offered by other aspects of the product (e.g., the can containing the floor cleaner that makes it easier to spread the product). Consequently, at the very heart of all product decisions is determining the key or core benefits a product will provide. From this decision, the rest of the product offering can be developed.

Actual Product

The core benefits are offered through the components that make up the actual product the customer purchases. For instance, when a consumer returns home from shopping at the grocery store and takes a purchased item out of her shopping bag, the actual product is the item she holds in her hand. Within the actual product is the consumable product, which can be viewed as the main good, service or idea the customer is buying.

For instance, while toothpaste may come in a package that makes dispensing it easy, the Consumable Product is the paste that is placed on a toothbrush. But marketers must understand that while the consumable product is, in most cases, the most critical of all product decisions, the actual product includes many separate product decisions including product features, branding, packaging, labelling, and more. Full coverage of several of these important areas is provided later in this tutorial.

Augmented Product

Marketers often surround their actual products with goods and services that provide additional value to the customer's purchase. While these factors may not be key reasons leading customers to purchase (i.e., not core benefits), for some the inclusion of these items strengthens the purchase decision while for others failure to include these may cause the customer not to buy. Items considered part of the augmented product include:

- *Guarantee:* This provides a level of assurance that the product will perform up to expectations and if not the company marketing the product will support the customer's decision to replace, have it repaired or return for a refund.
- *Warranty*: This offers customers a level of protection that often extends past the guarantee period to cover repair or replacement of certain product components.
- *Customer Service*: This consists of additional services that support the customer's needs including offering training and assistance via telephone or online.
- *Complementary Products:* The value of some product purchases can be enhanced with add-on products, such as items that make the main product easier to use (e.g., laptop carrybag), enhance styling (e.g., cellphone face plates) or extend functionality (e.g., portable keyboard for PDAs).
- *Accessibility:* How customers obtain the product can affect its perceived value depending on such considerations as how easy it is to obtain (e.g., stocked at nearby store, delivered directly to office), the speed at which it can be obtained, and the likelihood it will be available when needed.

KEY PRODUCT DECISIONS

The actual product is designed to provide the core benefits sought by the target market. The marketer offers these benefits through a combination of factors that make up the actual product. These factors include:

Consumable Product Features

Features are characteristics of a product that offer benefits to the customer. In most cases, the most important features are those associated with the consumable product since they are the main reason a customer makes a purchase. For this tutorial we separate the benefits of consumable product features into two groups: functional and psychological.

COMPETITIVE ENVIRONMENT IN CUSTOMER INTEGRATION MANAGEMENT (CIM)

Customer Interaction Management helps organisations execute effective and efficient interactions with their customers and prospects. These interactions must be consistent and tailored to the customer needs, based on the segment of the customer, the service required and the used channel.

IMPORTANT

Today's competitive environment requires companies to ensure that the customer has a consistent experience across interactions and channels, giving him a clear sense of brand value and differentiation.

Customer Interaction specialists at Deloitte focus on the following offerings:

- *Customer Experience*: We support the organisation in describing and assessing the experience of its customer or prospect across their lifecycle, providing actionable recommendations for enriching the customer experience.
- *Multi-channel interaction management*: We provide advice regarding the ways the organisation can best reach its customers. By implementing right-channelling, we help companies maximize interaction value in a cost-efficient way.
- *Service Organisational design*: Our organisational design methods consider people and processes in order to put in place the right service models, contact flows and escalation rules.
- *Service request and SLA management*: We provide methods and tools to improve service request management and implement the appropriate service level agreements.
- *Contact Centre Implementation and Transformation*: Deloitte has a proven track-record in implementing multi-channel interaction centres, including integration with CRM processes and tools.

PREDICTIVE CUSTOMER INTERACTION MANAGEMENT

Every business needs to efficiently manage outbound and inbound interactions with customers. These interactions can occur through many channels including the web, call centres branch offices, ATMs, and e-mail. With inbound interactions, customers offer their attention. They visit a web site, make a call, or access an ATM because they want something at that moment – information about a product or help with a problem.

These interactions usually present an opportunity to communicate with a customer who is engaged by choice and ready to share information regarding his or her wants and needs. Outbound interactions are typically used to target products to particular customer segments based on analysis of customer data. The success of these interactions – whether through e-mail, direct mail, or other channels – depends to a great extent on the organization's understanding of the customer's wants and needs at the time of the offer. This document describes an architecture that manages inbound and outbound interactions in a consistent manner to present a unified, real-time view of each customer.

Requirements for Effective Customer Interaction Management

The following list summarizes requirements for such an architecture:

- Provides consistent customer interaction management of outbound and inbound communications.
- Addresses the uniqueness and complexities of various inbound and outbound channels. For example, in an inbound call, the business logic might dictate that the CSR should not make an offer if the call time is greater than a given threshold.
- Allows businesses that are aligned along product lines to use both customer knowledge and data mining to publish product propensities.
- Allows customer data to be distributed across multiple systems.
- Combines rules, policies, inferencing, and analytics – both statistical and probabilistic – to produce complex models of reasoning via events, customer data, time, and analytics.
- Leverages existing investment in data mining tools such as SAS, SPSS, and others.
- Handles the low latency requirements of real-time customer interactions with sophisticated caching techniques.
- Provides flexibility, scalability, and high availability.

Key Aspects of Customer Interaction Management

How a business treats customers and manages customer relationships is a key differentiator and is critical to succeeding in highly competitive and dynamic environments.

The solution proposed in this document addresses three important aspects of customer interaction management:

1. Maintaining customer relationships using relationship events over time.
2. Driving up-sell and cross-sell opportunities using both inbound and outbound events.
3. Incorporating a feedback model to calculate the effectiveness of models over macro and micro dimensions.

Architecture

Effective customer interaction management requires an event-driven architecture that is application and database agnostic.

High-level components of such a solution include:

- Channel adapters.
- Customer interaction engine also referred to as a recomm-endation engine
  - Knowledge models maintained by business users.
  - Analytical models maintained by business users or reused from existing investments.
- Virtual data source
  - SOA platform to integrate customer and other information from various data sources. A typical implementation will require integration with customer and product data from operational stores and/or data warehouses

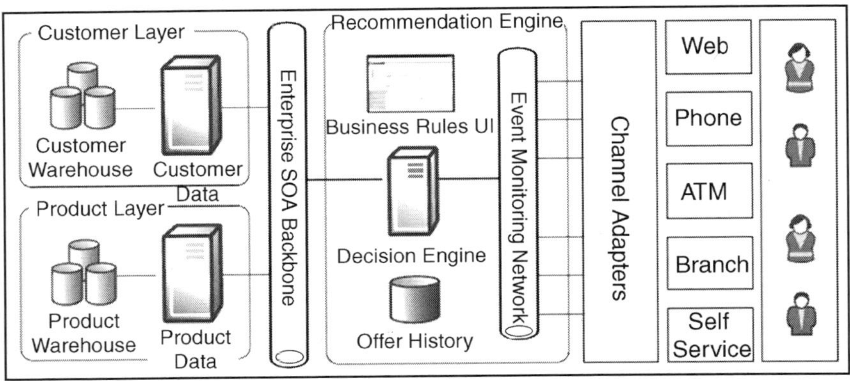

Channel Adapters

In the context of this solution, channel adapters have two key roles:

1. *Sense*: Channel adapters, either intrusively or non-intrusively, publish relevant events to the recommendation engine. The solution contains pre-defined adapters for various technologies used in the channels.

2. *Respond*: Channel adapters provide a mechanism to initiate a dialogue with the customer. The response is inferred and initiated by the recommendation engine to the channel adapters.

Recommendation Engine

The recommendation engine provides the following functions:

- A glossary of terms and vocabulary that form the basis of marketing strategies.
- Integration with channels using events.
- Pattern matching of a set of events with the policies, knowledge, and analytical models to generate a set of responses.
- Generic offers such as "Offer of the Day."
- Maintain history of offers and customer responses.
- A business user interface to create and represent marketing strategies or business "rules" based on the vocabulary of terms and events. TIBCO provides a recommendation engine based on TIBCO BusinessEvents™ software, a market-leading complex event processing application.

Virtual Data Source

The virtual data source integrates all relevant customer and product data. TIBCO BusinessWorks™ is an extensible SOA enablement platform that uses a no-coding approach to developing, deploying, and running integration projects and building serviceoriented architectures. It simplifies some of the more complex implementation issues that are critical for the glue and sequence between connected systems, such as process orchestration and transformation.

Customer Examples

Today's leading retail banks recognize that customers are their most important and strategic asset and are rapidly adopting customer-centric IT strategies to achieve competitive advantage.

This part presents a number of practical examples showing how a real-time, event-driven, multi-channel, application-agnostic architecture delivers immediate value to the retail banking business and a unique banking experience to their customers.

Retail banks have traditionally used customer resource management systems to capture the inbound customer data stream and store the information in a central repository. Using a post-processing procedure, data mining tools are then used to analyse the data and apply rules to execute marketing campaigns.

TIBCO's approach to customer interaction management uses CEP software to enable:

- Real-time matching of customer profiles and product lines across all banking channels.
- Real-time, rules-based product recommendations based on statistical, relationship, or experience models per business line.

Example: Multi-Channel Customer Interaction

The following example shows how banks can use real-time information to provide more effective service:

- Mick and his wife have a new baby girl named Nora.
- While using the bank's internet portal, Mick updates his Personal Profile to include the new family member.
- Still using the portal, he checks the bank's mortgage packages and requests several brochures because he is thinking about renovating or buying a new home.
- The next day he and his wife get a present from the bank congratulating them on the new family member and offering a baby savings account especially tailored for them.
- One week later, while visiting the local branch, the local branch officer congratulates Nick on Nora's birth, offers him an informational appointment with the bank's mortgage advisor, and offers to increase the credit limit on the family credit card at no charge and with no paperwork. In the example, complex event processing software allows the bank to:
- Capture all events through all channels in real-time.
- Seek out patterns and correlate information with the goal of identifying important events, such as the birth of a child.
- Consult historical information to determine, for instance, the customer's demographic profile and to estimate the bank's share of wallet
- Apply different models, or rules, to assess which marketing campaign, if any, is most suited to the customer.
- Execute appropriate marketing strategies and recommend products in real-time. By tracking customer interactions, capturing other vital, non-traditional customer events that help flesh out the customer profile – birth of a child, starting or ending school, landing a first job, getting married, renting a house, purchasing a new car, moving, changing a job, buying a house – and responding with relevant offers and services, banks have an opportunity to extend the customer relationship and demonstrate that the customer is the bank's most important asset.

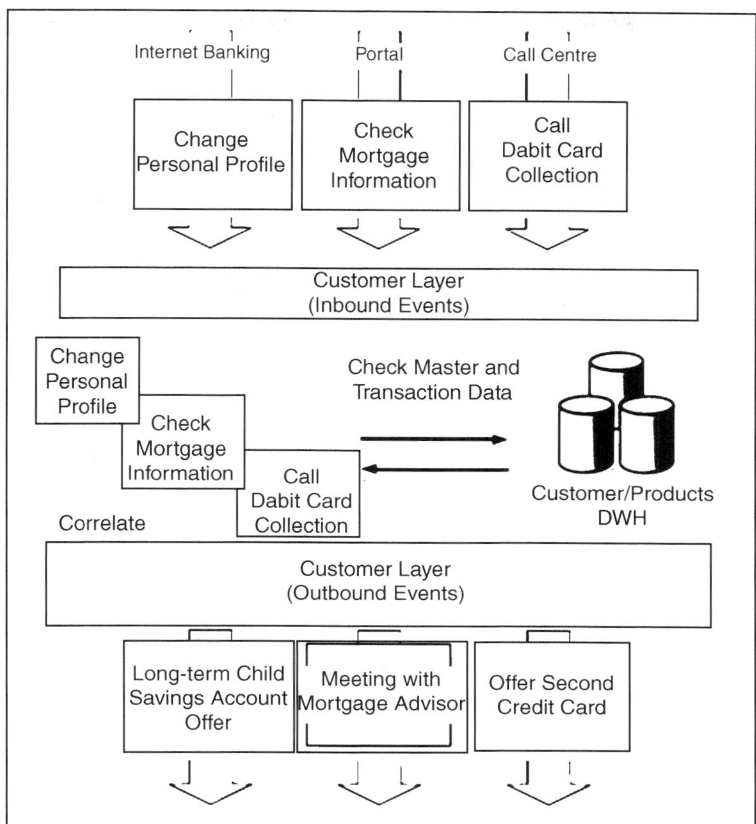

CONSUMER PROTECTION

Consumer protection laws are designed to ensure fair competition and the free flow of truthful information in the marketplace.

The laws are designed to prevent businesses that engage in fraud or specified unfair practices from gaining an advantage over competitors and may provide additional protection for the weak and those unable to take care of themselves. Consumer Protection laws are a form of government regulation which aim to protect the interests of consumers. For example, a government may require businesses to disclose detailed information about products—particularly in areas where safety or public health is an issue, such as food. Consumer protection is linked to the idea of "consumer rights" and to the formation of consumer organizations which help consumers make better choices in the marketplace.

Consumer is defined as someone who acquires goods or services for direct use or ownership rather than for resale or use in production and manufacturing. Consumer interests can also be protected by promoting competition in the markets which directly and indirectly serve consumers, consistent with economic efficiency, but this topic is treated in Competition law. Consumer protection can also be asserted via non-government organizations and individuals as consumer activism.

CONSUMER LAW

"Consumer protection law" or "consumer law" is considered an area of law that regulates private law relationships between individual consumers and the businesses that sell those goods and services. Consumer protection covers a wide range of topics, including but not necessarily limited to product liability, privacy rights, unfair business practices, fraud, misrepresentation, and other consumer/business interactions.

Such laws deal with credit repair, debt repair, product safety, service and sales contracts, bill collector regulation, pricing, utility turnoffs, consolidation, personal loans that may lead to bankruptcy and much more.

Germany

A minister of the federal cabinet is responsible for consumer rights and protection. In the current cabinet of Angela Merkel, this is Ilse Aigner. When issuing public warnings about products and services, the issuing authority has to take into account that this affects the supplier's constitutionally protected economic liberty.

Republic of China

Consumer Protection Law in the Republic of China is the national special law which specifically protects the interests and safety of end-user using the products or services provided by business operators. Consumer Protection Commission of Executive Yuan serves as an ombudsman supervising, coordinating, reporting any unsafe products/services and periodically reviewing the legislation.

United Kingdom

The United Kingdom, as member state of the European Union, is bound by the consumer protection directives of the EU. Domestic laws originated within the ambit of contract and tort but, with the influence of EU law, it is emerging as an independent area of law. In many circumstances, where domestic law is in question, the matter judicially treated as tort, contract, restitution or even criminal law. Consumer Protection issues are dealt with when complaints are made to the Director-General of Fair Trade.

The Office of Fair Trading will then investigate, impose an injunction or take the matter to litigation. The Office of Fair Trading also acts as the UK's official consumer and competition watchdog, with a remit to make markets work well for consumers, and at a local, municipal level by Trading Standards departments. General consumer advice can be obtained from Consumer Direct or via a local branch of the Citizen's Advice Bureau.

Other Commonwealth Countries

In Australia the corresponding agency is the Australian Competition and Consumer Commission or the individual State Consumer Affairs agencies. The Australian Securities and Investments Commission has responsibility for consumer protection regulation of financial services and products. In New Zealand, the corresponding agency is the Ministry of Consumer Affairs and the New Zealand Commerce Commission.

United States

In the United States a variety of laws at both the federal or state levels regulate consumer affairs. Among them are the federal Fair Debt Collection Practices Act, the Fair Credit Reporting Act, Truth in Lending Act, Fair Credit Billing Act, and the Gramm-Leach-Bliley Act. Federal consumer protection laws are mainly enforced by the Federal Trade Commission and the U.S. Department of Justice. At the state level, many states have a Department of Consumer Affairs devoted to regulating certain industries and protecting consumers who use goods and services from those industries.

For example, in the U.S. state of California, the California Department of Consumer Affairs regulates about 2.3 million professionals in over 230 different professions, through its forty regulatory entities. In addition, California encourages its consumers to act as private attorneys general through the liberal provisions of its Consumers Legal Remedies Act, Cal. Civil Code § 1750 et seq. California has the strongest consumer protection laws of any US state, partly because of rigorous advocacy and lobbying by groups such as Utility Consumers' Action Network, Consumer Federation of California and Privacy Rights Clearinghouse. Other states have been the leaders in specific aspects of consumer protection. For example Florida, Delaware and Minnesota have legislated requirements that contracts be written at reasonable readability levels as a large proportion of contracts cannot be understood by most consumers who sign them.

THE CONSUMER PROTECTION ACT, 1986

The Act enshrines all the consumers' rights which are internationally accepted. As per the Act, the consumer protection councils have been established at Central, State and District levels to promote and protect the consumer rights.

They are:

- *Right to Safety*: To be protected against the sale of goods and services which are spurious/hazardous for the life.

- *Right to Information*: To know the quality, quantity, weight and the price of goods/services being paid for, so that one is not cheated by unfair trade practices.
- *Right to Choose*: To be assured, wherever possible, access to a variety of goods and services at competitive prices.
- *Right to be Heard*: To be heard and to be assured that the interest would receive due consideration at appropriate fora.
- *Right to Seek Redressal*: To seek legal redressal against unfair or restrictive trade practices or exploitation.
- *Right to Consumer Education*: To have access to consumer education.

At present there are 35 State Commissions, one in each State/UT and 571 district forum besides the National Commission. The state governments are responsible to set up the district forum and the State Commissions. States have been empowered to establish additional District Forum and also additional members in the State Commission to facilitate constituting benches and also for holding circuit benches. The Central Government is required to set up the National Commission.

It has been empowered to appoint additional members to facilitate creation of more benches and holding of circuit benches. The second bench of the National Commission started functioning from 24 September 2003.

The government is monitoring the disposal of cases by the consumer courts through National Commission. Since its inception and up to March 2004, 32,910 cases were filed out of which 24,974 cases disposed of in the National Commission. Similarly 3,01,485 cases were filed and 1,97,797 cases disposed of in the State Commissions and 18,86,236 cases were filed and 16,46,698 cases disposed of in the district forum. Overall 18,69,469 cases have been disposed of out of 22,20,631 cases filed with a remarkable disposal rate of 84.2 per cent. The government has declared 24 December as 'National Consumer Day', since the President gave his assent on that day to the enactment of the historic Consumer Protection Act, 1986. Besides this, 15 March is observed as 'World Consumer Rights Day' every year.

8

Soft Skills and Communication Management

COMMUNICATION SKILLS

The ability to communicate is the primary factor that distinguishes human beings from animals. And it is the ability to communicate well that distinguishes one individual from another. The fact, is that apart from the basic necessities, one needs to be equipped with habits for good communication skills, as this is what will make them a happy and successful social being.

In order to develop these habits, one needs to first acknowledge the fact that they need to improve communication skills from time to time. They need to take stock of the way they interact and the direction in which their work and personal relations are going. The only constant in life is change, and the more one accepts one's strengths and works towards dealing with their shortcomings, especially in the area of communication skills, the better will be their interactions and the more their social popularity.

The dominating question that comes here is: How to improve communication skills? Well, the answer is simple. One can find plenty of literature on this. There are also experts, who conduct workshops and seminars based on communication skills of men and women. In fact, a large number of companies are bringing in trainers to regularly conduct sessions on the subject, in order to help their work force maintain better interpersonal work relations.

Today, an effective communication skill has become a predominant factor even while recruiting employees. While interviewing candidates, most interviewers judge them on the basis of the way they communicate. They believe that skills can be improvised on the job; but ability to communicate well is important, as every employee becomes the representing face of the company.

There are trainers, who specialize in delivering custom-made programmes on the subject. Through the session they not only facilitate better skills in the department of communications, but also look into the problems that come in the way of being able to convey messages effectively. They discuss these issues with the management and then sought to design programmes accordingly. For instance, time mismanagement becomes a cause for stress and frustration, which then hampers the possibility of healthy communications at work. Then in weeks to come the company organizes a programme on time management. Thus, a workshop on communication skills helps the management t to deal with the finer employee nuances about which they lack awareness. Communication is generally classified into a couple of types.

The classifications include:

- Verbal and non-verbal
- Technological and non-technological
- Mediated and non-mediated
- Participatory and non-participatory

COMMUNICATION SKILL TRAINING

Training has become an important aspect of corporate development and progress. In fact, an increasing number of companies have been identifying various areas where training is required; and the leading among them has been communication skills.

Management across the various industries have realised that improving communication skills amongst their staff not only helps them in communicating and negotiating better with clients, but also helps in maintaining better interpersonal relations at the workplace, which in turn brings about a harmonious and productive working environment. While conducting communication skills training, a trainer usually covers the following topics through the programme. However, the number and type of topics do vary according to training needs and the level being trained...

Here is a comprehensive and exhaustive list of communication skills topics that are included in the various training programmes:

- What are communication skills
- Business communication skills
- How to improve English speaking
- Taking responsibility for what is being communicated
- Listening skills
- Adaptation to differences
- Asking and accepting feedback-praises and criticism
- Assertive communicating skills
- Attentive listening skills
- Being aware of all communicated messages
- Being gently repetitive to drive in important points and messages
- Addressing people appropriately
- Ability to handle cognitive complexity
- Ability to resolve conflicts with a compromise
- Using specific examples with concrete examples

- Ability to confront a situation without upsetting the apple cart
- Speaking using descriptive language without being boring
- Using details and examples
- Filtering irrational thoughts and emotions
- Being empathetic
- Supportive communication skills
- Accepting manipulative criticism, without revolting
- Giving effective and needed feedback without being judgmental and aggressive
- Showing genuine interest through body languages, gestures and facial expressions
- Initiating the communication process
- Managing an interaction
- Ability to interpret without being biased or judgmental
- Recognizing emotions and being sensitive to other's feelings and emotions
- Taking responsibility for one's own feelings and emotions
- Paraphrasing without distorting original message
- Perceiving without letting one's own judgments cloud the actual perception
- Understanding what is being communicated from various perspectives
- Being polite
- Praising without being superfluous
- Making provisional statements
- Putting forth appropriate questions
- Remembering and recalling
- Revealing vital self-information
- Making supportive statements
- Being versatile
- Conflict resolution—win-win problem solving ability.

COMMUNICATION SKILLS COURSE OBJECTIVES

- Understanding how communications work
- Gaining active listening and responding skills
- Seeing things from other points of view
- Managing your assumption more effectively
- Understanding your own strengths
- How others may see you
- Looking at body language
- Increasing confidence
- Difficult people or situations
- Filling up your communications tool kit

Communication Skills Course Programme

The course content may include many of the exercises listed below, and any additional material that the trainers feel is relevant to the delegates on the day.

Introduction

Everything to be done is participative and interactive. There will be work in pairs, small group work, games, processes and exercises designed to stimulate, challenge and develop people's knowledge and skills. They are also fun!

What Else would you like out of a Communications Skills Course?

A chance for delegates to add anything they would like from the programme. The Communication Skills Course will be adapted and changed as we go along to better fit their needs.

Communications Dynamic-how it Works

This is an introduction to the dynamics of face-to-face communication skills-looking at what affects the participants and how they might take more charge of situations. It gives an overview of how communication works at its best, identifying where it can go wrong. The day will be based around this key aim, with delegates being given the opportunity to practice and experience each section.

Vocal Tone and Communication

There are a range of exercises which experiment with the effects of variations of tone. Each person will have the chance to identify their usual default style and also consider how their tone affects the way that they may be perceived. From there we will practice ways to turn up and down different aspects of our natural communications style. In unpicking how to achieve the tone you choose, participants can see how they can do so consistently.

How Words Communicate

We have fun looking at ways to deliberately mangle our message and bury its meaning under waffle, padding and jargon. The premise being that if we know how to make our communications worse, we can also see how to make them clearer. From here, we may get to share one of our best communication skills exercises which offers everyone a failsafe way to deliver a clear key message.

Impact of Body Language on Communication

There are a variety of exercises to demonstrate the power and control the listener has, through body language and attitude. Making ourselves consciously aware of our options means that we can remain on a front foot when it comes to communicating effectively.

What does your History have to do with Communication Skills?

What makes us who we are inside and outside of work? What is our history or our form with particular sorts of people, particular subjects in particular scenarios?

How Head Stuff Affects Communication Skills

What makes us who we are inside and outside of work and how does that impact on the sense we make of others and they of us? When was the last time you got something wrong? When you were last misunderstood? Mis-communication seems to happen most when we base what we do on assumptions, perceptions and misconceptions rather than upon objective fact.

Communication by Eye Contact

One of our most vital communication skills is eye contact and its effect upon the communications dynamic. Back to assumptions again, but what do we make of those who avoid looking at us directly or else those who seem to hold our gaze too long?

What does the Environment Communicate?

Being aware that non-verbal factors may either help or hinder effective communication is vitally important. How far do those more subtle or not so subtle details swing things one way or the other? As well as the physical environment generally and the effect of rearranging the furniture or opening a window, we will consider those other things that can make a difference. How does a family photo, symbols of status or the provision of simple or expensive refreshments affect a meeting, an interview or a difficult interaction?

In reality there may be things about the environment that we can't necessarily change, like the choice of space, the colour of the walls or the temperature. Of equal importance is the effect of breaking natural physical boundaries, we can investigate how they too affect our communication skills far more than we might realise.

Geography and Communication

What is the effect of being on your territory or theirs? We will look at how the familiarity of a place and where we are geographically can dictate who dances to whose tune. Certainly culture, in its widest sense, influences how our behaviour and words are perceived. Being attentive to what is likely to cause a ripple means that we can be deliberate in our intentions. Its obvious, but successful communicators are sensitive to the culture and geography of a place and can predict the effect of their words and behaviour.

Working to your Communication Strengths

Everyone will give a brief description of what they already do that they know works about them. They will then have chance to reflect upon how others see them through the feedback of others.

Communication Skills Course Support

The final exercise of the Communication Skills Course is for each delegate to devise a personal Plan of Action, identifying their personal take-out of the programme, where they know they will practise and areas for their development.

Finally there are people identify what will stop them putting this into practise and what support they need to help themselves put the *communication skills course* work into practise.

Presentation Skills Training Objectives:

- How Nervous Energy can be Harnessed
- Making the Best Use of Existing Strengths
- Freeing up Body Language
- Myths and Rules about Presenting
- What you Are and Are Not Allowed To Do
- Developing an Individual Presentation Style
- How to Stimulate Easy Interaction with an Audience
- Preparing for a Non-Linear Presentation
- Ways of Getting Ideas Across
- Call to Action (Closing a Sale)
- How to be Entertaining and Stimulating
- How to Create Effective Support Materials

Effective Presentation Skills

What might the most common Presentation Skills issue be?

The fact that for most people, even experienced presenters, getting up and presenting in front of an audience can be a terrifying and even phobic experience.

Yes! The number one phobia that most people share is making a presentation; speaking in front of a group of other people: colleagues, strangers, it doesn't seem to matter-it's scary. You may have people who are new to the presentation 'game' and who need to understand just what happens to them when they have to stand and deliver and how they can become confident and effective presenters. You may have people who have been around the presentation block and are in a rut, giving acceptable, but not brilliant presentations.

You may have people who have to present detailed and technical information without putting their audience to sleep. Presenting detailed information may be important but if the presenter's audience aren't engaged then they've made their job of putting across information even harder.

All of these people could benefit from confidence-building Presentation Skills programmes.

In addition, you may have individuals who have to:

- Give Key Note Speeches
- Make Presentations at Conference
- Pitch Crucial Clients Presentations
- Make Boardroom Presentations
- Pitch Ideas Internally
- Talk to the Public or Media
- Make Sales Presentations

Good Presentation Skills Training

Presentation Skills Training that concentrates on 'how to get it right' is available in all shapes and forms. However there is very little presentation skills training that really addresses the key issue of Working Your Audience.

Many presenters have no idea of what can be achieved. Most of us know the power of an audience. It is often the rather unnerving experience of being on the receiving end of twenty pairs of eyes looking at us in polite silence as if to say "Yes?... So?" It is this energy that can be harnessed to make dynamic, lively, memorable and effective presentations. It takes a little courage, but the rewards are enormous.

Our 'Working Your Audience' Presentation Skills Programme gives delegates clear insight into how the dynamic of a presenter and their audience works, enabling them to make really effective presentations. Tailored specifically to each group Working Your Audience is a Presentation Skills Training Course designed to develop delegates into powerful, persuasive presenters.

Tailored and in House Presentation Training

Tailored Advanced Presentation Training comes in many formats from one-to-one through to fully tailored company wide programmes. Many of us are now required to make presentations as a part of our job. Indeed for some people it will limit their career prospects if they are seen to be reluctant to make them. For the lucky few it doesn't seem to be a problem: they seem to have always been able to do it and thrive on it. For the rest of us, however, *presentation skills* are something we learn. Given that it can be a daunting and even frightening area of learning for most of us, it would seem sensible to use an approach that seeks to make it easy and enjoyable rather than one that makes it even more difficult. The difficult presentation skills path is the one where you learn to get it right first time, to be flawless in your delivery and to make no mistakes. This is "how to" learning. Learning what to do and what not do.

The easier path is the one where you learn how presentation skills work and develop a style, which includes your idiosyncrasies and quirks (this way you don't have to learn to behave differently when you present). Let me give you an example of what I mean. Most presenters are concerned about their body language when presenting, and rightly so: what you do matters as much as what you say. So you have a choice. You can learn the rules for what you are not allowed to do and apply them. For instance, as a presenter you shouldn't cross your arms, put your hands in your pockets, touch your ear or nose (apparently this means you're lying), sway from side to side. The list is a long one and fortunately you don't need it. You can take the easy route.

DEVELOPING COMMUNICATION AND PROFESSIONAL SKILLS

In Emphasizing Leadership Skill development in the business curriculum, the 1990 AACSB sponsored Porter and McKibbon report, "Management Education and Development: Drift or Thrust into the 21st Century?" fueled a major change within schools of management. It challenged universities to make students both technically and interpersonally competent. Recent studies of skills and competencies valued by employers continue to document the need for excellence in writing, speaking, and listening.

Equally significant are such interpersonal communi-cation skills as teamwork, working with culturally diverse populations, and adapting to change and the environment while maintaining a positive attitude. Wilhelm concludes the following from his-study of the expectations Arizona employers held for entry-level employees: "The highest valued skills and competencies by employers require for the most part an employee's ability to interact with and relate well with others in the workplace.

Of the top-rated nine skills and competencies, none were technical in nature and eight represented abilities to successfully interact in the workplace". Drucker states that professionals in the 21st century must be workers who manage themselves using "soft skills" to relate to others in the workplace. What are "soft skills?" In a recent conference presentation, "What do Employers Expect from Employees," three human resource managers representing three large American corporations agreed on the following "soft skills" as the most important characteristics of employees (in addition to good communication skills and a good appearance):

- "How-can-I-help" attitude.
- Good manners.
- Willingness to take ownership.
- Commitment.

- Initiative, including the initiative to be a leader through assuming responsibility.
- Adaptability.
- Teamwork.
- Relationship building through trust and respect for the firm and for individuals.
- Desire to advance.

McCall and Lombardo's comparison of business executives who failed in their career objectives reveals the importance of soft skills to executives' success. The failed executives exhibited insensitivity to others, arrogance, aloofness, a lack of trustworthiness, over dependence on others, and an excessive drive toward moving up the corporate ladder. Clearly, if students are to succeed in the workplace, they must obtain knowledge of soft skills and strengthen their communication skills including interpersonal negotiations and team skills. In a curriculum already squeezed with technical information also important to students' careers, the challenge is to develop innovative ways to provide professional development for future career success.

Furthermore, in an effort to validate the importance of business writing courses, AACSB has stressed the importance of assessment and accountability through value assessments emphasizing analysis of information, audience adaptation, and content through systematic analytical assignments.

This chapter discusses such an analytical assignment including:

- Skills developed.
- Historical background and description.
- Step-by-step implementation guide for a successful analytical report project.

SKILLS DEVELOPED

The analytical report assignment described in this chapter develops and integrates the following skills: oral communicating, interviewing, writing, presenting, listening, interpersonal communicating, and working in teams. Through the professional development topics chosen for the report, students research specific professional skills graduates need when beginning their careers and gain knowledge of the soft skills through content. Additionally, the project requires technical skills to incorporate software applications including word processing, spreadsheets for graphics, presentation design, and Internet usage for gathering secondary data and information about the companies where executives who will be interviewed work.

Specifically, through the analytical report, students will complete the following tasks:

- Identify and articulate the problem statement.
- Use the report-writing process to collect, analyse, interpret, and report data.

- Function effectively as a team member.
- Appraise the performance of a peer.
- Construct an effective questionnaire.
- Write a cover letter for a questionnaire.
- Schedule an on-site interview with a business executive.
- Interview a business executive.
- Follow up an interview.
- Share, compile, edit, and tabulate data.
- Use analytical thinking to discuss and present conclusions and recommendations.
- Prepare an effective oral presentation.
- Critically evaluate the oral presentations of peers.
- Present an effective team presentation to a business executive.
- Use computer technology (PowerPoint) to incorporate visuals in the oral presentation.
- Write a formal report.

Implementing the Assignment

The analytical report assignment was created six years ago for Managerial Report Writing, a junior/senior level writing course required for all business majors enrolled at Eastern Kentucky University. The intent of the report was to integrate and develop the skills mentioned above and to introduce students to professional skills they will need in the workplace. To date, approximately 1,400 students have completed the assignment.

Careful planning and instruction are necessary to implement this comprehensive project so that students, professors, and business executives are aware of the participants' expectations.

Perhaps one of the most important phases of the project is the actual assignment of the project. A memorandum authorizing the assignment is an effective way to include specific instructions for the report in a realistic format. The memo helps students understand the assignment and remain focused as the assignment progresses.

ASSIGNMENT TOPICS

Students must select one of several approved topics addressing a professional skill needed by college graduates beginning their careers. These professional-skills topics should apply to all disciplines.

Suggestions for topics might include:

- Team Building
- Ethics
- Conflict Resolution
- Time Management

- Impact of Diversity
- Leadership Skills
- Conducting Meetings
- Goal Setting
- Managing Change
- Global Communication
- Checklists for implementation

To integrate the multiple skills students need to display throughout a semester-long project, we provide many checklists.

- Assignment Checklist. The checklist provides written documentation of assignment details for both students and instructors. The assignment checklist also underlies the project-evaluation checklist.
- Specific Tasks Checklists. As part of the assignment, students compose a questionnaire, interview two executives each using their questionnaire as the research instrument, and follow up the interview with a thank-you letter.
- Evaluation Checklists. When the data have been collected and analysed, students write a long, formal report including an executive summary and give an oral presentation to visiting corporate executives. Checklists are used to evaluate each part of the final project. Visiting executives complete an open-ended form for each student and collectively for the team's oral presentation.

PROJECT OUTCOMES

Throughout the past six-year period, the analytical report assignment has been an effective way to integrate and develop communication, professional development, and technical skills in the report-writing classroom. Specifically, faculty's assessment and students' self evaluations indicate that the project provides the following benefits:

- Knowledge is gained regarding professional skills and the expectations of the workplace that goes beyond the traditional coverage of these topics in a report-writing classroom.
- Content, knowledge of professional skills is strengthened through listening to and evaluating other students' oral presentations.
- Team skills are developed.
- Time management skills and self-discipline are practiced through the length and complexity of the project.
- Students experience a sense of accomplishment through completing a challenging, multi-task project.
- Students gain confidence through their experiences of scheduling interviews and talking with executives.
- Students begin professional networking for their future careers.

Although the project is revised as new ideas emerge, the basic design has survived the test of time and has added a new dimension to students' professional development and career preparation. Executives who visit the classroom are favorably impressed with the content of the oral presentations through primary research and the delivery of the presentations using PowerPoint slides.

Through the interviews with executives, students have gained valuable information and resources for potential employment opportunities. While a considerable amount of time must be spent to develop, implement, and evaluate this project, the results merit the expenditures.

More recently, the last two decades have marked a period in which a series of reports from government, industry, and academia has called into question the state of engineering education and paved the way for including the professional skills as learning outcomes. In 1985, the National Research Council's Engineering Education and Practice in the United States: Foundation of our Techno-Economic Future called on universities to make faculty careers more attractive in order to fill vacancies.

This was followed by the NSF-supported Belmont Conference. Smerdon credits this conference with leading to the creation of the National Science Foundation's (NSF) undergraduate engineering education coalitions initiative, probably the one NSF programme that has had the greatest impact on engineering education to date. Starting in the early 1990s, a series of reports emerged that recognized serious deficiencies in engineering education and called for major reforms. The ASEE's Engineering Education for A Changing World proclaimed that "engineering education programmes must not only teach the fundamentals of engineering theory, experimentation, and practice, but be relevant, attractive, and connected," preparing students for a broad range of careers and lifelong learning.

It stated that engineering education must provide the "technical knowledge and capabilities, flexibility, and an understanding of the societal context of engineering". The NSF's complementary report, Restructuring Engineering Education: A Focus on Change, stressed similar themes. Among its recommendations is that engineering education should become flexible enough to support diverse career aspirations and engineering courses that would include a broad range of concerns: environmental, political and social issues; international, and historical contexts; and legal and ethical ramifications.

The National Research Council's Board of Engineering Education also recommended a number of actions for curriculum reform "including early exposure to 'real' engineering and more extensive exposure to interdisciplinary, hands-on, industrial practice aspects, team work, systems thinking, and creative design". Three leading educators, Bordogna, Fromm, and Ernst, called for educators to "create an intellectual environment where students can develop an awareness of the impact of emerging technologies, an appreciation of engineering as an integral process of societal change, and an acceptance of responsibility for civilization's progress".

At the 1992 Engineering Foundation Conference on "Engineering Education: Curriculum Innovation and Integration," Pister proposed reformulating the goals of engineering education as developing technical competence, understanding the practice of engineering as a social enterprise, acquiring clinical experience in practice, preparing for management and leadership roles in society, and building a foundation for lifelong learning. To Pister, examining the trade-offs among these objectives and selecting the appropriate weighting in a particular curriculum would present one of the more difficult challenges for faculty. As noted, the Belmont Conference's call to revitalize engineering education led the NSF to create its Engineering Education Coalitions programme, a bold initiative aimed at "revolutionizing" education.

In all, eight coalitions involving more than sixty schools were funded. Collectively, they produced (and are still producing) a large quantity of curricula innovations, a substantial number of which are archived in the proceedings of both the annual ASEE national meetings and the annual Frontiers in Education Conferences.

In addition, the NSF's Division of Undergraduate Education has funded a scries of "Course, Curriculum, and Laboratory Improvement" (CCLI) projects, many of which are directed at improving engineering education. The NSF also funded a series of "Action Agenda" projects aimed at implementing and expanding many of the collations' innovations.

Concomitantly, a group of leading engineering deans and educators, realizing that the current ABET engineering criteria were stifling innovation, began the process with strong input from industry that in 1996 led to EC2000. Of note was the Accreditation Process Review Committee, chaired by John Prados (1991-92 ABET president), which condensed a large number of issues into a four-page report that stated "the current criteria are too long and by their very nature, encourage a rigid, bean-counting approach that stifles innovation, even though the Engineering Accreditation Committee sincerely tries to avoid this".

In commenting on the newly adopted criteria, Prados noted that the major drivers had included a shift from defence to commercial competition with a resultant impact on engineering employment, the exploding information technology growth, corporate downsizing, outsourcing of engineering services, and the globalization of both manufacturing and service delivery. Employers were now emphasizing that success as an engineer required more than simply strong technical capabilities; also needed were skills in communication and persuasion, the ability to lead and work effectively as a team member, and an understanding of the non-technical forces that affected engineering decisions.

To do this would require a new engineering education paradigm built around active, project-based learning, horizontal and vertical integration of subject matter, the introduction of mathematical and scientific concepts in the context of application, close interaction with industry, broad use of information technology, and a faculty devoted to developing emerging professionals as mentors and coaches rather than all-knowing dispensers of information. Not surprisingly, these new criteria were consistent with the collective recommendations of the reports that preceded it.

Professional Skills Are Particularly Important

After ten years, these same drivers-rapidly changing technology, particularly information technology, corporate downsizing, outsourcing, and globalization-that provided the impetus for the professional skills are, if anything, even more critical today. This is especially true as industry views an increasingly larger portion of the science and engineering labour pool more like a commodity then a profession.

Consequently, a growing number of less developed countries, with lower wage rates and an abundance of young, intellectual capital are competing for work that less than four years ago was performed by highly paid U.S. professionals, many of whom were then in short supply. While we do not know the extent of this shift in work from the United States (and other G-8 nations) to offshore locations, we do feel that the trend is, for the most part, permanent and irreversible.

Hence, a new issue confronting engineering educators today is how to best ensure that our graduates will continue to bring value to a marketplace in which their salary demands are three to five times greater than their international competitors. Oberst and Jones put the question succinctly: "It is no longer just whether engineers are being treated as commodities, but how engineers and other highly educated technical people shape and are shaped by the emerging realities of a truly global workforce. Engineers as a professional group are thus the canaries in the mincshaft of the new world economy. Whether engineers manage the transition from local to international workplace environments will determine if the profession remains attractive".

They cite four major mega trends that affect the practice of engineering and necessitate the acquisition of more than technical skills:

- Changes forced by the fragile world economy;
- Student and professional mobility;
- Use of communications and instructional technology; and
- Increasingly loud voice of the social imperative.

To them, the so-called "soft skills" are much more than public speaking, management skills, and the ability to work well in teams. What is also needed is an understanding of how the growing social consciousness around the world is making it imperative that engineering students understand the implications of their work.

We propose that the mastery of these professional skills combined with an ability to innovate will add sufficient value to U.S. engineering graduates so that price does not become the primary determinant of who is hired in the global marketplace. From continuing skill development through lifelong learning that prevents technical obsolescence to the ability to do engineering within its global (and/or societal) context, the professional skills arc critical.

Hence, globalization, which now includes the globalization of the engineering profession, is forcing us to reconsider the role of future engineering graduates and the education required to meet that role. In 1994, Morrow (then National Academy Engineering president) in a farsighted consideration of the issues facing undergraduate engineering education noted that it is not a given that the U.S. engineering education system will always be globally pre-eminent. There is clear evidence that many U.S. corporations now seek their engineering talent wherever they can find it throughout the world. Engineering design quality, low-cost engineering services, and responsive engineering production capabilities are determinants of where engineering jobs will be. U.S. construction companies use civil engineers in Korea; automobile companies use design talents in Europe; software companies use software engineers in India.

A decade later, it is now evident that countries like China and India, with large, well-educated work forces, have learned how to move large segments of their populations into the advanced industrial economy in a manner similar to Japan, Korea, and Taiwan before them.

Further, like Korea and Taiwan, they are continuing to build universities to produce larger numbers of engineering and science talent and hence attract additional foreign direct investment, acquire advanced technology, and pursue export-led growth strategies. Further, another trend from the early '90s will continue to impact engineering education-an increasing number of engineeringgraduates may never practice engineering; rather, they choose to use their engineering education to enter a wide range of fields from business, medicine, law, and management among others.

Hence, as some have predicted, an undergraduate engineering education may become the liberal arts education of the twenty-first century. Certainly, the increasing number of engineering schools introducing general or interdiscip-linary degrees recognize this. Consistent with this trend, Purdue recently created the country's first Department of Engineering Education, followed a few months later by Virginia Tech's creation of the second department. Purdue's new department combines its existing freshman engineering and interdisciplinary engineering programmes. In the future, it plans to offer graduate degrees for students studying the science of learning and other topics in engineering education. There also are plans to add an engineering teaching certification programme for high school teachers and to pursue accredited undergraduate degrees in engineering education and interdisciplinary engineering. Virginia Tech has similar plans for its programme. Further, six states-Massachusetts, Arkansas, New Hampshire, Florida, Texas, and Maryland-have mandated engineering courscwork in high schools, a trend that is likely to spread to other states in the coming years.

Process and Awareness Skills

It is against this setting that we consider how to best teach and assess these professional skills. We believe that mastering these skills will be a major determinant of the future competitiveness of U.S. engineering graduates, enabling them to become highly innovative global "problem solvers," which, in fact, we propose is what much of engineering is all about.

To best examine these skills we have divided them into two categories: process skills-communication, teamwork, and the ability to recognize and resolve ethical dilemmas (a more advanced formulation of criteria) and awareness skills-understanding the impact of global and social factors, knowledge of contemporary issues, and the ability to do lifelong learning.

We designate the first set as process skills because students learn a robust process to address each one. In contrast, the awareness skills arc so designated because students learn how to be aware of the importance of each one and to include them in their problem-solving activities. In reviewing these skills, we cite examples of how some institutions are able to successfully teach them.

Process Skills

- *Communication:* We note that communication is the one skill that can certainly be taught and assessed. Indeed, most universities have departments of communications. The proceedings of both the Frontiers in Education conferences and the annual conferences of the American Society of Engineering Education are replete with examples of ways to integrate communication into the fabric of undergraduate engineering education. We are particularly impressed with those institutions now combining communication with global and social and ethical issues as part of design projects. Two noteworthy examples are Union College and the University of Utah.

At Union College, Spinelli has developed a course that examines the history of electrical engineering by combining the study of technological development within American and European civilizations with a concentration on writing, oral communication, and ethics. Certainly, placing technological developments within a social and human context is one way of approaching ABET's engineering criteria for ethics, communications, and broad education, in a course with significant technical content. In a similar spirit, faculty at the University of Utah are using funding from the Hewlett Foundation to bring together communication, leadership (team building), and ethics into the College of Engineering's eight programmes over the entire four-year curriculum. They are building upon a successful model communication programme in mechanical engineering, where teaching assistants from the humanities have been brought into the engineering classes so that communication skills can be taught as "situational" learning. A similar ethics component is to be added.

- Functioning on multidisciplinary teams: More and more engineering courses are being designed to give students the opportunity to experience teamwork firsthand. These range from short, decision-making exercises to project management or business simulations lasting the length of the course.

This team-based course design trend reflects industry practice, where teamwork has become the prevalent mode. Companies use teams as an integral part of their product development, process improvement, and manufacturing activities. Such management techniques as concurrent engineering, total quality management, and business process reengineering are founded upon the concept of people working effectively in teams. Engineering educators, recognizing these trends, are designing more and more courses around teams. Such programmes as Columbia's Gateway design course, MIT's undergraduate design course and its "New Products Programme", and Rowan University's Engineering Clinics Programme make extensive use of teams composed of students, faculty, and outside sponsors.

These project-driven classes provide students with the opportunity to experience team design work from idea conception to completion. When properly structured, such courses can teach students the skills necessary to work effectively in teams. However, too often educators incorporate student teams into their courses with little thought to their best use.

Minimal guidance is provided to students on group development, soliciting member input, consensus building, resolving conflict, and team leadership. Evaluation oftentimes is subjective and little more than a piecemeal integration of individual and group-level performance. Consequently, instructors often fail to capitalize on much of the learning that can occur through group dynamics and behaviour.

However, there are several outstanding examples where engineering educators have integrated teamwork and team skill-building activities into the classroom. An increasing number of engineering educators now realise that students cannot be thrown into team projects without support.

One of the primary methods created to help integrate team learning into the engineering classroom is the development of formal curricular modules that can be used by various faculty planning to have students work on team projects. Of note is the Clark School of Engineering, University of Maryland modular team training programme-Building Engineering Student Team Effectiveness and Management Systems (BESTEAMS).

Supported by the National Science Foundation, the goal of this programme is to provide a team curriculum that can be easily adopted by engineering faculty from various schools and at different levels of the undergraduate curriculum. This well-structured programme allows faculty to select from various modules, depending on the nature of the course and the knowledge level of the students, its three modules-introductory, intermediate, and advanced-cut across three major team skill domains-personal, interpersonal, and project management.

The engineering schools at both the University of Tennessee and the University of San Diego have adopted this modular approach to provide engineering faculty with the tools necessary to develop students' team skills. The underlying foundation of these training modules is based on learning style theory, enabling student problem solvers to apply newly acquired technical skills more effectively by improving interpersonal interactions.

All levels of undergraduates have used these modules, which can be customised based on developmental level and technical knowledge of the student. The modular nature of all three programmes makes them easily transportable in full or in parts, thus allowing faculty to customise based on class structure, project design, and course material. Another key component for teaching students team skills is the type of team project students will be exposed to in the classroom.

Recent literature is replete with examples from structured, simulated team experiences to authentic design projects, where students work on real problems for actual clients. As discussed later in this paper, there is now an emerging interest in using projects with global and/or humanitarian dimensions. Several experiential activities can help students better understand the behaviours and skills needed to be an effective team member.

At one end of the spectrum, there are literally hundreds of "off-the-shelf" group exercises designed to give participants hands-on experience. On the other end, there are many elaborate game simulations designed to provide realistic conditions that allow students to experience teamwork. The choice of team task depends on the educational objectives. For example, if the objective is to have students experience a specific aspect of teaming such as brainstorming, specific group exercises in which students practice common methods of group brainstorming to generate new ideas can be used. However, if the objective is for students to experience a broad range of team processes and behaviours, then more complex activities are suitable. Two guiding principles should be followed in choosing activities: fidelity and complexity.

Fidelity is defined as the similarity of the training situation to the students' present and future working conditions. The higher the fidelity, the more superior the transfer of learning to the workplace. The fidelity of a particular activity can be increased by matching the conditions of the work environment as closely as possible.

This may be difficult, especially when it comes to physical conditions, but many of the environmental conditions can be simulated. An example is "temporal environment," which involves such factors as time limits and deadlines the team may experience. Research has shown that time has a definite effect on team performance. Such conditions as actual time to complete the task or make decisions should be matched to real conditions where possible.

"Social context" is another environmental condition that can be manipulated. Few teams work in a vacuum; instead, they typically co-exist with other teams that are working within a similar context. The more that inter-group activities can be designed into the team activity, the more a team can engage in real-world team behaviours such as inter-group communication, coordination, and conflict.

Complexity is defined by two subfactors: task interdependence and cognitive effort. The more complex the activity, the more team skills are required by the participant. Activities also can range from high to low degrees of complexity. In general, the higher the fidelity and complexity of the activity, the better the transfer of team skills to the workplace.

For example, programmes like Purdue's EPICS provides highly realistic teaming activities, with all the complexities experienced by a product design team. Some computer-generated simulations also can be both highly realistic and very complex. An example is the Centre for Creative Leader-ship's COLAB simulation that places technology management students in cross-functional teams with a focus on making decisions on new polymer processes to be commercialized.

Each competing team's objective is to get the new process to the market in a timely manner. Students make decisions on the allocation of research and development resources, manufacturing processes, and marketing activities. There are both advantages and disadvantages to each type of activity. Experiential activities categorized as high fidelity/high complexity most resemble real workplace" conditions, but typically are more difficult for the instructor to manage, resource intensive, and time consuming for the student.

Activities that are lower in fidelity are typically more structured and easier to administer, but may be perceived as less relevant by the student, resulting in the experience having less of a learning impact. Finally, team activities that are lower in complexity may not challenge the team nor provide the environment necessary for intense interaction among team members.

- *Understanding professional and ethical responsibilities*: As part of their educational process, students should be sensitized to the potential ethical dilemmas they may confront in their professional life.

If an engineer is able to recognize a developing ethical dilemma, he or she should be better able to first clearly frame it and then begin the process of resolution. Stephan, in ques-tioning whether or not engineering ethics can be taught, quotes philosopher Michael Davis in giving four good things that can result if successful: students can become more aware of the ethical implications of their work, they can learn ethical standards, they can become better judges of ethical conduct, and they can become more willing to put their ethical knowledge into action.

To Stephan, the true test of engineering ethics education is how graduates behave in the workplace during their careers, certainly a difficult outcome to measure a priori. Much attention has focused on how engineers perceive, articulate, and resolve ethical dilemmas that arise when complex, advanced technologies are developed, such as the explosion of the Challenger, the Three Mile Island Nuclear Power Plant accident, Cherynobl, the DC-10 cargo door, or the Ford Pinto. In fact, an entire field, disaster ethics, has emerged from studying such events.

While we believe that such lessons remain relevant to practicing engineers, of more importance may be how to recognize and then resolve those dilemmas that may arise in the routine practice of engineering. Engineers frequently work under cost and schedule pressures, situations that can lead to increased risk. At what point is that increased risk no longer acceptable? In addition, the multiple loyalties of the practicing engineer also contribute to ethical dilemmas.

Certainly, engineers have a loyalty to their employer, but engineering practice typically also involves a client or contractor, creating a second level of loyalty. Then there is the public, where the "safety of the public" as declared by Cicero has become accepted as the responsibility of the engineer. Every engineering code of ethics places the safety of the public in a prominent position. Finally, the engineer has a loyalty to the profession and to him or herself.

The need to incorporate some form of ethics instruction into the engineering curriculum is no longer debated, largely because of the new ABET engineering criteria. A number of educators have noted the important relationship between ethics and engineering design and the value of integrating the two within the curriculum.

However, this is only a recent happening. Over the past fifty years, engineering educators have focused on providing students with tools and technical skills, but providing the education and skills for social decision making was not a priority. Consequently, until recently, little had been done to make students aware of the social dimensions of engineering. Stephan found that only 27 per cent of ABET-accredited institutions listed an ethicsrelated course requirement, even though an increasing number of philos-ophers, engineers, and ethicists focus their research and teaching on engineering ethics. The interest of practitioners and professional enginee-ring societies in engineering ethics has also increased. The Institute of Electrical and Electronics Engineers (IEEE) has been especially active. However, if the vision for understanding ethical and professional responsibilities as articulated in ABET is to become reality, educators must now answer a number of questions: What is the appropriate content?

What teaching methods and curriculum models are preferable? Which works best-required course, ethics across-thc-curriculum, integration of ethics and science, technology and society, or integration of the liberal arts into the engineering curriculum? Which outcome assessment methods are most suitable? Pinkus has provided an overview of these issues with emphasis on biomedical engineering.

Pfatteichcr proposes that a current engineering ethics educational 'dilemma' is how to provide meaningful ethics instruction to all students without overburdening faculty, increasing graduation requirements, or removing essential technical material from the curriculum. She notes that the ABET engineering criteria call for ensuring understanding rather than demonstrating that graduates arc ethical. Hence, students should be evaluated on knowledge and skills, not values and beliefs.

Pfatteicher proposes providing students with an understanding of the nature of engineering ethics, the value of engineering ethics as opposed to the values of an ethical engineer, and the resolution of ethical dilemmas. At the University of Virginia, Richards and Gorman have effectively used case studies to teach not only design, but ethics.

They have developed (researched and written) a set of case studies for teaching engineering ethics, engineering design, and environmental issues. These cases have been used in a course on invention and design and in other courses offered by the Division of Science, Technology, and Society, which Gorman chaired. They emphasize that cases promote active learning, team-based activities, and the ability to deal with open-ended problems. With cases, students can be exposed to realistic situations involving unstructured problems with multiple possible answers, key decision points, and trade-offs. The case method, which also fosters the development of higher-level cognitive skills, enables students to address problems that require analysis, judgment, decisions, perspective taking, role playing, independent thought, and critical thinking.

Awareness Skills

Broad education to understand the impact of engineering solutions in a global and societal context and knowledge of contemporary issues: A growing number of engineering programmes recognize that these two areas can be combined with issues related to globalization, sustainability, and development, especially in lesser developed countries, and are designing highly innovative educational programmes to meet this need. By introducing design projects into the mix, often as part of a service learning experience, they are finding effective ways to teach the gamut of professional skills while reinforcing the "harder" technical skills.

We highlight some of these exemplary programmes in this section, with a particular emphasis on those with a global orientation. While traditionally few engineering students study abroad or co-op/intern abroad-the most recent data indicate that only 4,670 students (2.9 per cent) participated in a study abroad programme in as noted here, this should change as innovative programmes are designed to provide engineering students with needed global and social experiences.

Lucena, one of the first academics to study globalization from an engineering perspective, notes that corporations, governments, and the engineers they hire face increasing challenges, such as mobility of capital and labour, organizational restructuring across national boundaries, and the development and implementation of more efficient production and manufacturing practices, among others.

Globalization depends on the availability of flexible workers to produce "just-in-time" products according to consumer demands and on the rapid dispersal of those products around the globe. This flexibility, demanded by globalization, presents special difficulties for engineering education and practice. Most engineers have no choice but to learn to cope with the practices changes that globalization is creating.

Lucena (who holds a B.S. and M.S. in engineering and a Ph.D. in anthropology) suggests that a more appropriate education to prepare engineers to deal with the challenges brought by globalization might be a liberal-arts-based education that teaches them first to recognize and deal with the political dimensions of their work and second to deal with the ambiguity that results from working, sharing, and even valuing perspectives other than their own.

Swearengen et al., concerned with outsourcing capturing an increasing percentage of engineering work, suggest that engineers will become "free agents" in a professional services market. To thrive, future engineers will have to be able to work productively with radically different cultures, educational backgrounds, technical standards, quality standards, professional registration requirements, and time zones. The manufacturing engineer must not only master the elements of global design, manufacture, marketing, and distribution, but also prepare to participate as a contractor in a "twenty-four-hour virtual enterprise".

Engineers must understand that in a global context, engineering solutions, whether consumer products or unintended consequences such as resource exhaustion and environmental pollution, increasingly cross or transcend international boundaries. Global sustainability, for example, may eventually outweigh technical and other aspects of manufacturing.

Engineering faculty are beginning to recognize that students who have participated in study abroad programmes are better problem solvers, have strong communication and cross-cultural communication skills, and arc able to work well in groups of diverse populations and understand diverse perspectives. Living overseas creates graduates who are more adaptable to new environments and have a greater under-standing of contemporary issues as well as engineering solutions in a global and social context. However, further research is required to fully support these findings.

Perhaps the prototype model for integrating international experience into an engineering education is the University of Rhode Island's (URI) International Engineering Programme. Founded in 1987 by John Grandin, professor of German, and Herman Viets, then dean of engineering, this innovative programme combines an undergraduate engineering degree with a degree in languages (initially German, but now expanded to French and Spanish).

In addition, students do an internship in a country where they must use their language skills, and many also do at least one term of study in that country. This five-year programme, which has been replicated by both the University of Connecticut and Rice University, has served to increase both the quality and quantity of URI engineering students; currently 20 per cent of incoming students participate.

Worchester Polytechnic Institute (WPI) is one of the leaders in enabling its students to study engineering within a global and social context. WPI's programme is centered on the Major Qualifying Project-the equivalent of a nine-credit capstone design experience-and provides a professional-level application of the students' knowledge in their major fields. It typically involves the design, synthesis, and realization of a solution to a real-world technical problem. WPI has established project centers, including ones in Ireland, Denmark, Hong Kong, Australia, Namibia, and Costa Rica. By 2002, 35 per cent of the electrical and computer engineering students were completing their senior design project in a project centre (10 weeks).

In total, more than half of the WPI students complete at least one degree requirement internationally. To make the programmes more affordable, WPI provides free passports and financial aid incentives. The University of Michigan has created a global concentration in engineering with an initial focus on China, the United Kingdom, and Mexico. The flexible framework enables all disciplines to participate. It requires international experience, global engineering course content, and a required cross-cultural course for engineers on global understanding. A motivation to establish the programme was to better prepare engineers to deal with the global supply chain by training engineers who possess not only the appropriate technical skills but also the cross-cultural skills based on knowledge of "other" cultures and their own cultural biases. Michigan faculty have also created an Engineering Global Leadership Honours Programme, where students select a regional focus and concentrate their humanities/social science electives in that area. Students also must complete two years of advanced language study. Teams of business and engineering students consult for a major corporation. Muzumdar and Bean feel that even though almost all business is conducted in English and students may not even work in a location where their second language is spoken, having a second language makes the student more likely to work well in any other culture.

Melsa, Holger, and Zachary have described Iowa State's Global Academic Industrial Network (GAIN), which provides U.S. students with international experiences in Germany to better prepare them for future job requirements. They note that the critical element in all international exchange programmes is the faculty; institutions must find ways to engage their faculty in international experiences, including extended stays at a foreign institution.

Programmes built around a single faculty member and his or her international connections are fragile and typically fail when that individual loses interest or moves. Further, funding cannot become the limiting factor with such programmes. Institutional support at the highest levels is essential. A promising, comprehensive programme is Purdue's Global Engineering Alliance for Research and Education (GEARE). This unique eighteen-month progra-mme, developed in partnership with Karlsruhe (Germany) and Shanghai Jiao Tong (China) Universities, integrates language education, cultural orientation, three-month domestic and three-month international internships at the same partner firm, study abroad, and a two semester face-to-face multinational design team project, with one semester abroad and one at home. The bilateral programme involves equal numbers of students from each university participating in the paired exchanges.

Another model programme for providing international experience is Old Dominion University's cluster concept. Here, students take a three-course cluster with an inter-national perspective, including two required courses-"Global Engineering and Project Management" and "Commu-nications Across Cultures"-and select one other from among "World Resources," "International Business Operations," or "Sustainable Development".

The cluster concept attempts to provide students with a basic understanding of the integrative nature of successful engineering practices that involve not only technical but international, cultural, communication, and busincss factors. It also attempts to provide students with the knowledge to work productively in an environment that encompasses difierent cultures, business practices, resources, communi-cation, and engineering practices.

The University of Kentucky has created an innovative combined B.S. Engineering-M.B.A. programme with a strong international component directed at producing manufactu-ring engineers and engineering managers. The engineering undergraduate degree, coupled with the M.B.A., allows students to explore immediate interests while building a solid, long-term career foundation.

This integration of business and economics courses with a traditional engineering programme over a five-year period results in students developing a broader, more holistic view of management principles and their application to an engineering environment. The students' senior year marks the beginning of the graduate M.B.A. courses and interaction with non-engineering M.B.A. students. During the summer prior to the fifth year, students participate in a study abroad programme designed expressly for the programme, thereby enhancing and broadening their cross-cultural experiences. For the summer of 2004, the Kentucky students participated in a second innovative initiative-the University of Pittsburgh's Manufacturing and the Global Supply Chain in the Pacific Rim as part of the Semester at Sea Programme.

That programme, a joint effort between the University of Pittsburgh's School of Engineering and the International Business Centre, offered three manufacturing courses with a global perspective as students visited China, Hong Kong, Japan, Korea, Russia, Taiwan, and Vietnam. Visits to in-country manufacturing sites complemented the class activities.

Amadei at Colorado has become a leader among the engineering educators now looking at sustainability issues in the less developed world. He suggests that most past engineering achievements have been developed with little consideration of their social, economic, and environmental impact on natural systems. In many instances, engineering projects have contributed to the degradation of the Earth's natural systems. Amadei is concerned with the education of engineers interested in addressing the problems that are most specific to developing communities-water provision and purification, sanitation, power production, shelter, site planning, infrastructure, food production and distribution, and communication.

These problems arc not usually addressed in U.S. engineering curricula, despite the fact that 20 per cent of the world's population lacks clean water, 40 per cent lacks adequate sanitation, 20 per cent lacks adequate housing, and 30 per cent live in conflict zones, transition, or situations of permanent instability.

As a result Amadei is helping to create a programme in Engineering for Developing Communities that will view the developing world as the classroom of the twenty-first century. This interdisciplinary effort will bring together engineering and non-engineering disciplines, thus supporting the learning of multiple professional skills. It will address a wide range of issues-water provision and purification, sanitation, health, power production, shelter, site planning, infrastru-cture, food production and distribution, communi-cation, and jobs and capital for various developing communities. The first phase involves an undergraduate certificate programme that should be in place by the time this chapter is published.

As part of this initiative, Amadei and his colleagues have formed Engineers without Borders-USA (EWB) at Colorado, which is dedicated to helping disadvantaged communities improve their quality of life by implementing environ-mentally and economically sustainablc engineering projects while developing internationally responsible engineering students.

Student projects that involve the design and construction of water, sanitation, and energy systems are ongoing in Belize, Mali, Mauritania, Nicaragua, Peru, Haiti, and Thailand. Rowan University faculty are incorporating EWB projects into their junior and senior clinics as a means of introducing open-ended problem solving in conjunction with developing synthesis, analysis, teamwork, communica-tion, business, and entrepreneurial skills.

A somewhat similar programme is being developed at Colorado School of Mines (CSM), with a focus on "humanitarian engineering." With support from the William and Flora Hewlett Foundation, the goal is to nurture a cadre of engineers that is sensitive to social contexts and committed and qualified to serve humanity by contributing to the solution of complex problems at regional, national, and international levels and locations around the world.

This goal is to be achieved through the development of a humanitarian component for the CSM engineering curriculum that will teach engineering students how to bring technical knowledge and skill, as well as cultural sensitivity, to bear on the real-world problems of the less materially advantaged. A complement of Engineers without Borders-U.S.A. is Engineers for a Sustainable World (ESW) (previo-usly known as Engineers without Frontiers-USA).

ESW originated in the College of Engineering at Cornell University in 2001 as a result of the efforts of Dr. Krishna S. Athreya, director of Minority and Women's Programmes in Engineering, and Regina R. L. Clewlow, a Cornell University graduate. ESW is based on the belief that engineers and community members can work together to identify and solve technology-based problems, employing solutions that can be locally sustained, leading to an improved quality of life. ESW believes that locally sustainablc engineering solutions are fundamental to the needs of communities in which issues such as lack of clean water, poor housing, and limited energy are barriers to adequate living conditions.

By establishing a national network in the United States for engineers to be of service to developing communities, ESW contributes to a better world and enriches the lives of engineering professionals who seek to participate in socially responsible endeavors. ESW has almost twenty chapters, with another thirty in the formation stage. Iowa State University and the Universities of Dayton and Seattle have joined together to form Engineers in Technical, Humanitarian Opportunities of Service Learning (ETHOS). Its purpose is to help students gain an awareness of the social and cultural fabric of the poorest of the world and perform design research focused on improving the ability of these individuals to meet their basic needs. Engineering activities are being implemented in a number of formats, ranging from classroom activities to multi-semester research studies. Both on-campus curricular and immersion service experiences arc included in its mission. Initial projects have focused on two non-governmental organizations' efforts to develop more efficient and more durable wood-burning stoves used for cooking by the world's poor.

Another example of service learning incorporated as part of undergraduate engineering education is the building of low-cost, energy-efficient houses in South Africa by students from Tuskegee University and the University of Fort Hare (South Africa). The idea behind this project is to develop a way for some of the economic benefit to stay in the local community. A number of faith-based institutions, notably Calvin, Drodt, Grove City, and Messiah Colleges, have combined engineering, service learning, and globally based humanitarian projects, thus meeting both social and student needs. However, Riley and Miller (Smith College) have raised concerns about involvement with faith-based projects, feeling that certain projects may be inappropriate if the development aid is tied to religious conversion and destroying indigenous cultures without regard for the community's traditions.

Smith College has developed an interdisciplinary project-based course that seeks to initiate critical study of the technological, cultural, and policy aspects of international development. This course requires students from different majors to share sophisticated disciplinary knowledge. Students address the promises and limitations of technology for development; the meanings of capitalism, colonialism, and globalization; and the implications of engaging in development work from places of privilege.

In developing a service component for the course, they seek to avoid sending students for only a few weeks to a country with which they have had no prior cultural experience-a situation that would make it difficult for students to acquire an adequate knowledge or sense of the community in which they are working.

Since the mid-1990s, an increasing number of programmes have incorporated international design team experiences, involving students from a U.S. and one or more partner international institutions. The original concept involved using the Internet and e-mail for communication, with the team coming together at the end of the project for a final meeting and presentation. Now, with the introduction of virtual design and virtual teaming concepts, the potential exists to do these types of programmes without having students leave home.

The need to train engineers to be well prepared to collaborate with their colleagues around the world and to work effectively in geographically distributed, multicultural teams was a motivation for Union College's creation of an International Virtual Design Studio (IVDS) in 1996. The IVDS initially brought together the mechanical engineering departments at Union College and Mideast Technical University (METU) in Ankara, Turkey, in response to the need to develop skills among students to better function in the emerging global environment in today's workplace.

In 1997, Queen's University (Kingston, Ontario) joined the partnership. Such projects provide international culture interaction, team building, communication, creative thinking, and project management experience. Each IVDS team has four to six members, two or three from each institution-METU and either Queens or Union. At Union, students select their project in spring term of the junior year.

Students must analyse, design, and build an autonomous robot for a given task and application. Since 1999, METU students have visited in November to compile and finish design reports. Final reports are presented before they leave. In January, after a prototype has been built, they go to Turkey for a competition at METU.

Sheppard et al. propose that virtual reality (VR) has the potential to have a major impact on engineering education by permitting students to explore environments that would be otherwise inaccessible. Specifically, VR will better facilitate teaming on an international and therefore multicultural level. Hence, faculty now must address educational collaboration in the virtual environment, testing and refining it at the institutional level, between institutions and across national boundaries.

A pilot implementation at Stevens Institute of Technology involves undergraduate student teams from three universities in three countries: Stevens is providing overall design and project coordination, the University of the Philippines (Quezon City, Philippines) is the manufacturing lead, and the National Institute of Technology (Warangal, India) is the simulation lead.

The project, "MEMS across the Globe" forms part of a larger pilot in virtual student design undertaken by a consortium of schools in collaboration with PTC Inc., a producer of industry standard design and collaboration tools. At Northern Arizona, language and engineering faculty are combining to utilize virtual reality to develop a pilot "Global Engineering College." When successfully implemented, it will inject international perspectives throughout the curriculum by leveraging technological, developments to create a "virtual" engineering college.

A recognition of the need for and the ability to engage in lifelong learning: Although the new ABET engineering criteria have brought lifelong learning to the forefront of engineering education, as Litzinger and his colleagues have pointed out, lifelong learning in engineering has been recognized as critical for decades. They note that the Final Report of the Goals Committee on Engineering Education contained a discussion of the importance of lifelong learning, and the theme of the 1978 ASEE Annual Meeting was "Career

Management-Lifelong Learning." A number of earlier studies that investigated the types of activities involved in lifelong learning, their frequency of use, the support systems required, the barriers, and impact of lifelong learning for individual engineers are summarized in a 1985 report by a National Research Council panel. Litzinger and his colleagues, who are at the frontier of studying lifelong learning relative to engineering education, note that a major issue is how to assess the extent to which students are prepared to engage in it and also their willingness to do so. With funding from the National Science Foundation, they have been investigating how best to assess lifelong learning.

Various engineering education researchers have defined elements of lifelong learning, including Henry and Rogers, whose RIRI model consists of four components: receiving, inquiring, reflecting, and integrating. Miller, Olds, and Pavelich purport that their Cogito system for measuring intellectual development (based on assessing reflective judgment) will, when fully validated, also assess lifelong learning. When we specified the attributes of lifelong learning as part of our NSF-funded Action Agenda study, we proposed that these include the ability to:

- Demonstrate reading, writing, listening, and speaking skills;
- Demonstrate an awareness of what needs to be learned;
- Follow a learning plan;
- Identify, retrieve, and organize information;
- Understand and remember new information;
- Demonstrate critical thinking skills; and
- Reflect on one's own understanding.

We propose that as students acquire the other professional skills, especially the other two awareness skills, as well as the process skills, that they will, in fact, acquire the ability to do lifelong learning. Hence, one will become a proficient lifelong learner as one becomes proficient in the broad spectrum of professional skills.

INTERPERSONAL SKILLS TRAINING

Interpersonal skills, in layman's terms, refer to the skills individuals need when they interact with other people. Also, the meaning of interpersonal skills has a number of synonyms, such as social skills, soft skills, people skills, or communication skills. The distinctions among the terms are not always clear, in many cases they are used interchangeably. Despite the significance of interpersonal skills in our life, research on interpersonal skills training is difficult to find.

One explanation for this might be because interpersonal skills are used unconsciously as a part of daily life; people view the interpersonal domain as inborn skills or characteristics, not skills or knowledge to be acquired consciously.

Another reason for this might be the overarching characteristics of interpersonal skills, which require the combination of cognitive, psychomotor and affective components simultaneously. Many researchers explain that interpersonal skills have complicated characteristics. Marlowe's social intelligence model shows multidimensional characteristics as consisting of: care for others, social self-efficacy, and the ability to understand others.

Similarly, Hargie identifies the following six characteristics of interpersonal skills:

- Goal-directedness and intentionality.
- Inter-related situationally appropriate social behaviours.
- Qualitative differences in social behaviour.
- A series of related skills in sequence.
- The composition of the sub-skills.
- The influence of cognitive control.

Similarly, Bailey and Butcher emphasized that effective interpersonal skills training should focus on developing perceptual, cognitive, and behavioural skills components together. That is, learners need to make reasonable judge-ments at the perceptual level to respond in a timely manner. At the cognitive level, the learners should understand the purpose of an interaction and have clear ideas of what appropriate behaviours are in specific situations.

Finally, the learners should demonstrate actual behavi-ours at the performance level to execute their individual interpersonal skills. These multidimensional characteristics of interpersonal skills require a different instructional approach from traditional approaches that focus on developing individuals' cognitive skills. Given the complexity of inter-personal skills characteristics, combining two or more methods that have different strengths and weaknesses may promise better results. This implies the necessity of an integrated approach for interpersonal skills training.

BEHAVIOUR MODELING TRAINING

Behaviour modeling has been recognized as the most appropriate instructional method for interpersonal skills training since 1970. It is primarily based on Bandura's social learning theory, which explains that people can learn by observing others. Noe defined behaviour modeling as "A training method in which trainees are presented with a model who demonstrates key behaviours to replicate and provides them with the opportunity to practice those key behaviours". The primary advantage of behaviour modeling is that it enables individuals to learn without a trial and error process.

Therefore, behaviour modeling serves as an efficient way to teach interpersonal skills by reducing the costs and time involved in a trial and error process. In addition to the efficiency of behaviour modeling, many research studies report its effectiveness. From the learning theory perspective, Simon and Werner explained that behaviour modeling is somewhere between direct instruction and exploration in the continuum of instructional methods because it provides learners with both cognitive instruction and the opportunities to explore learning content with practices. That is, behaviour modeling enhances learning effectiveness by combining bipolar approaches.

Decker and Nathan provided five components of behaviour modeling:

- Modeling.
- Retention process
- Behavioural rehearsal
- Feedback
- Transfer of training.

The graphic representation of the behaviour modeling training process is as follows:

First, modeling is the most distinct feature of the behaviour modeling approach. The objective of modeling is to facilitate the learners' attention towards the key behaviours, which is a set of behaviours intended for the students to learn. Decker and Nathan indicated that when a model's behaviour is "distinctive, meaningful to the observer, not too complex, and observable," the effectiveness of modeling is increased. Second, the retention process facilitates learners' memorization of what they learn from the models. As Bandura mentioned, if learners do not remember what they saw during the modeling, learning will not occur.

To facilitate the retention process, Decker and Nathan recommended using learning points, which are verbal instructions in words or phrases, to summarize or generalize key behaviours. Third, behavioural rehearsal provides the learners with opportunities to practice the modeled behaviours. Acquiring cognitive concepts of skills does not guarantee actual behaviour reproduction, so it is necessary to provide learners with practice opportunities to enhance the likelihood of obtaining desirable performances. Dick and Carey indicated that practice and feedback are key to the success of psychomotor skills acquisition.

Finally, the learners are asked to apply the new knowledge gleaned from the models to their real life. The significance of transfer of training cannot be overemphasized because it is expected to eventually lead to positive performance results, which is the ultimate goal of providing learners with training.

Online Interpersonal Skills Training

Some researchers are skeptical about the effectiveness of interpersonal skills training delivered by technology because of the limited interaction and feedback in the online environment. Meanwhile, others are enthusiastic about conveying interpersonal skills training through technology because of the cost-effectiveness it achieves by reducing training costs and its delivery time. The former are more concerned about learning effectiveness of online interpersonal skills training whereas the latter have high expectations of online learning for the cost-effectiveness reasons. In terms of cost-effectiveness of interpersonal skills training programmes, Campbell, Lison, Brosook, Hoover, & Arnold compared training programmes conveyed by way of computer/video technology and instructor-led programmes and found that there is no significant difference in learning gains between the two programmes.

As a result, they claimed that computer/video technology can reduce costs and instructors' working hours to half that which would be spent on instructor-led programmes. Despite Campbell and his colleague's study, the effects of interpersonal skills training delivered by technology are still controversial because of insufficient empirical evidence. However, in spite of the technical and pedagogical limitations of online environments for interpersonal skills training, given the proliferation of online learning and the magnitude of interpersonal skills in daily life, it is imperative to explore the most effective method to deliver interpersonal skills training online.

Based on the proven effectiveness of behaviour modeling for interpersonal skills training in classrooms, this study applied it to online environments. For this, some changes should be made because of the discrepancies between online and classroom learning environments. One change is model presentation. Given that models convey learning content, key behaviours, it is necessary to design instructionally effective models for learning outcomes. The model presentation formats can be live, video, audio, written scripts, or a combination of two or more of these methods. For enhancing the effectiveness of modeling, Decker and Nathan indicated that models' behaviours should be displayed in enough detail to convey the learning content. By contrast, from the cognitive load theory, some researchers insist that it is necessary to provide learners with the appropriate amount of information because of a learners' limited working memory.

Meanwhile, Bandura stated that the effectiveness of modeling is determined by the learners' cognitive development in interpreting key behaviours and the models' characteristics, such as its complicatedness. He also added that if the amount of information conveyed is identical, the presentation formats do not influence learning outcomes because the role of model presentations is to provide learners with information. However, when the results of information processing are defined broadly by processed amount, speed, accuracy, and cost-effectiveness, the model presentation formats may influence the learning outcomes in certain ways.

CONCEPTUALIZING COMMUNICATION COMPETENCE

Generally speaking, a competent communicator is one who has "knowledge of appropriate communication patterns in a given situation and the ability to use the knowledge". Correspondingly, the two major components of communication competence that have been most closely examined in the organizational communication literature are strategic and tactical communication.

Strategic communication pertains to knowledge of organizational realities, what things "mean" in the organization, and may vary from one organization to another. Tactical communication represents the skills one has available to use as instruments to accomplish personal, group, and organizational goals.

Strategic communication knowledge has been frequently studied using a social cognitive perspective. Some researchers employing this approach believe that the way to study organizational communication competence is to understand self and role responsibilities within the organization through examinations of individual differences among organizational members.

In particular, they operationalize competence in terms of an individual's cognitive complexity, perspective taking, empathy, persuasive ability, and self-monitoring. Research findings viewing competence in this way have shown that individuals who have more developed cognitive abilities are considered to be more competent in their organizations than those with less developed abilities.

Other researchers, such as Harris and Cronen, have applied a rules-based approach to conceptualize communi-cation competence. They define strategic communication competence as an individual's ability to interpret constitutive rules (i.e., accurate knowledge of organizational meanings) and tactical communication competence as an ability to follow and manipulate regulative rules (i.e., communication skills or performance capability to achieve personal, group, and organizational goals). However, Harris has also suggested that individuals' levels of competence depend upon the balance of the complexity and flexibility of their own intrapersonal system and the interpersonal environment.

Complexity refers to the extent to which an individual possesses the various communication behaviours that are required in an environment, whereas flexibility is defined as an individual's ability to adapt and/or an environmental capability to endure various communication behaviours.

Tactical communication has been often studied from a skill/performance perspective. Generally, these studies have attempted to identify communication skill requirements in organizations. According to these studies, the most common communication skills that organizational members see as important in their jobs are advising, persuading, instructing, interviewing, exchanging information, public speaking, leading discussions, giving orders, solving problems, and listening.

Jablin et al. noted, based on the results of surveys in this area, that commonalties across occupations and organizational roles regarding communication skill requirements are often suggested by the researchers conducting research in this area. To review, in this section, we have attempted to describe the basic dimensions - communication knowledge, communi-cation skills/behaviours - of the communication competence construct.

Although these dimensions appear to be applicable across cultures, the specific characteristics of each dimension are likely to vary across cultures because cultural communication can influence the way organizational members interact with each other within the same culture. Thus, cultural differences may be a major factor affecting the characteristics of communication competence in different organizational and national cultures.

Culture is usually viewed as a historically derived system of shared symbolic ideas and meanings, or interpretations of symbols, which are associated with the "ordering" of societies. Since cultural variability is considered to be a major factor affecting the way that individuals in different national cultures communicate in the interpersonal, group, and organizational contexts, it may be a key source from which members of different national cultures develop their understandings of the strategic communication knowledge and tactical skills necessary to be competent organizational communicators.

Consistent with the above position, in a study examining the influence of national culture on organizational culture, Sorod found that the national culture influenced organizati-onal/managerial values in 12 Thai-owned companies and 13 U.S.-owned companies in Thailand. In addition, she confirmed the generalizability of the characteristics of Thai culture found in Hofstede's earlier work (that is, Thai culture is characterized by low individualism, low masculinity, high power distance, and high uncertainty avoidance).

In particular, her research showed that Thai culture emphasizes group interests and loyalty, modesty, and quality of life (rather than material success), status, and the use of appropriate communication rules and norms in interactions with people in different societal strata. However, Sorod's study did not investigate the influence of the national culture on Thai organizational communication competence, nor did it explore how beliefs about what constitutes communication competence may vary depending on Thai organizational characteristics and traditions.

For example, as noted earlier, what is considered to be appropriate behaviour in Thai organizations is often closely tied to an individual's status, and is frequently associated with one's level in the organizational hierarchy and his or her role (supervisor, subordinate, peer), as well as personal characteristics (such as educational attainment, age, and gender). In addition, Komin's data suggest that what is considered competent organizational behaviour in Thailand may vary depending on the type of organization in which one works: government, state enterprise (at least 50% of the organization is owned by the state), or private business. For example, Komin reports that managers in Thai government and state enterprises have greater expectations that they should be experts who can answer almost all questions raised by subordinates than do managers in Thai business firms (who may be somewhat more participative as problem solvers than those working in traditional government organizations).

In turn, since much higher degrees of intense conflict appear to occur in government organizations than in state enterprises, it is likely that the sorts of skills and abilities associated with competent conflict management may vary across organizational types.

In light of these issues, this study poses the following research questions:

- *RQ* 1: What kinds of communication knowledge and skills/behaviours are most associated with communication competence in Thai organizations for supervisors, subordinates, and co-workers?
- *RQ* 2: Do perceptions of communicatively competent Thai supervisors, subordinates and co-workers vary in light of their organizational role (supervisory, non-supervisory), hierarchical level, the type of organization in which they work (public, state enterprise, private), or their personal characteristics (gender, age, education)?

Methodology

In order to acquire information representative of Thai organizations, data were collected from 14 different organizations. Five of these were public organizations which operated as part of the government, five were companies that were privately-owned business enterprises, and four were state-enterprise organizations (at least 50% of each organization is owned by the state).

The public organizations included a department of the Finance Ministry, a department from the Interior Ministry, a public school located in Bangkok (provided education from grades 1-12), a department from the Defence Ministry, and a department from the Education Ministry. The private companies included a manufacturer and distributor of construction materials, a petrochemical company, a private school, and two different commercial financial institutions. The four state-enterprise organizations included an airline, a mass transit organization, a telecommunications institution, and a provider of electric power.

The size of these organizations ranged from 150 to 28,000 employees; with respect to the size of the units from which data were collected for this study, the number of employees ranged from 35 to 3,000. Usable data were collected from 413 members of the 14 organizations (89% response rate). However, because of missing data, the number of subjects reported in some of our analyses totals less than 413.

Of the respondents, 31% worked in government positions, 25% were employees of state-enterprises, and 43% worked in privately own companies. Participants represented a wide range of occupations including jobs as educators (15%), personnel officers (12%), accountants/auditors (11%), sales/marketing representatives (9%), administrators/managers (5%), clerks/secretaries (7%), non-clerical support staff (7%), financial officers (6%), information/data programmers (7%), public relations officers (6%), professionals (i.e., engineers, architects, and lawyers, 4%), cashiers/bank tellers (5%), maintenance/physical plant staff members, and other miscellaneous positions.

Approximately half of the respondents were male and half female, and they ranged in age from 15 to 59 (Mean = 34.5 years of age). Approximately one-third of the subjects worked in supervisory positions and two-thirds in non-supervisory jobs. The typical respondent had 10 years of work experience and had worked in her/his current positions for 4 years.

With respect to educational backgrounds of members of the sample, 7.5% had a high school certificate, 10% had an Associate's degree, 60% had an undergraduate college degree, and 18% had graduate degrees. Regarding the educational profile of members of this sample, it is important to note that this group had received more schooling than the average Thai citizen. According to census statistics 93% of the Thai people are "literate."

Among those considered literate, 75% have at least a compulsory education (six years in school), 15% have a high school certificate, 5.5% have an undergraduate degree, and 4.5% have others types of educational backgrounds (e.g., trade school, seminary). Thus, the sample of respondents in our study is more representative of well-educated versus poorly or moderately educated members of Thai society.

SCALE DEVELOPMENT AND PILOT TEST OF QUESTIONNAIRES

Original items were generated to reflect two bodies of literature, one concerned with organizational communication competence, and the other with Thai cultural and organizational characteristics, and to tap into the two dimensions of organizational communication competence discussed earlier: strategic communication knowledge and tactical communication skills.

Strategic communication knowledge, as we have seen, refers to the ability to know when and where specific behaviours are situationally appropriate and includes the ability to describe, explain, and interpret messages by assigning meaning to codes, and predict other's behaviour in various communication settings/activities.

Items measuring strategic communication knowledge explored two issues. The first issue focused on the relationship between Thai cultural communication behaviours and communication competence in Thai organizations and in particular four characteristics of Thai culture: low individualism, low masculinity, high power distance, and high uncertainty avoidance.

The second issue involved the relationship between individuals' cognitive abilities (empathy and cognitive complexity) and communication competence in Thai organizations. The communication skills that our literature analysis suggested might be relevant to Thai communication competence included giving feedback, receiving feedback, writing reports/memos, providing information, receiving information, seeking information, giving instructions/orders, taking instructions/orders, advising, persuading/motivating, and networking.

A pilot test was conducted by administering a preliminary questionnaire to five Thai graduate students at a university in the southwestern United States. These students were asked if the design, instructions, and items were clear, if they knew why each item was being asked, and if any items were unnecessary. The results revealed that some items needed to be reworded in order to enhance clarity and consistency and that the format needed slight adjustment to make it easier for individuals to respond. In addition, the questionnaire was shortened by eliminating nonessential and redundant items.

Since the actual study was to be conducted in Thailand, the revised English version of the questionnaire was then translated in format and content into Thai by one of the researchers and several graduate students who were natives of Thailand. Subsequently, the Thai-version was given to a bilingual speaker for back translation. Afterwards, a group of five Thai graduate students were asked to review the Thai-version for clarity and adequacy. To further insure the success of the study, the final revision of the Thai questionnaire was given to ten members of an organization in Thailand for examination. After some slight revisions, the final set of 80 items that were included in the questionnaire were randomized to minimize order effects.

At least ten individuals who were in supervisory positions were asked to respond to the supervisor form of the questionnaire, ten to the subordinate/follower form, and ten to the coworker form (individuals in these latter two groups could be either supervisors or non-supervisors). Of the 413 respondents, 30% responded to the supervisor form of the questionnaire, 37% to the subordinate form and 33% to the coworker version. The questionnaires were divided into two major sections. The first section contained ten items and sought demographic information: gender, age, highest level of education, the division or department in which they worked, organizational tenure, job tenure, position/nature of job, supervisor's span of control, number of employees in their organization, and their approximate position within the organization chain of command/hierarchy.

The second section consisted of the 80 randomly ordered items describing potential communicative behaviours/skills and forms of knowledge expected to be associated with communicatively competent organizational members. Respondents were asked to think of the most communi-catively competent supervisor/subordinate/coworker they knew. Those responding to the supervisor form were asked to think of the most communicatively competent subordinate who worked or had worked for them. Those completing the subordinate form were asked to think of the most communicatively competent supervisor for whom they worked or had worked. Similarly, those responding to the coworker version of the questionnaire were asked to think of the most communicatively competent coworker with whom they worked or had worked.

Although the "targets" (supervisor/subordinate/coworker) about whom individuals responded varied across the questionnaire forms, the items were the same; across all questionnaires subjects were asked to indicate on five-point, Likert-type scales (1 = strongly agree, 5 = strongly disagree) the extent to which they associated the various communicative skills, behaviours and forms of knowledge with the target.

DATA ANALYSIS

Given the nascent nature of this research, we conducted an exploratory factor analysis (principal components, varimax rotation) of the responses to the questionnaire instrument (by combining data across the questionnaires) to identify key dimensions of communication competence. Initial results indicated a multi-factor solution; an examination of a scree plot and eigenvalues suggested a simple structure of no more than ten factors. A second principal components analysis was conducted limiting the number of factors to ten. In total, the ten factors accounted for 41.7% of the variance; however, only the items in the first factor met basic criteria for factor integrity (given the exploratory nature of this research, an item needed to load at least 50 on one factor and no more than 30 on any other factor).

This one factor was comprised of 21 items, was highly reliable (alpha =.88) and accounted for 15.6% of the variance. Consequently, the items from this factor were summed to form a competence scale. In order to understand why our final factor analysis solution contained only 25% of the items in the competence instrument, we reexamined the descriptive statistics associated with our questionnaire data.

Inspection of these statistics revealed a general low level of variability in the responses of subjects to the questionnaire items (standard deviations for most items were in the 60-90 range and few exceeded 1.0), thus constraining the magnitude of the correlations possible among the variables and limiting our ability to make use of many of the questionnaire items in the factor analysis.

As a consequence, and in light of our goal of identifying the kinds of communication knowledge and skills most associated with communication competence, we conducted a secondary analysis of our questionnaire data that maximized the variability that was present in our data. First, frequency distributions, means, and standard deviations were examined for each item, allowing the researchers to rank the mean scores of the 80 items from highest to lowest for each of the three groups of respondents (supervisors, subordinates, co-workers) as well as for the respondents as a whole. Subsequently, those items in the combined data for which the means were 2.5 or less, or greater than 3.5 were isolated for further analysis. Items that had means of 2.5 or less included all items for which there was overall "agreement" that the item described a knowledge or skill closely associated with communication competence. Items that had means of 3.5 or above included all items for which there was overall "disagreement" that the item described a knowledge or skill closely associated with communication competence. In total, 33 items met these criteria (this included all items contained in 21 item competency scale).

We decided to examine the kinds of knowledge and skills that respondents least associated with communication competence, as well as those they most associated with competence, because we suspected that to some degree the two sets of items would complement one another; if this was the case, it would offer support for the internal validity of our results.

Second, separate multivariate analyses of variance were calculated for the high agreement items (n = 24) and low agreement items (n = 9) across the three "targets" that subjects evaluated with respect to communication competence: super-visors, subordinates, and coworkers. If a Manova test were statistically significant then 1 × 3 Anova results were examined with respect to each of the questionnaire items associated with the multivariate test. If a univariate F test was significant for an item, then post hoc multiple comparison tests were computed to determine specific difference among the mean for the three "target" groups (supervisors, subordinates, co-workers).

Inspection of the results of factor analysis suggests that communicatively competent members of Thai organizations are expected to understand norms associated with polite, tactful, and respectful communication, display empathic listening skills and high levels of cognitive complexity, and have the ability to seek, give, and process information in a situationally appropriate manner.

In order to determine if respondents' perceptions of competence varied according to the target they evaluated, a one-way analysis of variance was computed across the three groups - supervisors, co-workers, and subordinates - with respect to their scores on the competence scale. Results of this analysis revealed a non-significant F-ratio and showed minimal differences among the groups.

For all, communication competence was associated with the extent to which an individual is open to his/her super-visor's/subordinates'/co-workers' questions, proficient in adapting his/her speaking approach and choice of words to people in varying organizational positions and/or situations, knowledgeable about how to address others with whom she/he communicates in different situations, makes use of the information he/she receives, and knows when, where and with whom to express respectfulness when interacting with others. However, there were also a number of distinctions in the knowledge and skills most closely associated with communicatively competent supervisors, subordinates and co-workers. The ability to present job-related information in both oral and written forms was more closely associated with communicatively competent supervisors than co-workers.

In addition, the ability to understand and explain things going on in the organization, speak thoughtfully and calmly even in a crisis, and to socialize with people in all levels of the organization were more closely associated with communication competence for supervisors than for subordinates (the ability to socialize with people in all levels of the organization was also more closely associated with communicatively competent co-workers than subordinates). It was less appropriate for supervisors and co-workers not to try to give advice to others than for subordinates.

In fact, among all the behaviours assessed in the questionnaire, failing to give advice to others was rated as the communication behaviour least associated with communicatively competent supervisors and co-workers.

Respondents were in general agreement that the following forms of knowledge and skill were not highly associated with communicatively competent supervisors, subordinates, or co-workers: Speaking, listening and working all at the same time without looking at the other person, not desiring to receive feedback from others, socializing only with people in the same level or higher in the organization, not questioning the feedback received from others even though it is not clear, and talking about any topic anytime the person wants to (with respect to this latter competency, ANOVA results approached statistical significance, suggesting that while respondents believed this behaviour to be inappropriate for all targets, they perceived it as especially inappropriate for supervisors.

Research Question

The second research question sought to determine if respondents' perceptions of communicatively competent Thai supervisors, subordinates and co-workers vary in light of their organizational role (supervisory, non-supervisory), hierarchical level, the type of organization in which they work (public, state enterprise, private), and their personal characteristics (gender, age, education).

Results associated with the competence scale showed no differences in the scores of supervisors as compared to non-supervisors, individuals at various levels of their organizational hierarchies, between males and females, among employees of varying ages (29 years of age and younger, 3038 years of age, and 39 years of age and older), or across individuals with various levels of formal education (high school, Associate's degree, Bachelor's degree, graduate degree).

However, results did reveal differences in perceptions among those who worked in public organization, state enterprise organizations, and private companies. More specifically, individuals employed in private concerns agreed more with the notions expressed in the communication competence scale than those who worked in state enterprises, or in public organizations. In addition to the above analyses, RQ 2 was explored by computing MANOVAs for the items most and least associated with communication competence to discover the presence of interaction effects between the "target" group respondents evaluated (supervisor, subordinate, coworker) and the individual and organizational characteristics noted above. For the group of items least associated with communication competence there were no significant multivariate interaction effects between the target evaluated and any of the organizational and individual characteristics; in addition, there were no significant main effects for any of the characteristics. Results of the tests associated with those items that were perceived as most closely associated with communication competence indicated there were no significant multivariate interaction effects between the "target" evaluated and respondents' gender, age, education, level in the organization hierarchy, the type of organization in which they worked (public, state enterprise, private), or their position (supervisory, non-supervisory).

In addition, with one exception, there were no significant multivariate main effects associated with any of the individual and organizational characteristics. The one significant multivariate main effect that was discovered was associated with the type of organization in which respondents reported working.

An inspection of the univariate ANOVAs revealed significant main effects for twelve of the twenty-four items. These items are reported along with the results of post-hoc Newman-Keuls multiple comparison tests that were computed to determine the nature of the specific differences in responses among those working in the different types of organizations.

Examination of these results suggests, generally speaking, that those working in private companies perceived the behaviours and forms of knowledge described in the various questionnaire items as more indicative of organizational communication competence than those who worked in state enterprises or in public organizations.

This research sought to determine the kinds of communication knowledge and skills that are most associated with communicatively competent members of Thai organizations. Accordingly, questionnaire data were collected from a cross-section of individuals working in fourteen different Thai organizations (including public, private and state enterprises) concerning their perceptions of the kinds of skills/behaviours and forms of knowledge that are characteristic of the most communicatively competent supervisors, subordinates or co-workers with whom they work (or have worked). The study was founded on the notion that communication competence in Thai organizations requires consideration of unique characteristics of Thai culture (and that "western" approaches to conceptualizing competence needed to be applied to Thai organizations in a cautious manner).

However, it is also important to recognize that the Thai organizational members who participated in this research represent a group with a higher overall level of education than workers in Thailand generally. Thus, just as much of what we know about communication competence in the "west" is limited to white, middle-class persons, the generalizability of our results is limited to middle-class, well-educated Thais (78% of the research participants had at least a bachelor's degree).

Overall results suggest that Thai organizational members perceive communication competence in terms of knowledge of normative communication behaviours, especially with respect to how to communicate with persons in different organizational roles and/or status, one's communication skills repertoire, and related cognitive abilities.

As expected, the forms of communication knowledge that Thais perceived to be associated with competence were related to and consistent with the forms of cultural variability that Hofstede, among others, has suggested typify Thai society: low individualism, high power distance, high uncertainty avoidance, and low masculinity.

More specifically, findings suggest that highly competent Thai organizational members are expected to know how to communicate so as to avoid conflict with others, display respect, control their emotions, tactfulness, modesty and politeness, and know the appropriate pronouns to use in addressing others.

For Thais, communication competence was associated with knowing when, where and with whom to express respectful manner in the organization, knowledge of chain of command communication, knowing how to communicate with and honour senior organizational members and show respect for their experience. These finding support the Thai belief that people who assume high social or organizational positions have "boon" (merit), "ba-ra-me" (prestige and influence), and "metra" (compassion) and thus not only know how to use their power to influence others, but also are thoughtful and kind to their subordinates.

In turn, people who are in lower social or organizational positions recognize that they are suppose to be obedient and respectful to those in higher positions. Essentially, these results support the notion that the Thai approach to management is one of benevolent paternalism, and that competent individuals display behaviours consistent with "Orn nork khaeng nai".

Results also showed that for Thais communication competence also involves knowing how to avoid conflict with others (for example, by not discussing things without regard to the person being referred to, recognizing the inappropriateness of responding negatively to colleague's opinions, and being able to control the expression of emotions). As noted earlier, Thais believe that inner freedom is best preserved in an emotionally and physically stable environment, and that social harmony is best maintained by avoiding unnecessary friction in contacts with others. Thus, it is not surprising that the Thai societal belief in "kreng jai" (extreme reluctance to impose on anyone or disturb his/her personal equilibrium by direct criticism, challenge or confrontation) is embedded in the implicit norms that guide Thai organizational communication behaviour. Thais do not value aggressive and competitive behaviour, "tend to be subtle and deferential", and like to use networking/ contacts or "Len sen" (knowing somebody) to resolve disputes informally.

The ability to use correct pronouns and carefully select words and speaking approaches in interacting with people in different levels were also identified as important forms of knowledge associated with communication competence. These findings may reflect the high uncertainty avoidance that other researchers have found to characterize Thai culture. By knowing that they are expected to communicate with a gentle tone of voice, display a smiling and pleasant face and friendly manner, use specific respectful pronouns in addressing persons of higher status, and adopt body posture that communicates required levels of respect, deference and intimacy, Thai organizational members reduce a considerable amount of uncertainty they might otherwise experience in their interactions with others. At the same time, however, it is important to recognize that the use of particular first- and second-person pronouns in conversations among Thai organizational members, as well as related body gestures, serve as structurational forces that produce and reproduce what some western critics might consider to be a problematic class-based social hierarchy in Thai organizations.

Given that Thai culture is considered to be "high context," it was not surprising to find that communication competence among Thais was associated with fairly high levels of cognitive complexity and empathy. For instance, communicatively competent workers were expected to be able to propose new ideas related to their jobs and to know the personal backgrounds of others well enough that they can analyse, predict, and accurately respond to the other party's needs, without having to be asked to do so. These sorts of skills and knowledge appear to be particularly important in superior-subordinate relationships since subordinates are expected to provide their bosses with all the information that they need to perform their jobs and maintain face. In turn, their bosses are expected to "reciprocate by providing for the welfare" of those who work for them.

In general, our results with respect to the kinds of communication skills associated with communication competence in Thai organizations were similar to those frequently identified as important for workers in "western" organizations. These skills include giving instructions, feedback and advice, providing, seeking and receiving information; and writing, listening, networking, and persuading. However, our results also suggest that in Thai organizations individuals also place a very high value on a person's ability to speak in a gentle, calm, and thoughtful manner. Although it is possible that these speaking attributes may be valued in some "western" organizations, assertive/aggressive approaches to oral communication have been more frequently identified as typical in western countries. In sum, with a few exceptions, the major source in variance in perceptions of communication competence in Thai organizations, in comparison to those in North America, centres on the knowledge/culture dimension of competence (knowing appropriate ways to use communication to achieve goals) and not on the skill dimension.

Although findings generally supported our expectations, several results were unexpected and provide a somewhat different perspective concerning competent communication in Thai organizations. In particular, while our literature review indicated that supervisors/managers in Thai organizations are not generally interested in soliciting opinions from their subordinates (since those in authority have traditionally exercised their power without consulting followers), our results revealed that supervisors/managers perceived fairly consultative and to some extent participative approaches to communication with subordinates as associated with communication competence.

If, as the literature suggests, Thai managers are expected to know everything for which they are responsible, they may find they can obtain more useful information from their subordinates by encouraging them to be more open in expressing their opinions, providing them with positive feedback for the upward communication of bad as well as good news, and rewarding them for generating new, unsolicited ideas for improving job performance. Consistent with this contention, supervisors rated those subordinates who provide complete information to them, as well as those who ask their supervisors questions about unclear matters, as highly competent communicators. Thus, to some degree, a shift may be occurring in contemporary Thai organizations, such that employee behaviour indicative of higher levels of individualism and lower levels of power distance is becoming more highly regarded than in the past. The developing shift toward consultative/participative management approaches may also reflect the influence of the large number of Thai managers who have attended colleges in the United States, and/or have participated in management programmes offered by western business schools that operate branches in Thailand.

Paradoxically, while communicatively competent subordinates in Thai organizations are expected to be open and straightforward, they are also expected to know how and when to communicate to avoid conflict and interpersonal problems with their supervisors. Thus, to some extent the leader-follower relationship in Thai organizations represents a balance of "supervision" and "leadership" exchanges.

In essence, followers need to walk a fairly high and narrow wire: they must avoid conflict and maintain harmony in their relationships with their supervisors while at the same time they are forthright and complete in sharing information with them. The difficulty in maintaining such a balance is evident in other of our research findings. Specifically, communicatively competent supervisors were seen as being more open in their communication with their subordinates than communicatively competent subordinates were in their communication with their supervisors.

However, the tradition in many Thai organizations of using a "luug maw" (old hand) as an intermediary in helping to resolve conflicts between supervisors and subordinates may also allow subordinates to informally share problematic information with their bosses while at the same time maintaining harmony in their relationships. The role of the "luug maw" in mediating communication problems between supervisors and followers should be explored in future research.

Results of our study also suggest that communicatively competent supervisors are not only expected to have the ability to talk to anybody about anything in any situation, and to be able to communicate a clear vision of organizational concepts to their subordinates, but they are also expected to network with people in all levels of the organization and display "connection power" As noted earlier, "connection power" is associated with networking and may be especially important for Thai supervisors since highly personalized approaches to influence are common in Thai organizations.

Although findings from the present study did not reveal many distinctive characteristics of communicatively competent co-workers in Thai organizations, results suggest that co-workers value peers who excel in their advising and empathic listening skills.

That is, a communicatively competent coworker listens to the problems and opinions of others, gives substantial advice, and commits him/herself to give assistance if it appears the other party needs it. In addition, it appears that the oral exchange of information, without any written follow-up, is considered more acceptable in coworker communication than in interactions between supervisors and their direct reports.

Our results also showed that perceptions of commun-ication competence varied across the three different kinds of organizations we examined: public, state enterprise, and private. In particular, those working in private firms seemed to place a higher value on the communication competencies we examined in this research than those working in public organizations or state enterprises.

Given the competitive nature of for-profit organizations (and the existence of lifetime employment practices in many public and state enterprise organizations), proficiency in communication may be more instrumental to individual success (and thus be more highly valued by workers) in these settings, than among those employed in public or state enterprise organizations.

At the same time, these results also indicate that while there may be many consistencies in individuals' perceptions of communication competence across types of organizations within any national culture, particular qualities associated with competence may be more or less salient depending on the type of organization in which one works. In considering the results of this research, several limitations, in addition to constraints associated with our sample, should be kept in mind. In particular, due to lack of variability in responses the great majority of competence items were not included in the communication competence scale that resulted from our factor analysis of the competence measure.

At the same time, however, it should be noted that the factor that did emerge was highly reliable and, generally speaking, was associated with knowledge of politeness/deference norms in communicating with others. Not surprisingly, many of the items associated with this scale were the same ones that were identified as most or least associated with communicatively competent supervisors, subordinates, and co-workers (thus adding support to our findings).

In light of our fairly elaborate efforts to pilot test the questionnaires prior to collecting data, possible reasons for the lack of variability in responses to these instruments warrants consideration. One possible reason for constrained variation in responses may be associated with the manner in which Thais approach the completion of questionnaire items that utilize Likert-type response formats (strongly agree to strongly disagree).

Given Thai cultural norms associated with conflict avoidance, deference, politeness, etc., our respondents may have felt that it was inappropriate to strongly agree or disagree with many of the statements presented in the questionnaire items.

Ancillary data collected as part of this study, but not reported earlier, support this interpretation. Specifically, data gathered in moderately structured interviews (lasting approximately 40-60 minutes each) conducted with managers from seven of the ten organizations participating in the research (one interview/organization) produced results very similar to those obtained from the questionnaire data.

Thus, the same norms that may have been operating to limit variability in responses to questions asked in our paper-and-pencil competence measure may have affected our efforts to elicit information from respondents in face-to-face interviews. In light of this possibility, we recommend that future research explore the interaction between values and norms associated with Thai culture and the methods that researchers use to collect data. More generally, alternatives to traditional western research methodologies may require development if we are to obtain valid, representative, and useful data about communication in organizations in non-western countries/cultures such as Thailand.

9

Consumer Behaviour and Management

AN OVERVIEW

The study of consumers helps firms and organizations improve their marketing strategies by understanding issues such as how.

- The psychology of how consumers think, feel, reason, and select between different alternatives;
- The psychology of how the consumer is influenced by his or her environment;
- The behaviour of consumers while shopping or making other marketing decisions;
- Limitations in consumer knowledge or information processing abilities influence decisions and marketing outcome;
- How consumer motivation and decision strategies differ between products that differ in their level of importance or interest that they entail for the consumer; and
- How marketers can adapt and improve their marketing campaigns and marketing strategies to more effectively reach the consumer.

One "official" definition of consumer behaviour is "The study of individuals, groups, or organizations and the processes they use to select, secure, use, and dispose of products, services, experiences, or ideas to satisfy needs and the impacts that these processes have on the consumer and society."

Although it is not necessary to memorize this definition, it brings up some useful points:

- Behaviour occurs either for the individual, or in the context of a group or an organization.
- Consumer behaviour involves the use and disposal of products as well as the study of how they are purchased. Product use is often of great interest to the marketer, because this may influence how a product is best positioned or how we can encourage increased

consumption. Since many environmental problems result from product disposal this is also an area of interest.

- Consumer behaviour involves services and ideas as well as tangible products.
- The impact of consumer behaviour on society is also of relevance. For example, aggressive marketing of high fat foods, or aggressive marketing of easy credit, may have serious repercussions for the national health and economy.

There are four main applications of consumer behaviour:

- The most obvious is for *marketing strategy*—i.e., for making better marketing campaigns. For example, by understanding that consumers are more receptive to food advertising when they are hungry, we learn to schedule snack advertisements late in the afternoon. By understanding that new products are usually initially adopted by a few consumers and only spread later, and then only gradually, to the rest of the population, we learn that
  - Companies that introduce new products must be well financed so that they can stay afloat until their products become a commercial success and
  - It is important to please initial customers, since they will in turn influence many subsequent customers' brand choices.
- A second application is *public policy*. In the 1980s, Accutane, a near miracle cure for acne, was introduced. Unfortunately, Accutane resulted in severe birth defects if taken by pregnant women. Although physicians were instructed to warn their female patients of this, a number still became pregnant while taking the drug. To get consumers' attention, the Federal Drug Administration took the step of requiring that very graphic pictures of deformed babies be shown on the medicine containers.
- *Social marketing* involves getting ideas across to consumers rather than selling something. Marty Fishbein went on sabbatical to work for the Centres for Disease Control trying to reduce the incidence of transmission of diseases through illegal drug use. The best solution, obviously, would be if we could get illegal drug users to stop. This, however, was deemed to be infeasible. It was also determined that the practice of sharing needles was too ingrained in the drug culture to be stopped. As a result, using knowledge of consumer attitudes, Dr. Fishbein created a campaign that encouraged the cleaning of needles in bleach before sharing them, a goal that was believed to be more realistic.
- As a final benefit, studying consumer behaviour should make us better consumers. Common sense suggests, for example, that if you buy a

64 liquid ounce bottle of laundry detergent, you should pay less per ounce than if you bought two 32 ounce bottles. In practice, however, you often pay a size *premium* by buying the larger quantity. In other words, in this case, knowing this fact will sensitize you to the need to check the unit cost labels to determine if you are *really* getting a bargain.

There are several units in the market that can be analysed. Our main thrust in this course is the *consumer*. However, as suggested, also need to analyse our own firm's strengths and weaknesses and those of *competing firms*. Suppose, for example, that we make a product aimed at older consumers, a growing segment. A competing firm that targets babies, a shrinking market, is likely to consider repositioning toward our market. To assess a competing firm's potential threat, we need to examine its assets against pressures it faces from the market. Finally, we need to assess conditions. For example, although we may have developed a product that offers great appeal for consumers, a recession may cut demand dramatically.

PROCESSES OF CONSUMER BEHAVIOR

Consumer behavior involves the psychological processes that consumers go through in recognizing needs, finding ways to solve these needs, making purchase decisions (e.g., whether or not to purchase a product and, if so, which brand and where), interpret information, make plans, and implement these plans (e.g., by engaging in comparison shopping or actually purchasing a product).

SOURCES OF INFLUENCE ON THE CONSUMER

The consumer faces numerous sources of influence. Often, we take *cultural* influences for granted, but they are significant.An American will usually not bargain with a store owner.This, however, is a common practice in much of the World.*Physical* factors also influence our behavior. We are more likely to buy a soft drink when we are thirsty, for example, and food manufacturers have found that it is more effective to advertise their products on the radio in the late afternoon when people are getting hungry. A person's *self-image* will also tend to influence what he or she will buy—an upwardly mobile manager may buy a flashy car to project an image of success.*Social* factors also influence what the consumers buy—often, consumers seek to imitate others whom they admire, and may buy the same brands.The social environment can include both the mainstream culture (e.g., Americans are more likely to have corn flakes or ham and eggs for breakfast than to have rice, which is preferred in many Asian countries) and a subculture (e.g., rap music often appeals to a segment within the population that seeks to distinguish itself from the mainstream population). Thus, sneaker manufacturers are eager to have their products worn by admired athletes. Finally, consumer behavior is influenced by *learning*—you try a hamburger and learn that it satisfies your hunger and tastes good, and the next time you are hungry, you may consider another hamburger.

CONSUMER CHOICE AND DECISION MAKING

One model of consumer decision making involves several steps. The first one is *problem recognition*—you realize that something is not as it should be. Perhaps, for example, your car is getting more difficult to start and is not accelerating well. The second step *is information search*—what are some alternative ways of solving the problem? You might buy a new car, buy a used car, take your car in for repair, ride the bus, ride a taxi, or ride a skateboard to work. The third step involves *evaluation of alternatives.* A skateboard is inexpensive, but may be ill-suited for long distances and for rainy days. Finally, we have the *purchase* stage, and sometimes a post-purchase stage (e.g., you return a product to the store because you did not find it satisfactory). In reality, people may go back and forth between the stages. For example, a person may resume alternative identification during while evaluating already known alternatives.

Consumer *involvement* will tend to vary dramatically depending on the type of product. In general, consumer involvement will be higher for products that are very expensive (e.g., a home, a car) or are highly significant in the consumer's life in some other way (e.g., a word processing program or acne medication).

It is important to consider the consumer's motivation for buying products. To achieve this goal, we can use the Means-End chain, wherein we consider a logical progression of consequences of product use that eventually lead to desired end benefit. Thus, for example, a consumer may see that a car has a large engine, leading to fast acceleration, leading to a feeling of performance, leading to a feeling of power, which ultimately improves the consumer's self-esteem.

A handgun may aim bullets with precision, which enables the user to kill an intruder, which means that the intruder will not be able to harm the consumer's family, which achieves the desired end-state of security. In advertising, it is important to portray the desired end-states. Focusing on the large motor will do less good than portraying a successful person driving the car.

INFORMATION SEARCH AND DECISION MAKING

Consumers engage in both *internal* and *external* information search. *Internal* search involves the consumer identifying alternatives from his or her memory. For certain low involvement products, it is very important that marketing programs achieve "top of mind" awareness. For example, few people will search the *Yellow Pages* for fast food restaurants; thus, the consumer must be able to retrieve one's restaurant from memory before it will be considered. For high involvement products, consumers are more likely to use an *external* search. Before buying a car, for example, the consumer may ask friends' opinions, read reviews in *Consumer Reports*, consult several web sites, and visit several dealerships. Thus, firms that make products that are selected predominantly through external search must invest in having information available to the consumer in need—e.g., through brochures, web sites, or news coverage.

A *compensatory* decision involves the consumer "trading off" good and bad attributes of a product. For example, a car may have a low price and good gas mileage but slow acceleration. If the price is sufficiently inexpensive and gas efficient, the consumer may then select it over a car with better acceleration that costs more and uses more gas. Occasionally, a decision will involve a *non-compensatory* strategy. For example, a parent may reject all soft drinks that contain artificial sweeteners. Here, other good features such as taste and low calories *cannot* overcome this one "non-negotiable" attribute.

The amount of effort a consumer puts into searching depends on a number of factors such as the *market* (how many competitors are there, and how great are differences between brands expected to be?), *product characteristics* (how important is this product? How complex is the product? How obvious are indications of quality?), *consumer characteristics* (how interested is a consumer, generally, in analysing product characteristics and making the best possible deal?), and *situational* characteristics (as previously discussed).

Two interesting issues in decisions are:

- *Variety seeking* (where consumers seek to try new brands not because these brands are expected to be "better" in any way, but rather because the consumer wants a "change of pace," and
- *"Impulse" purchases*—unplanned buys. This represents a somewhat "fuzzy" group. For example, a shopper may plan to buy vegetables but only decide in the store to actually buy broccoli and corn. Alternatively, a person may buy an item which is currently on sale, or one that he or she remembers that is needed only once inside the store.

A number of factors involve consumer choices. In some cases, consumers will be more *motivated*. For example, one may be more careful choosing a gift for an in-law than when buying the same thing for one self. Some consumers are also more motivated to *comparison shop* for the best prices, while others are more *convenience* oriented. *Personality* impacts decisions. Some like variety more than others, and some are more receptive to stimulation and excitement in trying new stores. *Perception* influences decisions. Some people, for example, can taste the difference between generic and name brand foods while many cannot.

Selective perception occurs when a person is paying attention only to information of interest. For example, when looking for a new car, the consumer may pay more attention to car ads than when this is not in the horizon. Some consumers are put off by perceived *risk*. Thus, many marketers offer a money back guarantee. Consumers will tend to change their behavior through *learning*—e.g., they will avoid restaurants they have found to be crowded and will settle on brands that best meet their tastes. Consumers differ in the *values* they hold (e.g., some people are more committed to recycling than others who will not want to go through the hassle). We will consider the issue of lifestyle under segmentation.

THE FAMILY LIFE CYCLE

For purposes of this discussion, a "couple" may either be married or merely involve living together. The breakup of a non-marital relationship involving cohabitation is similarly considered equivalent to a divorce. In real life, this situation is, of course, a bit more complicated. For example, many couples undergo divorce. Then we have one of the scenarios: Single parenthood can result either from divorce or from the death of one parent. Divorce usually entails a significant change in the relative wealth of spouses. In some cases, the non-custodial parent (usually the father) will not pay the required child support, and even if he or she does, that still may not leave the custodial parent and children as well off as they were during the marriage. On the other hand, in some cases, some non-custodial parents will be called on to pay a large part of their income in child support. This is particularly a problem when the non-custodial parent remarries and has additional children in the second (or subsequent marriages).

As a person gets older, he or she tends to advance in his or her career and tends to get greater income (exceptions: maternity leave, divorce, retirement). Unfortunately, obligations also tend to increase with time (at least until one's mortgage has been paid off). Children and paying for one's house are two of the greatest expenses.

Note that although a single person may have a lower income than a married couple, the single may be able to buy more discretionary items. Note that although a single person may have a lower income than a married couple, the single may be able to buy more discretionary items.

FAMILY DECISION MAKING

Individual members of families often serve different roles in decisions that ultimately draw on shared family resources. Some individuals are *information gatherers/holders*, who seek out information about products of relevance. These individuals often have a great deal of power because they may selectively pass on information that favours their chosen alternatives. *Influencers* do not ultimately have the power decide between alternatives, but they may make their wishes known by asking for specific products or causing embarrassing situations if their demands are not met. The *decision maker(s)* have the power to determine issues such as:

- Whether to buy;
- Which product to buy (pick-up or passenger car?);
- Which brand to buy;
- Where to buy it; and
- When to buy.

Note, however, that the role of the decision maker is separate from that of the *purchaser*. From the point of view of the marketer, this introduces some problems since the purchaser can be targeted by point-of-purchase (POP) marketing efforts that cannot be aimed at the decision maker. Also note that the distinction between the purchaser and decision maker may be somewhat blurred:

- The decision maker may specify what kind of product to buy, but not which brand;
- The purchaser may have to make a substitution if the desired brand is not in stock;
- The purchaser may disregard instructions (by error or deliberately).

It should be noted that family decisions are often subject to a great deal of conflict. The reality is that few families are wealthy enough to avoid a strong tension between demands on the family's resources. Conflicting pressures are especially likely in families with children and/or when only one spouse works outside the home. Note that many decisions inherently come down to values, and that there is frequently no "objective" way to arbitrate differences. One spouse may believe that it is important to save for the children's future; the other may value spending now (on private schools and computer equipment) to help prepare the children for the future. Who is right? There is no clear answer here. The situation becomes even more complex when more parties—such as children or other relatives—are involved.

Some family members may resort to various strategies to get their way. One is *bargaining*—one member will give up something in return for someone else. For example, the wife says that her husband can take an expensive course in gourmet cooking if she can buy a new pickup truck. Alternatively, a child may promise to walk it every day if he or she can have a hippopotamus. Another strategy is *reasoning*—trying to get the other person(s) to accept one's view through logical argumentation. Note that even when this is done with a sincere intent, its potential is limited by legitimate differences in values illustrated above. Also note that individuals may simply try to "wear down" the other party by endless talking in the guise of reasoning. Various manipulative strategies may also be used. One is *impression management*, where one tries to make one's side look good (e.g., argue that a new TV will help the children see educational TV when it is really mostly wanted to see sports programming, or argue that all "decent families make a contribution to the church"). *Authority* involves asserting one's "right" to make a decision (as the "man of the house," the mother of the children, or the one who makes the most money). *Emotion* involves making an emotional display to get one's way (e.g., a man cries if his wife will not let him buy a new rap album).

THE MEANS-END CHAIN

Consumers often buy products not because of their attributes *per se* but rather because of the ultimate benefits that these attributes provide, in turn leading to the satisfaction of ultimate values. For example, a consumer may not be particularly interested in the chemistry of plastic roses, but might reason as follows:

The important thing in a means-end chain is to start with an *attribute*, a concrete characteristic of the product, and then logically progress to a series of consequences (which tend to become progressively more abstract) that end with a *value* being satisfied.

Thus, each chain *must start with an attribute and end with a value*. An important implication of means-end chains is that it is usually most effective in advertising to *focus on higher level items*. For example, in the flower example above, an individual giving the flowers to the significant other might better be portrayed than the flowers alone.

ATTITUDES

Consumer attitudes are a composite of a consumer's (1) beliefs about, (2) feelings about, (3) and behavioural intentions toward some "object"—within the context of marketing, usually a brand, product category, or retail store. These components are viewed together since they are highly interdependent and together represent forces that influence how the consumer will react to the object.

Beliefs: The first component is *beliefs*. A consumer may hold both positive beliefs toward an object (e.g., coffee tastes good) as well as negative beliefs (e.g., coffee is easily spilled and stains papers). In addition, some beliefs may be neutral (coffee is black), and some may be differ in valance depending on the person or the situation (e.g., coffee is hot and stimulates—good on a cold morning, but not good on a hot summer evening when one wants to sleep). Note also that the beliefs that consumers hold need not be accurate (e.g., that pork contains little fat), and some beliefs may, upon closer examination, be contradictory.

Affect: Consumers also hold certain feelings toward brands or other objects. Sometimes these feelings are based on the beliefs (e.g., a person feels nauseated when thinking about a hamburger because of the tremendous amount of fat it contains), but there may also be feelings which are relatively independent of beliefs. For example, an extreme environmentalist may believe that cutting down trees is morally wrong, but may have positive affect toward Christmas trees because he or she unconsciously associates these trees with the experience that he or she had at Christmas as a child.

Behavioural intention: The behavioural intention is what the consumer plans to do with respect to the object (e.g., buy or not buy the brand). As with affect, this is sometimes a logical consequence of beliefs (or affect), but may sometimes reflect other circumstances—e.g., although a consumer does not really like a restaurant, he or she will go there because it is a hangout for his or her friends.

Changing attitudes is generally *very difficult*, particularly when consumers suspect that the marketer has a self-serving "agenda" in bringing about this change (e.g., to get the consumer to buy more or to switch brands). Here are some possible methods:

- *Changing affect*. One approach is to try to change affect, which may or may not involve getting consumers to change their beliefs. One strategy uses the approach of *classical conditioning* try to "pair" the product with a liked stimulus. For example, we "pair" a car with a beautiful woman. Alternatively, we can try to get people to like the advertisement and hope that this liking will "spill over" into the purchase of a product. For example, the Pillsbury Doughboy does not really emphasize the conveyance of much information to the consumer; instead, it attempts to create a warm, "fuzzy" image. Although Energizer Bunny ads try to get people to believe that their batteries last longer, the main emphasis is on the likeable bunny. Finally, products which are better known, through the *mere exposure* effect, tend to be better liked—that is, the more a product is advertised and seen in stores, the more it will generally be liked, *even if consumers to do not develop any specific beliefs about the produc*t.
- *Changing behavior*. People like to believe that their behavior is rational; thus, once they use our products, chances are that they will continue unless someone is able to get them to switch. One way to get people to switch to our brand is to use temporary price discounts and coupons; however, when consumers buy a product on deal, they may justify the purchase based on that deal (i.e., the low price) and may then switch to other brands on deal later. A better way to get people to switch to our brand is to at least temporarily obtain better shelf space so that the product is more convenient. Consumers are less likely to use this availability as a

rationale for their purchase and may continue to buy the product even when the product is less conveniently located.

- *Changing beliefs*. Although attempting to change beliefs is the obvious way to attempt attitude change, particularly when consumers hold unfavorable or inaccurate ones, this is often difficult to achieve because consumers tend to resist. Several approaches to belief change exist:
- *Change currently held beliefs*. It is generally very difficult to attempt to change beliefs that people hold, particularly those that are strongly held, *even if they are inaccurate*. For example, the petroleum industry advertised for a long time that its profits were lower than were commonly believed, and provided extensive factual evidence in its advertising to support this reality. Consumers were suspicious and rejected this information, however.
- *Change the importance of beliefs*. Although the sugar manufacturers would undoubtedly like to decrease the importance of healthy teeth, it is usually not feasible to make beliefs less important—consumers are likely to reason, why, then, would you bother bringing them up in the first place? However, it may be possible to strengthen beliefs that favour us—e.g., a vitamin supplement manufacturer may advertise that it is extremely important for women to replace iron lost through menstruation. Most consumers already agree with this, but the belief can be made stronger.
- *Add beliefs*. Consumers are less likely to resist the addition of beliefs *so long as they do not conflict with existing beliefs*. Thus, the beef industry has added beliefs that beef (1) is convenient and (2) can be used to make a number of creative dishes. Vitamin manufacturers attempt to add the belief that stress causes vitamin depletion, which sounds quite plausible to most people.
- *Change ideal*. It usually difficult, and very risky, to attempt to change ideals, and only few firms succeed. For example, Hard Candy may have attempted to change the ideal away from traditional beauty toward more unique self expression.
- *One-sided vs. two-sided appeals*. Attitude research has shown that consumers often tend to react more favourably to advertisements which either (1) admit something negative about the sponsoring brand (e.g., the Volvo is a clumsy car, but very safe) or (2) admits something positive about a competing brand (e.g., a competing supermarket has slightly lower prices, but offers less service and selection). Two-sided appeals must, contain overriding arguments why the sponsoring brand is ultimately superior—that is, in the above examples, the "but" part must be emphasized.

PERCEPTION

Our perception is an approximation of reality. Our brain attempts to make sense out of the stimuli to which we are exposed. This works well, for example, when we "see" a friend three hundred feet away at his or her correct height; however, our perception is sometimes "off"—for example, certain shapes of ice cream containers look like they contain more than rectangular ones with the same volume.

Subliminal stimuli. Back in the 1960s, it was reported that on selected evenings, movie goers in a theater had been exposed to isolated frames with the words "Drink Coca Cola" and "Eat Popcorn" embedded into the movie. These frames went by so fast that people did not consciously notice them, but it was reported that on nights with frames present, Coke and popcorn sales were significantly higher than on days they were left off. This led Congress to ban the use of subliminal advertising. First of all, there is a question as to whether this experiment ever took place or whether this information was simply made up. Secondly, no one has been able to replicate these findings. There is research to show that people will start to giggle with embarrassment when they are briefly exposed to "dirty" words in an experimental machine. Here, again, the exposure is so brief that the subjects are not aware of the actual words they saw, but it is evident that something has been recognized by the embarrassment displayed.

ORGANIZATIONAL BUYERS

A large portion of the market for goods and services is attributable to *organizational*, as opposed to individual, buyers. In general, organizational buyers, who make buying decisions for their companies for a living, tend to be somewhat more sophisticated than ordinary consumers. However, these organizational buyers are also often more risk averse. There is a risk in going with a new, possibly better (lower price or higher quality) supplier whose product is unproven and may turn out to be problematic. Often the fear of running this risk is greater than the potential rewards for getting a better deal. In the old days, it used to be said that "You can't get fired for buying IBM." This attitude is beginning to soften a bit today as firms face increasing pressures to cut costs.

Organizational buyers come in several forms. *Resellers* involve either wholesalers or retailers that buy from one organization and resell to some other entity. For example, large grocery chains sometimes buy products directly from the manufacturer and resell them to end-consumers. Wholesalers may sell to retailers who in turn sell to consumers. *Producers* also buy products from sub-manufacturers to create a finished product. For example, rather than manufacturing the parts themselves, computer manufacturers often buy hard drives, motherboards, cases, monitors, keyboards, and other components from manufacturers and put them together to create a finished product. *Governments* buy a great deal of things. For example, the military needs an incredible amount of supplies to feed and equip troops. Finally, large *institutions* buy products in huge quantities. For example, UCR probably buys thousands of reams of paper every month.

Organizational buying usually involves more people than individual buying. Often, many people are involved in making decisions as to (a) whether to buy, (b) what to buy, (c) at what quantity, and (d) from whom. An engineer may make a specification as to what is needed, which may be approved by a manager, with the final purchase being made by a purchase specialist who spends all his or her time finding the best deal on the goods that the organization needs. Often, such long purchase processes can cause long delays. In the government, rules are often especially stringent—e.g., vendors of fruit cake have to meet fourteen pages of specifications put out by the General Services Administration. In many cases, government buyers are also heavily bound to go with the lowest price. Even if it is obvious that a higher priced vendor will offer a superior product, it may be difficult to accept that bid.

CONSUMER RESEARCH METHODS

Market research is often needed to ensure that we produce what customers really want and not what we *think* they want. Primary vs. secondary research methods. There are two main approaches to marketing. *Secondary* research involves using information that others have already put together. For example, if you are thinking about starting a business making clothes for tall people. *Primary* research, in contrast, is research that you design and conduct yourself. For example, you may need to find out whether consumers would prefer that your soft drinks be sweater or tarter.

Research will often help us *reduce risks* associated with a new product, but it *cannot take the risk away entirely*. It is also important to ascertain whether the research has been complete. For example, Coca Cola did a great deal of research prior to releasing the New Coke, and consumers seemed to prefer the taste. However, consumers were *not* prepared to have this drink replace traditional Coke. Sources of influence on the consumer. The consumer faces numerous sources of influence.

Often, we take cultural influences for granted, but they are significant. An American will usually not bargain with a store owner. This, however, is a common practice in much of the World. Physical factors also influence our behaviour. We are more likely to buy a soft drink when we are thirsty, for example, and food manufacturers have found that it is more effective to advertise their products on the radio in the late afternoon when people are getting hungry.

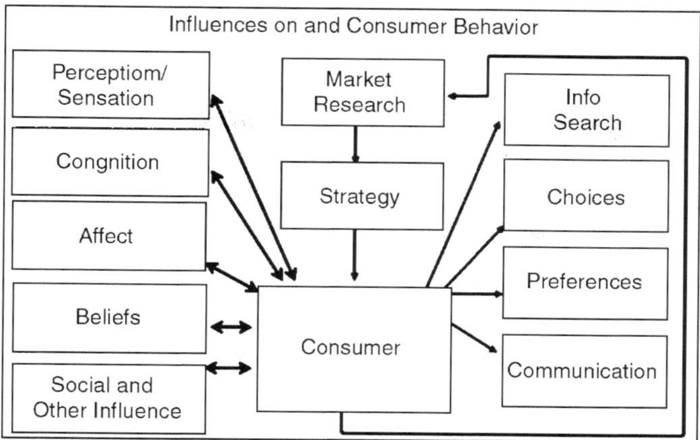

A person's self-image will also tend to influence what he or she will buy-an upwardly mobile manager may buy a flashy car to project an image of success. Social factors also influence what the consumers buy-often, consumers seek to imitate others whom they admire, and may buy the same brands. The social environment can include both the mainstream culture and a subculture. Thus, sneaker manufacturers are eager to have their products worn by admired athletes. Finally, consumer behaviour is influenced by learning-you try a hamburger and learn that it satisfies your hunger and tastes good, and the next time you are hungry, you may consider another hamburger.

CONSUMER CHOICE AND DECISION-MAKING: PROBLEM

One model of consumer decision making involves several steps. The first one is problem recognition-you realise that something is not as it should be. Perhaps, for example, your car is getting more difficult to start and is not accelerating well. The second step is information search-what are some alternative ways of solving the problem? You might buy a new car, buy a used car, take your car in for repair, ride the bus, ride a taxi, or ride a skateboard to work. The third step involves evaluation of alternatives. A skateboard is inexpensive, but may be ill-suited for long distances and for rainy days. Finally, we have the purchase stage, and sometimes a post-purchase stage. In reality, people may go back and forth between the stages. For example, a person may resume alternative identification during while evaluating already known alternatives.

Consumer involvement will tend to vary dramatically depending on the type of product. In general, consumer involvement will be higher for products that are very expensive or are highly significant in the consumer's life in some other way. It is important to consider the consumer's motivation for buying products. To achieve this goal, we can use the Means-End chain, wherein we consider a logical progression of consequences of product use that eventually lead to desired end benefit. Thus, for example, a consumer may see that a car has a large engine, leading to fast acceleration, leading to a feeling of performance, leading to a feeling of power, which ultimately improves the consumer's self-esteem. A handgun may aim bullets with precision, which enables the user to kill an intruder, which means that the intruder will not be able to harm the consumer's family, which achieves the desired end-state of security. In advertising, it is important to portray the desired end-states. Focusing on the large motor will do less good than portraying a successful person driving the car.

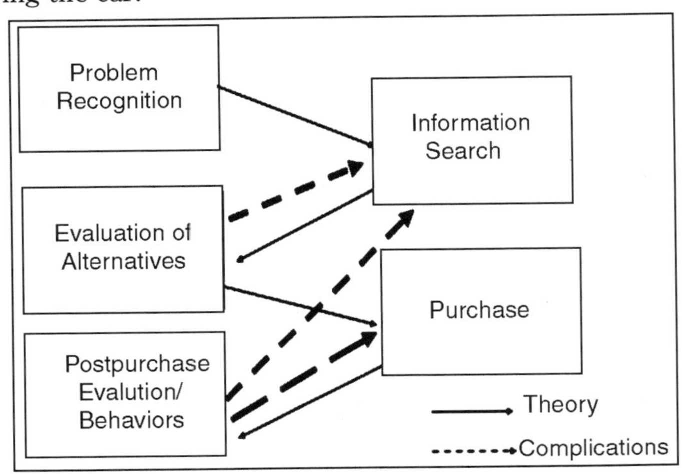

INFORMATION SEARCH AND DECISION-MAKING

Consumers engage in both internal and external information search. Internal search involves the consumer identifying alternatives from his or her memory. For certain low involvement products, it is very important that marketing prigrammes achieve"top of mind" awareness. For example, few people will search the Yellow Pages for fast food restaurants; thus, the consumer must be able to retrieve one's restaurant from memory before it will be considered. For high involvement products, consumers are more likely to use an external search. Before buying a car, for example, the consumer may ask friends' opinions, read reviews in Consumer Reports, consult several web sites, and visit several dealerships. Thus, firms that make products that are selected predominantly through external search must invest in having information available to the consumer in need-e.g., through brochures, web sites, or news coverage.

A compensatory decision involves the consumer"trading off" good and bad attributes of a product. For example, a car may have a low price and good gas mileage but slow acceleration. If the price is sufficiently inexpensive and gas efficient, the consumer may then select it over a car with better acceleration that costs more and uses more gas. Occasionally, a decision will involve a non-compensatory strategy. For example, a parent may reject all soft drinks that contain artificial sweeteners. Here, other good features such as taste and low calories cannot overcome this one"non-negotiable" attribute.

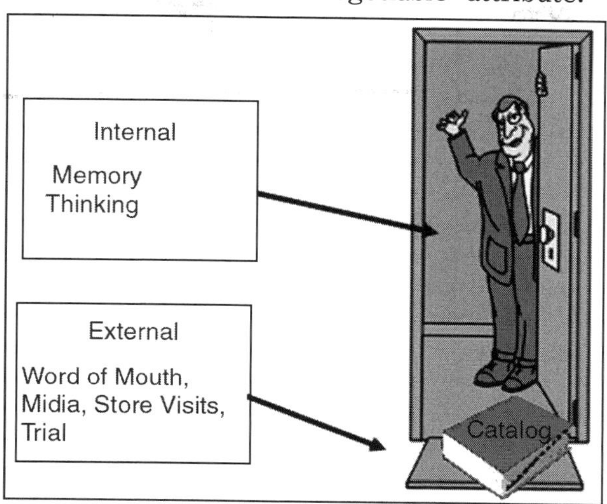

The amount of effort a consumer puts into searching depends on a number of factors such as the market, product characteristics, consumer characteristics, and situational characteristics.

Two interesting issues in decisions are:

- *Variety seeking* where consumers seek to try new brands not because these brands are expected to be "better" in any way, but rather because the consumer wants a "change of pace," and
- *"Impulse" purchases*—unplanned buys. This represents a somewhat "fuzzy" group. For example, a shopper may plan to buy vegetables but only decide in the store to actually buy broccoli and corn. Alternatively, a person may buy an item which is currently on sale, or one that he or she remembers that is needed only once inside the store.

A number of factors involve consumer choices. In some cases, consumers will be more *motivated*. For example, one may be more careful choosing a gift for an in-law than when buying the same thing for one self. Some consumers are also more motivated to *comparison shop* for the best prices, while others are more *convenience* oriented. *Personality* impacts decisions. Some like variety more than others, and some are more receptive to stimulation and excitement in trying new stores. *Perception* influences decisions.

Some people, for example, can taste the difference between generic and name brand foods while many cannot. *Selective* perception occurs when a person is paying attention only to information of interest. For example, when looking for a new car, the consumer may pay more attention to car ads than when this is not in the horizon. Some consumers are put off by perceived *risk*.

Thus, many marketers offer a money back guarantee. Consumers will tend to change their behaviour through *learning*—e.g., they will avoid restaurants they have found to be crowded and will settle on brands that best meet their tastes. Consumers differ in the *values* they hold. As suggested, consider the issue of lifestyle under segmentation.

CUSTOMER VALUE AND SATISFACTION

CUSTOMER VALUE

As it is used in the business world, customer value is the amount of benefit that a customer will get from a service or product relative to its cost. Some businesspeople explain customer value as "realization" compared to "sacrifice." Realization is a formal term for what customers get out of their purchases. Sacrifice is what they pay for the product or service.

Businesses of all sizes use customer value as part of a greater analysis to determine how well they are supplying their customer base. Detailed research might include what customers generally do with the products they receive, or how they use services to increase the value of assets like real estate. Businesses also look at the prices of their products in order to price them competitively. Businesses that identify the value of their wares to customers might go a step further and consider other similar ideas. In order to generate more thought about customer value, and to reach out to a customer base, a business might promote a customer value proposition. The customer value proposition is basically a promise of benefits from a vendor to customers.

We see examples of customer value propositions all the time in advertising. Companies pinpoint the benefits that they believe a customer will realise, and display them in advertising to attract more customers. The question is whether these propositions are made in good faith, or whether they may not be entirely true. When business leaders and others are talking about customer value, it is important that everyone at the table understands that customer value does not relate to the value of customers, but to the value that customers receive from the business. Those who are talking about how valuable customers are to a business might use terms like customer retention, or refer to the customer base as "valued customers," or VIPs. Since customer service is also a critical element for many businesses, it's possible that these two ideas might sometimes get confused.

Along with the basic idea of customer value, other terms help further define that value precisely. Relative performance identifies how the product or service gives customer value relative to what competitors offer. Access cost is something that business analysts add into the mix as an estimated cost of the effort involved in purchase. Value propositions often include these levels of detail to help leaders look at how well a business is serving its intended audience.

SATISFACTION

Customer satisfaction, a business term, is a measure of how products and services supplied by a company meet or surpass customer expectation. It is seen as a key performance indicator within business and is part of the four of a Balanced Scorecard. In a competitive marketplace where businesses compete for customers, customer satisfaction is seen as a key differentiator and increasingly has become a key element of business strategy. There is a substantial body of empirical literature that establishes the benefits of customer satisfaction for firms.

Measuring Customer Satisfaction

Organizations need to retain existing customers while targeting non-customers;. Measuring customer satisfaction provides an indication of how successful the organization is at providing products and/or services to the marketplace. Customer satisfaction is an abstract concept and the actual manifestation of the state of satisfaction will vary from person to person and product/service to product/service. The state of satisfaction depends on a number of both psychological and physical variables which correlate with satisfaction behaviours such as return and recommend rate. The level of satisfaction can also vary depending on other factors the customer, such as other products against which the customer can compare the organization's products.

Work done by Parasuraman, Zeithaml and Berry between 1985 and 1988 delivered SERVQUAL which provides the basis for the measurement of customer satisfaction with a service by using the gap between the customer's expectation of performance and their perceived experience of performance. This provides the researcher with a satisfaction "gap" which is semi-quantitative in nature. Cronin and Taylor extended the disconfirmation theory by combining the "gap" described by Parasuraman, Zeithaml and Berry as two different measures into a single measurement of performance relative to expectation.

The usual measures of customer satisfaction involve a survey with a set of statements using a Likert Technique or scale. The customer is asked to evaluate each statement in terms of their perception and expectation of performance of the service being measured.

Improving Customer Satisfaction

Published standards exist to help organizations develop their current levels of customer satisfaction. The International Customer Service Institute has released The International Customer Service Standard. TICSS enables organizations to focus their attention on delivering excellence in the management of customer service, whilst at the same time providing recognition of success through a 3rd Party registration plan. TICSS focuses an organization's attention on delivering increased customer satisfaction by helping the organization through a Service Quality Model. TICSS Service Quality Model uses the 5 P's - Policy, Processes, People, Premises, Product/Services, as well as performance measurement. The implementation of a customer service standard should lead to higher levels of customer satisfaction, which in turn influences customer retention and customer loyalty.

CONSUMERISM

Consumerism is a social and economic order that is based on the systematic creation and fostering of a desire to purchase goods or services in ever greater amounts. The term is often associated with criticisms of consumption starting with Thorstein Veblen or, more recently by a movement called Enoughism. Veblen's subject of examination, the newly emergent middle class arising at the turn of the twentieth century, comes to full fruition by the end of the twentieth century through the process of globalization. In economics, consumerism refers to economic policies placing emphasis on consumption. In an abstract sense, it is the belief that the free choice of consumers should dictate the economic structure of a society.

DECISIONS OF CONSUMER PURCHASE MANAGEMENT

Consumers are faced with purchase decisions nearly every day. But not all decisions are treated the same. Some decisions are more complex than others and thus require more effort by the consumer. Other decisions are fairly routine and require little effort. In general, consumers face four types of purchase decisions:

- *Minor New Purchase*: These purchases represent something new to a consumer but in the customer's mind is not a very important purchase in terms of need, money or other reason (e.g., status within a group).
- *Minor Re-Purchase*: These are the most routine of all purchases and often the consumer returns to purchase the same product without giving much thought to other product options (i.e., consumer is brand loyalty).
- *Major New Purchase*: These purchases are the most difficult of all purchases because the product being purchased is important to the consumer but the consumer has little or no previous experience making these decisions. The consumer's lack of confidence in making this type of decision often (but not always) requires the consumer to engage in an extensive decision-making process..
- *Major Re-Purchase*: These purchase decisions are also important to the consumer but the consumer feels confident in making these decisions since they have previous experience purchasing the product.

For marketers it is important to understand how consumers treat the purchase decisions they face. If a company is targeting customers who feel a purchase decision is difficult (i.e., Major New Purchase), their marketing strategy may vary greatly from a company targeting customers who view the purchase decision as routine. In fact, the same company may face both situations at the same time; for some the product is new, while other customers see the purchase as routine. The implication of buying behaviour for marketers is that different buying situations require different marketing efforts.

WHY CONSUMERS BUY

Customers make purchases in order to satisfy needs. Some of these needs are basic and must be filled by everyone on the planet (e.g., food, shelter) while others are not required for basic survival and vary depending on the person. It probably makes more sense to classify needs that are not a necessity as wants or desires. In fact, in many countries where the standard of living is very high, a large portion of the population's income is spent on wants and desires rather than on basic needs. In this tutorial when we mention the consumer we are referring to the actual buyer, the person spending the money. But is should also be pointed out that the one who does the buying is not necessarily the user of what is bought and that others may be involved in the buying decision in addition to the actual buyer. While the purchasing process in the consumer market is not as complex as the business market, having multiple people involved in a purchase decision is not unusual. For example, in planning for a family vacation the mother may make the hotel reservations but others in the family may have input on the hotel choice. Similarly, a father may purchase snacks at the grocery store but his young child may be the one who selected it from the store shelf.

So understanding consumer purchase behaviour involves not only understanding how decisions are made but also understanding the dynamics that influence purchases.

WHAT INFLUENCES PURCHASING

As we discussed the decision-making process for consumers is anything but straight forward. There are many factors that can affect this process as a person works through the purchase decision. The number of potential influences on consumer behaviour is limitless. However, marketers are well served to understand the KEY influences. By doing so they may be in a position to tailor their marketing efforts to take advantage of these influences in a way that will satisfy the consumer and the marketer (remember this is a key part of the definition of marketing).

For the purposes of this tutorial we will break these influences down into three main categories: Internal, External and Marketing. However, those interested in learning more about customer buying activity may want to consult one or more consumer behaviour books where they will find additional methods for explaining consumer buying behaviour. For the most part the influences are not mutually exclusive. Instead, they are all interconnected and, as we will see, work together to form who we are and how we behave. For each of the influences that are discussed we will provide a basic description and also suggest its implication to marketers. Bear in mind we only provide a few marketing implications for each influence; clearly there are many more.

INTERNAL INFLUENCES

We start our examination of the influences on consumer purchase decisions by first looking inside ourselves to see which are the most important internal factors that affect how we make choices.

Perceptual Filter

Perception is how we see ourselves and the world we live in. However, what ends up being stored inside us doesn't always get there in a direct manner. Often our mental makeup results from information that has been consciously or subconsciously filtered as we experience it, a process we refer to as a perceptual filter. To us this is our reality, though it does not mean it is an accurate reflection on what is real. Thus, perception is the way we filter stimuli (e.g., someone talking to us, reading a newspaper story) and then make sense out of it.

Perception has several steps:

- *Exposure*: Sensing a stimuli (e.g. seeing an ad)
- *Attention*: An effort to recognize the nature of a stimuli (e.g. recognizing it is an ad)
- *Awareness*: Assigning meaning to a stimuli (e.g., humorous ad for particular product)
- *Retention*: Adding the meaning to one's internal makeup (i.e., product has fun ads)

How these steps are eventually carried out depends on a person's approach to learning. By learning we mean how someone changes what they know, which in turn may affect how they act.

There are many theories of learning, a discussion of which is beyond the scope of this tutorial, however, suffice to say that people are likely to learn in different ways. For instance, one person may be able to focus very strongly on a certain advertisement and be able to retain the information after being exposed only one time while another person may need to be exposed to the same advertisement many times before he/she even recognizes what it is. Consumers are also more likely to retain information if a person has a strong interest in the stimuli.

If a person is in need of new car they are more likely to pay attention to a new advertisement for a car while someone who does not need a car may need to see the advertisement many times before they recognize the brand of automobile.

Marketing Implications

Marketers spend large sums of money in an attempt to get customers to have a positive impression of their products. But clearly the existence of a perceptual filter suggests that getting to this stage is not easy. Exposing consumers to a product can be very challenging considering the amount of competing product messages (ads) that are also trying to accomplish the same objective (i.e., advertising clutter). So marketers must be creative and use various means to deliver their message. Once the message reaches consumer it must be interesting enough to capture their attention (e.g., talk about the product's benefits). But attending to the message is not enough. For marketers the most critical step is the one that occurs with awareness. Here marketers must continually monitor and respond if their message becomes distorted in ways that will negatively shape its meaning. This can often happen due in part to competitive activity (e.g., comparison advertisements). Finally, getting the consumer to give positive meaning to the message they have retained requires the marketer make sure that consumers accurately interpret the facts about the product.

Knowledge

Knowledge is the sum of all information known by a person. It is the facts of the world as he/she knows it and the depth of knowledge is a function of the breadth of worldly experiences and the strength of an individual's long-term memory. Obviously what exists as knowledge to an individual depends on how an individual's perceptual filter makes sense of the information it is exposed to.

Marketing Implications

Marketers may conduct research that will gauge consumers' level of knowledge regarding their product. As we will see below, it is likely that other factors influencing consumer behaviour are in large part shaped by what is known about a product. Thus, developing methods (e.g., incentives) to encourage consumers to accept more information (or correct information) may affect other influencing factors.

Attitude

In simple terms attitude refers to what a person feels or believes about something. Additionally, attitude may be reflected in how an individual acts based on his or her beliefs. Once formed, attitudes can be very difficult to change. Thus, if a consumer has a negative attitude toward a particular issue it will take considerable effort to change what they believe to be true.

Marketing Implications

Marketers facing consumers who have a negative attitude toward their product must work to identify the key issues shaping a consumer's attitude then adjust marketing decisions (e.g., advertising) in an effort to change the attitude.

For companies competing against strong rivals to whom loyal consumers exhibit a positive attitude, an important strategy is to work to see why consumers feel positive toward the competitor and then try to meet or beat the competitor on these issues. Alternatively, a company can try to locate customers who feel negatively toward the competitor and then increase awareness among this group.

Personality

An individual's personality relates to perceived personal characteristics that are consistently exhibited, especially when one acts in the presence of others. In most, but not all, cases the behaviors one projects in a situation is similar to the behaviors a person exhibits in another situation.

In this way personality is the sum of sensory experiences others get from experiencing a person (i.e., how one talks, reacts). While one's personality is often interpreted by those we interact with, the person has their own vision of their personality, called Self Concept, which may or may not be the same has how others view us.

Marketing Implications

For marketers it is important to know that consumers make purchase decisions to support their self concept. Using research techniques to identify how customers view themselves may give marketers insight into products and promotion options that are not readily apparent.

For example, when examining consumers a marketer may initially build marketing strategy around more obvious clues to consumption behaviour, such as consumer's demographic indicators (e.g., age, occupation, income).

However, in-depth research may yield information that shows consumers are purchasing products to fulfill self-concept objectives that have little to do with the demographic category they fall into (e.g., senior citizen may be making purchases that make them feel younger). Appealing to the consumer's self concept needs could expand the market to which the product is targeted.

Lifestyle

This influencing factor relates to the way we live through the activities we engage in and interests we express. In simple terms it is what we value out of life. Lifestyle is often determined by how we spend our time and money.

Marketing Implications

Products and services are purchased to support consumers' lifestyles. Marketers have worked hard researching how consumers in their target markets live their lives since this information is key to developing products, suggesting promotional strategies and even determining how best to distribute products. The fact that lifestyle is so directly tied to marketing activity will be further examined as we discuss developing target market strategies.

Roles

Roles represent the position we feel we hold or others feel we should hold when dealing in a group environment. These positions carry certain responsibilities yet it is important to understand that some of these responsibilities may, in fact, be perceived and not spelled out or even accepted by others. In support of their roles, consumers will make product choices that may vary depending on which role they are assuming. As illustration, a person who is responsible for selecting snack food for an office party his boss will attend may choose higher quality products than he would choose when selecting snacks for his family.

Marketing Implications

Advertisers often show how the benefits of their products aid consumers as they perform certain roles. Typically the underlying message of this promotional approach is to suggest that using the advertiser's product will help raise one's status in the eyes of others while using a competitor's product may have a negative effect on status.

Motivation

Motivation relates to our desire to achieve a certain outcome. Many internal factors we have already discussed can affect a customer's desire to achieve a certain outcome but there are others. For instance, when it comes to making purchase decisions customers' motivation could be affected by such issues as financial position (e.g., *Can I afford the purchase?*), time constraints (e.g., *Do I need to make the purchase quickly?*), overall value (e.g., *Am I getting my money's worth?*), and perceived risk (e.g., *What happens if I make a bad decision?*).

Marketing Implications

Motivation is also closely tied to the concept of Involvement, which relates to how much effort the consumer will exert in making a decision. Highly motivated consumers will want to get mentally and physically involved in the purchase process. Not all products have a high percentage of highly involved customers (e.g., milk) but marketers who market products and services that may lead to high level of consumer involvement should prepare options that will be attractive to this group. For instance, marketers should make it easy for consumers to learn about their product (e.g., information on website, free video preview) and, for some products, allow customers to experience the product (e.g., free trial) before committing to the purchase.

EXTERNAL INFLUENCES

Consumer purchasing decisions are often affected by factors that are outside of their control but have direct or indirect impact on how we live and what we consume.

Culture

Culture represents the behaviour, beliefs and, in many cases, the way we act learned by interacting or observing other members of society. In this way much of what we do is shared behaviour, passed along from one member of society to another. Yet culture is a broad concept that, while of interest to marketers, is not nearly as important as understanding what occurs within smaller groups or Sub-Cultures to which we may also belong. Sub-cultures also have shared values but this occurs within smaller groups. For instance, sub-cultures exist where groups share similar values in terms of ethnicity, religious beliefs, geographic location, special interests and many others.

Marketing Implications

As part of their efforts to convince customers to purchase their products, marketers often use cultural representations, especially in promotional appeals. The objective is to connect to consumers using cultural references that are easily understood and often embraced by the consumer. By doing so the marketer hopes the consumer feels more comfortable with or can relate better to the product since it corresponds with their cultural values. Additionally, smart marketers use strong research efforts in an attempt to identify differences in how sub-culture behaves. These efforts help pave the way for spotting trends within a sub-culture, which the marketer can capitalize on through new marketing tactics (e.g., new products, new sales channels, added value, etc.).

Other Group Membership

In addition to cultural influences, consumers belong to many other groups with which they share certain characteristics and which may influence purchase decisions. Often these groups contain Opinion Leaders or others who have major influence on what the customer purchases. Some of the basic groups we may belong to include:

- *Social Class*: Represents the social standing one has within a society based on such factors as income level, education, occupation
- *Family*: One's family situation can have a strong effect on how purchase decisions are made

- *Reference groups*: Most consumers simultaneously belong to many other groups with which they associate or, in some cases, feel the need to disassociate

Marketing Implications

Identifying and understanding the groups consumers belong to is a key strategy for marketers. Doing so helps identify target markets, develop new products, and create appealing marketing promotions to which consumers can relate. In particular, marketers seek to locate group leaders and others to whom members of the group look for advice or direction. These opinion leaders, if well respected by the group, can be used to gain insight into group behaviour and if these opinion leaders accept promotional opportunities could act as effective spokespeople for the marketer's products.

Purchase Situation

A purchase decision can be strongly affected by the situation in which people find themselves. In general, a situation is the circumstances a person faces when making a purchase decision, such as the nature of their physical environment, their emotional state, or time constraints. Not all situations are controllable, in which case a consumer may not follow their normal process for making a purchase decision. For instance, if a person needs a product quickly and a store does not carry the brand they normally purchase, the customer may choose a competitor's product.

Marketing Implications

Marketers can take advantage of decisions made in uncontrollable situations in at least two ways. First, marketers can use promotional methods to reinforce a specific selection of products when the consumer is confronted with a particular situation. For example, automotive services can be purchased that promise to service vehicles if the user runs into problems anywhere and at anytime.

Second, marketers can use marketing methods that attempt to convince consumers that a situation is less likely to occur if the marketer's product is used. This can also be seen with auto products, where marketers explain that using their product will prevent unexpected damage to their vehicles.

FACTORS INFLUENCING CONSUMER BEHAVIOUR

Consumer purchases are influenced strongly by or there are four factors.

1.	Cultural Factor	2.	Social Factor
3.	Personal Factor	4.	Psychological Factor.

CULTURAL FACTOR

Cultural factor divided into three sub factors:

1. Culture
2. Sub Culture
3. Social Class

- *Culture*:
  - The set of basic values perceptions, wants, and behaviours learned by a member of society from family and other important institutions. Culture is the most basic cause of a person's wants and behaviour. Every group or society has a culture, and cultural influences on buying behaviour may vary greatly from country to country.
- *Sub Culture*:
  - A group of people with shared value systems based on common life experiences and situations.
  - Each culture contains smaller sub cultures a group of people with shared value system based on common life experiences and situations. Sub culture includes nationalities, religions, racial group and geographic regions. Many sub culture make up important market segments and marketers often design products.
- *Social Class*:
  - Almost every society has some form of social structure, social classes are society's relatively permanent and ordered divisions whose members share similar values, interests and behaviour.

SOCIAL FACTORS

A consumer's behaviour also is influenced by social factors, such as the:

1. Groups
2. Family
3. Roles and status

- *Groups*:
  - Two or more people who interact to accomplish individual or mutual goals.
  - A person's behavious is influenced by many small groups. Groups that have a direct influence and to which a person belongs are called membership groups.
  - Some are primary groups includes family, friends, neighbours and coworkers. Some are secondary groups, which are more formal and have less regular interaction. These includes organizations like religious groups, professional association and trade unions.
- *Family*:

- Family members can strongly influence buyer behaviour. The family is the most important consumer buying organization society and it has been researched extensively. Marketers are interested in the roles, and influence of the husband, wife and children on the purchase of different products and services.

- *Roles and Status*:
  - A person belongs to many groups, family, clubs, organizations.
  - The person's position in each group can be defined in terms of both role and status.
  - For example. M & "X" plays the role of father, in his family he plays the role of husband, in his company, he plays the role of manager, etc. A Role consists of the activities people are expected to perform just as to the persons around them.

PERSONAL FACTORS

- *It includes*:

  i. Age and life cycle stage
  ii. Occupation
  iii. Economic situation
  iv. Life Style

  (v) Personality and self concept.

  - *Age and Life cycle Stage*:
    i. People changes the goods and services they buy over their lifetimes. Tastes in food, clothes, furniture, and recreation are often age related. Buying is also shaped by the stage of the family life cycle.
  - *Occupation*:
    i. A person's occupation affects the goods and services bought. Blue collar workers tend to buy more rugged work clothes, whereas white-collar workers buy more business suits. A Co. can even specialize in making products needed by a given occupational group. Thus, computer software companies will design different products for brand managers, accountants, engineers, lawyers, and doctors.
  - *Economic situation:*
    i. A person's economic situation will affect product choice
  - *Life Style:*
    i. Life Style is a person's Pattern of living, understanding these forces involves measuring consumer's major AIO dimensions.
    ii. i.e. activities interest and opinions
  - *Personality and Self concept*:
    i. Each person's distinct personality influence his or her buying behaviour. Personality refers to the unique psychological

characteri-stics that lead to relatively consistent and lasting responses to one's own environment.

PSYCHOLOGICAL FACTORS

- It includes these Factors.
  - Motivation
  - Perception
  - Learning
  - Beliefs and attitudes
- *Motivation*:
  - Motive a need that is sufficiently pressing to direct the person to seek satisfaction of the need
- *Perception*:
  - The process by which people select, Organize, and interpret information to form a meaningful picture of the world.
- *Learning*:
  - Changes in an individuals behaviour arising from experience.
- *Beliefs and attitudes:*
  - Belief is a descriptive thought that a person holds about something
  - Attitude, a Person's consistently favourable or unfavourable evaluations, feelings, and tendencies towards an object or idea

CONSUMER BUYING BEHAVIOUR

Consumer Buying Behaviour the decision processes and acts of final household consumers associated with evaluating, buying, consuming, and discarding products for personal consumption. Consider the purchase an automobile.

You generally will not consider different options until some event triggers a need, such as a problem needing potentially expensive repair. Once this need has put you "on the market", you begin to ask your friends for recommendations regarding dealerships and car models.

After visiting several dealerships, you test drive several models and finally decide on a particular model. After picking up your new car, you have doubts on the way home, wondering if you can afford the monthly payments, but then begin to wonder if instead you should have purchased a more expensive but potentially more reliable model.

Over the next five years, the car has several unexpected breakdowns that lead you to want to purchase a different brand, but you have been very happy with the services of the local dealership and decide to again purchase your next car there.

In this particular case, the following generic model of consumer decision making appears to hold:

- Need recognition
- Information search
- Evaluation of alternatives
- Purchase decision
- Postpurchase behaviour

Now consider the purchase of a quart of orange juice. This product when you do your grocery shopping once per week. You have a favourite brand of orange juice and usually do your grocery shopping at the same store. When you buy orange juice, you always go to the same place in the store to pick it up, and never notice what other brands are on the shelf or what are the prices of other brands.

How is it that the generic model works differently in this second scenario? Why does it work differently? Why would we generally need the ministrations of a sales person in the sale of a car, but we generally do not need the help of a salesperson in the purchase of orange juice?

How can the marketer of orange juice get a consumer like you to exert more effort into information search or to consider alternative products? How is it that the marketer of your brand got you to ignore alternative competing brands? What is the involvement of salespeople in *sales promotions* that might be associated with products such as orange juice? Consumer behaviour researchers are not so interested in studying the validity of the above generic model, but are more interested in various factors that influence how such a model might work.

GROUP INFLUENCES ON CONSUMER BEHAVIOUR

Culture

Culture the set of basic values, beliefs, norms, and associated behaviours that are learned by a member of society

Note that culture is something that is *learned* and that it has a relatively long lasting effect on the behaviours of an individual. As an example of cultural influences, consider how the salesperson in an appliance store in the U.S. must react to different couples who are considering the purchase of a refrigerator. In some subcultures, the husband will play a dominant role in the purchase decision; in others, the wife will play a more dominant role.

Social Class

Social Class a group of individuals with similar social rank, based on such factors as *occupation*, *education*, and *wealth*

Reference Groups

Reference groups, often temporary, that affect a person's values, attitude, or behaviours:

- E.g., your behaviours around colleagues at work or friends at school are probably different from your behaviours around your parents, no matter your age or stage in the family life cycle. If you were a used car salesperson, how might you respond differently to a nineteen year old prospect accompanied by her boyfriend from one accompanied by two girlfriends?
- Opinion leadera person within a reference group who exerts influence on others because of special skills, knowledge, personality, etc.
  - You might ask the webmaster at work for an opinion about a particular software application. Software manufacturers often give away free beta copies of software to potential opinion leaders with the hope that they will in turn influence many others to purchase the product.

TYPES OF CONSUMER PROBLEM-SOLVING PROCESSES

Routenized

- Used when buying frequently purchased, low cost items
- Used when little search/decision effort is needed
- E.g., buying a quart of orange juice once per week

Limited Problem Solving

- Used when products are occasionally purchased
- Used when information is needed about an unfamiliar product in a familiar product category

Extended Problem Solving

- Used when product is unfamiliar, expensive, or infrequently purchased
- E.g., buying a new car once every five years

POST-PURCHASE CONSUMER BEHAVIOUR

Satisfaction

After the sale, the buyer will likely feel either satisfied or dissatisfied. If the buyer beleives that s/he received more in the exchange than what was paid, s/he might feel satisfied. If s/he believes that s/he received less in the exchange than what was paid, then s/he might feel dissatisfied. Dissatisfied buyers are not likely to return as customers and are not likely to send friends, relatives, and acquaintences. They are also more likely to be unhappy or even abusive when the product requires post-sale servicing, as when an automobile needs warranty maintenance.

The idea can be modeled as Homans' basic exchange equation:

Profit = Rewards–Costs

Unfortunately, even a buyer who "got a good deal" with respect to price and other terms of the sale might feel dissatisfied under the perception that the salesperson made out even better.

This idea is called equity theory, where we are concerned with:

Outcomes of A Inputs of A

vs.

Outcomes of B Inputs of B

Consider value is listed at $16,000. You are probably delighted with the purchase until you accidentally meet the prior owner who had received a trade-in of $10,000 on the car just a few days before. That the dealer appears to have received substantially greater benefit than you could lead to extreme dissatisfaction, even though you received good value for the money spent.

An issue related to this is attribution theory. Attribution theory, people tend to assign cause to the behaviour of others. Mary's life insurance agent advises her to purchase a whole life policy, while her accountant advises her, "buy term insurance and invest the difference.". The reason, explains the accountant, "is that insurance agents receive substantially higher commission payments on sales of whole life policies."

If Mary believes that the insurance agent is recommending a product merely because he receives a higher commission, she will likely be displeased with the relationship and will not take his recommendation. If the agent is able to show Mary that the recommended product is the best solution for her situation, then she will likely attribute his recommendation to having her best interests in mind and will not be concerned about how it is that he is compensated for his services.

Cognitive Dissonance

cognitive dissonance has to do with the doubt that a person has about the wisdom of a recent purchase.

It is very common for people to experience some anxiety after the purchase of a product that is very expensive or that will require a long term commitment. Jane and Fred, for example, signed a one year lease on an apartment, committing themselves to payments of $1500 per month. A week later, they are wondering if they should have instead leased a smaller $900 apartment in a more rough part of town; they are not sure if they really can afford this much of a monthly obligation. Dick and Sally, on the other hand, ultimately rented the $900 apartment, and now are wondering if the savings in rent will be offset by noisy and sometimes unsafe conditions in this neighbourhood.

Perhaps neither couple would be experiencing this anxiety if their landlords had given them just the smallest of assurances that they had made a good decision. After a close on products that are expensive or that require a long term commitment, the salesperson should provide the prospect with some reasons to be happy with the decision. Allow the car buyer to reinforce her own positive feelings by calling her a week after the purchase to ask how things are going. Call the new life insurance policy holder after two months to see if there are any questions; a lack of questions can only help the buyer to convince himself that he did the right thing.

BUYING DECISION PROCESS

Whenever folks make a buying decision, that decision represents the culmination of a process. It may take place almost instantaneously or stretch out over a long period of time–but it's a process, not an event.

No matter how long the process takes, the buying decision always begins when folks become aware of a need. Once they have identified that need, they begin to search for and explore possible avenues for meeting it. While gathering information, they refine and evaluate all the buying criteria that will affect the decision to purchase and narrow the field of choice to the "best few" alternatives.

Once they reach a decision and choose, they take action by making a purchase. The final step in the process involves a reevaluation of the decision and its results.

To summarize, the steps of the buying decision process are:

- Identify
- Search
- Evaluate
- Decide
- Purchase
- Reevaluate

NATURE OF THE BUY

The way folks make buying decisions depends on the complexity of the problem they are trying to solve and the complexity of each step in the decision process. This will affect how you manage the sale.

If their needs and the decision-making process are simple, all you need to do is make your visitors aware of you, build confidence, differentiate yourself, demonstrate value and guide them through a very simple shopping and buying process. This is why lower-end, branded products sell so well.

If the needs and the decision-making process are highly complex, then you need to make people aware of you, build relationships, educate them show sensitivity to the different decision-makers, influencers and groups, and resolve conflicting needs, so you can custom-tailor your solutions and make the buying process as painless and positive as possible. Think of purchasing a multi-million dollar piece of equipment that needs five departments to sign off to close the deal.

It also helps if you understand and incorporate how folks think about buying what you offer. Are they going to compare similar models in different brands? Are they looking for the range offered by one manufacturer? Do they think of the purchase in terms of a hierarchy of benefits, with some more important than others? Is the best way to showcase your product or service to compare it with someone else's stuff?

PROPENSITY TO BUY

You get four types of traffic, and each group is primed with a different level of motivation and preparedness - the classic"propensity to buy." First, you've got the to-die-for perfect visitors; they are the ones who know exactly what they want and come to you looking for features, brands, and model numbers.

Then you've got the visitors who sort of know what they want. These are folks who have identified a strongly felt need, but they're still in the process of narrowing down their search criteria.

Then there are the window shoppers, folks who aren't sure they want anything, but might buy if they saw something that interested them. They have no strongly felt need in mind, but one could be suggested to them.

The fourth group aren't really prospects. They're lost or there by mistake. Be happy when they go away.

You don't know where your visitors are in the process when they land on your site, so you've got to plan for each possibility. You've got to help the folks who know exactly what they want get to it quickly; make them jump through too many hoops and they're gone. You've got to help the ones still mulling it over by offering pertinent information where and when they are most likely to need it, as well as persuading them you're the logical business choice. You've got to be most engaging and appealing for the window shopper.

It also helps to consider that not all your visitors are prepared or even inclined to make a decision when they first visit your site–sometimes a successful conversion is the result of multiple visits. So you'd like to give folks a reason to come back.

BUYING IS AN EMOTIONAL DECISION

It really is the piece that pulls it all together. Folks rationalize the decision to buy based on facts, but they make the decision to buy based on feelings. The single biggest motivator in buying is emotional response. And that takes place on two levels. In part, it's the emotional response that comes when folks imagine themselves enjoying the benefits of what you offer. Put them in the driver's seat, and they are that much closer to being able to see themselves making the decision to buy. "Ditch the features?" Absolutely not. You should make your features available and present them as corollaries to benefits. After all, some of your visitors, particularly analytic types who will pointedly look for this stuff, feel more comfortable emotionally with facts and specifications.

And that brings me to the other aspect of emotional response. Folks buy when they feel comfortable, when they feel they can trust you, when the process feels natural and reassuring, and when they come to believe that buying will make them feel good. Ignore this, and most of your visitors will bail out. Tap into it, and watch your conversion rate climb. Because, at then end of the day, it's not facts that convince customers to go with your company. It's emotion.

PACKAGE BUYING WITH SELLING

The persuasive architecture of your entire site must recognize every step of the buying decision process. Each step feeds and leads to the others. Although the process ultimately is linear, there can be feedback loops within the process as folks reevaluate information. So, it's not unusual to address multiple steps on a single page.

To successfully get your visitors to take action you must be able to see the world from their "buying" point of view. So learn how to address and package the buying process within your selling process. It will make a world of difference!

CONSUMER ADOPTION PROCESS

Adoption is an individual's decision to become a regular user of a product.

Sequence of events beginning with consumer awareness of a new product leading to trial usage and culminating in full and regular use of the new product. Over time the adoption process resembles a bell curve formed by innovators, early adopters, the majority of consumers, late adopters, and laggards.

An innovation is any good, service, or idea that is perceived by someone as new. The idea may have a long history, but it is an innovation to the person who sees it as new. Innovations take time to spread through the social system. Rogers defines the innovation diffusion process as "the spread of a new idea from its source of invention or creation to its ultimate users or adopters."

The consumer-adoption process focuses on the mental process through which an individual passes from first hearing about an innovation to final adoption.

Adopters of new products have been observed to move through five stages:

1. *Awareness*: The consumer becomes aware of the innovation but lacks information about it.
2. *Interest*: The consumer is stimulated to seek information about the innovation.
3. *Evaluation*: The consumer considers whether to try the innovation.

4. *Trial*: The consumer tries the innovation to improve his or her estimate of its value.
5. *Adoption*: The consumer decides to make full and regular use of the innovation.

The new-product marketer should facilitate movement through these stages. A portable electricdishwasher manufacturer might discover that many consumers are stuck in the interest stage;they do not buy because of their uncertainty and the large investment cost. But these same consumers would be willing to use an electric dishwasher on a trial basis for a small monthly fee.The manufacturer should consider offering a trial-use plan with option to buy.

FACTORS INFLUENCING THE ADOPTION PROCESS

People differ in their approach towards change. Some differ in adopting new fashion, some in adopting new appliances, some doctors are hesitant to apply new medicines and still some farmers do not apply new implements. This is called adoption culture. After the early adoption, they increase the use and then others follow. Others are late adopters by nature.

Let us categorize these customers into three units:

- *One who are early adopters*: They are very quick in their response. These people are venture some and willing to try new ideas. In fact they are innovators in life and early adopters.
- *Secondly Early Majority*: They are very careful people and take time to adopt things. They tend to collect information about the change or the product, study carefully and then adopt on the basis of their merits.
- *The third ones are late majority and traditionalists*: They are the ones who adopt late and then use the product.

As marketing managers, we must study the demographics, the psychographics and media characteristics of the product and also keep the theme of advertising message on these lines. We must find the innovators of the product and also opinion leaders and keeping in view the financial stature of the consumers and their category. Then there are certain areas where product change is imminent and quicker while some areas change or innovation in the product is least desired or welcomed.

FINANCING THE CONSUMER

To facilitate the process of consumption, some goods are sold to the ultimate consumer on credit, or loans of cash are made to him. The subject was analyzed as one determinant of consumer behaviour. At this point, consumer finance is treated as a marketing activity, with attention given both to its business and social implications.

NATURE OF CONSUMER CREDIT

The credit granted to ultimate consumers for the purpose of facilitating the process of consumption is known as consumer credit. Theoretically, it is the power which an individual uses in obtaining goods and services, or in borrowing money, for consumption purposes, on the promise to repay an equivalent at an agreed future time. Broadly conceived, consumer credit includes all credit extensions for personal use, whether granted by manufacturers that sell directly to consumers, by retailers, professional men, service businesses, or by the various types of financial institutions. Reasons for and Basic Types of Consumer Credit From the standpoint of creditors, the principal reason for credit is profit. To the retailer, credit spells increased sales volume and remunerative business; to the money lender, it means a worth-while return on his investment. To the ultimate consumer, however, the matter is not so simple.

In general, however, the consumer is prompted to use credit by one or more of three sets of motives: *convenience, a desire for immediate improvement in his standard of living,* and *necessity.* Each of these motives constitutes, in the main, the fundamental explanation for a different type of consumer credit: *the charge account, instalment sale credit, and consumer cash credit, respectively.*

Importance and Composition of Consumer Credit

The importance of consumer credit may be judged in several ways. First, it may be pointed out that about one-third of all retail store sales is made on a credit basis, with about two-thirds of such credit sales being made on a charge account basis and about one-third on some type of instalment credit arrangement. The importance of credit sales varies considerably among different lines of trade, being of greatest significance to large establishments, with a wide range of merchandise classifications, serving a relatively permanent clientele.

For example, department stores, which account for only 6.7 per cent of retail store sales, hold 19 per cent of the total consumer indebtedness arising out of the use of charge accounts in all retail stores, including credit card plans. Another indication of the importance of consumer credit is the volume of credit outstanding at a particular time. Such data, which are published regularly in very comprehensive fashion, measure the amount due creditors as of a particular date rather than the volume of credit granted during a particular period. Nevertheless, trends in such data at least reflect increasing or decreasing use of various means of financing consumption through credit.

In 1960, for example, consumers owed $54 billion in connection with previous uses of all forms of short-term and intermediateerm instalment credit. This was the equivalent of 15 per cent of total disposable personal income during that year. On an annual basis, consumer credit outstanding (debt) has tended to increase gradually but consistently, from 9.2 per cent in 1950 to 15 per cent of disposable personal income in 1960. Greater use of consumer credit, as so measured, is explained by a variety of factors, including:

- Growing acceptance of credit as an institution of modern society, as opposed to a puritanical aversion to indebtedness;
- Increasing levels of per family income which has enhanced the demand for types of goods commonly sold on a credit basis and caused a larger proportion of the population to qualify as acceptable credit risks;
- A wider variety of credit or financing arrangements, available from a growing number of marketing and financial institutions, especially designed to meet the particular needs of families in different income groups and financial circumstances.

Of total consumer indebtedness in 1960, 78 per cent arose out of the use of one form or another of instalment credit and 22 per cent reflected noninstalment credit. Instalment debt was, however, only 11.7 per cent, or less than one-eighth, of total annual disposable personal income. It appears, therefore, that the total population could safely carry considerably larger amounts of instalment financial obligations, without impairing its ability to repay on a reasonable basis, provided such debt is of high quality by virtue of being wisely extended in the vast number of individual cases that comprise the aggregate.

The composition of consumer credit, in terms of debt outstanding. These data do not correspond with the magnitude of consumer expenditures made on a credit basis since expenditures which involve long-term financing tend to be overstated in terms of marketing significance and those which are short-term obligations tend to be understated. However, provide a frame of reference for appraising the composition of consumer credit by major parts or uses and by various sources of credit (holders), and do serve as a background for discussion of types of credit and kinds of financial institutions.

Charge Accounts

Consumers utilize charge accounts chiefly because it is convenient for them to obtain goods on that basis. Orders can be placed by telephone, better service can be obtained from stores, several members of a family may buy on an account, home budgeting may be facilitated, and family budgeting may be controlled through monthly payments.

Merchants who operate on a charge account basis do so for several reasons. It is claimed that charge accounts serve to build regular customers who tend to concentrate their purchases and to buy more merchandise. Credit customers are believed to be less resistant to sales and advertising appeals and are more likely to buy on considerations of quality and style rather than price. Stores extending charge account credit also have a more uniform distribution of sales than do cash stores which experience pronounced peaks in business on and following paydays and lulls in activity between such times.

In spite of the advantages explained above, many stores do not choose to make charge accounts available to their customers. If the basic appeal of an establishment is price, all services, including credit, are usually minimized. Charge accounts are not usually used in the sale of goods of low unit value, as in the case of variety store items, for which customers are accustomed to paying cash. Furthermore, merchants with limited financial resources are often forced to operate on a cash basis because charge accounts involve financing consumer purchases for periods of 50 or 60 days on the average.

Retail store charge accounts have tended to be a relatively stable or declining component of total consumer credit out standings, but service credit, which is closely akin to charge accounts, has increased significantly in the post-World War II era. Service credit consists principally of amounts owed to doctors, hospitals, and public utility companies. Its steady growth reflects wider acceptance of credit financing of medical and household operation expenses, but is also partly attributable to the increased relative significance of service expenditures in the typical family budget.

Most charge accounts involve a relationship between an individual retail store and an individual consumer; however, some group arrangements are of interest. In some cities, numerous independent retailers and service establishments sell on credit through bank charge account plans. Usually a number of stores are affiliated with a given bank; the bank makes credit investigations and approves the accounts; customers may make charge purchases in any of the participating stores; the retailer receives cash for the sale, minus a service charge, at the daily presentation of the sales checks to the bank; and the bank bills the customer monthly for all purchases he made in all participating stores. Major oil companies have promoted the use of credit cards or credit check books which are accepted by any of the independent dealers associated with the company and by the dealers of other affiliated companies. National credit card plans, such as Carte Blanche of Hilton Hotels Corporation and the American Express Company Credit Card, are similar in many respects but are used to a greater extent for handling business travel and entertainment expense than for financing ultimate consumption. Such group arrangements have made it possible for many individual firms to offer charge account services when they would otherwise have found it impossible or uneconomical to do so.

Instalment Sale Credit

Instalment sale credit differs from charge account credit in one major way. Instead of paying the full amount of the bill at the end of a given period of time, the purchaser, when using instalment credit, agrees to pay his obligation in fixed portions or instalments at stated intervals. Other common, although not universal, distinctions are that a down payment is often made on instalment transactions and that a finance charge is levied on the unpaid balance.

Although it is an old business practice, the instalment method did not evoke much attention until about the middle of the 1920's when its use was greatly extended together with the expansion of the automobile market. During the 1930's the method became more common as it was extended to numerous types of durable goods and even to "soft" goods which have been later sold extensively on deferred multiple payment plans. Instalment sale credit accounts for about one-third of total credit sales of retail establishments in nonwar years.

During war years and periods of national emergency marked by scarcities of durable goods, the total volume of instalment sale credit has been as little as one-fourth of total credit sales and as low as less than 5 per cent of the total sales of retail establishments. More than one-half of the *instalment sale* credit *extended* annually represents automobile financing. Other lines of business in which instalment sale credit is of great significance are furniture stores, household appliance stores, jewelry stores, automobile tire and accessory stores, and department stores.

Instalment selling has also been applied to the marketing of various kinds of services. Airlines, for example, have made it possible for consumers to take expensive vacation trips which are financed over a number of months. Similarly, many doctors, dentists, and hospitals have made arrangements with financing institutions so that people with limited incomes may finance major medical expenses on definite instalment arrangements.

Sales Finance Companies and Instalment Sale Credit

Finance companies are of two types: *consumer* or *personal finance companies* engaged chiefly in making cash loans and which are discussed at a later point, and *sales finance companies* engaged principally in financing the sale of products.

Sales finance companies, in turn, may be divided into two principal classes: manufactured-owned companies, such as General Motors Acceptance Corporation, and independent financial institutions, as illustrated by Commercial Credit Corporation. Regardless of ownership, both types of companies do the bulk of their business in connection with automotive sales, but both types also are heavily engaged in financing sales of appliances, electronic products, furniture, and other durable goods. The nature of their operations may be illustrated with respect to automobile financing.

When an automobile is sold on the instalment plan (and the same applies to other articles financed by sales finance companies), a promissory note covering the transaction is made out by the purchaser. The note, secured by a chattel mortgage on the car, or by a conditional sales contract, is indorsed by the dealer, with or without recourse, as the case may be, and is then discounted by the finance company. Prior to acceptance of the risk by the finance company, a credit investigation is made in order to determine the purchaser's willingness and ability to meet the instalments when due. An agreement must be reached on the amount of down payment and the number of, and the amount of time between, instalment payments.

On automobiles, the usual down payment required has, from time to time, varied from about 10 per cent to 15 per cent to onethird of the purchase price; the time interval between payments is generally one month; and the number of payments has varied from about 12 to 36. In some cases, however, automobiles are sold on terms involving no down payment and with terms of 48 months.

In determining the amount to be paid under the instalment sales contract a regular service charge is added to the unpaid balance. This charge, which is all too often confused and compared with pure interest rates, must cover interest on the money lent, credit and collection expense of the lending agency, a reasonable allowance for bad debt losses, allowance for expenses involved in repossession, reconditioning, and sale of cars of delinquents, and certain types of insurance as specified.

This charge is quoted in terms of a *nominal* rate, *i.e.*, the amount of service charge expressed as a percentage of the total unpaid amount on a per annum basis, that is, on the total initial unpaid balance. The *actual* effective rate of charge is generally about twice the nominal rate because the debtor is constantly decreasing the outstanding balance by monthly payments made throughout the period.

Instalment Credit Handled by Retailers

Instalment credit is generally used in many types of retail stores that operate without assistance from sales finance companies. Department stores, mail order companies, furniture stores, and home appliance stores are some of the major types of establishments that maintain their own instalment credit departments, make credit investigations, and handle collections, which are accepted at accounts receivables offices in the store or are made by consumers by mail. Many of these stores finance their receivables through commercial banks or other financial institutions. Some large-scale retailers have subsidiary corporations which have been established to handle their time-sales financing activities and which operate in the same manner as sales finance companies.

Durable goods items of high unit value are usually sold on straight instalment contracts which customarily involve a down payment and payments of a specified amount for a definite number of weeks or months. Since about the middle 1940's, various types of "budget," "revolving" or "optional" credit plans have been adopted extensively by department stores, mail order companies, and apparel retailers, to facilitate the sale of soft goods on instalments. According to a common arrangement, the consumer contracts to pay a certain amount each month and thus is granted a credit limit which is a multiple of the monthly payment. In a 12-month revolving account, if the customer contracts to pay $20 per month the credit limit is set at $240. The consumer can make purchases of any kind of goods sold by the store, so long as the credit limit is not exceeded. Each month a carrying charge is added to the outstanding balance as of the end of the month.

The "optional" or multiple-purpose account used by many retailers serves either as a regular charge account or as a deferred payment account. If the customer wishes to pay the total amount of the monthly billing, he may do so, and there is no service charge. On the other hand, if the billing is large (*e.g.*, owing to seasonal purchases such as at school opening time, Christmas, or Easter) payments may be spread over several or many months, with a service charge added to the outstanding balance, as in the case of revolving credit. The various forms of revolving credit are classified, for statistical purposes, along with regular instalment credit. Their popularity in the 1950's and early 1960's has resulted in the shifting of some debt balances from the category of charge account to instalment.

Arguments for Instalment Credit

The real nature of instalment credit can be but little understood merely from a knowledge that it involves periodic payments. Instalment credit is not merely a technique; rather it is a pervasive influence and an explanation of its nature must be sought in the effects it has upon all whom it touches. These effects are reputedly both beneficial and detrimental. The advantages of instalment credit may be considered from the standpoint of the business establishments that use it as a selling technique and from the view of the consumer and society in general. To merchants selling on the instalment plan, it is not a matter of conjecture that the plan tends to increase sales volume. It does increase the total demand for goods of the type that may be sold on this plan, and it brings people into stores at frequent intervals to make payments. Each such call is an opportunity to make additional sales, with payments for one purchase leading to still additional purchases and greater familiarity with the credit-granting establishment.

From the standpoint of society, the instalment plan is desirable, first, because it *enables people to obtain, without delay, many commodities of high unit value and much usefulness,* without the necessity of waiting long periods before they are acquired, or of doing without them altogether. The buyer is thus enabled to use the article while paying for it; as a result he can enjoy life more fully than would otherwise be possible.

A second social advantage, and one contrary to much popular opinion, is that instalment buying *tends to encourage thrift.* It is an enforced form of saving, *provided* that the terms of payment are such that the consumer's equity in the purchased article is increased at a rate greater than the rate at which the article is used up or consumed. Many people will economize in order to be able to meet instalments when they come due, even though they may be unable, or lack the discipline, to economize merely for the sake of accumulating money for future use. Third, *because instalment credit has widened the market for the type of consumer goods sold in this manner, it has contributed to lower prices on such goods.*

Most of the industries manufacturing durable goods of high unit value operate on a decreasing cost basis; consequently, as their output is increased, the unit cost is materially reduced. The advantage of lower prices resulting from market expansions attributable to consumer credit inures to the benefit, therefore, of cash and credit customers alike. There can be no doubt, furthermore, that instalment credit *has contributed to a substantially higher standard of living for large segments of the consuming public.*

This argument is a natural corollary of the two just stated, in that it results both from the savings feature of the plan and the broadening of the market through price reductions of many types of goods. Standards of living are judged in large measure by the number and kinds of durable goods and costly articles in the possession of consumers, as well as by the consumption of items yielding cultural and aesthetic satisfaction.

Much of the income that is now used for purchasing automobiles, television, radios, dishwashers, washing machines, garbage disposals, vacuum cleaners, floor coverings, furniture, and refrigerators would be expended upon highly perishable satisfactions in the absence of instalment credit. Furthermore, in the absence of economies of scale enjoyed by industries manufacturing such goods, unit prices would necessarily be much higher and at such a level that it would be impossible for the masses to purchase items of this kind.

Objections to Instalment Credit

Instalment credit is sufficiently well established as a business practice that it is only upon rare occasions that objections to it arise from within the business community. Some strong arguments have been set forth against it, however, by those who view the subject from a consumer or social standpoint. Most such objections are either made by those who have no understanding of this type of credit, or objections are directed to abuses rather than to sound applications of it. Among the most common criticisms is that it causes people to live beyond their means by the consumption of luxuries to which they are not entitled on the basis of current income. Tastes and desires of different individuals vary so much, however, as to make any attempt to dictate that one commodity be purchased instead of another, or that it be bought on a certain basis, the height of absurdity. A second and somewhat related objection is that instalment credit has led consumers to mortgage their future incomes, both through the consumption of luxuries and overconsumption in general, to the extent that the slightest interruption in normal earnings would effect a very serious and straitened condition in their ability to meet obligations. Such criticisms are apparently based upon two assumptions:

- That a person's income is static
- That instalment purchases are made on top of what would be normally bought in the absence of such purchases. In numerous individual cases the person who bought an expensive article on the instalment plan may justly expect an increase in his present earnings during the life of the contract. Again, he may so reapportion and redirect his purchases that less of other types of goods will be bought, or he may have been saving to the extent that this distribution of his income can be modified without impairing his security. Furthermore, many buyers on the instalment plan have resources other than their immediate income, which can be converted into cash if desired or necessary in order to meet obligations.

One of the most serious objections to instalment credit is its costliness. In operating on a charge account basis, there is but one collection to be made for purchases during the credit period and, ordinarily, only one chance that payment will be delayed or not made at all. From the standpoint of the store or finance company, there are repetitive chances that the instalment purchaser will become delinquent. Elaborate collection machinery must be established to insure that payments are kept forthcoming and that the purchaser remains satisfied with the goods and the service of the selling establishment. In addition to collection expenses, carrying charges must also include, as previously indicated, interest on the funds used, bookkeeping and clerical costs, credit investigation expense, reserves for bad debt losses, and allowances for the cost of repossession and resale of articles.

An objection voiced by many is that charges are exorbitant, that is, even greater than warranted by actual costs of carrying instalment accounts. This criticism arises in part from misunderstanding and in part because certain less reputable vendors have taken advantage of the ignorance of some consumers. All too often the carrying charge on instalment purchases is inappropriately related to the economic concept of interest which involves merely a price paid for the use of money.

Learning that the actual rate of instalment charge per annum on a given transaction is, for example, 12 or 18 per cent per annum, a consumer may unrealistically compare this rate with a rate of interest, say 3 or 4 per cent, that his funds will yield if deposited in a savings account. The conclusion may be drawn that the charge is exorbitant, without cognizance of the fact that interest is only a fraction of the total charge which must cover all of the various costs detailed in the preceding paragraph. In other cases, the charge of exorbitance results from the practice of certain vendors who do not quote any percentage rate of instalment charge, but emphasize in the sales presentation merely the amount of the down payment and the amount of the periodic payments. Apparently there are many consumers who are unable or too indifferent to figure the cost of purchasing on the instalment plan at the time purchases are made if the amount of the monthly or weekly payment is something they feel they can reasonably afford. Consequently, certain stores have been able to make very high charges on instalment transactions and under such circumstances that the amount of the charge is not actually known by many customers. Fortunately, this is a practice that has never been common among more reputable dealers. A fifth important criticism of instalment credit is concerned solely with *abuses,* as for example, when carrying charges are not disclosed or are misrepresented. Many vendors and finance companies have quoted only nominal rather than actual rates of charge per annum and, even so, have failed to indicate whether the rate applied to the unpaid balance after the deduction of the down payment or to the full purchase price of the article. With respect to this criticism, it is significant that steps have been taken in the direction of regulation relating to the use of clear forms of instalment contracts which reveal just what the customer gets and how much he is paying for the product and how much for the financing of it.

Cash Credit as a Supplement to Instalment Sale Credit

Consumer cash credit may be distinguished from instalment sale credit in that consumers obtain cash funds, rather than merchandise, in exchange for a promised future repayment. A large proportion of such credit has its origin in human want and misery and is explained by the urgent need for immediate funds in order to cope with emergency situations. To an important extent, however, cash credit is a supplement to instalment sale credit; and in this respect it is of great significance as a factor in the marketing of goods. There are numerous instances in which a consumer has a choice as to the type of credit he might use.

For example, in buying a major electrical appliance, he might make the purchase on the instalment plan, arranging for payments with the store from which the purchase is made. On the other hand, he might obtain a cash loan from a lending agency, pay cash to the store selling the merchandise, and repay the loan to the lending agency in periodic instalments. In some instances, the latter procedure may be used to circumvent the down payment that is required by the store selling on the instalment plan. There are no statistics that reveal the extent to which cash credit directly supplements instalment sale credit and to what extent it is used for emergency purposes arising out of unforeseen events or from past financial mismanagement. That cash credit is of considerable significance in facilitating the sale of goods is, however, generally recognized, both by marketing authorities and by those engaged in the cash-lending business.The principal sources of consumer cash credit are as follows:

- Consumer or personal finance companies: These are lending agencies licensed under state laws to engage in the business of lending money to consumers. Typical examples are Household Finance Company, Personal Finance Company, and City Loan Company.
- Banks: Most commercial and industrial banks have consumer loan departments. In general, they make loans of larger amounts at lower rates of instalment payment charges than is the case with personal finance companies, owing to their tendency to confine lending activities to high-grade credit risks.
- Credit Unions: Cooperative organizations formed for the purpose of encouraging thrift among members and making loans to them at relatively low rates are known as credit unions. Such organizations are chartered under, and regulated by, state or federal law. Members are ordinarily otherwise affiliated in some way, as employees of a particular company or members of the same church, labour union, or lodge. Since much of the work of the credit union is done by members without compensation, because its facilities are often subsidized by employers or other associated institutions, and because of certain tax advantages owing to status as cooperatives, loans are made at lower rates than are available from financial institutions. Credit is, however, available only to members.

Control of Consumer Credit

As consumer credit has grown in stature in the course of this century, it has led to ever-broadening concepts of its social and economic significance. Consumer credit, particularly of the instalment sale or instalment cash type, has been, accordingly, the subject of increasing control and regulation by state and federal government. This control is of two types, quality and quantity control.

Quality Control

Regulations pertaining to the quality of consumer credit are designed to prevent usurious, deceptive, unfair, or monopolistic practices by credit-granting agencies. At the beginning of this century, many consumers in need of cash funds were forced to look to illegal lenders or "loan sharks" as a source for loans, and had to pay exorbitant rates. The reason for this was that the usury laws of most states limited interest rates to 6 per cent per annum or, in the presence of a special contract, to 8 per cent. Such rates were inadequate to attract agencies to make consumer loans in small amounts at inevitable high costs. After making a thorough study, the Russell Sage Foundation, a philanthropic organization working for the improvement of social conditions, drafted a model bill for submission to state legislatures in 1916. This Uniform Small Loan Law, has subsequently been enacted, in some cases with modifications, in 44 states. The main provisions of the law permit specially authorized rates on loans up to $300. A charge of 3 ½ per cent per month on unpaid balances of $100 or less and 2 ½ per cent per month on the remainder up to the $300 limit is recommended. The law provides that no special fees may be collected on the loans, nor may any charges be made other than the rates applying on the unpaid balance. Companies operating under the law are licensed and bonded and are subject to state inspection.

State laws concerning the control of instalment sale credit were first enacted in the 1930's but have since been passed in more than 30 states containing more than three-fourths of the population. Some of these laws pertain solely to automobile financing whereas others cover all kinds and types of instalment sale credit. Practically all of them are intended to combat excessive finance charges and nonprice abuses by requiring instalment sellers to provide written contracts that give a dollar itemization of the following: commodity price, down payment, finance charge, and insurance and/or other charges, if any. In a few states, such laws have specific provisions establishing maximum allowable finance charges. The broadening interest in the quality of available instalment sale credit is also evident from a code of fair trade practices covering certain aspects of automobile sale financing. Rules promulgated by the Federal Trade Commission Trade Commission in 1951 prohibited a variety of abusive or deceptive practices which had become somewhat common among less scrupulous automotive dealers. These rules apply, of course, only to dealers engaged in interstate commerce and subject to the jurisdiction of the FTC.

From time to time there has been considerable sentiment in favour of a federal law which would prescribe standard conditions of disclosure of credit terms in all cash and sale instalment credit transactions. One proposal bill, the improperly designated "Truth in Lending Act," was the subject of much publicity in 1961. If enacted, it would require that the instalment charge in every transaction be stated in terms of simple "interest" per annum. Owing to the wide variety of instalment plans in use, it would be practically impossible to comply with the terms of such a law in each particular retail transaction. Moreover, referring to such a charge as "interest" is fallacious when due consideration is given to the other, and quantitatively more significant, types of clerical and operating costs which must be recovered in instalment finance charges. Such a law would, furthermore, greatly extend federal control of local and retail business activity and duplicate to a substantial extent the provisions of numerous and increasing state laws on the same subject but which, significantly, require disclosure of finance charges only in amounts or in some other simple fashion.

Bibliography

Anil K. Rai 'Ankit': *Communication Management : Listening Versus Hearing*, Shree Publication, Delhi, 2006.

Anil Mishra, Ruchi Gupta: *Customer Service In Retailing, Indian Text Ed*, Dreamtech Press, Delhi, 2005.

Bhanu Pratap Singh: *Communication Management in Journalism*, Anmol Publication, Delhi, 2011.

CARLAW & DEMING: *The Big Book of Customer Service Training Games*, Tata McGraw-Hill Publication, Delhi, 2004.

D S Verma: *Media and Communication Management*, Pearl Books Publication, Delhi, 2007.

Darryl S Doane and Rose D Sloat: *50 Activities for Achieving Excellent Customer Service*, Ane Books Pvt. Ltd., Delhi, 2004.

Dileeep A.S. and V. Harikumar: *Customer Service in Co-Operative Banks*, Sonali Publication, Delhi, 2010.

Girish Saxena; *Advanced Media and Communication Management*, Vista International Publication, Delhi, 2010.

Kojo Yankah, Dilip Kumar Sarma, Ujjwal K. Chowdhury and Rupak Ghosh: *An Introduction to Branding and Marketing Communication Management*, Manak Publication, Delhi, 2007.

Lynda Byron and Michael Quinn: *Superior Customer Service: The Prompt Approach To Success*, PHI Learning Publication, Delhi, 2010.

Lynn Jurewicz and Todd Cutler: *High Tech, High Touch : Library Customer Service Through Technology*, Ess Ess Publication., Delhi, 2009.

M C Metti, *Customer Service and Hotel Management*, Anmol Publication, Delhi, 2008.

M. Thomas: *Business Communication Managemen*, Cyber Tech Publication, Delhi, 2011.

Manikant Singh: *Communication Management : A Global Perspective for Identification and Corporate Branding*, Global India Publication, Delhi, 2011.

Manoj Kumar Singh: *Communication Management in Journalism*, Mohit Publication, Delhi, 2007.

Narendra Tripath: *Communication Managementi*, Reference Press, Delhi, 2005.

Neil Russell-Jones: *Marketing, Sales and Customer Service*, Ane Books Pvt. Ltd., Delhi, 2009.

Pauline Rowson: *Successful Customer Service : Get Brilliant Results Fast*, Viva Books Publication, Delhi, 2011.

Renee Evensen: *Award-Winning Customer Service : 101 Ways To Guarantee Great Performance*, PHI Learning Publication, Delhi, 2004.

S B Nageswara Rao and C Madhavi: *Customer Service Excellence : Trends and Strategies*, Kanishka Publication, Delhi, 2004.

Sandhir Sharma, Pavitar Parkash Singh and Rajpal Kaur: *Communication Management*, Deep and Deep Publication, Delhi, 2005.

Shashi Kanta Varma; Nishi Sethi; Sushma Kaushik; Seema Rani and Ramesh K Goyal: *Extension and*

Communication Management, Agrotech Publication Academy, Delhi, 2012.

Index

I

L

M

N

O

Q

R

S

T

U

V